Praise for

THE FAULTS OF MEAT

"This book explores the historical debate over vegetarianism in Tibet and breathes life into the important issues surrounding the relationship between compassion in action and the more subtle aspects of the Tibetan Buddhist perspective. To read these well-presented accounts, some from centuries long past and others more recent, highlights the fact that today there is more need than ever for people to treat the world around them with respect, and to approach ethical and ideological conundrums with an open, courageous heart rather than an opportunistic, self-serving attitude. Just as important, however, is to be wary of turning the bodhisattva path into a dogmatic ideology that elevates puritanical morality over the wisdom and skillful means that are so essential to it. In particular, it is the vast array of wisdom-based skillful means that makes the Vajrayāna so extraordinary and profound."
—Jigme Khyentse Rinpoche

"This book presents an excellent array of texts, all translated for the first time, addressing the gamut of issues related to animal slaughter and meat eating within the context of Tibetan Buddhism, from the cultivation of compassion for animals to the ritual mis/uses of meat. It reveals a long tradition of reflection on the ethics of meat abstention in a climate where it had to have been particularly challenging, given the narrow range of food options. A superb resource both for teachers and students of Tibetan Buddhism and for practicing (or would-be) vegetarians and vegans from any climate."
—Janet Gyatso, Harvard University, author of *Being Human in a Buddhist World: An Intellectual History of Medicine in Early Modern Tibet*

"If we aspire to live with compassion toward all beings, how should we approach meat eating? In Tibetan Buddhism, this question has been debated since the eleventh century. The texts compiled and discussed in *The Faults of Meat* shed light on conversations about vegetarianism in ways that are at times surprising and always illuminating. This book is highly valuable for scholars of Buddhism, but also for people in the vegan, vegetarian, reducetarian, and omnivore communities who care about animals and grapple with the ethics of our current food system."
—Barbara J. King, author of *Personalities on the Plate: The Lives and Minds of Animals We Eat*

"*The Faults of Meat* is without doubt the most comprehensive and rich account of Buddhist arguments against meat eating available in English. Simultaneously rigorous and accessible, the fascinating millennia-long arc of debates it documents reveal central values and tensions within Tibetan Buddhist traditions. The volume's carefully curated and contextualized anthology of primary sources will be of great interest not only to Buddhists themselves but to scholars of religion, animal studies, or food studies who want to engage Buddhist views on animals, meat, and even ethics as such. I can think of few texts on any religious tradition that capture the history, depth, and existential stakes of eating animals with such force, balance, and nuance. We are indebted to Barstow for this landmark work of scholarship."
—Aaron S. Gross, author of *The Question of the Animal and Religion*

"My gratitude to Geoffrey Barstow for compiling and editing the writings of these great teachers of Tibetan Buddhism, and to those who care for innocent beings like the animals. Adopting a plant-based diet is not only a matter of personal faith or tradition but is also a wonderful way to care for our health and well-being. This volume also benefits the environment, so that our Mother Earth could remain a little longer in the service of human beings, as we all know that if we continue to disregard the planetary consequences of a meat-based diet, we will regret it within two or three decades."
—Pema Wangyal Rinpoche, founder, Padmakara Translation Group

The Faults of Meat

Tibetan Buddhist Writings on Vegetarianism

Compiled and Edited by Geoffrey Barstow

Wisdom

Wisdom Publications
199 Elm Street
Somerville, MA 02144 USA
wisdompubs.org

Library of Congress Cataloging-in-Publication Data is available.

Names: Barstow, Geoffrey, compiler.
Title: The faults of meat: Tibetan Buddhist writings on vegetarianism / compiled and edited by Geoffrey Barstow.
Description: Somerville, MA: Wisdom Publications, 2019. | Includes bibliographical references and index.
Identifiers: LCCN 2019002930 (print) | ISBN 9781614294818 (pbk.: alk. paper)
Subjects: LCSH: Vegetarianism—Religious aspects—Buddhism. | Buddhism—Tibet Region—History.
Classification: LCC BQ4570.V43 F38 2019 (print) | LCC BQ4570.V43 (ebook) | DDC 294.3/5693—dc23
LC record available at https://lccn.loc.gov/2019002930
LC ebook record available at https://lccn.loc.gov/2019980101

ISBN 978-1-61429-481-8 ebook ISBN 978-1-61429-505-1

23 22 21 20 19 5 4 3 2 1

Cover design by Jim Zaccaria. Interior design by Gopa&Ted2. Typesetting by Kristin Goble. Set in Diacritical Garamond Pro 10.5/13.

Wisdom Publications' books are printed on acid-free paper and meet the guidelines for permanence and durability of the Production Guidelines for Book Longevity of the Council on Library Resources.

♻ This book was produced with environmental mindfulness. For more information, please visit wisdompubs.org/wisdom-environment.

Printed in the United States of America.

FSC www.fsc.org MIX Paper from responsible sources FSC® C005010

Please visit fscus.org.

Contents

Foreword by Khenpo Tsultrim Lodrö

Vegetarianism is nonharmful and peaceful in nature. In itself, it generates tremendous, long-lasting benefit for the natural environment and all the creatures who live within it. Because of this, for several thousand years, many tens of thousands of people who like and admire world peace have embraced a vegetarian diet.

Moreover, Shakyamuni Buddha and other compassionate great leaders of humankind have frequently praised vegetarianism and encouraged its adoption. Both the sūtric and tantric systems of the Buddhist Mahāyāna tradition hold that all meat should be abandoned. The key purpose for this is to avoid causing harm to sentient beings and to increase one's own compassion.

As for Tibetans of the Land of Snows, the whole nation is one that practices and has faith in the Buddhist teachings. Thus, by rights, vegetarianism should have been widespread in Tibet; but this was not the case. The primary reasons were environmental in nature—namely, the Tibetan Plateau's limited variety of vegetables, inconvenient transport, intense cold, and so forth. The fact that most Tibetan monastics followed the practice of consuming what is known as "meat with threefold purity" also hinges on these factors. It is important to understand, therefore, that the rationale for consuming meat was environmental rather than religious.

Nonetheless, it is not the case that there were no vegetarians in Tibet. Not only were there many lamas, spiritual teachers, and learned and accomplished noble beings who practiced vegetarianism, but they also composed many writings on the subject that exerted a positive influence. What they said was extremely clear. In light of the great difficulties in adopting vegetarianism faced by those in Tibet—compared with other places—these writings are an undeniable sign of the strong importance that was placed on the practice.

It is a cause for great joy that nowadays, unlike in the past, an increasing number of monastics and lay Buddhists in Tibet are becoming vegetarian. However, for the sake of protecting the environment, advancing the equality of all living beings, and increasing loving compassion, we still need to continue making unflagging efforts on the vegetarian front.

On this occasion, it is my hope that the work of my American friend Dr. Geoffrey Barstow (known as Tenzin Wangchuk in Tibetan), in compiling Tibetan writings on vegetarianism and producing this new volume, will be of immense benefit, both directly and indirectly, for the environment and the living beings within it.

Written by Tsultrim Lodrö on the 10th day of the last month of spring in the Tibetan year of the earth pig (May 10, 2019). Translated from the Tibetan by Catherine Hardie.

Foreword by Matthieu Ricard

Of all the great religions, only Jainism has consistently preached strict vegetarianism and unconditional nonviolence toward animals. Buddhism comes next. According to Buddhism, "buddha nature" is present in every sentient being, even in those who do not have the intellectual faculties necessary to actualize it, such as animals. The special quality of human beings is their ability to draw on buddha nature fully in order to achieve enlightenment. This places immense value on being human, but it far from gives humans a reason to look down on other life forms. In fact, this realization should encourage them to feel greater compassion for beings who are floundering in ignorance and incite them to do everything in their power to alleviate the sufferings of these beings. From the point of view of Buddhism, it is therefore out of the question to use human intelligence for the purpose of exploiting other sentient beings.

In *Food of Sinful Demons*,[1] Geoffrey Barstow gave us the first comprehensive study showing that vegetarianism has always existed in Tibetan culture, has been motivated by compassion for the animals, and has been thought to represent the highest ethical standards. Avoiding meat eating has been advocated by highly respected masters from Milarepa to Shabkar (1781–1851), the author of several texts on this subject, including *Food of Bodhisattvas*,[2] and Patrül Rinpoché (1808–1887), the author of *The Words of My Perfect Teacher*.[3] In *The Faults of Meat*, Barstow and his coauthors present us with a most interesting array of views expressed by great luminaries of Tibetan Buddhism and Bön about the consumption of meat. This body of literature constitutes a

1. Geoffrey Barstow, *Food of Sinful Demons: Meat, Vegetarianism, and the Limits of Buddhism in Tibet* (New York: Columbia University Press, 2018).

2. Shabkar Tsogdruk Rangdrol, *Food of Bodhisattvas: Buddhist Teachings on Abstaining from Meat*, trans. Padmakara Translation Group (Boston: Shambhala Publications, 2004).

3. Patrul Rinpoche, *The Words of My Perfect Teacher*, trans. Padmakara Translation Group (Boston: Shambhala Publications, 1998).

solid scholarly contribution to the issue of vegetarianism in Buddhism in general and in Tibetan Buddhism in particular.

In Tibetan Buddhism, the various viewpoints concerning meat eating can be best viewed according to the perspectives of the Three Vehicles, respectively related to Prātimokṣa, Mahāyāna, and Vajrayāna teachings.

At the level of Prātimokṣa, one is chiefly concerned with individual liberation from samsaric sufferings. Meat eating is tolerated to a certain extent, under the rule of so-called threefold purity (*rnam gsum dag pa'i sha*): (1) that one has not killed the animal oneself, (2) that one has not ordered its killing, and (3) that it has not been purposely killed for one's own consumption. The principle of meat with the threefold purity applies chiefly to monks who receive their daily food by begging and are not supposed to discriminate among the various kinds of alms they receive, accepting whatever they are offered. But even at the Prātimokṣa level, one should remember that when entering the Buddhist path by taking refuge, one takes the following precept: "In taking the Dharma as refuge, I promise not to harm any being." This pledge undoubtedly applies to animals.

In the Mahāyāna, it is compassion all the way. It thus becomes inconceivable to inflict unnecessary suffering and death on others. In Buddhism, "others" indeed includes all sentient beings, not just humans. Only the meat of animals who have died of natural or accidental causes is therefore suitable to be eaten, which is not a very common occurrence. In Mahāyāna sūtras it is explained that applying the rule of threefold purity is a way to become more aware and responsible, and, accordingly, it encourages one to stop eating meat. It is not suggesting that even though these three conditions may have been met, eating meat is suitable for a compassionate Buddhist practitioner.

In addition to that, one should realize that all these sentient beings have been, in one lifetime or another, one's kind parents, siblings, or children. One should therefore develop love and compassion for all sentient beings, considering each of them as though they were our own dear children. In the *Laṅkāvatāra Sūtra* (often said to be "the quintessence of the Buddha's words") the Buddha says, "Those who practice loving-kindness should consider all sentient beings as their own children; therefore, they must give up eating meat," and in the *Mahāparinirvāna Sūtra*, he says that "the eating of meat annihilates the seed of compassion."

Likewise, in the Land of Snows, the great hermit Milarepa once sang:

> When pricked by thorns, you cannot bear the pain,
> and yet you kill and eat the flesh of living beings.
> How harsh will be the prickles of Reviving Hell,

when skin will be flayed from your burning limbs!
So, take away your dreadful blood-red meat.[4]

As for the argument sometimes put forward by Mahāyāna meat eaters—that one should eat meat out of compassion, since eating the flesh of a slaughtered animal creates a connection with this animal in favor of whom one can direct the full power of one's compassionate prayers—Shabkar points out that this is a serious misunderstanding of compassion. One may also argue that if an advanced practitioner has the power to affect the fate of others through prayer alone, he or she may as well pray for the sake of the animals free and alive rather than over the flesh of their corpse killed for one's consumption. If one genuinely cares about animals, rather than praying over their dead bodies it is more effective to buy them from butchers and set them free in their natural environment after praying for them.

One of my teachers, Pema Wangyal Rinpoché (1945–), often says that if a practitioner is able to bring back a slaughtered animal to life simply by snapping his fingers—as Tilopa (988–1069) is said to have done with the remnants of fish he had caught and eaten, and as Do Khyentse Yeshe Dorje (1800–1866) did with the leftovers of a sheep after eating it—then he should joyfully eat as much meat as he pleases. Otherwise, he'd better beware of dreadful karmic consequences of unnecessarily killing a sentient being. As Shabkar said in his autobiography, assuming the voice of old ewes:

When some lamas enter someone's house
and seat themselves comfortably upon the throne,
we are being slaughtered right outside the door—
don't pretend you don't know what's going on!

When there is nothing on earth
you lamas don't know,
how can you not know about this?

We pray to you from the bottom of our hearts
that, at that moment, you may say something to reprieve us.
When we are gagged and being smothered,
if we could but draw a single breath,
it would be the greatest goodness on earth.
. . . .

4. Shabkar, *Food of Bodhisattvas*, 83.

> We are just being slaughtered and slaughtered one lifetime after
> another—
> don't let your wisdom, compassion and power be so weak![5]

As for the Vajrayāna, contrary to the common belief that only the Mahāyāna sūtras condemn meat eating, one actually finds unforgiving indictments of eating meat in several tantras. The *Tantra of the Great Compassionate One Who Dredges the Depths of Samsara*,[6] for instance, says that the result of eating meat is rebirth in the hell realm for one kalpa.

Within the practice of Vajrayāna, during a gaṇacakra feast offering, one is meant to consume what is known as the "five meats" (of cow, dog, elephant, horse, and human) as samaya substances, allowing one to transcend the concepts of "pure" and "impure" and cultivate pure vision (*dag snang*), the root of Vajrayāna practice. As the Fourteenth Dalai Lama explains: "In this regard, someone might try to justify eating meat on the grounds that he or she is a practitioner of Highest Yoga Tantra. But this person must not forget that included in the five nectars and five meats are substances that are normally considered dirty and repulsive. A true practitioner of Highest Yoga Tantra does not discriminate by taking the meat but not the dirty substances. Yet, we cover our noses if such dirty substances are anywhere near us, let alone actually ingesting them."[7]

Consuming the five meats in such ways has nothing in common with eating meat as daily food. As Patrül Rinpoché reminds us in *The Words of My Perfect Teacher*: "Even those five acceptable kinds of meat may only be used if you have the power to transform the food you eat into ambrosia. . . . To eat them casually in the village, just because you like the taste, is what is meant by heedless consumption contrary to the samayas of relishing, and is also a transgression."[8] It is indeed most unlikely that people who grant themselves permission to eat meat because of their tantric practice would be eager to consume a large quantity of human flesh. In normal practice, these five meats are found as minute traces in pills made to fulfill the injunction of including them in the gaṇacakra offering. A single one of those pills is often used to make many others and the five meats thus become diluted until they are of symbolic quantity only.

5. Shabkar Tsogdruk Rangdrol, *The Life of Shabkar: The Autobiography of a Tibetan Yogin*, trans. Matthieu Ricard et al. (Ithaca, NY: Snow Lion Publications, 2001), 193–94.

6. Tib: *Thugs rje chen po 'khor ba dong sprug gyi rgyud.*

7. The Dalai Lama, *The World of Tibetan Buddhism: An Overview of Its Philosophy and Practice* (Boston: Wisdom Publications, 1995), 112.

8. Patrul Rinpoche, *The Words of My Perfect Teacher*, 208.

According to Patrül Rinpoché, making a gaṇacakra offering out of the fresh meat of an animal slaughtered for consumption is a complete aberration. It is like inviting the buddhas and bodhisattvas to a banquet and offering them the flesh of their own children.[9] Shabkar also explains in his *Emanated Scripture of Compassion* that "when in the Secret Mantra teachings, it is said that one should eat meat, this is not an explicit teaching. In the commentary on the *Ocean of Ḍākinīs Tantra*,[10] it is specified that the eating of meat refers to the 'devouring of discursive thoughts.'"[11] Along the same lines, I also heard some of my teachers say that according to some tantras—that I have not had the leisure to identify—regarding the inclusion of meat (*sha*) and alcohol (*chang*) in gaṇacakra feast offering, one may consider all solid food as "meat" and all liquid substances as ritual "alcohol."

To add to the list of contemporary Tibetan masters who have adopted and advocated a nonviolent diet, my root teacher Kangyur Rinpoché (1898–1975) was not only a strict vegetarian but could also be considered as a Tibetan pioneer of veganism, since, in addition to abstaining from eating meat, fish, and eggs, he also avoided consuming salt and tea because in Tibet these products were carried for weeks over long distances on the backs of sheep (in the case of salt from Central and Western Tibet) and mules (in the case of tea coming from China). Among Kangyur Rinpoché's children, Pema Wangyal Rinpoché and Jigme Khyentse Rinpoché (1963–) have not only actively advocated veganism but have also purchased nearly ten million live animals and freed them in their natural environment (mostly sea animals) as well as saved domestic animals from being slaughtered. In Tibet, these animals were entrusted to herders who vowed to care for them until they died from natural causes, according to the Tibetan tradition of "freeing lives" (*tshe thar*), while in Western countries they were entrusted to animal sanctuaries.

I therefore welcome with gratitude this inspiring and insightful collection of texts that will make any Buddhist practitioner think twice before continuing to nourish their own life through the suffering and death of fellow sentient beings.

9. Patrul Rinpoche, *The Words of My Perfect Teacher*, 208.

10. Skt: *Ḍākārṇava Tantra*. Tib: *Mkha' 'gro rgya mtsho'i rgyud.*

11. Shabkar Tsokdruk Rangdrol (Zhabs dkar tshogs drug rang grol), *Snying rje sprul pa'i glegs bam*, in *Zhabs dkar tshogs drug rang grol gyi bka' 'bum*, vol. 7 (*ja*) (New Delhi: Shechen, 2003), 395; BDRC: W23893. Quoted in Shabkar, *Food of Bodhisattvas*, 35.

Acknowledgments

A BOOK LIKE THIS is the product of many people's labor. I would like to begin by thanking the translators who have contributed to this volume. Translating is a difficult and time-consuming task, and these individuals have done this work well and in a timely manner. I have enjoyed collaborating with each of them and am grateful for their willingness to work on this project.

I would also like to thank the many Tibetan teachers who have contributed their knowledge to this work. Some introduced me to new texts, others patiently answered my questions about this material, and still others simply offered their good will and encouragement. Some of these teachers are named in the various chapters of this book, while others, particularly those inside the PRC, remain anonymous. Whether I have named them here or not, however, I remain deeply grateful to all of them.

The funding for this research came from many sources over many years. I particularly want to thank the Fulbright US student program, Otterbein University, and the Center for the Humanities at Oregon State.

The editors and staff at Wisdom Publications have been nothing short of a delight to work with. I particularly wish to thank Daniel Aitken and David Kittelstrom for their early and enthusiastic encouragement, Mary Petrusewicz for her tireless editing work, Ben Gleason for overseeing the production of the book, and Brianna Quick and Kestrel Slocombe for their work marketing it.

Finally, I would like to thank Eliza and Meg, who have believed in this book from the beginning and whose support has been unflagging.

Conventions

THE TIBETAN LANGUAGE is notoriously difficult to render in the Roman alphabet, at least in a way that is easily pronounceable. The standard system for rendering Tibetan in Roman letters (Wylie) accurately reproduces most elements of the Tibetan alphabet but is largely unintelligible to those who do not already read Tibetan. In order to make Tibetan terms pronounceable, this volume employs the THL system of Tibetan phonetics. Rather than trying to reproduce every Tibetan letter accurately, THL phonetics aims to standardize pronunciation based on Lhasa-dialect Tibetan. Rather than the Wylie *bsgrubs*, THL simply gives us *drub*, a fairly accurate version of how this word is pronounced. This volume employs THL phonetics throughout for the convenience of a general audience, while using Wylie transliteration in footnotes for those who read Tibetan.

Most of these texts are full of quotations from canonical and noncanonical scriptures. Many of these texts were originally composed in Sanskrit, others in Tibetan. Throughout this volume, when an author refers to an Indic text originally composed in Sanskrit, we have referred to the text by its Sanskrit title (i.e., "the *Laṅkāvatāra Sūtra* says . . ."). This is primarily because most of these texts are already well known by their Sanskrit titles. Further, many of these texts have already had their titles translated into English in a plethora of different ways. Using the Sanskrit titles, then, has the advantage of familiarity as well as avoiding the confusion of adding yet another English title to the mix. When a text composed in Tibetan is cited, however, the title is rendered in English (i.e., "the *Faults of Meat* says . . ."). This is because the Tibetan titles of these Tibetan texts are not, generally speaking, well known to an English language audience. Rendering them in English, therefore, was deemed the best way to help readers keep track of which text was which.

The translations included in this volume are the work of several individuals. Each of us has our own translation style and preferred terminology. We have, generally speaking, tried to standardize terminology across the various translations so that the same Tibetan word is rendered with the same English term. Further, we have tried to standardize the translations of canonical quotations so that when the same quotation appears in different texts, the English rendering is more or less the same. While this was our general practice, however, some translators have chosen to provide their own translations of both individual terms and longer canonical quotations. This is particularly true of the *Laṅkāvatāra* and *Mahāparinirvāṇa Sūtras*, quotations from which show up repeatedly throughout these texts, sometimes resulting in notably different readings of the same passages than are found in chapter 1. These differences of opinion serve as a reminder that the end result is a product of the translator's efforts and not simply a perfect mirror of the original.

Introduction

THIS VOLUME COLLECTS fourteen texts, all of which relate to the question of whether Tibetan Buddhists should eat meat. As these texts make clear, Tibetans have argued this point among themselves for at least a thousand years. Some of those voices argued that eating meat was morally acceptable. But others felt that meat was at least somewhat problematic. This was not a simple debate, however, and different authors could agree that meat eating was less than ideal, while also disagreeing on why that was the case and what should be done in response. For some, the only solution was to adopt—and demand that others adopt—full vegetarianism. Other authors stopped short of this dramatic step but still felt uncomfortable with the casual consumption of meat and tried to curb it in one way or another. It is the goal of this volume to introduce the contours of this debate and the range of voices and positions within it.

Some History[1]

Over the last few decades, vegetarianism has emerged as a point of tension in Tibetan communities. Some lamas and other religious leaders have argued that meat eating is against Buddhist ideals and should be abandoned. Others have argued that eating meat is a traditional part of Tibetan culture and should be maintained. In order to support this argument, many of those opposed to vegetarianism argue that it is an innovation, a practice not found in traditional forms of Tibetan Buddhism.[2] As the texts in this volume amply illustrate, however, claims like this are simply untrue. Not all Tibetans were vegetarian by any measure. As far as I can tell, most were not. But a significant minority were vegetarian, and, perhaps more important, some of these individuals were prominent enough to ensure that the debates over meat

1. A longer and more detailed history of vegetarianism in Tibet can be found in chapter 2 of Barstow, *Food of Sinful Demons.*

2. For an analysis of one particular response, see Buffetrille, "A Controversy on Vegetarianism."

eating never disappeared. Vegetarianism may not have been the norm, but it was certainly present and was an important aspect of Tibetan Buddhist practice.

The first well-attested examples of Tibetan Buddhists adopting vegetarianism come from the early centuries of the period known as the "second dissemination" of Buddhism in Tibet.[3] This period, beginning in the late tenth century, was characterized by renewed interest in monastic Buddhism and new translations of Indian texts into Tibetan. Among these practices was a distinct concern for the moral status of meat. This can be seen in a number of early textual sources, including the seminal eleventh-century Indian master Atiśa's (982–1054) dialogues with his Tibetan disciple Dromtön (1004–1064), contained in the *Book of Kadam*.[4] At roughly the same time, the Bön[5] master Metön Sherab Özer (1058–1132) criticized meat eating in his *Vinaya Compendium*, one of the earliest Bön texts on the Vinaya, the formal rules for monks and nuns. Like generations of Tibetan authors after him, Metön Sherab Özer's critique focuses specifically on the question of compassion, the single most important point in the debates over meat. His claims are brief but provide perhaps the earliest clear statement against meat eating, foreshadowing the more elaborate arguments that came later:

> By definition, this thing called "meat" comes from the killing of animals. Being without mercy sends one to hell. With great regret, abandon eating it. This thing called "meat" comes from a father and a mother. These are its causes and conditions. If you saw this with your eyes, you would tremble with fear. How pitiful it would be to take it in your hands! Just smelling it brings on nausea. Once it is tasted by the tongue, how can it be kept down? For these reasons, it should be abandoned.[6]

3. There are some hints that vegetarianism may also have been practiced in the "first dissemination," which began in the seventh century. But the records are spotty and incomplete, so I do not wish to make any definitive claims. For more, see Barstow, *Food of Sinful Demons*, 30–31.

4. For an English translation of these passages, see Thubten Jinpa, *Book of Kadam*, 25–28.

5. The Bön tradition has its roots in Tibet's pre-Buddhist era and continues to conceive of itself as distinct from the Buddhist tradition. Nevertheless, by the eleventh century Bön had begun to adopt many Buddhistic practices and norms, including monasticism and tantric ritual. Metön Sherab Özer himself was a seminal figure in this transition, particularly in founding Bön monasticism. For more on this, see Cech, "A Bonpo Bca' Yig," 69.

6. I have not managed to locate a complete copy of this text. This passage is quoted in the fifteenth-century work by Nyamé Sherab Gyaltsen, *'Dul bab mdor bsdus kyi 'grel pa*, 49.

There is also some good evidence for vegetarianism in the community centered around the twelfth-century master Pakmodrupa (1110–1170). Some later Tibetan sources claim that Pakmodrupa himself was vegetarian, though I have not found evidence for this in early material.[7] It would make sense, however, as at least two of Pakmodrupa's students are well-attested vegetarians: Jigten Sumgön (1143–1217, founder of the Drikung Kagyü) and Taklung Tangpa (1142–1209, founder of the Taklung Kagyü). Taklung Tangpa's student Rinchen Gön (1191–1236) was also a vegetarian, as were at least some of his students.[8] Overall, this cluster of vegetarians suggests that a meatless diet may have been common early on in this lineage.

While vegetarianism may have been common in this community, however, none of these lamas wrote about it extensively. The first significant discussion in Tibet does not emerge, in fact, until Dolpopa Sherab Gyaltsen (1292–1361), the thirteenth-century founder of the Jonang lineage. His *Refraining from Meat and Alcohol*, translated in chapter 2 of this volume, discusses the faults of drinking alcohol and eating meat at some length. Of particular importance is Dolpopa's division of his work into three sections based on the three different sets of vows that Tibetan Buddhists often adopt: the vows of individual liberation, the bodhisattva vow, and the tantric samayas. Dolpopa is the first Tibetan that I am aware of to organize his discussion of meat eating along these lines, developing a schema that would become common throughout these debates and that is reflected in many of the texts translated here.

A century after Dolpopa, Ngorchen Künga Sangpo (1382–1456) wrote his *Epistle Benefitting Students*, the most extensive Tibetan work on meat eating to that point and one of the most influential such works ever written. Translated in chapter 3 of this volume, Ngorchen followed Dolpopa's approach, discussing meat according to each of the three vows. Ngorchen's commitment to vegetarianism, however, went well beyond this single text. When he founded Ngor Ewam Chöden Monastery in 1429, Ngorchen insisted on strict adherence to the Vinaya, including vegetarianism.[9] Further, many of his disciples and successors are known to have practiced and promoted vegetarianism, including Gorampa (1429–1489), whose criticism of meat eating is translated in chapter 5 of this book. It seems, in fact, that vegetarianism may have been common at

7. For one such claim, see Shabkar Tsokdrük Rangdröl, *Rmad byung sprul pa'i glegs bam*, 58. For an English translation, see Shabkar, *Food of Bodhisattvas*, 82.

8. For brief references to these masters' vegetarianism, see Gö Lotsawa Shonu Pal, *Ddeb ther sngon po*, 707, 727. For an alternate English translation, see Roerich, *The Blue Annals*, 599, 617.

9. For more on the banning of meat at Ngor, see Jörg Heimbel's introduction in chapter 3 of this book. See also Heimbel, *Vajradhara in Human Form*, 251.

Ngor Ewam Chöden for several centuries after its founding, making it one of the few places in Tibet where vegetarianism ever became normative.

At roughly the same time, Khedrup Jé (1385–1438), a foundational figure in the up-and-coming Geluk lineage, also wrestled with the question of meat eating. Khedrup competed with Ngorchen for patronage and disagreed with him on a host of intellectual issues. His opinions on meat eating, therefore, can be seen in part as a critique of Ngorchen's uncompromising call for vegetarianism among monks. In fact, Khedrup's fullest treatment of this topic—contained in his *Polishing the Jewel of the Sage's Teachings: A Brief and Conclusive Presentation on the Three Vows* and translated in chapter 4 of this volume—amounts to the most robust defense of meat eating that I am aware of in premodern Tibetan literature.[10] He argues that the Vinaya rules are clear that monks can eat meat as long as it has threefold purity, and asserts that the *Laṅkāvatāra Sūtra* does not actually mandate or suggest vegetarianism—despite this sūtra's seemingly plain anti-meat stance. That said, even though Khedrup argues against Ngorchen (and others') vegetarianism, he does not go so far as to suggest that eating meat casually, without reflection, is acceptable. In particular, he accepts that the Buddha restricted certain types of meat, that meat without threefold purity is unacceptable, and that some beginner bodhisattvas should avoid meat in order to revese their instinct toward craving. Further, it is worth noting that some later Tibetans present Khedrup as a (partial) proponent of vegetarianism.[11] Nevertheless, it is clear that Khedrup stakes out a position in opposition to Ngorchen, Dolpopa, and other earlier authors.

Perhaps because of Khedrup's stance on meat and the political ascendancy of his Geluk lineage, references to vegetarianism begin to decline in the fifteenth and sixteenth centuries, at least in Central Tibet. This is not to say that it disappeared entirely, of course. Vegetarianism continued to be important at Ngor for several centuries, as well as within the Karma Kagyü lineage. The eighth Karmapa, Mikyö Dorjé (1507–1554), was particularly important in the latter, penning several critiques of meat eating—including the short work translated in chapter 6 of this volume—and instituting vegetarianism at Tsurpu, his home monastery. Despite these individuals and communities, it is clear that on the whole, the practice of vegetarianism declined in Central Tibet from the mid-fifteenth century onward.

While vegetarianism may have been declining in Central Tibet, however,

10. As a defense of meat eating, Khedrup's text is obviously an outlier in this volume. It was included here in order to give readers a fuller sense of the arguments and debates that surrounded meat eating.

11. See, for instance, Shabkar, *Food of Bodhisattvas*, 87–90, 105–6, 112, 117–18.

it was on the rise in the eastern Tibetan region known as Kham. In the mid-seventeenth century, Karma Chakmé (1613–1678) wrote an extended critique of meat eating, as well as a prayer to be said before eating it, both of which are translated in chapter 7. I do not know if there was already a tradition of vegetarianism in Kham prior to Karma Chakmé, but it is clear that his influence was felt for the next several generations. While he himself never held the abbacy, Karma Chakmé was instrumental in the founding of Pelyül Monastery in 1665, and the first and second abbots of this institution were vegetarian themselves and also encouraged it among their monks. This tradition does not seem to have lasted more than a century, but for a time Pelyül may have rivaled Ngor as a center of institutionalized vegetarianism.

Like his predecessors, Karma Chakmé structures his work around the three vows. He also draws on previous texts, particularly Ngorchen's *Epistle*, for many of his basic arguments and the scriptural passages he cites. His work, however, takes these arguments further than any his predecessors, providing the most detailed take on the three-vow approach to meat eating that I am aware of. This is fitting, as Karma Chakmé's work is the last of the major scholastic treatises on vegetarianism. Up to and including Karma Chakmé, all of the Tibetan authors I am aware of focused their works on a close parsing of the sūtras, tantras, and other authoritative scriptures. The goal, it seems, was to use scholastic methods to determine the Buddha's take on meat eating so that Buddhists could do likewise. The result is texts that are dense and full of scriptural citations, often assuming an argumentative posture that sometimes even uses the technical vocabulary usually found in debate courtyards.

After Karma Chakmé, however, the writing style used in these texts shifts dramatically. In his memoirs of life in a Tibetan monastery, Georges Dreyfus—the first European or American to earn the prestigious geshé degree—describes the Tibetan educational system as essentially scholastic. What he means by this is that Tibetan education centers on reading and commenting on classical Buddhist scriptures illuminated by the light of previous generations of commentary. "I believe the most distinctive feature of scholasticism," he writes, "to be its emphasis on interpreting the great texts constitutive of the tradition within the confines of its authority, using the intellectual tools handed down from previous generations."[12] Such an approach to scholarship is evident in the texts on vegetarianism written prior to the eighteenth century. Dolpopa, Ngorchen Künga Sangpo, Khedrup Jé, Gorampa, and Karma Chakmé all center their writings on a detailed analysis of scriptural precedent,

12. Dreyfus, *The Sound of Two Hands Clapping*, 11. Dreyfus earned the geshé lharampa, the highest degree in the curriculum of Tibetan Buddhist monastic universities, in 1985.

including both canonical works by the Buddha and texts written by previous Indian and Tibetan scholars. They parse and dissect these texts with great subtlety, and each come to their own conclusions, but they all come to these conclusions based on their analysis of scripture and textual precedent. The result is texts that are full of quotations and that feel almost legalistic in tone. This is a powerful mode of argumentation, particularly for a Buddhist audience that accepts the authority of the scriptures.

In the late eighteenth century, however, there is a striking shift in the rhetoric used to support vegetarianism. This shift has its roots, as far as I have been able to discover, in the writings of the Nyingma visionary Jigmé Lingpa (1730–1798).[13] To the best of my knowledge, Jigmé Lingpa did not compose any texts specifically focused on meat eating or vegetarianism, and his work is therefore not included in this volume. Short passages that display a deep concern for animal welfare, however, are woven throughout his extensive literary corpus. He calls meat a "sinful food"[14] and suggests that his followers should avoid it whenever possible. Unlike his predecessors, however, he largely eschews the scholastic approach when expressing this concern for animal welfare, replacing detailed scriptural exegesis with powerful descriptions of animals suffering. Instead of asking his readers to balance competing scriptural claims, he simply asks them to have an affective, emotional response to the lived experience of the animals themselves. Perhaps nowhere is this approach as clear as in the following passage from his autobiography:

> Having now become animals, your fathers, mothers, siblings, and friends from previous lives tremble with fear in the butcher's sinful hands, tears streaming from their eyes, and panting for breath. In that state they wonder what to do. Alas, there is no refuge! There is nowhere to go! Thinking that, right now in this place, they may be killed, their urgent suffering is great. In such a state, like one approaching a terrifying pit of hell-fire, their body is turned upside down, their muzzle is tied up, and their eyes move wildly with lights shining forth. What they see is their stomach being opened up. With their feet perpendicular, they are set on the path to the next life without even a quiver.[15]

13. For a more detailed look at Jigmé Lingpa's attitude toward vegetarianism, see Barstow, "Buddhism Between Abstinence and Indulgence."

14. Jigmé Lingpa, *Ri bong shin tu brtan pa'i gtam brag ri'i mgu la rgyan*, 4:772.

15. Jigmé Lingpa, *Yul lho rgyud du byung ba'i rdzogs chen pa rang byung rdo rje mkhyen brtse'i 'od zer gyi rnam thar pa legs byas yongs 'du'i snye ma*, 9:125–26.

Jigmé Lingpa's affective arguments against causing animal suffering were picked up and adopted by later writers. Perhaps the most famous of these was Shabkar Tsokdrük Rangdröl (1781–1851), a master from Amdo associated with both the Nyingma and Geluk lineages. Shabkar was himself a deeply committed vegetarian, and his autobiography recalls a powerfully emotional conversion experience: he was walking along the pilgrimage circuit in Lhasa when the sight of sheep lined up for slaughter prompted him to reflect, with great distress, on the suffering that meat eating caused. He immediately went before the Jowo Shakyamuni statue and took a lifelong vow to never again eat meat.[16] Further, Shabkar promoted vegetarianism relentlessly, writing with pride of the three hundred disciples who became vegetarian under his influence.[17] Shabkar also wrote prolifically about vegetarianism, composing three extended works decrying meat eating in the strongest terms. As two of these texts are already widely available in the Padmakara Translation Committee's excellent English translation, these longer works have been left out of this volume.[18] But Shabkar also addressed the question of vegetarianism in several poems and shorter works, and four of these are included here in chapter 8. Shabkar's work on vegetarianism is extensive, and he certainly includes plenty of scholastic analysis. He tends, however, to follow Jigmé Lingpa and emphasize the experience of the animals themselves, seemingly in an attempt to prompt an emotional, affective response among his readers.

This approach is also reflected in the work of Patrül Rinpoché (1808–1887), another famed nineteenth-century master. Patrül's primary discussion of meat eating is found in his *Words of My Perfect Teacher*, a famous text that is already widely available in English and so has not been included in this volume.[19] Like Jigmé Lingpa and Shabkar, Patrül focuses on creating vivid images of the slaughtering and meat-eating process intended to prompt an affective response among his readers:

> These days, those who have the appearance of lamas are drawn in when a patron slaughters a fat, greasy sheep and cooks the quivering meat with the gullet and organs, piling the lot atop the still-trembling ribs of a yak. These lamas pull their monastic shawls over

16. Shabkar Tsokdruk Rangdrol, *The Life of Shabkar*, 232.

17. Shabkar Tsokdruk Rangdrol, *The Life of Shabkar*, 542.

18. The Padmakara Translation Committee's translation of Shabkar is a must read for anyone interested in the question of Tibetan Buddhist vegetarianism: Shabkar, *Food of Bodhisattvas*.

19. Patrul Rinpoche, *The Words of My Perfect Teacher*, esp. pages 70, 103–4, 201–3.

their heads and suck away at the entrails like a baby sucking at its mother's breast.[20]

Jigmé Lingpa, Shabkar, and Patrül's works mark not only a shift in rhetorical strategy but also the increasing popularity of vegetarianism in nineteenth-century Kham. Earlier, I noted that the thirteenth through sixteenth centuries marked something of a high-water mark for vegetarianism in Central Tibet. The same can be said for nineteenth- and early twentieth-century Kham. Important individual lamas such as Rigdzin Garwang (1858–1930), Ngawang Lekpa (1864–1941), Sera Khandro (1892–1940), and many others personally practiced vegetarianism. Further, interviews I have conducted with elderly Tibetans who remember this time suggest that vegetarianism may have been widespread in certain communities. The writings of Nyala Pema Dündul (1816–1873, chapter 9 of this volume) and Shardza Tashi Gyaltsen (1859–1935, chapter 10) are both part of this broader movement. For his part, Nyala Pema Dündul continues the emphasis on emotional imagery begun by Jigmé Lingpa, describing a dream sequence in which the bodhisattva Avalokiteśvara gives him a tour of the various punishments that await meat eaters in hell. Shardza, on the other hand, was arguably the most important Bön scholar of his generation, so it is not surprising that his *Faults of Meat* marks something of a return to the scholastic style, with numerous quotations from canonical sources. Even here, however, traces of the more emotional, affective style remain. In some ways, then, it is fitting that Shardza's work is the final pre-Communist work included here. It captures many of the broad trends and concerns we see across these texts, distilling them down into a short yet surprisingly nuanced work.

But the history of vegetarianism in Tibet did not end with the arrival of Communist Chinese forces in the early 1950s. The arrival of communism marked the beginning of rapid and painful transformations in Tibet, first into a centrally organized socialist system and then into today's market economy. Periods of relative peace alternated with extended periods during which all things religious were attacked—sometimes violently. Religious leaders were publicly criticized, arrested, and sometimes killed, while monasteries, texts, and art were destroyed.[21] This process was particularly disastrous during the decades of high Maoism (roughly from the Great Leap Forward in 1958 until

20. Patrül Rinpoché, *Snying tig sngon 'gro'i khrid yig kun bzang bla ma'i zhal lung*, 7:103. For an alternate English translation, see Patrul Rinpoche, *The Words of My Perfect Teacher*, 70.

21. There has been a plethora of books on the changes in Tibet since the Communist takeover. Many, however, are deeply biased or otherwise incomplete. For reliable studies, see the three

the death of Mao in 1976), but it has never fully abated. Despite the hardships, however, vegetarianism never fully disappeared. I have interviewed two elderly lamas who claim to have maintained their personal vegetarianism through the entire Communist period, despite the fact that food of any type was often hard to come by.[22]

More recently, vegetarianism has experienced a surge of popularity over the last two decades. It is impossible to know what percentage of the present Tibetan population is vegetarian, but anecdotal evidence suggests it is considerable. Many restaurants, for instance, now offer extensive vegetarian menus, and vegetarian foods are produced and marketed directly to Tibetans. I am no longer at all surprised to hear that someone I am talking to is a vegetarian or to overhear people discussing it among themselves.

Like vegetarianism in pre-Communist Tibet, the contemporary movement is essentially a religious movement, and its foremost proponents are all religious leaders. There have been quite a few voices raised in support of this vegetarianism movement, and improvements in technology—particularly the Internet and smart phones—mean that almost anyone who wishes can weigh in on this issue. Nevertheless, there are a few individual religious leaders whose religious standing and personal charisma have gone a long way to supporting contemporary vegetarianism. Among those religious leaders active in the exile community, the current Dalai Lama (1935–) and Karmapa[23] (1985–) deserve special mention. Both (though particularly the Karmapa) have spoken out in support of vegetarianism, and their position on this question is well known to Tibetans in Tibet.[24] In addition, numerous other exile leaders have argued for vegetarianism, including Arjia Rinpoché, a contemporary Mongolian lama based in Bloomington, Indiana. Arjia Rinpoché became a vegetarian in 1994 and has actively promoted the diet ever since. An interview with him is included as chapter 11.

Most Tibetans, however, live in Tibet rather than in exile, amplifying the importance of those lamas inside Tibet who support vegetarianism. Among these, the most significant is Khenpo Tsultrim Lodrö (1961–), whose *Clear*

volumes in Melvyn Goldstein's *History of Modern Tibet* series, and particularly Tsering Shakya, *The Dragon in the Land of Snows*.

22. I am withholding the names of these individuals in order to preserve their anonymity.

23. There are currently two claimants to the throne of the Karmapa. This is not the place to discuss the merits of either candidate, except to note that within Tibet itself, Ogyen Trinle Dorjé is almost universally recognized as the true Karmapa. When I refer to the current Karmapa, this is who I am discussing.

24. For more on the stance of these two towering figures on vegetarianism, see His Holiness the Dalai Lama, "Non-Vegetarian Food," and Karmapa Ogyen Tinle Dorjé, "Talk on Vegetarianism."

Mirror of Advice has been translated in chapter 12 of this volume. Khenpo Tsultrim Lodrö is the Dharma heir of the renowned Khenpo Jigmé Püntsok (1933–2003), founder of Larung Gar Buddhist Academy. Khenpo Tsultrim Lodrö himself spent more than a decade leading the Larung Gar community, which—at least prior to a round of government-sponsored destruction in the summer of 2016—had been the largest monastic community in world history.[25] And he has published numerous texts, posters, and video disks in support of vegetarianism and regularly incorporates it into his public teachings. His stance on this issue is so well known that when I ask Tibetans in Tibet about vegetarianism, I am always invariably pointed in his direction. Between the Karmapa, Arjia Rinpoché, Khenpo Tsultrim Lodrö, and the many other contemporary proponents of vegetarianism, it seems clear that concern with meat eating—indeed, with animal ethics more broadly—is likely to remain an issue in Tibetan religion for the foreseeable future.

Before concluding, it is important to remember that vegetarianism never became normative in pre-Communist Tibet. Most Tibetans—both monastic and lay—ate meat regularly. At the same time, however, there was a consistent concern about the ethics of a meat-eating diet, particularly among the devout. In some cases, this led to the adoption of vegetarianism on the part of individual practitioners. Less commonly, there were times (thirteenth- to sixteenth-century Central Tibet and nineteenth- to twentieth-century Kham) and places (Ngor Ewam Chöden and Pelyül Monasteries) where vegetarianism was strikingly common and perhaps even the norm. The texts contained in this volume demonstrate that while vegetarianism was a minority practice, it was nonetheless an important practice worth taking seriously.

What Is "Vegetarianism"?

I have used the word "vegetarian" repeatedly in this introduction. And yet what exactly this word means in a Tibetan context is not altogether clear. "Vegetarian" is a slippery word, even in English, with some people suggesting that one can be vegetarian while still eating fish, and others arguing that only a fully vegan diet counts as true vegetarianism. The situation is even more complex in Tibetan, where there is no single word (or concept) that maps easily onto the English term "vegetarian." In modern Tibetan, the closest equivalent is *karsé* (*dkar zas*), meaning "white food," and contrasted against *marsé* (*dmar zas*), "red food." As this color coding suggests, the central distinction here

25. I am not aware of any firm figures, but there were likely between twenty and thirty thousand monks and nuns at Larung Gar at its peak.

involves blood: eating karsé food does not involve killing an animal, whereas eating marsé food does. But while karsé and marsé are now in common use, they are actually neologisms, new words unattested in traditional literature.[26]

The only word used in pre-Communist literature that approaches the concept of "vegetarianism" is *dokar*, meaning something like "white ingedients."[27] When used, dokar means that a person has made a choice to not eat meat on an ongoing basis, something quite similar to the English word "vegetarian." Dokar, however, is not used universally in Tibetan literature, appearing primarily in works of the Drigung Kagyü and, sometimes, Ngor Sakya lineages. Elsewhere, when Tibetan authors wanted to get across the idea that a particular individual had given up meat, they simply described the situation rather than referring to a specific diet. *The Biography of Ngawang Lekpa*, for instance, simply states, "Since the time he requested monk's vows, he abandoned eating meat, drinking alcohol, and eating after noon."[28] Here the author does not use a specific term or concept like *karsé* or *dokar* to define Ngawang Lekpa's diet. Instead, he simply states that Ngawang Lekpa stopped eating meat. This same pattern is found throughout Tibetan literature and is far and away the most common way to explain that someone does not eat meat.

Thus Tibetan literature tends to conceptualize vegetarianism as a negation (giving up meat) rather than an affirmation (adopting a specific diet). This approach to vegetarianism is broad and allows a lot of flexibility in what can be considered vegetarian. This flexibility is important because, as the texts in this volume demonstrate, individual Tibetans gave up meat to different degrees and in different ways. Some, of course, gave it up entirely. Others, however, simply reduced how much meat they ate or gave it up for a certain period of time. These practices do not adhere to a single, clearly defined "vegetarian" diet, but they do all involve the intentional rejection of meat in one way or another. When I speak of vegetarianism in this volume, I am referring to this flexible conception of vegetarianism, loosely defined as intentionally avoiding meat in one way or another.

26. While these specific terms are unattested, the white/red color coding does exist, especially in the context of religious offerings. There, offerings without meat are called *karchö* (*dkar mchod*) "white offerings," while those that include meat are *marchö* (*dmar mchod*), "red offerings."

27. Tib: *rdor/sdor dkar*. The term *dokar* is discussed extensively in note 167 to Jörg Heimbel's translation of Ngorchen Künga Sangpo's *Epistle Benefitting Students* in this volume. See also Hou Haoran, "Some Remarks on the Transmission of the Ascetic Discipline of the 'Single Mat,'" 206.

28. Künga Tenpé Gyaltsen, *Rje bla ma rdo rje 'chang ngag dbang kun dga' legs pa'i 'byung gnas ye shes rgyal mtshan dpal bzang po'i rnam par thar pa ngo mtshar nor bu'i 'phreng ba*, 9.

Themes and Arguments

The texts in this volume approach the question of meat eating from a variety of perspectives. Each author brought his own concerns and experiences to this issue, and the result is, not surprisingly, that they each emphasized different things. That said, there are several important themes and concerns that run throughout these works, and over the next few pages I will highlight some of the most important.

Compassion

Without doubt, the central concern driving these authors is compassion. Tibetan Buddhism self-consciously adheres to the Mahāyāna form of Buddhism. And like Mahāyāna Buddhism elsewhere, compassion is a central concern of Tibetan religiosity, perhaps even *the* central concern. As Shardza says in the opening lines of his *Faults of Meat*, "Compassion is the essence of all the Buddha's teachings."[29] Compassion, for Shardza and most other Tibetans, was not simply a side effect or byproduct of religious practice, it was the central aim, the essence, of Buddhism itself. And that compassion was not limited to other humans. Humans, of course, should be treated compassionately. But that compassion should also extend to all other sentient beings as well, including animals (as well as ghosts, hell-beings, and any other sentient being). Further, compassion should be more than just a mental state; it should include active engagement with the world in order to lessen the suffering of others. Once again, Shardza summarizes this discussion well: "Become completely absorbed with this, so that you guard beings with great compassion, steadfast and immeasurable. Motivate yourself with the aim of establishing all beings in both temporary and ultimate happiness! With this as your intention, perform positive actions of body and speech."

In Tibetan perspective, there is no question that killing animals causes them to suffer and is therefore highly sinful and completely incompatible with the Buddhist call to compassion. The question about eating meat, then, is not about the ethics of killing animals but rather whether or not eating meat is connected with the act of killing. Some Tibetans—drawing on the rule of threefold purity, discussed below—understood eating meat to be largely or wholly separate from the act of killing. The killing, they argued, was already complete by the time they entered the butcher shop: all they were doing was buying a product after the fact. Not surprisingly, many of the authors included

29. See the full translation in chapter 10 of this volume.

in this volume argued strongly against this position. To do so, they usually pointed out the causal connection between consumers buying meat and butchers killing. As the Eighth Karmapa Mikyö Dorjé puts it, "If the consumer is not present as the initial observed condition, then the later empowering condition [i.e., the butcher's desire to kill] will not arise and the act of killing will not happen. If that exists, then this happens."[30] In addition to their own words, many authors also relied on canonical quotations in order to make this connection between the consumption of meat and the killing of the animal, particularly the *Laṅkāvatāra Sūtra*, which notes, "People pay money for meat, causing animals to be killed for profit. Both the killer and buyer own this sinful karma and will boil in the Crying Hell." Others cited similar passages in the *Kālacakra Tantra*[31] and the *Mañjuśrī Pradarshana*.[32]

A more literary approach to this issue can be found in Jigmé Lingpa's *Story of the Hunted Deer*. Here Jigmé Lingpa tells a story in which a hunter meets a hermit deep in the mountains. The hermit chastises the hunter for the sinful nature of his work, but the hunter pushes back, arguing that it is the people who buy the meat of the animals he kills that are truly sinful: "Even if it is hunters like me who do the actual killing, the meat is bought and eaten by all of the so-called religious ascetics. It is laughable to claim there is a difference between the sin of killing and the sin of eating."[33] Whether they made their argument using logic, scriptural citations, or simply by telling a story, all of these authors insist that eating meat is directly connected to the act of killing, even if the purchaser did not personally order the death of the specific animal in question. Butchers kill in order to sell meat. Those who purchase it are therefore deeply implicated in the death of the animal even though they

30. This line is from Mikyö Dorjé's *Letter on the Unsuitability of Eating the Meat of Our Old Mothers*. I had initially intended to include a translation of this text in this volume, but the only manuscript known to me is difficult to read in many places, so, in the end, this text has been left out. Those interested in reading it themselves can find the microfilm of the manuscript via the Nepal German Manuscript Preservation Project (reel no. E 2943/4): Mikyö Dorjé, *Gangs ri'i khrod na gnas pa gtso bor gyur pa skyabs med ma rgan tshogs la sha zar mi rung ba'i springs yig sogs*, 9.

31. See Dolpopa's *Refraining from Meat* (chapter 2 of this volume), Khedrup Jé's *Polishing the Jewel of the Sage's Teachings* (chapter 4), Gorampa's *Commentary on Distinguishing the Three Vows* (chapter 5), Karma Chakmé's *Faults of Meat* (chapter 7), and Khenpo Tsultrim Lodrö's *Clear Mirror* (chapter 12).

32. See Gorampa's *Commentary on Distinguishing the Three Vows* (chapter 5 of this volume), Karma Chakmé's *Faults of Meat* (chapter 7), and Khenpo Tsultrim Lodrö's *Clear Mirror* (chapter 12).

33. Jigmé Lingpa, *Ri dwags kyi gtam nges 'byung gi pho nya*, 4:759. For an alternate English translation, see Jigmé Lingpa, "The Story of the Hunted Deer."

did not wield the knife. Given this understanding, and given the importance of applied compassion in Tibetan Buddhism, it is not hard to see why these authors would suggest that eating meat should be abandoned.

Meat in the Vinaya

For most of the authors represented in this book, the need to be compassionate toward animals by reducing their suffering is the core argument in favor of vegetarianism. It is striking, however, how little many of these texts actually discuss compassion. Discussions of compassion appear, of course, but they often take up far fewer lines of text than other issues, particularly in the scholastic works by Dolpopa, Ngorchen, Khedrup, Gorampa, Karma Chakmé, and Khenpo Tsultrim Lodrö. Instead, the majority of these texts are dedicated to rebutting arguments in opposition to vegetarianism. That is, these authors tend to briefly lay out their own position in favor of vegetarianism and then spend the majority of their time defending that position against counterarguments.

Of particular concern for these authors was the Vinaya, and particularly the rule of threefold purity.[34] This rule is found in multiple passages in the *Mūlasarvāstivāda Vinaya* followed by Tibetan monastics, but perhaps the clearest formulation is found in the *Bhaiṣajya* chapter of the *Vinayavastu*:[35]

> I say that meat that is not suitable by the three ways should not be eaten. What are these three? Meat that has been seen to have been prepared for one's own sake is unsuitable to be eaten. Meat that you have heard from trustworthy sources to have been prepared for your own sake is unsuitable to be eaten. Meat that you think, based on suspicions that have arisen in your mind, to have been prepared for your own sake is unsuitable to be eaten.[36]

In essence, this rule states that a monk or nun may eat meat as long as they do not even suspect that the meat was prepared for their own sake. All Tibetans that I am aware of, including the proponents of vegetarianism included in

34. Tib: *snang / rnam gsum dag pa'i sha*; Skt: *tikoṭiparisuddha.*

35. *The Chapter on Medicine* (Tib: *Sman gyi gzhi*). One of seventeen chapters in the *Vinayavastu* (Vinaya Chapters; Tib: *'Dul ba'i gzhi*) of the *Mūlasarvāstivāda Vinaya.*

36. This passage is translated from the edition of the *Vinayavastu* found in the Degé edition of the Kangyur, vol. 3, 25a–25b. For a translation of the corresponding passage from the Pali canon, which features several important differences, see Horner, *The Book of the Discipline*, 324–25.

this volume, understood this rule to be the authentic speech of the Buddha, and thus canonical. They could not, therefore, attack it directly. Instead, those Tibetan authors who supported vegetarianism tended to argue that the rule of threefold purity was never meant to be definitive. The rule of threefold purity, they argue, was made because a strict rule requiring vegetarianism would have driven some people away from Buddhism. Once these people had been Buddhists for a while and had developed some discipline, then they could give meat up entirely. Gorampa makes this argument clearly: "My own view is that the Vinaya allows beginners to eat meat while they gradually practice the foundational discipline. Later, having perfected this foundational discipline and having studied the *Laṅkāvatāra Sūtra* and *Mahāparinirvāṇa Sūtra*, meat is forbidden."[37] As Gorampa suggests, Tibetan authors found support for this position in canonical texts such as the *Laṅkāvatāra Sūtra* and *Mahāparinirvāṇa Sūtra*, both of which explicitly state that the Buddha allowed meat with threefold purity only in order to avoid alienating beginners.

This argument was bolstered by an appeal to the theory and literature surrounding what is known as the "three vows."[38] Devout Tibetans typically adopt three distinct sets of vows: the monastic vows of individual liberation,[39] the bodhisattva vow,[40] and the tantric samayas.[41] Each of these three sets of vows are distinct, and while they usually agree with one another, they do sometimes conflict. In such instances, most three-vow theorists argued that practitioners should follow the higher set of vows.[42] Meat eating is one such point of conflict. The rule of threefold purity is found in the monastic vows of individual liberation. The call to compassion, however, is the core of the

37. For the full quote in context, see chapter 5 of this book.

38. Tib: *sdom gsum*.

39. Tib: *so sor thar pa'i sdom pa*; Skt: *prātimokṣa*. The vows that form the core of the monastic lifestyle. These vows focus on restraint and are common across all Buddhist traditions, Mahāyāna and non-Mahāyāna. While the vows of individual liberation are usually associated with monastics, there is a set of five basic vows sometimes taken by lay practitioners as well.

40. Tib: *byang chub sems pa'i mon lam*; Skt: *bodhisattvapraṇidhāna*. The vow (literally aspiration) to attain enlightenment not for one's own sake but in order to effectively benefit others. In the Tibetan tradition, taking the bodhisattva vow marks entry to the bodhisattva path.

41. Tib: *dam tshig*; Skt: *samaya*. The tantric samayas are the vows undertaken by all who enter into tantric practice. For more on these very complex vows, see van Schaik, "The Limits of Transgression"; Wedemeyer, *Making Sense of Tantric Buddhism*.

42. For more on three-vow theory, see Sobisch, *Three-Vow Theories in Tibetan Buddhism*. For two examples of Tibetan texts clarifying the three vows and their relationship to one another, see Sakya Paṇḍita Kunga Gyaltshen, *A Clear Differentiation of the Three Codes*; Dudjom Rinpoche, *Perfect Conduct*.

bodhisattva vow, which is almost universally considered to be higher than the vows of individual liberation. For many of the authors translated in this volume, this means that even if the rule of threefold purity is relevant for śrāvakas and other non-Mahāyāna Buddhists, it is superseded by the bodhisattva vow's call to compassion. Since Tibetans adhere to the Mahāyāna and adopt the bodhisattva vow, the argument goes, they should not eat meat despite the permissions granted by the rule of threefold purity. Sakya Paṇḍita articulates this point clearly in his *Distinguishing the Three Vows*, in the passage that Gorampa comments on in chapter 5 of this volume. "Śrāvakas," he says, "may eat meat that has threefold purity. . . . In the Mahāyāna, meat is forbidden."[43]

There are some exceptions to this, of course, and Khedrup Jé's *Polishing the Jewel of the Sage's Teachings*, in chapter 4 of this volume, is notable for his insistence that the bodhisattva vow does not conflict with the rule of threefold purity, at least for ordinary practitioners. Despite such outliers, however, most Tibetan authors who wrote about meat eating concluded that it was opposed to the bodhisattva vow. Because of this, the rule of threefold purity simply didn't apply.

Meat in Tantra

Three-vow theory holds that since the bodhisattva vow is more advanced and represents a further stage of the Buddhist path, it supersedes the monastic vows of individual liberation. The same logic, however, holds that the tantric samayas supersede the bodhisattva vow. These commitments are the vows taken whenever someone receives initiation into a particular tantric practice. Since most Tibetans practiced some form of tantric Buddhism, they were bound by these commitments. And while different tantric lineages espouse different sets of commitments, they all include a requirement that practitioners drink alcohol and eat meat. This requirement was, not surprisingly, something of a stumbling block for those Tibetan religious leaders who were promoting vegetarianism. It is not surprising, therefore, that they devoted considerable space in their works to dealing with the question of meat in tantra.

The discussions of meat found in the tantras[44] are complex and detailed, and the texts translated in this volume approach the issue with more diversity and detail than I can in this introduction. In general, however, the tantric

43. Sakya Paṇḍita, *Sdom pa gsum gyi rab tu dbye ba'i bstan bcos*, 34. For an alternate English translation, see Sakya Paṇḍita Kunga Gyaltshen, *A Clear Differentiation of the Three Codes*, 66.

44. "Tantra" is a textual genre, akin to the sūtras, but with esoteric content. Like the sūtras, the tantras are said to have been taught by the Buddha himself.

samayas require practitioners to consume meat as part of ritual feast offerings, known as *tsok* in Tibetan.[45] During the course of these rituals, practitioners offer food to one or more tantric deities. In the process, that food is ritually transformed from normal, everyday fare into divine nectar, suitable for consumption by the deities themselves. The actual food offered can include a wide variety of substances, but most tantric texts say that meat must be included.

That meat, however, is not just any meat. Instead, most tantras say, practitioners must use what are known as the five meats. The exact list of these five can vary slightly from one individual tantra to the next, but a fairly standard list is found in the *Vimalaprabhā*,[46] Puṇḍarīka's seminal commentary on the *Kālacakra Tantra*.[47] "The five meats," Puṇḍarīka explains, "are cow, dog, elephant, horse, and human."[48] All of these meats were taboo in ancient India, where the tantras were written.[49] Pro-vegetarian authors liked to point out, therefore, that consuming the five meats was part of a specific, antinomian ritual and did not give license to eat meat on a normal, daily basis. Patrül Rinpoché makes precisely this argument in his *Words of My Perfect Teacher*: "Eating [the five meats] wantonly in towns, because you are attached to the taste of meat, is the fault known as 'behaving carelessly with the tantric commitment of consumption.'"[50] Patrül does not deny the need to include the five meats in the ritual feast. He does, however, argue that the need to include meat in the ritual does not mean that meat—even the five meats—should be eaten casually as part of a regular diet. Rather than upholding the tantric samayas, he argues, eating the five meats outside of the feast offering ritual is actually a violation of those same commitments.

Along with their concern about eating the five meats only in their ritual context, several of these authors also suggested that meat should only be used by those who are truly capable of transforming it into divine nectar. Through

45. Tib: *tsok*; Skt: *ganachakra*. This is a ritual event where a group of practitioners gathers and makes offerings to a particular tantric deity.

46. *Stainless Light* (Tib: *Dri ma med pa'i 'od*). The most important commentary on the *Kālacakra* cycle.

47. *The Wheel of Time* (Tib: *Dus kyi 'khor lo'i rgyud*). Among the most important tantric cycles in Tibet, now widely transmitted around the world by the current Dalai Lama. For more on this text, see Newman, *A Brief History of the Kalachakra*; Khendrup Norsang Gyatso, *Ornament of Stainless Light*.

48. Puṇḍarīka, *Dri ma med pa'i 'od*, 12:5b.

49. For a thorough study of the five meats in India, see Wedemeyer, *Making Sense of Tantric Buddhism*.

50. Patrül Rinpoché, *Snying tig sngon 'gro'i khrid yig kun bzang bla ma'i zhal lung*, 7:323. For an alternate English translation, see Patrul Rinpoche, *The Words of My Perfect Teacher*, 208.

the process of the ritual feast, the meat and other offerings are believed to be transformed or transmuted so that they lose their impure, worldly qualities and become pure, divine nectar. But, many authors sympathetic to vegetarianism claimed, it takes an advanced practitioner to effect this transformation, and those who are unable should avoid using actual meat in their feast offerings. Dolpopa, for one, argues that while it is appropriate for powerful practitioners who are truly capable of benefitting others to eat pills made of the five meats,[51] others should not do so. In *Refraining from Meat*, translated in chapter 2 of this volume, he says, "These [five meats] are mixed with the juniper berry to make ambrosia pills that yogis eat not merely out of lip service but for the sake of their tantric vows—they need to increase the strength of their body, abate various arrogances, and guide sentient beings. With this in mind, yogis who eat meat but are incapable of guiding sentient beings should stop eating meat of any kind."

Others laid out specific benchmarks that a practitioner must attain before consuming the five meats. Karma Chakmé argues in his *Faults of Meat*, translated in chapter 7, that before someone is able to use the five meats in ritual, they "must be able to either truly transform the meat into divine nectar or, if they do not transform it into divine nectar, they must be able to transform their body so that they appear as a burial-ground jackal, a tiger, a lion, or the like. After that they can eat. Other than that, if someone eats human flesh or the rest, then it is a violation of all three vows at once!"

A more detailed take on this argument is provided by Mikyö Dorjé, the eighth Karmapa. In his *Great Commentary on the Vinayasūtra*, translated in chapter 6, Mikyö Dorjé directly confronts those who assert that meat is necessary in the feast ritual. Assuming a debate posture, he asks his unnamed adversary to declare whether or not the meat must be literally transmuted. If his opponent declares that it does not, he argues, then it is worldly food and not an appropriate offering for the wisdom deities. But if the opponent says that it does need to be transmuted, then Mikyö Dorjé points out that only a very advanced practitioner is capable of truly transmuting it, and he says, in summary, "When thinking about putting actual meat and alcohol in the torma, I say that since you are unable to truly transmute it into suchness, you should not use real meat or alcohol. This is my prayer."

Even among those who accepted that meat does in fact need to be included in ritual feast offerings, there was still the question of how much was appropri-

51. In practice, the five meats are often consumed in the form of small pills. These pills are prepared using the five meats and other ingredients (Dolpopa mentions juniper) and then used in the ritual. If no other meat is used, the actual amount of meat consumed is thus very small.

ate to use. In his *Faults of Meat*, Karma Chakmé admits that meat is necessary in tsok ritual feasts, saying: "If you completely refuse to eat meat during the feast ritual, you will be committing the thirteenth root downfall [i.e., breaking your tantric samayas]." But, he goes on to say, the actual amount of meat used should be minuscule. "During the ritual feast," he argues, "it is not appropriate to consume more than a small amount of meat, the equivalent of the leg of an insect."

As Karma Chakmé's comments suggest, the overall concern driving these authors is a fear that the ritual feast will turn into an actual feast, with deliberate ritual conduct replaced by casual—or even gluttonous—consumption of otherwise forbidden foods. Toward this end, it is worth noting that none of these authors ever suggest that meat should never, under any circumstances, be included in the tsok ritual. Even Mikyö Dorjé allows that it is appropriate for someone who is truly capable of transmuting meat into nectar to use meat in their offerings. But, these authors seem to suggest, practitioners need to honestly evaluate their own level of realization and not perform sinful actions in the name of tantric rituals that they are not truly capable of. In his *Nectar for the Mind*, Rigdzin Garwang recalls a group of students asking their teacher, Nyala Pema Dündul, about including meat in tsok. Nyala Pema Dündul's response is a pithy and self-effacing summary of this position. "Who among you," he asks, "is able to benefit by using the flesh and blood of your father and mother? I am not."[52]

Affective Rhetoric

The authors whose works appear in this volume were scholars known for their learning and erudition. Their writings often included nuanced debates over the finer points of the sūtras and tantras. At other times, however, they set aside this scholastic approach and sought to produce an emotional, affective response in their listeners. Sometimes they did this by describing, in vivid and upsetting language, the suffering that animals experience as they are slaughtered, as Jigmé Lingpa does in the passage from his autobiography quoted above. In other cases, authors used loaded and powerful language to convince their readers to reconsider their diet. Shardza calls meat nauseating, and

52. *Nectar for the Mind* is Rigdzin Garwang's extensive treatise on meat eating. It has not been included in this volume for reasons of space and because it largely reproduces arguments found elsewhere. Nyala Pema Dündul's own work on vegetarianism is translated here in chapter 9. Rigdzin Garwang, *Sha zos pa'i nyes pa byams snying rje gsod pa'i zas gcod sems kyi bdud rtsi*, 2:153.

several authors insist that eating animal flesh is no different from eating the flesh of one's own parents. As Shabkar puts it in one particularly vivid passage:

> Amidst heaps of flesh and bones from beings who were once our mothers,
> the monks, wielding knives, stuff their gaping mouths.
> Alas! If Buddhists dare do this to beings,
> let's not speak of non-Buddhists![53]

In other instances, the language serves to highlight the negative impact of meat on the consumer, particularly the negative births awaiting those who eat meat. Eating meat, these authors claim, generates powerful negative karma, so much so that meat eaters will find themselves reborn in hell for many eons. Shardza claims, "It is certain that consuming the meat and blood of beings out of desire will result in being flung to the lower realms. For this reason, it is important to abandon meat forever." For his part, Shabkar argues that the karmic results of meat eating do not end once a being is released from hell. Instead, those who formerly ate meat "will be reborn as yaks, goats, and sheep, and will likewise experience being killed a hundred times by having their mouths and snouts bound.[54] In this way, beheaded and disemboweled, their life force will be severed."

While this argument is found in many of the texts collected here, Nyala Pema Dündul elevates it to a new level, structuring his *Song of Advice for Giving Up Meat,* translated in chapter 9 of this volume, entirely around the karmic repercussions of meat eating. In this work he recalls a visionary experience in which the bodhisattva Avalokiteśvara gives him a tour of hell. During this sojourn, he observes beings as they are tortured by animal-headed demons: "Many of the servants held sharp weapons in their hands, with which to slice apart and devour the flesh of their victims. Time and again they cut, and time and again flesh grew back. Victims did not expire until their karma was fully exhausted." When he asks what these beings had done to deserve their punishment, Avalokiteśvara explains that in previous lives all of these beings had eaten meat.

Whether they are explaining the suffering that animals experience as they

53. From the final of several poems by Shabkar in chapter 8 of this volume.

54. Animals in Tibet are often slaughtered by having their muzzles tightly bound until they suffocate. This method of slaughter is said to produce tasty meat rich in blood but was a frequent target of authors concerned not only with eating meat but also with the ethics of the slaughtering process itself.

are slaughtered or the suffering that humans who eat meat will experience in the future, all of these works share a vividly graphic vocabulary that seeks to elicit an emotional response from the viewer. Animals are terrified, cry out in pain, are repeatedly compared to one's own mother. The tortures of hell are presented in full detail. These passages are an appeal to the heart rather than the head, seeking to bring home the consequences of meat eating in a way that cannot be easily dismissed.

A Graded Path

A final theme to explore in this introduction is the fact that many of these authors did not see the question of meat eating as an all-or-nothing, black-and-white issue. Vegetarianism, as I will discuss in the next section of this introduction, was always seen by Tibetans as a difficult diet. No matter how well-justified by religious or other arguments, giving up meat was simply a difficult thing to do. And many of these authors recognized that difficulty. In response, they often suggested practices that stopped short of full vegetarianism but that also forced practitioners to recognize and respond to the sinful nature of eating meat.

One such strategy was to suggest that if meat had to be eaten, it was better to eat meat with threefold purity than without. As Shabkar says in the second of several poems translated in chapter 8, "If you are not able to give it up completely, then eat it in the faultless way that involves 'threefold purity.'" It is important to recognize that neither Shabkar nor others who adopt this approach are claiming that meat with threefold purity is fully acceptable. But it is, they argue, better than regular meat that does not adhere to this standard. Another strategy was to suggest that if meat must be eaten, the consumer should say prayers for the animal before (and sometimes after) doing so. The recommended prayers varied, but often included the famous *maṇi* mantra of Avalokiteśvara, as well as the purificatory mantra of Akṣobhya. And sometimes the prayers were much longer than simply reciting a few *maṇis*. Karma Chakmé, for one, composed a three-page prayer to be recited prior to eating meat (translated in full in chapter 7). Reciting prayers before eating meat may not seem to have much impact, as it does not change the fact that the animal was slaughtered. Such prayers, however, reinforce the idea that eating meat is something sinful, requiring expiation. And in so doing they help to promote and maintain an awareness of vegetarianism as an ideal.

For several of these authors, one strategy for partial vegetarianism was not enough. Instead, they created a graded path, with full vegetarianism as the ideal but with multiple lower stages for those who feel that full vegetarianism is too difficult. Such graded paths are found in several of the texts included here, but perhaps the clearest articulation is found at the end of Karma Chakmé's *Faults of Meat*:

> For all these reasons, the best option is to perform the holy act of relinquishing all meat. When you perform a ritual feast, use meat with threefold purity in order to guard your samaya. At that time, it is very important simply to not reject meat, alcohol, or dough. Eat only a little, however, an amount equivalent to the leg of an insect. The middle option is to give up meat that was slaughtered for your own sake, or, if you eat other meat, to eat only a little. The least option is to give up the meat of animals killed that day, meat of animals of a similar species, and human meat. When you do eat it, bless it as divine nectar and consume it as an inner fire offering. Then give rise to great compassion, purifying the animal's obscurations through prayers, mantras, and the names of buddhas.

For Karma Chakmé, vegetarianism was the ideal. But recognizing that this was a difficult ideal for many people, he created a structure in which those who found full vegetarianism too difficult could still participate.

Why Eat Meat?

With all of the arguments against eating meat deployed by these authors, readers may reasonably start to wonder why any Tibetans continued to eat it at all.[55] This is a complex question, and many different theories have been advanced to explain the centrality of meat in the Tibetan diet. Among the most common explanations is the notion that vegetables didn't grow in Tibet because of the high altitude, necessitating a meat-based diet. No less an authority than the current Dalai Lama has advanced this theory. "In Tibet," he writes, "the difficult geographical conditions—its climate and altitude—were not suitable for growing vegetables and the people have always had to depend on meat and dairy products to survive."[56] While it is certainly true that growing fruit and many types of vegetables was difficult in Tibet, this argument perhaps overstates the role of meat in the diet of many Tibetans in the pre-Communist era. With the exception of some nomad communities, tsampa—roasted bar-

55. I have explored this question in far more detail in chapters 5, 6, and 7 of *Food of Sinful Demons*.

56. His Holiness the Dalai Lama, "Non-Vegetarian Food," 57.

ley flour—was the main dietary staple, along with butter and other forms of dairy. Even among nomads, as Arjia Rinpoché notes, meat was a seasonal staple, consumed primarily in the winter. At other times, tsampa and other foods provided most of a person's daily calories. Overall, then, the evidence suggests that meat was more of a seasonal staple or an occasional treat than a true everyday staple.[57] Furthermore, there is also the simple fact that there were a sizable number of vegetarians. So clearly nonmeat foods were available, despite the altitude and generally harsh environment.

But if it was not an environmental necessity, and if many—perhaps most—lamas saw meat eating as ethically problematic, why didn't more Tibetans adopt vegetarianism? I have argued elsewhere that there are two major cultural factors militating in favor of meat eating.[58] The first of these is the widespread belief that meat is important for human health and that without it the body will become weak and feeble. Tibetan medicine suggests that the body contains three humors—wind, phlegm, and bile—and that these three need to be in balance if the body is to be healthy. Meat, according to Tibetan medicine, keeps the wind humor from becoming too strong. Without it, there is a risk that the wind humor will come to dominate and that the body will therefore become weaker.

Because of this belief, many Tibetans felt that eating meat was necessary. This did not mean, however, that they thought it was a good or moral thing to do. There was, it seems, a sizable group of Tibetans who saw meat as a necessary evil. They acknowledged that it was unethical, but simply felt that they had to eat it anyway. As the eighteenth-century nun Orgyen Chökyi puts it, "When I put goat's meat in my mouth, my mind is sad. But set in this human life, I need food."[59] This argument is made even more elaborately, and somewhat surprisingly, in Shardza's *Faults of Meat*. In this work Shardza discusses, at some length, why one should not eat meat. Then, in the last few lines, he abruptly changes direction, arguing that practitioners actually *must* eat it. To justify this, he points to the idea that without meat a practitioner would not have the strength to perform virtue. This does not, of course, negate any of

57. To the best of my knowledge, there were no systematic surveys of what Tibetans ate in the pre-Communist era. This conclusion, therefore, is based on an analysis of numerous other sources, including biographies, catalogs, reports of travelers, and other texts. For more detail, see chapter 5 of *Food of Sinful Demons*.

58. See *Food of Sinful Demons*, especially chapters 5 and 6.

59. Orgyen Chökyi, *Mkha' 'gro ma o rgyan chos skyid kyi rnam thar*, 8–9. For an alternate English translation, see Schaeffer, *Himalayan Hermitess*, 138.

his previous criticisms of meat. Instead, it simply posits that eating meat is an unfortunate part of life. It is a necessary evil.

Second, while the Buddhist authors translated in this volume all condemn meat to one degree or another, other aspects of Tibetan culture actually celebrated it. For while Buddhism was obviously an important aspect of Tibetan culture, other perspectives also existed and influenced how Tibetans lived their lives. And sometimes meat was viewed differently from these perspectives than it was from a Buddhist one. One such perspective promoted and idealized the accumulation of wealth as an appropriate life aim. In this economic perspective, human flourishing did not depend on Buddhist renunciation, but rather on skillfully conducting business so as to acquire wealth—the more the better. When viewed from this perspective, raising animals for slaughter can be seen in a positive light, as a skillful way to accumulate wealth. Meat itself, according to this economic orientation, also becomes an object of conspicuous consumption. It was often more expensive than other foods, and so consuming a lot of it, particularly at festivals and special events, was a way to telegraph an individual's wealth and status.

Another perspective that viewed meat in a positive light was what might be called heroic masculinity. In this perspective, the good life is characterized by physical strength, skill at arms, and a general sense of toughness. This heroic masculine ideal found expression in Tibet's famous horse races, in archery and firearm contests, and, more problematically, in widespread banditry and warlordism. For those who subscribed to this masculine ideal, meat served as both a support for physical strength (again, the assumption was that someone who did not eat meat would become weak) and as an expression of the ability to dominate and control animals. The medical perspective discussed above saw meat as a necessary evil. In doing so, it acknowledged and to some degree respected the Buddhist stance on meat. The economic and heroic masculine perspectives, on the other hand, invert the Buddhist view entirely. Instead of a necessary evil, they portray meat as a positive good, an integral part of a life well lived.

An individual's decision to eat meat or not is a complex choice. For many Tibetans, that choice was influenced not only by Buddhist ideals but also by other cultural norms, such as those outlined above. Beyond these, there is also the simple fact that Tibetans always seem to have felt that meat was quite tasty. Giving it up meant giving up something pleasant and enjoyable. Whether because of cultural reasons such as the medical, economic, and masculine perspectives, or simply because they like it too much, giving up meat was a difficult choice. Driven by their religious convictions, many Tibetans did make the hard choice to become vegetarian. But for the majority, such a step was simply too difficult.

Texts Included and Excluded

The texts included in this volume do not represent the entirety of Tibetan literature on vegetarianism by any measure. Rather than attempting to be comprehensive, these particular texts were selected to provide as broad an overview of these debates as possible, ranging from Shabkar's strident vegetarianism to Khedrup Jé's meat apologetics. All of the major lineages of Tibetan Buddhism—including Bön—are represented, as are texts from a wide variety of time periods and geographical locations. While I have attempted to capture as many facets of the vegetarian debate as possible, the physical limitations of this volume mean that some texts had to be excluded. Usually the choice to not include a particular text was made because I felt that the arguments in it were similar to those made in a text that was either included here or published elsewhere.

Some of these works are stand-alone treatises solely focused on vegetarianism. Others are extracts from longer—sometimes much longer—works on broader topics. In all cases, however, these are long, multipage reflections on meat eating. Much of the Tibetan literature on meat, however, comes in the form of very short passages, sometimes only one or two lines. Given the difficulty of adequately introducing and contextualizing each of these brief references, I have decided not to include any of them among the translations in this volume (though some have snuck into this introduction). Readers should, however, be aware that there are many of these brief references to meat eating and vegetarianism scattered across Tibetan literature.[60] I have tried to curate a representative selection of Tibetan texts on vegetarianism, but this volume is far from complete or exhaustive.

Conclusions

The texts included in this volume represent voices in an ongoing debate. They share a topic and some foundational ideals—the need for compassion, fidelity to the Buddhist canon, and so on. But they also showcase a remarkable diversity in their approaches to the question of vegetarianism. For some, this was an emotional question with a simple answer: Buddhists who cultivate

60. I have drawn heavily on these sources for my monograph, *Food of Sinful Demons*. Readers who wish for more detail should consult that work.

compassion have no business eating meat. For others, meat eating was not a simple issue at all, and multiple competing concerns and arguments needed to be balanced against one another. Sometimes these competing concerns were canonical, as when the need for compassion seemed to conflict with the rule of threefold purity or the tantric samayas. In other cases, even when an author might feel that the Buddhist perspective clearly comes down against meat, they still had to balance that stance against a popular culture in which meat eating was deeply entrenched. Further, as these texts amply demonstrate, the debate over meat eating in Tibet was never fully resolved. For almost a thousand years, Tibetan authors continued to debate this issue without coming to a firm conclusion.[61] And these debates continue to the present with active vegetarian movements among Tibetans in Tibet, Tibetans in exile, and Western practitioners. It is my hope that the texts that follow will illustrate the contours of the traditional debates over vegetarianism and, in so doing, will help to inform these same debates in the contemporary world.

61. This unresolved nature of the debates over vegetarianism is in striking contrast to some other Buddhist cultures, where vegetarianism either became normative for devout Buddhists (as in Chinese Buddhism) or was simply not an issue (as is largely true of Theravāda Buddhism).

Canonical Sources

Vinayavastu (*'Dul ba gzhi*). In *Sde dge bka' 'gyur*, vols. 1–4. BDRC: W4CZ5369.
Laṅkāvatāra Sūtra (*Lang kar gshegs pa'i mdo*). In *Sde dge bka' 'gyur*, vol. 49, 56a–191b. BDRC: W4CZ5369.
Prātimokṣa Sūtra (*So sor thar pa'i mdo*). In *Sde dge bka' 'gyur*, vol. 5, 1a–20b. BDRC: W4CZ5369.
Puṇḍarīka (Padma dkar po). *Vimalaprabhā* (*Bsdus pa'i rgyud kyi rgyal po dus kyi 'khor lo'i 'grel bshad rtsa ba'i rgyud kyi rjes su 'jug pa stong phrag bcu gnyis pa dri ma med pa'i 'od; Dri ma med pa'i 'od*). In *Sde dge bstan 'gyur*, vols. 11, 107b–277a, and 12, 1a–297b. BDRC: W23703.
Mahāparinirvāna Sūtra (*Myang 'das chen po'i mdo*). In *Sde dge bka' 'gyur*, vols. 52–53. BDRC: W4CZ5369.

Other Tibetan Sources

Gö Lotsawa Shonu Pal ('Gos lo zhon nu dpal). 1984. *Deb ther sngon po* (*The Blue Annals*). Chengdu: Si khron mi rigs dpe skrun khang. BDRC: W1KG5762.
Jigmé Lingpa ('Jigs med gling pa). n.d. *Ri bong shin tu brtan pa'i gtam brag ri'i mgu la rgyan* (*The Well-Established Rabbitt*). In *'Jigs med gling pa gsung 'bum*, vol. 4, 765–73. Degé Edition. BDRC: W27300.
———. n.d. *Ri dwags kyi gtam nges 'byung gi pho nya* (*Story of the Hunted Deer*). In *'Jigs med gling pa gsung 'bum*, vol. 4, 753–65. Degé Edition. BDRC: W27300.
———. n.d. *Yul lho rgyud du byung ba'i rdzogs chen pa rang byung rdo rje mkhyen brtse'i 'od zer gyi rnam thar pa legs byas yongs 'du'i snye ma* (*The Autobiography of Jigmé Lingpa*). In *'Jigs med gling pa gsung 'bum*, vol. 9, 125–26. Degé Edition. BDRC: W27300.
Künga Tenpé Gyaltsen (Kun dga' bstan pa'i rgyal mtshan). 1981. *Rje bla ma rdo rje 'chang ngag dbang kun dga' legs pa'i 'byung gnas ye shes rgyal mtshan dpal bzang po'i rnam par thar pa ngo mtshar nor bu'i 'phreng ba* (*The Biography of Ngawang Lekpa*). New Delhi: Gönpo Dorjé. BDRC: W2CZ6645.
Mikyö Dorjé (Mi bskyod rdo rje). n.d. *Gangs ri'i khrod na gnas pa gtso bor gyur pa skyabs med ma rgan tshogs la sha zar mi rung ba'i springs yig sogs* (*A Letter on the Unsuitability of Eating the Meat of Our Old Mothers*). NGMPP Reel No. E 2943/4.
Nyamé Sherab Gyeltsn (Mnyam med shes rab rgyal mtshan). n.d. *'Dul bab mdor bsdus kyi 'grel pa* (*Commentary on the Received Vinaya*). Unpublished manuscript.
Orgyen Chökyi (Orgyan chos skyid). n.d. *Mkha' 'gro ma o rgyan chos skyid kyi rnam thar* (*Biography of the Ḍākinī Orgyen Chökyi*). Unpublished manuscript.
Patrül Rinpoché (Dpal sprul o rgyan 'jigs med chos kyi dbang po). 2009. *Snying tig sngon 'gro'i khrid yig kun bzang bla ma'i zhal lung* (*The Words of My Perfect Teacher*). In *Dpal sprul o rgyan 'jigs med chos kyi dbang po'i gsung 'bum*, vol 7. Chengdu: Si khron dpe skrun tshogs pa and Si khron mi rigs dpe skrun khang. BDRC: W1PD107142.
Rigdzin Garwang (Rig 'dzin Gar gyi dbang phyug). n.d. *Sha zos pa'i nyes pa byams snying rje gsod pa'i zas gcod sems kyi bdud rtsi* (*Nectar for the Mind: The Faults of Meat and Virtue of Cutting Off the Food Destroys Love and Compassion*). In *Rig 'dzin gar gyi dbang phyug gi gsung 'bum*, vol. 2, 149–94. 'Chi med byang chub gling. BDRC: W19884.

Sakya Paṇḍita (Sakya Paṇḍita Kun dga' rgyal btshan). 1999. *Sdom pa gsum gyi rab tu dbye ba'i bstan bcos* (*Distinguishing the Three Vows*). Dpal sa skya'i smon lam chen mo'i dran rten. BDRC: W1KG1686.

Shabkar Tsokdrük Rangdröl (Zhabs dkar tshogs drug rang grol). 2003. *Rmad byung sprul pa'i glegs bam* (*The Wondrous Emanated Scripture*). In *Zhabs dkar tshogs drug rang grol gyi bka' 'bum*, vol. 8, 1–214. New Delhi: Shechen. BDRC: W23893.

Secondary Sources

Barstow, Geoffrey. 2013. "Buddhism Between Abstinence and Indulgence: Vegetarianism in the Life and Works of Jigmé Lingpa." *Journal of Buddhist Ethics* 20: 73–104.

———. 2017. "Bold Judgements on Eating Meat." In *A Gathering of Brillian Moons: Practical Advice from the Rimé Masters of Tibet*, edited by Holly Gayley and Joshua Schapiro, 97–108. Boston: Wisdom Publications.

———. 2018. *Food of Sinful Demons: Meat, Vegetarianism, and the Limits of Buddhism in Tibet*. New York: Columbia University Press.

———. 2019. "On the Moral Standing of Animals in Tibetan Buddhism." *Études Mongoles et Sibériennes, Centrasiatiques et Tibétaines* 50: n.p.

Buffetrille, Katia. 2014. "A Controversy on Vegetarianism." In *Trails of the Tibetan Tradition: Papers for Elliot Sperling*, edited by Roberto Vitali, 113–27. Dharamsala: Amye Machen Institute.

Cech, Krystina. 1988. "A Bonpo Bca' Yig: The Rules of sMan-Ri Monastery." In *Tibetan Studies: Proceedings of the 4th Seminar of the International Association for Tibetan Studies*, edited by Helga Uebach and Jampa L. Panglung, 69–85. Munich: Kommission Für Zentralasiatische Studien.

Chatral Rinpoche. 2005. *Compassionate Action: The Teachings of Chatral Rinpoche*. Edited by Zach Larson. Ithaca, NY: Snow Lion Publications.

Dreyfus, Georges B. J. 2003. *The Sound of Two Hands Clapping: The Education of a Tibetan Buddhist Monk*. Berkeley: University of California Press.

Dudjom Rinpoche. 1999. *Perfect Conduct: Ascertaining the Three Vows*. Translated by Gyurme Samdrup and Sangye Khandro. Boston: Wisdom Publications.

Finnigan, Bronwyn. 2017. "Buddhism and Animal Ethics." *Philosophy Compass* 12.7: n.p.

Gaerrang. 2016. "Tibetan Identity and Tibetan Buddhism in Trans-Regional Connection: The Contemporary Vegetarian Movement in Pastoral Areas of Tibet (China)." *Études Mongoles et Sibériennes, Centrasiatiques et Tibétaines* 47: n.p.

Gayley, Holly. 2013. "Reimagining Buddhist Ethics on the Tibetan Plateau." *Journal of Buddhist Ethics* 20: 247–86.

———. 2017. "The Compassionate Treatment of Animals." *Journal of Religious Ethics* 45.1: 29–57.

Goldstein, Melvyn C. 1991. *A History of Modern Tibet, 1913–1951: The Demise of the Lamaist State*. Berkeley: University of California Press.

———. 2009. *A History of Modern Tibet*, vol. 2, *The Calm before the Storm, 1951–1955*. Berkeley: University of California Press.

———. 2013. *A History of Modern Tibet*, vol. 3, *The Storm Clouds Descend, 1955–1957*. Berkeley: University of California Press.

Harvey, Peter. 1998. "Buddhist Attitudes to and Treatment of Non-Human Nature." *Ecotheology: Journal of Religion, Nature & the Environment* 5.4: 35–50.

Heimbel, Jörg. 2017. *Vajradhara in Human Form: The Life and Times of Ngor chen Kun dga' bzang po*. Lumbini: Lumbini International Research Institute.

His Holiness the Dalai Lama. 2003. "Non-Vegetarian Food." In *'Tshe Sems 'Joms Pa'i Sman Zhun: The Remedy for Cold Heart*, edited by Tsa ri ba rab gsal, 57–58. Dharamsala: The Private Office of H. H. the Dalai Lama.

Horner, I. B., trans. 1951. *The Book of the Discipline*, vol. 4, *Mahavagga*. London: Luzac.

———. 1967. "Early Buddhism and the Taking of Life." *The Wheel*, no. 104.

Hou Haoran. 2015. "Some Remarks on the Transmission of the Ascetic Discipline of the 'Single Mat' within the 'Bri Gung Bka' Brgyud Pa Tradition." In *The Illuminating Mirror: Tibetan Studies in Honour of Per K. Sørensen on the Occasion of His 65th Birthday*, edited by Guntram Hazod and Olaf Czaja, 87–100. Weisbaden: Dr. Ludwig Reichert Verlag.

Huber, Toni. 2003. "The Chase and the Dharma: The Legal Protection of Wild Animals in Pre-Modern Tibet." In *Wildlife in Asia: Cultural Perspectives*, edited by John Knight, 36–55. Man and Nature in Asia 5. London: Routledge.

Jigmé Lingpa. 2006. "The Story of the Hunted Deer: The Messenger of Renunciation." Translated by Lama Kunzang Dorjée and Jeffrey Wenger. www.shabkar.org/download/pdf/The_Story_of_the_Hunted_Deer.pdf.

Kapleau, Roshi Philip. 1981. *To Cherish All Life: A Buddhist View of Animal Slaughter and Meat Eating*. Rochester, NY: The Zen Center.

Karmapa Ogyen Trinley Dorjé. 2007. "Talk on Vegetarianism." Presented at the 24th Annual Great Kagyü Monlam, Bodhgaya, India, January 3. http://www.shabkar.org/download/pdf/Talk_on_Vegetarianism.pdf.

———. 2017. *Interconnected: Embracing Life in Our Global Society*. Somerville, MA: Wisdom Publications.

Khendrup Norsang Gyatso. 2001. *Ornament of Stainless Light: An Exposition of the Kalachakra Tantra*. Translated by Gavin Kilty. Boston: Wisdom Publications.

Kieschnick, John. 2005. "Buddhist Vegetarianism in China." In *Of Tripod and Palate: Food, Politics, and Religion in Traditional China*, edited by Roel Sterckx, 186–212. New York: Palgrave Macmillan.

Lama Phurbu Tashi Rinpoche. 2017. *A Buddhist Perspective on the Faults of Eating Meat*. Dharamsala: Library of Tibetan Works & Archives.

Newman, John R. 1985. "A Brief History of the Kalachakra." In *The Wheel of Time: The Kalachakra in Context*, edited by Geshe Lhundub Sopa, Roger R. Jackson, and John R. Newman, 51–90. Madison, WI: Deer Park Books.

Patrul Rinpoche. 1998. *The Words of My Perfect Teacher*. Translated by Padmakara Translation Group. Boston: Shambhala Publications.

Ricard, Matthieu. 2016. A *Plea for the Animals: The Moral, Philosophical, and Evolutionary Imperative to Treat All Beings with Compassion*. Boston: Shambhala Publications.

Roerich, George, trans. 1976 [1951]. *The Blue Annals*. Delhi: Motilal Banarsidass.

Sakya Paṇḍita Kunga Gyaltshen. 2002. *A Clear Differentiation of the Three Codes: Essential Differentiations among the Individual Liberation, Great Vehicle, and Tantric Systems*. Translated by Jared Douglas Rhoton. Albany: State University of New York Press.

Schaeffer, Kurtis R. 2004. *Himalayan Hermitess: The Life of a Tibetan Buddhist Nun*. New York: Oxford University Press.

van Schaik, Sam. 2010. "The Limits of Transgression: The Samaya Vows of Mahayoga." In *Esoteric Buddhism at Dunhuang: Rites and Teachings for This Life and Beyond*, edited by Matthew T. Kapstein and Sam van Schaik, 61–83. Leiden: Brill.

Schmithausen, Lambert. 2005. "Meat-Eating and Nature: Buddhist Perspectives." In *Buddhism and Nature: Supplement to the Bulletin of the Research Institute of Bukkyo University*, 183–201. Kyoto.

Shabkar Tsogdruk Rangdrol. 2001. *The Life of Shabkar: The Autobiography of a Tibetan Yogin*. Translated by Matthieu Ricard. Ithaca, NY: Snow Lion Publications.

Shabkar [Tsogdruk Rangdrol]. 2004. *Food of Bodhisattvas: Buddhist Teachings on Abstaining from Meat*. Translated by Padmakara Translation Group. Boston: Shambhala Publications.

Sobisch, Jan-Ulrich. 2002. *Three-Vow Theories in Tibetan Buddhism*. Weisbaden: Dr. Ludwig Reichert Verlag.

Stewart, James. 2010. "The Question of Vegetarianism and Diet in Pāli Buddhism." *Journal of Buddhist Ethics* 17: 99–140.

———. 2015. *Vegetarianism and Animal Ethics in Contemporary Buddhism*. London: Routledge.

Sulek, Emilia Róza. 2016. "Caterpillar Fungus and the Economy of Sinning: On Entangled Relations between the Religious and Economic in a Tibetan Pastoral Region of Golog, Qinghai, China." *Études Mongoles et Sibériennes, Centrasiatiques et Tibétaines* 47: n.p.

Tan, Gillian G. 2016. "'Life' and 'Freeing Life' (tshe thar) among Pastoralists of Kham: Intersecting Religion and Environment." *Études Mongoles et Sibériennes, Centrasiatiques et Tibétaines* 47: n.p.

Thubten Jinpa, trans. 2008. *The Book of Kadam: The Core Texts*. Library of Tibetan Classics, vol. 2. Boston: Wisdom Publications.

Tsering Shakya. 1999. *The Dragon in the Land of Snows: A History of Modern Tibet since 1947*. New York: Columbia University Press.

Wedemeyer, Christian K. 2012. *Making Sense of Tantric Buddhism: History, Semiology, and Transgression in the Indian Traditions*. New York: Columbia University Press.

1. Canonical Precedents: The *Laṅkāvatāra* and *Mahāparinirvāṇa Sūtras*

By Geoffrey Barstow

As the founder of the tradition, the Buddha himself holds a particular authority for Buddhist audiences. It is not surprising, therefore, that Buddhist authors frequently cite the words of the Buddha to support their positions. The Tibetan authors translated in this volume are no exception. Even a cursory reading reveals that the texts are full of quotations from canonical scriptures, including a wide variety of both sūtras and tantras.[62] While these authors cited dozens of different canonical texts, two particular sūtras stand out, both for the frequency with which they appear and the impact their arguments had on the debates over meat eating in Tibet. These texts are the *Laṅkāvatāra Sūtra* and *Mahāparinirvāṇa Sūtra*.

The importance of these two sūtras for Tibetan discussions of meat eating cannot be overstated. Quotations from one or both of these sūtras appear in seven of the ten texts translated in this volume, usually more than once. Further, in some cases these quotations are the only argument presented. In his *Epistle Benefitting Students*, for instance, Ngorchen Künga Sangpo's entire discussion of meat eating in the Mahāyāna is comprised of a single long quotation from the *Laṅkāvatāra Sūtra*. Nothing more, it seems, needs to be said. Beyond the quotations themselves, these sūtras provide the basic arguments picked up and used by later authors. They are both Mahāyāna texts grounded in the rhetoric of compassion, and both articulate a vision in which the person consuming meat bears moral responsibility for the death of the animal that provided it. Drawing on this vision, both texts also question the relevance of such non-Mahāyāna doctrines as the rule of threefold purity, asserting that

62. Generally speaking, the Buddhist canon preserved in Tibet contains two types of texts: sūtras and tantras. Both genres are defined as having been taught by a buddha, either the historical Shakyamuni Buddha or a celestial buddha. The sūtras are, speaking broadly, those works that deal with exoteric subjects, whereas the tantras deal primarily with esoteric, tantric topics.

this and other permissive attitudes toward meat found in the Vinaya do not apply in a Mahāyāna context. As the texts in this volume make clear, these basic arguments, first articulated in these sūtras, form the foundation of later Tibetan debates over meat.

Laṅkāvatāra Sūtra

Modern scholarship suggests that the *Laṅkāvatāra Sūtra* was composed early in the first millennium CE, most likely during the third or fourth century.[63] It is a member—though not a particularly early member—of the Mahāyāna movement, a shift that may have begun as early as the first century BCE and that emphasized compassion for others over the pursuit of personal liberation. Given these dates, scholars broadly agree that the text does not in fact contain the words of the Buddha himself, but that it most likely was the work of more than one later author, probably over several generations.

That said, for Tibetan scholars the *Laṅkāvatāra Sūtra* was understood to be authentic teachings from the Buddha himself. It was included in the Kangyur, the Tibetan canon of texts said to have been spoken by the Buddha, and its status as a sūtra was never, to my knowledge, seriously questioned. Despite what we now know or guess about the circumstances of its composition, for the Tibetan authors included in this volume, the *Laṅkāvatāra Sūtra* was *buddhavacana*, the authentic words of the Buddha.

The *Laṅkāvatāra Sūtra* takes the form of a series of dialogues between the Buddha and the bodhisattva Mahāmati.[64] In each scene, Mahāmati asks a question and the Buddha answers it, first in an extended passage in prose and then in a verse summary. Most of these dialogues are focused on Buddhist philosophy, particularly the idea of "buddha nature."[65] It is these discussions

63. The precise dating of Indian texts is notoriously difficult and is based on a number of factors, including internal textual evidence, references to other texts, and the dates on which the text was translated into other languages. In the case of the *Laṅkāvatāra Sūtra*, we know that it was first translated into Chinese in 420 CE, meaning that a version of this text must have been extant prior to that date. Among many works on this topic, see Suzuki, *Studies in the Lankavatara Sutra*; Takasaki, "Analysis of the Lankavatara."

64. Tib: *blo gros chen po*. Mahāmati's name roughly translates as "Great Intelligence" or "Great Wisdom."

65. Buddha nature refers to the mind's infinitely vast potential; the mind can be the basis for both the dukha of saṃsāra (the unpurified mind) and the bliss and fulfillment of nirvāṇa (the purified mind). For more on the philosophical vision of the *Laṅkāvatāra Sūtra*, see Forsten, *Between Certainty and Finitude*; Sutton, *Existence and Enlightenment in the Lankavatara-Sutra*; Suzuki, *Studies in the Lankavatara Sutra*.

that have given the *Laṅkāvatāra Sūtra* its great fame, particularly in Zen and other East Asian forms of Buddhism. The extract translated here—chapter 7 of the Tibetan edition—eschews these metaphysical discussions in favor of a straightforward discussion of the ethics of meat eating. It begins with a lengthy request by Mahāmati, asking the Buddha to explain the faults of meat. The Buddha responds by presenting a number of reasons why meat should be avoided. These arguments approach the issue from a variety of perspectives, but at their core they present an ethic of compassion. Eating meat, the Buddha emphasizes over and over, harms animals and must therefore be relinquished. Compassionate bodhisattvas, he points out early on, see all creatures as no different from their own children, so how could they eat them?

It is noteworthy that the Buddha explicitly rejects the idea that eating meat is somehow distinct from the act of killing itself. Many Buddhists, both in India and later in Tibet, argued that it was acceptable to eat meat that they had purchased in the market, since they had neither personally killed the animal nor asked a butcher to kill a specific animal for them. The Buddha rejects this argument. "If someone gives up meat," he tells Mahāmati, "then animals will not be killed. This is because innocent beings are usually killed for money; other reasons are rare." Butchers do their work only because people buy meat. So eating meat, the Buddha argues, is economically connected to the act of killing, whether or not the eater has specifically requested that that particular animal be killed.

The prose body of this text concludes with an extended prophesy that future generations would forget his teachings on vegetarianism. "Mahāmati," he warns, "in the future there will be stupid people who are ordained in my tradition, who call themselves 'children of the Śākya,' and who bear aloft the saffron victory banner, but whose minds are spoiled by wrong views. Their ego-clinging will be vast, and they will lust for the taste of meat. Speculating on subtle distinctions in the Vinaya rules, they will find all kinds of justifications for eating meat." As the texts in this volume demonstrate, this prophesy was not wrong. Many Tibetans did, in fact, argue that eating meat was acceptable, often supporting their claims by pointing to the rule of threefold purity and other permissions found in the Vinaya. In response, those Tibetan authors sympathetic to vegetarianism could—and frequently did—point to this prophesy, suggesting that their interlocutors were not reading the Vinaya honestly but were simply trying to find ways to satisfy their own desire for meat.

Overall, it is not hyperbole to claim that no canonical sūtra or tantra has had a bigger impact on Tibetan views on meat eating than the *Laṅkāvatāra Sūtra*. It is cited repeatedly and extensively in most of the texts contained in this volume, as well as many other works on meat eating that are not included here. It provides a clear and unambiguous critique of meat eating, along with a nuanced defense of vegetarianism against a variety of objections, all backed by the authority of the Buddha himself.

Mahāparinirvāna Sūtra

Like the *Laṅkāvatāra Sūtra*, the *Mahāparinirvāna Sūtra* is a Mahāyāna text, likely composed in the first centuries CE. Again, however, this modern scholarly understanding differs significantly from how the text was understood by traditional Tibetans. In the perspective of the authors whose works are translated in this book, the *Mahāparinirvāna Sūtra* was an authentic sūtra, recording the literal speech of the Buddha himself. It was therefore an authoritative—yet still interpretable—statement of the Buddha's views.

Also like the *Laṅkāvatāra Sūtra*, the *Mahāparinirvāna Sūtra* largely focuses on philosophical ideas such as "buddha nature" and is of particular importance for Zen and other East Asian forms of Buddhism. It takes the form of a dialogue, this time between the Buddha and the bodhisattva Kāśyapa, and the discussion of meat eating and vegetarianism is only a small part of the larger text.

The anti-meat arguments found in the *Mahāparinirvāna Sūtra* align well with those found in the *Laṅkāvatāra Sūtra*, though they are significantly less extensive and varied. Perhaps the most important point raised in this text concerns the rule of threefold purity. This rule states that monks and nuns are allowed to eat meat as long as they are not personally responsible for the death of the animal. That is, they must not (1) have killed the animal themselves, (2) heard that the animal was killed specifically for them, or (3) even suspect that the animal might have been killed specifically for them. Like the *Laṅkāvatāra Sūtra* but with more elaboration, the Buddha asserts in the *Mahāparinirvāna Sūtra* that he made this rule only to make things easier for those of limited ability and self-control to nonetheless engage with Buddhism. "Kāśyapa," he explains, "I taught that it was acceptable to eat meat that had been examined in the three ways as a skillful method so people could gradually cut it off entirely." The rule of threefold purity, in this presentation, is merely a first step on the path to full vegetarianism.

The second half of the *Mahāparinirvāna Sūtra* contains another extended prophesy. Much like the prophesy found in the *Laṅkāvatāra Sūtra*, this prophesy claims that in future generations people will pervert the Buddha's teachings. Driven by their desire for the taste of meat, the Buddha says, they will falsely claim that the Buddha ate meat and that he said it was appropriate for his monks to do likewise. "They may wear saffron robes," he says, "but they will be just like hunters. They may walk slowly with downcast eyes, but this is only like a cat chasing a rat."

Overall, then, the discussion of meat in the *Mahāparinirvāna Sūtra* is strikingly consistent with the one found in the *Laṅkāvatāra Sūtra*. In both texts the Buddha explains that he allowed meat with threefold purity in the past, but only as a method to ease entry onto the Buddhist path. From now on, both texts claim, meat is no longer allowed. Despite this clear prohibition, however, the Buddha predicts that future generations of monks will pervert these teachings, claiming that meat is allowed and even wholesome.

About the Translations

The *Laṅkāvatāra Sūtra* currently exists in a number of different languages and Buddhist canons. In addition to the Tibetan version, there are no less than three extant Chinese translations[66] of the text as well as a Sanskrit edition.[67] For this translation, I have relied on the Tibetan edition preserved in the Degé edition of the Kangyur.[68] I chose this edition because it made sense to translate the *Laṅkāvatāra Sūtra* from the version that would have been known to the Tibetan authors in this volume. There have also been several English translations of the full *Laṅkāvatāra Sūtra*, most prominently including D. T. Suzuki's classic translation from the Sanskrit[69] and Red Pine's translation from the Chinese (Red Pine relies primarily, but not exclusively, on Guṇabhadra's Chinese translation).[70] The Padmakara Translation Committee has also translated a version of this present chapter on meat eating in *Food of Bodhisattvas*, where it is quoted by Shabkar as part of his *Wondrous Emanated Scripture*.[71] All of these editions have been open in front of me as I translated the *Laṅkāvatāra Sūtra*, and all have been useful when I confronted difficult passages or for suggesting particular phrasing. I am grateful to the work of all of these translators.

Like the *Laṅkāvatāra Sūtra*, the *Mahāparinirvāna Sūtra* currently exists in several editions and in several different canons.[72] There is no complete extant

66. Taishō canon, 670, 671, and 672.

67. Bunyu Nanjio, *The Laṅkāvatāra Sūtra*.

68. *Laṅkāvatāra Sūtra*, 49:56a–191b.

69. Suzuki, *The Lankavatara Sutra*.

70. Red Pine, *The Lankavatara Sutra*.

71. Shabkar, *Food of Bodhisattvas*, 47–59.

72. For a concise discussion of this text, see Buswell and Lopez, *The Princeton Dictionary of Buddhism*, 504–5.

Sanskrit edition, though there are several extant fragments. There are also three complete translations of the text into Chinese.[73] More important for readers of this volume, there are two distinct translations of this text contained in the Tibetan Kangyur. The first is much longer, comprising two full volumes in the Degé Kangyur, and was translated by Jinamitra, Jñāgarbha, and Devacandra from the Chinese version originally translated from Sanskrit by Dharmakṣena. The other, much shorter version was translated directly from the Sanskrit by Wang Phan zhun, Gewé Lodrö, and Gyatso Dé.[74] Both versions are found in the *Denkarma* catalog, so they must have been completed by the mid-ninth century.[75] The version translated below comes from the longer version of the text, originally translated from Dharmakṣena's Chinese.[76] I have relied primarily on the version contained in the Degé Kangyur, for the same reason as outlined above. While I have translated the longer version of the text here, the Tibetan authors translated in other chapters of this volume also sometimes quoted the shorter version, originally translated directly from the Sanskrit. One significant result of this is that the passages quoted in these texts sometimes have no corresponding passage in the full translation found in this chapter. Despite these discrepancies, I have decided to translate the longer, more extensive version of the sūtra.

There have been several notable translations of the *Mahāparinirvāna Sūtra* into English. Kosho Yamamoto has translated the full text of the so-called southern version of Dharmakṣena's Chinese translation,[77] while Mark Blum has so far completed one volume—including the relevant passage about vegetarianism—of a planned four-volume translation of the same text.[78] As with the *Laṅkāvatāra Sūtra*, Shabkar also cites the entirety of the *Mahāparinirvāna Sūtra*'s discussion of meat in his *Wondrous Emanated Scripture*,[79] drawing on the same, longer version of the sūtra that I translate here. Shabkar's work, including his quotations from the *Mahāparinirvāna Sūtra*, has been translated by the Padmakara Translation Committee in *Food of Bodhisattvas*. Again, my work here builds on these earlier translations.

73. Taishō, 374, 375, and 376.

74. For more on these different versions, see Hodge, "The Mahāyāna Mahāparinirvāna Sūtra."

75. The *Denkarma* (Tib: *Ldan dear ma*) is a catalog, composed in the first half of the ninth century, of Tibetan translations completed to that point.

76. As with the *Laṅkāvatāra Sūtra*, I have relied on the version of this text found in the Degé Kangyur, vols. 52 and 53.

77. Kosho Yamamoto, *The Mahayana Mahaparinirvana-Sutra*.

78. Blum, *The Nirvana Sutra*.

79. Shabkar, *Food of Bodhisattvas*, 59–64.

As I have noted repeatedly, these two sūtras are cited extensively by later Tibetan authors. Those authors, however, did not always reproduce the source material with perfect accuracy. In fact, these Tibetan works are full of misspellings, misquotes, and sometimes outright mistakes. Karma Chakmé, for instance, twice attributes quotations from the *Laṅkāvatāra Sūtra* to an entirely different text, the *Saddharmasmṛtyupasthāna Sūtra*! Throughout this volume, I have tried to translate these quotations in a way that uses language consistent with my translations of the source sūtras (contained in this chapter) while also reflecting the misquotes and idiosyncrasies found in each text.

Finally, I wish to thank the many friends and colleagues who assisted with these translations. In particular, I want to express my gratitude to Anna Johnson and Jörg Heimbel, who offered valuable thoughts and insights on earlier versions, as well as Yangsi Rinpoché of Maitripa University and Khenpo Jorden of the International Buddhist Academy, both of whom generously helped me decipher difficult passages in these texts. Without their help, this translation would remain riddled with errors. Any errors that remain are of course my own.

The Laṅkāvatāra Sūtra

Translated by Geoffrey Barstow

Then the great bodhisattva Mahāmati offered some verses and supplicated the Buddha, saying, "Bhagavān, Tathāgata, Arhat,[80] Perfect Buddha, please explain how to view the faults of meat! Explain how I and other great bodhisattvas of the present and future can remove the desire for the taste of meat felt by those who are infused with a tendency toward eating the flesh of beings. By what means can we cleanse their attachment to the taste of beings' flesh? Explain how, turning to the taste of the Dharma, they may regard all beings as their own children, achieving a state of loving-kindness toward all of them. Explain how, having done this, they will cleanse the stages of the bodhisattva path and swiftly come to perfect, unsurpassed buddhahood! If not this, explain how, having rested at the level of śrāvakas and pratyekabuddhas,[81] they will then attain the unsurpassed level of a buddha.

"Lord Buddha, even those extremists with wrong views of the Dharma—those who cling to the world, who uphold positions of either existence or non-existence, or who are eternalists or nihilists—refuse to seek out meat. Even they do not seek it! But you are the protector of the world, and your teachings are indistinguishable from compassion. It is the teaching of all the perfect buddhas. Yet we Buddhists seek out meat. We have not put an end to seeking it. Therefore, Lord Buddha, please explain the faults of seeking out meat, so that I and the other great bodhisattvas may teach the Dharma to others just as it is. Please explain this, for the sake of that affection with which you regard all beings everywhere with equal love, as if they were your only child."

The Buddha replied, "Your request is excellent and I will teach you. So listen well, Mahāmati, and remember!" So the great bodhisattva Mahāmati listened carefully to the Buddha.

"Mahāmati," the Buddha said, "bodhisattvas who embody compassion

80. Titles of the Buddha. They roughly translate as "Blessed One," "Thus Gone One," and "Foe Destroyer," respectively.

81. *Śrāvakas* and *pratyekabuddhas* ("listeners" and "solitary realizers," respectively) are two categories of Buddhist practitioner. In Mahāyāna texts such as the *Laṅkāvatāra Sūtra*, they are generally classed as practitioners of the so-called Hīnayāna, or Lesser Vehicle, and are considered to be below the level of bodhisattvas.

do not eat meat for innumerable reasons, only some of which I will explain. Mahāmati, it is not easy to find someone who was not once your father, mother, brother, sister, son, daughter, kinsman, friend, or the like at some point during the long ages of saṃsāra. Your friends and relatives in the past, they have now changed their form and become wild animals, domestic animals, and birds, whatever their karma dictates. Bodhisattvas and great beings aspire to the Buddha's Dharma, aspire to become like me. So how could they eat the meat that comes from these beings, now born as animals? Mahāmati, even demons turn away from eating meat when they hear the wholesome Dharma of the tathāgatas, turning away from their demonic nature toward compassion. So what need is there to speak of those who aspire to the true Dharma? In that way, Mahāmati, bodhisattvas look on all beings of the here and now as the transformations of their previous relatives and friends. Therefore they cultivate looking on each of them as their only child. Because of this, bodhisattvas—the embodiment of compassion—do not eat any type of meat.

"Mahāmati, it is mistaken and unsuitable for engaged bodhisattvas to eat meat, so they should not eat any type of meat. Mahāmati, worldly people do not eat the meat of donkeys, camels, dogs, cows, or humans (even though butchers claim that it is wholesome and sell it on the streets in order to make some money). Therefore, Mahāmati, bodhisattvas do not eat any meat. Mahāmati, bodhisattvas who aspire to purity do not eat meat, as it comes from semen and blood.

"Not wanting to scare living beings, Mahāmati, bodhisattvas who posses the yoga[82] of kindness do not eat any type of meat. It is the case, Mahāmati, that when a dog sees, even at a great distance, a butcher, outcast, fisherman, or anyone else that eats dog meat, it is thrown into a state of fear. Thinking, 'they will come and kill me,' the dog almost dies of fear! It is similar, Mahāmati, with those tiny beings that live in the air, on the earth, or in water. As soon as they see a distant meat eater, or when they detect one with their subtle sense of smell, then, fearing death, they quickly turn aside, just as a human might turn from a demon. Mahāmati, since bodhisattvas who abide in kindness do not want to cause fear, they do not eat meat. Mahāmati, eating meat gives ordinary, non-noble beings a gross and disagreeable smell that makes them repulsive. Noble beings abandon this, and so bodhisattvas should not eat meat.

82. Modern readers should be aware that the term "yoga," as it is used here, does not refer exclusively or even primarily to contemplative practices that involved physical bodily positions. Instead, it conveys its classical meaning, where it refers to spiritual practices in general and sometimes carries a sense of spiritual discernment.

Mahāmati, noble beings eat the food of sages, without meat or blood. Therefore bodhisattvas should also not eat meat.

"Mahāmati, compassionate bodhisattvas do not eat meat in order to avoid scandalizing people so that they disparage my teachings. So it is, Mahāmati. There are some in the world who speak ill of my teachings, saying, 'Alas, what type of virtue do those people have? Though they say it is important to act purely, they have abandoned the food of their own previous sages. Wandering throughout this world, like carnivorous animals, they fill their bellies with meat, terrifying those small animals that live in the sky, on the earth, and in the water. Their virtuous practice has declined! They have stopped turning aside from evil! They do not have any Dharma and they do not have any discipline!' Thus these people use many critical comments to disparage the teachings. Therefore, Mahāmati, since they desire to avoid scandalizing people who would then disparage my teachings, bodhisattvas who embody compassion do not eat any type of meat.

"Mahāmati, the smell of corpses is gross and disagreeable. Meat is no different, so bodhisattvas should not eat meat. Mahāmati, there is no difference between the smell of a roasting human corpse and the smell of the roasting flesh of some other kind of being. Both have the same disgusting smell. This is another reason, Mahāmati, that bodhisattvas who possess yoga and aspire to purity do not eat any type of meat. Mahāmati, yogis who dwell in charnel grounds, who live in forest monasteries, who sleep in remote hermitages haunted by spirits, who engage in yoga, who abide in kindness, who are adepts accomplished in knowledge-mantras, or who aspire to accomplish knowledge-mantras all understand that eating meat is an obstacle to liberation. Therefore all those accomplished yogis who are my sons and daughters and who abide in the Mahāyāna do not eat any type of meat. They see it as an obstacle to benefitting themselves and others, so these bodhisattvas do not eat any type of meat.

"Attachment arises based on the awareness of having a body, so that this body becomes identified with a being's self-identity. This is why bodhisattvas who embody compassion do not eat any type of meat. Mahāmati, even the gods abandon it, so bodhisattvas who embody affectionate kindness do not eat any type of meat. Even in this life, Mahāmati, eating meat causes one's breath to stink, so bodhisattvas do not eat any meat.

"Meat eaters suffer when they are asleep and suffer when they are awake. They have dark dreams: you can see the hairs rise on their bodies. Dwelling in empty houses or alone in isolated places, they are haunted by spirits that steal their life force. Sometimes they get angry or have sudden feelings of fear and dread. They eat gluttonously, without a sense of proportion. They cannot digest the nourishment in their food, drink, and other sustenance. Worms grow in their stomachs, and they are prone to leprosy and many other illnesses. Despite such unpleasant experiences, they do not understand the cause.

"I have explained that food can be medicinal or as unwholesome as the flesh of children. Mahāmati, ordinary, non-noble beings eat meat. Noble beings give it up. Meat causes the accumulation of much nonvirtue and the relinquishment of much virtue. This food is unpleasant and unsuitable: it is food for the unwise. How could I permit my disciples to eat flesh and blood? Mahāmati, I say that eating the food of noble beings brings much virtue and gets rid of nonvirtue. Sages of the past delighted in foods like rice, barley, wheat, various large and small beans, butter, oil, honey, sugar, molasses, and sugarcane. These are wholesome foods, and you should be understand that I have permitted them. Mahāmati, in the future benighted beings will speculate about the Vinaya. Proposing many subtle distinctions, they will conclude that meat is acceptable food. But in truth this is because they are predisposed to eating meat and are attached to its taste.

"Mahāmati, I teach this for the sake of those great bodhisattvas who do the work of the buddhas of the past, who cultivate virtue, who have faith, and who are without conceptions. They are the children of Śākyamuni's lineage, my human sons and daughters who are not attached to body, life, or enjoyments. Unattached to sense pleasures, they are not greedy for tasty food. Endowed with compassion, they aspire to be like me. They cherish all beings, as if they were their only child. I teach this for their sake.

"Mahāmati, in the past there was a king named Sengé Bangzang. He ate meat, including types that are normally forbidden. He was so attached to the taste that he even ate human flesh! All those who lived in his cities and villages abandoned him, even his wife, his ministers, his relatives, and his friends. Thus abandoned, his suffering was very great!

"Mahāmati, at the time when Indra had become king of the gods, even he had strong tendencies toward eating meat. Because of this fault, he sometimes took the form of a hawk and tormented Viśvakarmā, who took the form of a pigeon. The blameless and compassionate king Śibi was forced to put his flesh on the scales in order to ransom a dove, causing the king great pain.[83] Thus, Mahāmati, the tendency toward eating meat that has built up over many lifetimes is the source of problems for both yourself and others. This is true even if you are born as Indra, king of the gods, let alone as a lesser being!

83. This refers to a passage in the *Mahābhārata* in which King Śibi ransoms a dove (an avatar of the god Agni) from a hawk (Indra) by placing increasingly large pieces of his own flesh on a scale. For a complex discussion of this story, see Jörg Heimbel's translation of Ngorchen Künga Sangpo's *Epistle* in chapter 3, note 234. See also Doniger, *The Hindus*, 272.

"Mahāmati, there was once another king of men. One day this king was carried off by a powerful horse into a wild and unruly forest. After wandering for a long time, he began living with a lioness in order to survive. Eventually they had sons, one of whom was named Kangtra. At that time in the past, being accustomed to living with lions, Kangtra and the others were meat eaters. Because of these evil tendencies, Kangtra continued to eat meat over a succession of lives, even when he became a king of men. Mahāmati, in this present life Kangtra has been born in the city of Kimdün, and he is very attached to meat, to the extent that he even eats forbidden meats. Because of this, in the future he will be born as a malevolent male or female animal-headed spirit that consumes human flesh. Even after that life, Mahāmati, his strong, ongoing attachment to meat will cause him to fall into exceptionally fierce birth states, such as lions, tigers, leopards, wolves, cats, foxes, owls, and other carnivorous animals. He will even be born as a cannibal demon that eats a lot of meat. After such a fall, it will be hard for him to again achieve a human life, let alone achieve nirvāṇa!

"Mahāmati, these are the faults of eating meat, and this is what happens to those who eat a lot of it! Giving it up, however, brings much virtue. Mahāmati, ordinary, childish beings do not comprehend these virtues, faults, and so on. Mahāmati, I have taught this so that bodhisattvas who embody compassion will see these virtues and faults and stop eating any kind of meat.

"If someone gives up meat, Mahāmati, then animals will not be killed. This is because innocent beings are usually killed for money; other reasons are rare. Craving the taste of meat can be terribly overwhelming, Mahāmati, and can even lead people to eat human flesh, let alone the flesh of wild animals, domestic animals, birds, and other animals. Mahāmati, those tormented by a craving for the taste of meat create all manner of nets and traps. Using these, hunters, butchers, and fishermen kill all sorts of innocent animals that live in the sky, on the earth, and in the water. Such people, Mahāmati, endowed with fierce hunters' minds, are devoid of compassion, just like rākṣasa demons.[84] Anyone who recognizes that a being is alive and yet kills and eats it anyway can never develop compassion.

"All meat is unsuitable, Mahāmati, whether it is the type that I have allowed my dear śrāvakas to eat, the type I have not allowed, or so-called unexamined meat. Mahāmati, in the future there will be stupid people who are ordained

84. Rākṣasas are a type of demon common in South Asian literature, particularly known for eating a lot of meat and sometimes for cannibalism. See Buswell and Lopez, *Princeton Dictionary of Buddhism*, 695.

in my tradition, who call themselves 'children of the Śākya,' and who bear aloft the saffron victory banner, but whose minds are spoiled by wrong views. Their ego-clinging will be vast, and they will lust for the taste of meat. Speculating on subtle distinctions in the Vinaya rules, they will find all kinds of justifications for eating meat. They will spread these justifications to others, so that people ridicule me, saying I am not pure. They will examine the histories of the doctrine and will say, 'In these history books, it is clear that the Buddha allowed the consumption of meat. Far from being unsuitable, it is a wholesome food!' They will even say that that I myself ate it! But, Mahāmati, in none of my teachings have I ever permitted eating meat. I have never said that it is wholesome or permitted.

"Mahāmati, some may think that I have permitted it, or that I have allowed it in order to appease my śrāvaka disciples. But I have forbidden eating any type of meat for those yogis who abide with love, and for all my sons and daughters who are on the pure path of the Mahāyāna. I have forbidden it so that they can practice seeing all beings as their only child. Mahāmati, I have forbidden eating any type of meat to all my sons and daughters who aspire to the Dharma and who follow any of the vehicles. This includes those who dwell in charnel grounds, those who abide in love, those who dwell in forests, and those who practice yoga. Indeed, I have forbidden eating any type of meat to anyone who does contemplative practice and who thinks of all beings as their own children.

"When I spoke this or that teaching, I arranged the precepts in gradual stages, like the rungs of a ladder. I created the rule of threefold purity with this in mind, prohibiting such types of meat. This is why, in the past, I did not forbid the meat of animals that have died from the ten types of natural causes.[85] But now, in these times, I strongly forbid it to everyone, no matter what method they follow. Just so, Mahāmati, I do not permit anyone to eat meat. It is not permitted and will not become permitted. Mahāmati, I declare that the consumption of meat is unsuitable for anyone who has ordained as a monk.

"Mahāmati, foolish people whose past karmic defilement drives them to ridicule me by saying that even the Tathāgata ate meat will endure meaningless suffering for a long time, devoid of joy. Mahāmati, my noble śrāvakas do not eat ordinary, vulgar food, so what need is there to speak of unsuitable foods like meat and blood? Mahāmati, my śrāvakas, pratyekabuddhas, and bodhisattvas all eat the food of Dharma, not worldly food. What need is there

85. For a detailed discussion of the ten types of natural death mentioned here, see Khenpo Tsultrim Lodrö's commentary on this line in chapter 12, as well as note 329 in chapter 4.

to speak of what the Tathāgata eats? Mahāmati, tathāgatas possess the body of Dharma and are sustained by the food of Dharma. They do not have a worldly body and do not sustain themselves with any type of worldly food. They have abandoned all inclination to seek after mundane existence and the affairs of the world, and they do not have any inclination toward disturbing emotions. Their mind and insight have been completely liberated. They are all-knowing and all-seeing. They see all beings as the same as their only child and possess great compassion. In just this way, Mahāmati, I regard all beings as the same as my only child, and how could I permit the śrāvakas to eat the flesh of my child? What need is there to speak of my own food? Mahāmati, it is wrong to say that I have allowed my śrāvakas to eat meat, or that I have eaten it myself. Thus have I spoken."

Bodhisattvas of strong mind,
do not consume meat,
alcohol, garlic, or onions.
The Victor, supreme among all, has taught this.
Because they lack noble kindness,
others consume such disgusting fare.

Meat is a food for carnivorous animals;
the Great Sage has declared it to be unsuitable.
You should bear in mind, Mahāmati,
the faults of eating meat,
and the virtues of giving it up—
remember everything that comes from eating meat.

Whether of confused animals[86] or one's own friends,
all meat comes from semen and blood.
Yogis do not eat meat,
as consuming it causes other beings to fear.

All meats, garlic, onions,
all types of alcohol,

86. The Tibetan word I am translating as "animals" is *'khrul ba*, which usually means "mistaken," or "confused." These ordinary meanings do not fit this context, however, so after consulting with several Tibetan scholars, I am translating it as "animals," with the sense that animals are those who are confused about the world.

wild onions, and white garlic—
yogis abandon all of these!

They abandon rubbing with oil,
and since small beings live in the
open spaces inside mattresses,
yogis do not sleep on beds.[87]

Food gives rise to pride in oneself,
and from this conceptual pride,
desirous cravings arise with force.
So do not eat such foods!

Desire arises from concepts,
and desire leads to mental confusion.
Confusion then transforms into a body,
and the birth process is not liberated.

People pay money for meat,
causing animals to be killed for profit.
Both the killer and buyer own this sinful karma
and will boil in the Crying Hell.

All those who go against the Buddha's words,
and eat meat with an ignoble mind,
destroy their lives, both now and in the future,
and defile the conduct found in the Śākya's teachings!

Those people endowed with sinful karma,
go to hells that are thoroughly terrifying.
Those who eat meat will be boiled
in the Crying Hell.

87. This is another somewhat obscure passage. Padmakara interprets it differently: "And since it is on a bed/ that living beings enter into the womb of pain/ on such yogis do not sleep or take their rest." I originally interpreted this line in the same way that Padmakara did but changed my mind after a long and interesting discussion with Khenpo Jorden of the Internaional Buddhist Academy. The concern, in my present reading, is that small insects live inside the cushions on a bed, and that if someone sits or lies on the bed, they might injure the insects.

Meat that has threefold purity,
free of being considered, requested,
or coerced, does not exist.[88]
So do not eat meat!

Yogis do not eat meat.
This is my teaching,
and that of all other buddhas.

Beings that eat one another
take birth as carnivores.
Or they become madmen,
foul smelling with low reputations.
Again and again they are born
as outcasts, dog eaters, and dyers.
Or they are born as animal-headed gods,
or among flesh-eating demons.
After this present human life,
they come back as demons or cats.

This is why I teach that meat is utterly base,
in sūtras such as the *Hastikakṣya*,[89]
Mahāmega,[90] *Parinirvāṇa*, and *Aṅgulimālīya*,[91]
as well as this *Laṅkāvatāra Sūtra*.

Buddhas, bodhisattvas, and śrāvakas,
all decry it as base.
This food, whose essence is turbulent,
always leads to birth as a madman.

Abandoning meat, on the other hand,
leads to birth as a brahman or yogi,
or one endowed with wisdom and wealth.

88. This is an unusual formulation of the rule of threefold purity, which usually refers to meat that you have not (1) seen to have been killed for your own sake, (2) heard was killed for your own sake, or (3) suspect was killed for your own sake.

89. *The Elephant's Power Sūtra* (Tib: *Glang po'i rtsal gyi mdo*), Degé Kangyur, 62:254–88.

90. *The Great Cloud Sūtra* (Tib: *Sprin chen po'i mdo*), Degé Kangyur, 64:225–468.

91. *The Angulīmāla Sūtra* (Tib: *Sor mo'i phreng ba la phan pa'i mdo*), Degé Kangyur, 62:253–414.

Meat that you have seen, heard, or suspected:
all of it is utterly base.
But those born in meat-eating families
do not understand, despite their cleverness.
Desire creates an obstacle to liberation.
In just this way, meat and alcohol
are also obstacles to liberation.

In future times,
ignorant supporters of meat eating
will say that meat is sinless and suitable,
and will claim that I say the same.

Thinking of food as no different than medicine,
and of meat as the flesh of their own children,
yogis eat moderately,
not so much that they cannot digest it.

I, who abide in love,
always and in every way reproach
those who associate with lions,
tigers, foxes, and the like.

Since it is in opposition to achieving liberation,
and since it causes others to fear,
do not eat meat.
This is the noble banner of victory!

This is the seventh chapter of the Laṅkāvatāra Sūtra, the essence of the teaching of all buddhas, which explains not eating meat.

The Mahāparinirvāna Sūtra

Translated by Geoffrey Barstow

Then the bodhisattva Kāśyapa spoke these words to the Bhagavān: "The Bhagavān is not interested in meat, and giving you meat would be unsuitable.[92] If I were asked why this is, I would say that those who have no interest in meat are seen to possess eight great qualities.

"Very good!" the Bhagavān answered Kāśyapa. "You understand my purpose very well. This is the understanding of those bodhisattvas who guard the Dharma. Child of my lineage, from now on I do not allow even the servants of the śrāvakas to eat meat. If lay donors give some because of their faith, they should perceive it as the flesh of their child."

The bodhisattva Kāśyapa said, "Bhagavān, why did you, the Tathāgata, not allow seeking out[93] meat?" The Bhagavān replied, "Child of my lineage, eating meat severs the lineage of compassion!" Kāśyapa replied, "In the past, didn't you allow seeking out meat that had been examined in the three ways?"[94] The Bhagavān replied, "Kāśyapa, I taught that it was acceptable to eat meat that had been examined in the three ways as a skillful method so people could gradually cut it off entirely." The bodhisattva Kāśyapa said, "Why did you not

92. The Tibetan text here uses the important word *'tshal*, usually meaning to "seek out" or "ask" for something. In this case, that would be, "The Bhagavān does not seek out meat." Commentaries on this text, however, seem to take this term to simply mean "eat," producing "The Bhagavān does not eat meat." After discussing this term with multiple Tibetan scholars, I have settled on the translation here: "The Bhagavān is not interested in meat," with the hope that it conveys a sense that it is not simply the refusal to eat meat, but the sense that he simply has no interest in it. The eight qualities, therefore, inhere not necessarily in someone who gives up meat even though they would like it, but in someone who simply has no interest in it at all.

93. The verb here is the same problematic term encountered earlier, *'tshal*, which I rendered as "interested in" in the first paragraph of this translation. Here I have reverted to the more literal sense of "seeking out." It is worth noting, however, that the term is found only in Kāśyapa's questions, not in the Buddha's replies. Kāśyapa keeps asking why the Buddha allowed his disciples to seek out meat. But when the Buddha replies, he speaks of eating meat in general, not merely seeking it out.

94. Throughout this volume, I have generally translated this idea as "threefold purity" (Tib: *rnam gsum dag pa'i sha*). The *Mahāparinirvāna Sūtra*, however, uses an unusual phrasing for this idea, found, to the best of my knowledge, in no other canonical text (Tib: *sha brtags pa rnam gsum 'tshal du*). I have changed the translation to acknowledge this shift in phrasing, though the underlying idea remains the same.

allow seeking other meat, from the ten types of unexamined meats to the nine types of examined meat?"[95] The Bhagavān replied, saying, "This too I taught so that people could gradually cut it off entirely. In short, my teaching is to stop eating meat!"

"Bhagavān," the bodhisattva Kāśyapa asked, "why did you, the Tathāgata, declare that fish was wholesome food?" The Bhagavān replied, "Child of my lineage, I did not say that fish was wholesome food! Sugarcane, rice, molasses, rye, barley, milk, curd, butter, oil, and so on: I have said that these are wholesome foods. I have also said that my followers are allowed to wear many types of clothing. But even though I have allowed this, the clothes must be dyed the correct color! What need is there to speak of attachment to the flesh of fish?"

"Tathāgata," Kāśyapa said, "since you did not allow seeking out meat, then would it not be appropriate to forbid other things, such as the five tastes, milk, yogurt, buttermilk, white butter, ghee, sesame oil, and so on, as well as wearing fine robes, garlands, leather boots, and carrying bowls made of gold or silver?" The Bhagavān replied, "Child of my lineage, my teachings do not align with the view held by the naked ascetics.[96] When I, the Tathāgata, made the disciplinary rules, I was thinking about individual situations. Therefore I had a specific intention when I allowed eating meat that had been examined in the three ways. At another time, with another motivation, I forbade the ten types of meat. In yet another context, I did not allow eating any type of meat, even from animals that had died naturally. But from this time forward, Kāśyapa, I declare that it is unsuitable for those who are my disciples to eat any type of meat.

"Kāśyapa, no matter what they are doing—be it walking, sitting, lying down, or sleeping—meat eaters terrify any animal that can smell them, just as the smell of a lion terrifies any human. Child of my lineage, those who eat garlic have a disagreeable smell, so others dislike and avoid them. What need is there to discuss the flaws of such food? It is the same with those who eat meat. When beings encounter the smell of meat, they are afraid. The fear of death arises in them. Saying 'this is our enemy!' those animals that dwell in the water, on the land, or fly in the sky all turn aside and flee. This is why I do not permit bodhisattvas to eat meat. For the sake of liberating beings, they may manifest the appearance of eating meat. But in truth they do not eat it, even if

95. The sūtra does not make clear what the "ten types of unexamined meat" and the "nine types of examined meat" are, and despite consulting with several Tibetan scholars, I have been unable to find references to these lists elsewhere.

96. Refers to those Indian religious traditions in which practitioners perform extreme asceticism, such as never wearing clothes.

it looks like they are. Child of my lineage, bodhisattvas do not even eat thoroughly pure food, so what need is there to even speak about meat?

"Child of my lineage, after I have passed into final nirvāṇa, and after even those sages who are endowed with long life and who have accomplished the four noble paths have also entered nirvāṇa, the noble Dharma will decline. Monks will only appear to uphold the discipline and will only rarely read or recite the sūtras. They will desire food to nourish their bodies and will wear unwholesome, rough clothing. Their color will darken and their bodies will lack luster. They will care for cows and sheep and will carry wood and hay. They will have long hair and nails. All this will happen. They may wear saffron robes, but they will be just like hunters. They may walk slowly with downcast eyes, but this is only like a cat chasing a rat. They will repeatedly say, 'I am an arhat,' but they will be tormented by illness, pain, torpor, and impurity.[97] Outwardly they will maintain the semblance of religious practice, but inwardly their mind will be overwhelmed by jealousy and desire. In this way they will be just like brahmans and others who uphold false doctrines. Those who are not themselves virtuous will teach virtue to others. Beyond just holding wrong views, they will actually denigrate the pure Dharma!

"The Tathāgata taught the Vinaya, the path of activity, and the fruit that is perfect liberation, along with the morality that accompanies these. But these people heedlessly abandon this Dharma. Instead they create unsuitable teachings. They intend to speak profoundly, but they say only unsuitable things. In this way, they each propound teachings and disciplines of their own. In this way, they will say, 'The Tathāgata allowed us to eat meat.' They will write it down, then insist, 'The Buddha said this!' Then they will fight among themselves, each declaring, 'I am the heir of the virtuous Śākya!'"[98]

"Child of my lineage, at that time monks will also hoard a lot of grain and consume fish meat extensively. They will keep vessels for butter, jeweled umbrellas, and leather boots. When they teach kings, ministers, and other householders, they will only speak of interpreting omens, astrology, divination, and medicine. These monks will have male and female servants and will keep gold and silver, as well as jewels, gems, crystals, pearls, corals, topaz, and jeweled garlands. They will eat all kinds of fruit. Moreover, they will engage in sports, painting, and sculpture. They will teach students to read[99] and will

97. An arhat is an advanced practitioner who has conquered all emotions. Having disciplined and tamed the emotions, a true arhat would not be bothered by these things.

98. "Śākya" is the name of the Buddha's clan.

99. The problem here is likely that these monks act as professional tutors, teaching for money. It is, presumably, a good thing for older monks to teach young monks to read.

both plow and reap their fields. They will practice sorcery, spells, and compound medicines. They will learn all kinds of things, like how to sing, dance, and play, as well as how to make incense, flowers garlands, ornaments, and other games. All of this will happen. But you should know that if a monk abandons unwholesome things like these, then that one is truly my disciple."

Then Kāśyapa again spoke to the Bhagavān, asking, "Bhagavān, monks and nuns as well as male and female laypeople all depend on donors. When they beg for alms to support themselves, sometimes there is some meat mixed in with the food they receive. What should they do? How should they investigate?" The Bhagavān replied, saying, "They should take the meat out of the other food and wash the food with water. Then they can eat it. If their bowl was defiled by the meat but does not have any smell or taste left, then there is no fault in using it. If someone places a large amount of meat in their bowl, they should not accept it. If meat is mixed in with their other food, they should not eat it. If they do eat it, they are committing an offense. If I were to fully explain why meat is not allowed, I would never end! But the time has come for me to enter final nirvāṇa, so I have explained this only briefly."

Source Texts

Laṅkāvatāra Sūtra (*Lang kar gshegs pa'i mdo*). In *Sde dge bka' 'gyur*, vol. 49, 56a–191b. BDRC: W4CZ5369.

Mahāparinirvāṇa Sūtra (*Myang 'das chen po'i mdo*). In *Sde dge bka' 'gyur*, vols. 52–53. BDRC: W4CZ5369.

Secondary Sources

Blum, Mark, trans. 2014. *The Nirvana Sutra*, vol. 1. Berkeley, CA: BDK America.

Bunyu Nanjio, ed. 1923. *The Laṅkāvatāra Sūtra*. Kyoto: Otani University Press.

Buswell, Robert E., and Donald S. Lopez. 2013. *The Princeton Dictionary of Buddhism*. Princeton, NJ: Princeton University Press.

Doniger, Wendy. 2010. *The Hindus: An Alternative History*. New York: Penguin.

Forsten, Aucke D. 2006. *Between Certainty and Finitude: A Study of Laṅkāvatārasūtra Chapter Two*. Berlin: LIT Verlag Münster.

Hodge, Stephen. 2010. "The Mahāyāna Mahāparinirvāna Sūtra: The Text and Its Transmission." Presented at the Second International Workshop on the Mahāparinirvāna Sūtra, Munich.

Kosho Yamamoto, trans. 1975. *The Mahayana Mahaparinirvana-Sutra*. 3 vols. Karin Buddhological Series 5. Ube: Karin Bunko.

Red Pine, trans. 2012. *The Lankavatara Sutra: A Zen Text*. Berkeley, CA: Counterpoint.

Shabkar [Tsogdruk Rangdrol]. 2004. *Food of Bodhisattvas: Buddhist Teachings on Abstaining from Meat*. Translated by Padmakara Translation Group. Boston: Shambhala Publications.

Sutton, Florin Giripescu. 1991. *Existence and Enlightenment in the Laṅkāvatāra-Sūtra: A Study in the Ontology and the Epistemology of the Yogacara School of Mahayana Buddhism*. Albany: State University of New York Press.

Suzuki, D. T. 1930. *Studies in the Lankavatara Sutra*. Tokyo: Sanshusa.

———, trans. 1956. *The Lankavatara Sutra: A Mahayana Text*. London: Routledge & Keegan.

Takasaki, Jikido. 1980. "Analysis of the Lankavatara: In Search of Its Original Form." In *Indianisme et Bouddhisme: Mélanges offerts à Mgr Etienne Lamotte*, edited by D. Donnet, A. Bareau, and H. Bechert, 339–52. Louvain-la-Neuve: Université Catholique de Louvain, Institut Orientaliste.

2. Dolpopa Sherab Gyaltsen on Refraining from Meat

By Michael Sheehy

Dolpopa Sherab Gyaltsen (1292–1361)[100] was a giant among contemplative scholars in fourteenth-century Tibet. He lived during a crescendo moment for the intellectual experimentation and synergism of Buddhist scholasticism during which his own creative contributions would prove critical to the reformulation of Tibetan philosophical discourse. Having been born in the wake of the monastic principalities that shaped Buddhism up through the mid-twelfth century in Central Tibet, Dolpopa lived under the lordship of the Mongols and Sakya rule prior to Tsongkapa Lobzang Drakpa (1357–1419) and the rise of the Geluk order. His intellectual contemporaries included the Karma Kagyü incarnation and master of mahāmudrā, the Third Karmapa Rangjung Dorjé (1284–1339); the entrepreneurial editor in chief of the Buddhist canon at Zhalu Monastery, Butön Rinchen Drup (1290–1364); and the Nyingma virtuoso who synthesized the Dzokchen seminal heart tradition,[101] Longchen Rabjam Drimé Ödzer (1308–1364). Like Dolpopa, the intellectual titans who lived during his lifetime would also make their mark on Tibetan Buddhist thought.

Renowned by his epithet—Buddha from Dolpo[102]—Sherab Gyaltsen was born in the Pumdo[103] valley of the Dolpo region of northern Nepal.[104] Dolpopa received novice monk ordination at twelve years of age, and then at age seventeen, in 1309, began his life in Central Tibet. In 1322, after having visited Jonang Monastery a year earlier, Dolpopa returned to the valley of Jomonang to request the full transmission of the Dro Kālacakra tradition along with oral instructions on the sixfold vajrayoga completion-stage practices

100. Tib: Dol po pa Shes rab rgyal mtshan.

101. Tib: *snying thig.*

102. Tib: *Dol po sangs rgyas.*

103. Tib: *Spu mdo.*

104. Kapstein, *The 'Dzam-Thang Edition*, 7. For a full biography of Dolpopa, see Stearns, *The Buddha from Dolpo*.

from the throneholder at Jonang, Ketsun Yontan Gyatso (1260–1327).[105] The night preceding Dolpopa's arrival at Jonang, Yontan Gyatso is said to have dreamed that the emperor of Shambhala, King Puṇḍarīka, visited him and raised the Buddha's victory banner over the Jomonang valley. With this auspicious omen, Dolpopa was summoned the next morning for Yontan Gyatso to bestow the entirety of the Kālacakra initiation and its related esoteric instructions on him.[106] Enthroned a year before Yontan Gyatso's passing, Dolpopa ascended to the throne and assumed leadership at Jonang in 1326.[107] From 1330 to 1333, while constructing the Great Stūpa at Jonang in commemoration of Yontan Gyatso, Dolpopa served as editor in chief of the retranslation of the *Kālacakra Tantra*[108] and its commentary, the *Vimalaprabhā*.[109] Simultaneously, he was formulating his realizations and meditative experiences into a system that would eventually be coined *zhentong*.[110]

The confluence of these multiple events, including the construction of the Great Stūpa at Jonang, the retranslation of the *Kālacakra Tantra*, and Dolpopa's immersive time in solitary retreat, came to a zenith in 1333. During this year, Dolpopa metaphorically describes how the construction of the stūpa felt parallel to the raising of the axis mundi—Mount Meru—comparable only to blessings from the king of Shambhala. This enabled his realizations to gush forth from his deep internal reservoirs like a geyser springing from cosmic oceans.[111] With a new translation of the *Kālacakra Tantra* as his basis, and with the salience of his meditative experiences, Dolpopa employed a new Dharma language (*chos skad*) to describe his realizations. This doctrinal language was framed in the context of the Kālacakra cosmology and identified his teachings with the cosmic eon of the Kṛtayuga or the Dharma of the

105. Sheehy, "A Lineage History of Vajrayoga and Tantric Zhentong from the Jonang Kālacakra Practice Tradition," 224–26.

106. Stearns, *The Buddha from Dolpo*, 15–16.

107. Yontan Gyatso passed away in 1327. Kapstein, *The 'Dzam-Thang Edition*, 13; Stearns, *The Buddha from Dolpo*, 19.

108. *Wheel of Time* (Tib: *Dus kyi 'khor lo*).

109. *Stainless Light* (Tib: *'Dri med 'od*). This Jonang Kālacakra translation was completed by Dolpopa's main disciples Jonang Lotsawa Lodrö Pal (1313–1397) and Sazang Mati Paṇchen Lodrö Gyaltsen (1294–1376).

110. Tib: *gzhan stong*. Stearns, *The Buddha from Dolpo*, 24–29.

111. Stearns, *The Buddha from Dolpo*, 19–22.

Perfect Eon.[112] This teaching included terms such as *rangtong*[113] and *zhentong* to describe two modes of emptiness: (a) *rangtong*, emptiness that is devoid of an intrinsic relative nature, and (b) *zhentong*, emptiness that is not other than the continuously abiding nature of buddhahood, *tathāgatagarbha*. These innovative teachings and rearticulations of Indian Buddhist doctrines culminated in Dolpopa's masterpiece, *Mountain Dharma: An Ocean of Definitive Meaning*.[114]

Dolpopa's Ethic of Refrain

In 1314 Dolpopa vowed not to eat slaughtered meat for the rest of his life. He was twenty-three at the time, had received full monastic ordination that same year, and was on a tour of the preeminent scholastic institutions in Central Tibet.[115] The text that is partially translated here is his *Advice and Quotes about Refraining from Meat and Alcohol*, composed in 1325, the same year that he first taught at Jonang and was requested by his teacher Yontan Gyatso to assume leadership of the Jonang yogi community.[116] While there is certainly precedent for a meatless diet among spiritual masters in Tibet prior to Dolpopa, with early Kagyü masters including Pakmodrupa (1110–1170) and his disciples Jigten Sumgön (1143–1217) and Taklung Tangpa (1142–1209) being noteworthy exemplars, Dolpopa's advice is among the earliest Tibetan writings on vegetarianism.[117]

This work follows a familiar compositional style for Dolpopa, one that resembles his *Mountain Dharma* and several of his other writings. Arranging

112. Tib: *rdzogs ldan chos*. This is based on the cosmology derived from the *Lokadhātupaṭala*, or *Chapter on World Systems*, in the extensive *Vimalaprabhā* commentary on the *Kālacakra Tantra* that delineates four cosmic eons (*yuga*): (1) Kṛtayuga (*rdzogs ldan*), (2) Tretayuga (*gsum ldan*), (3) Dvāparayuga (*gnyis ldan*), and (4) Kaliyuga (*rtsod ldan*). According to Dolpopa, zhentong is in alignment with the dharma of the Kṛtayuga or Perfect Eon, while rangtong is in alignment with the dharma of the Tretayuga, or Third Eon. Stearns, 79–81, 86–98; Kapstein, *The 'Dzam-Thang Edition*, 110–19; Sheehy, "The Dharma of the Perfect Eon."

113. Tib: *rang stong*.

114. For a translation of *Mountain Dharma*, see Hopkins, *Mountain Doctrine*.

115. In a brief biography of Dolpopa, it reads that he vowed, "I take the vow not to eat slaughtered meat for the rest of this life" (Tib: *Tshe gcig ring bsad sha mi gsol ba'i dam bca' mdzad.*) *Shes bya'i gter mdzod*, vol. 2, 405. For the translation of this vow in the context of his biography, see Kapstein, *The 'Dzam-Thang Edition*, 12; Stearns, *The Buddha from Dolpo*, 14.

116. According to the colophon, this is a *shing mo glang*, a female wood-ox year, corresponding to the year 1325. For the biographical details of his teaching at Jonang, see Stearns, *The Buddha from Dolpo*, 16.

117. Shabkar, *Food of Bodhisattvas*, 79.

his advice and quotes (*lung 'dren rnams*), Dolpopa utilizes the relatively common Tibetan genre convention of compiling select passages from canonical sources, including sūtras and tantras, to make a single argument. In this case, Dolpopa is arguing against eating meat. He organizes his work into three distinct sections corresponding to the three sets of vows: (1) the śrāvaka, (2) the bodhisattva or Mahāyāna, and (3) the Secret Mantra or tantric samayas of the Vajrayāna.[118] While the quotes that Dolpopa selects for the Śrāvaka and Bodhisattva Vehicles are relatively straightforward, including anticipated verses from the *Laṅkāvatāra Sūtra*, his section on the Vajrayāna reads less obviously. This section on the Vajrayāna is further divided into the literal (*sgra ji bzhin pa*) and the nonliteral (*sgra ji bzhin ma yin pa*) interpretations, making a parallel with a sequence that he would employ frequently in his philosophical writings on zhentong emptiness: the distinction between those doctrines that are provisional in meaning (*drang don*) in relation to those that are definitive in their meaning (*nges don*).[119]

As he makes explicit in his text, refraining from meat is not merely at the śrāvaka level of ethical restraint that avoids killing, nor even at the bodhisattva level that is motivated by compassion. For Dolpopa, not eating meat is tantric. In discussing the literal meaning in accord with the precepts of the Secret Mantra, Dolpopa first advises that "slaughtered meat is not condoned" in tantra. The *Kālacakra Tantra* states that the karmic retribution for killing is being reborn as a wild animal and that those monks who continually "thirst to have the tastes and flavors of meat on their tongues" imagine suicide in hell.

Such punitive statements, however, follow the normative rhetoric of Mahāyāna verse on abstaining from meat. The distinct tantric contribution to the discourse on meat eating is made explicit in the quote from the *Kālacakra Tantra* that reads: "For many monks, meat possesses the ten powers. So, this is no different than overcoming death." Here we have a shift in the discourse from retributive consequences for eating meat to the consumption of power,

118. This organizational schema is common for a general treatise across Tibetan genres. In this volume, Ngorchen Künga Zanpo, Khedrup Jé, Gorampa, and Karma Chakmé all use a similar framework. For more on this genre, see the discussion of scholasticism and three-vow genre in the general introduction to this volume, 3–8.

119. Dolpopa distinguishes rangtong emptiness to be provisional in meaning (*drang don*), while zhentong is definitive in meaning (*nges don*). This rubric is similarly applied to the canonical literature that supports this doctrinal claim. For a reference to eating meat, Zhabs dkar (1781–1851) also makes use of a quote that Dolpopa references in his work to state that according to the Secret Mantra, eating meat is not a literal teaching, quoting the commentary on the *The Ocean of Ḍākinīs Tantra* that discusses the devouring of discursive thoughts or eating conceptuality. Shabkar, *Food of Bodhisattvas*, 35.

and more specifically, the ten powers[120] of a perfectly enlightened buddha. At this juncture, Dolpopa interjects by rhetorically asking, "How are the five meats explained?" And in response, he explains:

> Now, the five meats are not killed for the purpose of meat but have died naturally. These [five meats] are mixed with the juniper berry to make ambrosia pills that yogis eat not merely out of lip service but for the sake of their tantric vows—they need to increase the strength of their body, abate various arrogances, and guide sentient beings. With this in mind, yogis who eat meat but are incapable of guiding sentient beings should stop eating meat of any kind.

These five kinds of meat—human, cow, dog, elephant, and horse—consist of a set of indispensable foods for tantric samayas, eaten in the ritual context of self-creation during a tantric feast.[121] These five meats, as well as their corresponding five ambrosias—feces, urine, semen, blood, and brain fluid—were forbidden substances to consume in first-millennia India when they were introduced into Buddhist ritual context.[122] Both the five meats and five ambrosias are taboo substances, perceived to be polluted and disgusting, and it is precisely this repulsiveness that these substances symbolize to the tantric adept. These meats and ambrosia are signifiers meant to trigger realization of nondual enlightened wisdom in the process of ritual consumption while re-creating one's identity.[123] Paradoxically, according to the *Kālacakra Tantra*, not eating these meats and ambrosia would be a transgression against the pledge not to disavow the tantric samayas during a tantric feast.[124] So here we have a tantric conundrum, to eat meat outside of the ritual feast context is a

120. Tib: *stobs bcu.*

121. The five meats and their corresponding ambrosia are found throughout the tantric literature, particularly in the self-creation stages of the Mahāyoga and Anuttarayoga Tantra traditions. For discussion on the semiotics of the five meats and five ambrosias in the context of the Mahāyoga traditions, see Wedemeyer, *Making Sense of Tantric Buddhism*, 118–21.

122. Wedemeyer, *Making Sense of Tantric Buddhism*, 119.

123. Wedemeyer discusses beef as a signifier in the process of ritual consumption meant to signify the attainment of nondual wisdom (*advayajñāna*). Wedemeyer, *Making Sense of Tantric Buddhism*, 121–22.

124. It should also be noted that among the twenty-five root tantric samayas, detailed in chapter 3 of the *Kālacakra Tantra*, it includes not killing (*hiṃsā*) as well as the avoidance of the five types of killing (which includes the killing of a cow), unwholesome food (*sāvadya-bhojya*), and abandoning the tantric samayas (*samaya*) during a tantric feast. Wallace, *The Inner Kālacakratantra*, 242n9.

fault while not eating meat during a ritual feast would violate a root vow. Reiterating this tantric virtuosity, and the seriousness of these high stakes, Dolpopa warns that if a yogi is not capable of guiding beings, he should not eat meat.[125]

In the next section, explaining the nonliteral meaning, Dolpopa discusses his ethic of refraining from meat in relation to the inner yogic life. The ethic of refrain that Dolpopa advances is no different from the practice of refrain included in the observance of ethical discipline prescribed by the *Kālacakra Tantra*. This involves refrain from engaging in the five sense objects and keeping the twenty-five tantric samayas, which are prerequisites for the sixfold vajrayoga practice.[126] He begins this section by stating that "while you abide within meditative equipoise, your eyes and other five sense faculties should not rush toward their sense objects." This is a reference to the yoga of withdrawal, the first exercise in the sixfold vajrayoga sequence of the Kālacakra completion-stage process.[127] Based on fundamental Buddhist models of the mind-body complex, adapted to the tantric context, this yoga intentionally retracts the five sense faculties (*dbang po lnga*) from their engagement with the five corresponding sense objects (*yul lnga*).[128] This meditative process is enacted by withdrawing the subtle life energies[129] from the left and right channels and merging them into the central channel. By ceasing the flow of energy within the left and right channels, the connections between the five sense faculties and their corresponding sense objects are severed. This disengages the six types of ordinary awareness[130] from the external world, rendering these faculties inept, while giving rise to extrasensory perception.[131]

With ordinary operations of cognition ceased, awareness is subsumed by

125. Dolpopa here is referencing one of the twenty-five root tantric samayas in the *Kālacakra Tantra*, that it is proscribed to give a secret offering of sublime bliss to an immature spiritual person, meaning a śrāvaka. Wallace, *The Inner Kālacakratantra*, 242n9.

126. Restraint (*niyama*) is a prerequisite to the Kālacakra sixfold vajrayoga, present in each phase of the yoga as qualifying conditions, and thereby not considered to be a separate phase. Wallace, *The Inner Kālacakratantra*, 26.

127. Skt: *pratyāhāra*; Tib: *so sor sdud pa*. The sixfold (*ṣaḍaṅgayoga*) vajrayoga of the Kālacakra completion stage are: (1) withdrawal (*pratyāhāra, so sor sdud pa*), (2) meditative concentration (*dhyāna, bsam gtan*), (3) harnessing life force (*prāṇāyāma, srog rtsol*), (4) retention (*dhāraṇā, 'dzin pa*), (5) recollection (*anusmṛti, rjes dran*), (6) meditative absorption (*samādhi, ting nge 'dzin*).

128. Wallace, *The Inner Kālacakratantra*, 203–4.

129. Skt: *prāṇa*; Tib: *rlung*

130. Skt: *vijñāna*; Tib: *rnam shes*

131. Wallace, *The Inner Kālacakratantra*, 158–61.

nondual wisdom or pristine awareness.[132] To explain this, Dolpopa links it with the theme of his text by quoting the tenth-century Indian scholar Padmavajra's large commentary on the *Ḍākārṇava Tantra*,[133] which states, "Supreme wisdom eats conceptualization." At this point, he has employed the full semiotics of refrain, making clear to his reader that meat is a signifier for the taste of pristine awareness—nondual enlightened wisdom—and that the tantric adept eats the meat of conceptuality. Situating this within the tantric ritual context, Dolpopa writes:

> To eat the five meats is to devour the five sense faculties of ordinary awareness that rush toward the five sense objects, and to expand the powers of nonconceptuality. Without moving, reside in the center of the outer maṇḍala of the five energies. Eat all the meat of conceptuality that gives rise to the five upsetting emotions. Eating the five meats will expand the powers of pristine awareness.

Here, and in the text that precedes it, Dolpopa is arranging a maṇḍala in quintets. In typical tantric fashion, he is symmetrically correlating a matrix of the five sense faculties with the five sensory objects, the five meats with the five ambrosias, the five sense faculties with the five meats, the five ambrosias with the five aggregates, the five lamps with the five sense faculties, the five sensory objects with the five energies, and the five energies with the five upsetting emotions.[134] In so doing, he is not only inviting his reader into a reflection on the Buddhist tantric ethic of eating meat but also welcoming them into a symbolic universe wherein what they taste is irresistibly more delicious.

Translating Dolpopa's Advice and Quotes

This translation is based on the xylograph text from the edition of Dolpopa's *Collected Works* that was printed at Dzamthang Tsangwa Monastery in Sichuan. During the process of translation, I consulted the Wylie transliterated

132. Skt: *jñāna*; Tib: *ye shes*. Sheehy, "Rangjung Dorjé's Variegations of Mind," 70–72.

133. *The Ocean of Ḍākinīs Tantra* (Full Skt: *Ḍākārṇavamahāyoginī Tantrarāja*; Tib: *Mkha' 'gro rgya mtsho chen po rnal 'byor ma'i rgyud kyi rgal po*). This tantra and its commentary by Padmavajra detail the maṇḍala of *ḍākārṇava*, with the central deity Cakrasaṃvara, organized concentrically in twelve circles with a retinue of 1,500 distinct subsidiary deities. Dolpopa references this tantra in his *Mountain Dharma*, citing how equal taste abides in the limitless mind. Hopkins, *Mountain Doctrine*, 241.

134. Not unlike the generation stage descriptions in the *Kālacakra Tantra*. Wallace, *The Inner Kālacakratantra*, 27–77.

version by Kaie Mochizuki, the 2011 Paltsek computer input publication, and the 1992 cursive (*dbu med*) edition published by Matthew Kapstein. Though I have made significantly different choices in phrasing as well as interpretation of meaning compared with the Mochizuki translation, I found that work to be helpful. For the sake of consistency throughout this book, the passages quoted from the *Laṅkāvatāra Sūtra* were adapted from the translation by Geoffrey Barstow and the suggested translation choices for technical terms were kept, with the exception of a few personal preferences.

The one relatively cryptic and highly interpretable passage is from the commentary on the *Ḍākārṇava Tantra* where it is translated: "A vajra-like lotus on a ship is said to be 'cow meat.' It is taught that a cow is bound by the faculty of the ear." The Tibetan phrase translated here as "cow meat" is *pala sha* (pala meat). The Tibetan term for cow used in the second line is *balang* (*ba lang*). After a fruitful conversation with Professor Kunchok Gyaltsen of Tso-Ngon University Tibetan Medical College in Qinghai, to whom I am grateful, we chose the current translation. The logic is that the term *pala* here refers to the *balang*, both referring to beef or the meat of a cow.

An alternative translation could be: "A vajra-like lotus on a ship is said to be a 'palash flower.' It is taught that a cow is bound by the faculty of the ear." This translation would follow a literal rendering of the Tibetan *pala sha*, which is the word for a species of the Butea flowering plants found on the Indian subcontinent. This is plausible, particularly because the word "palash" is common in Sanskrit literature and several Indian vernaculars for this species of flower. The species *Butea monosperma* is associated with past buddhas and the fire-red blossoms of this flower are referenced throughout Indian poetry. This would mean that the Tibetan-language commentary on the tantra from which Dolpopa was quoting used a phonetic rendering of the Sanskrit rather than translating the term into Tibetan.[135] It would also mean that *sha*, which means "meat" in Tibetan, would not be referring to cow in the second part of the phrase, thus making less sense in the current context of writing about meat.

135. It should be noted that this is the interpretation that Mochizuki followed, translating this quote as "'A lotus in a ship is a parāśa tree by diamond' means an ox bound by auditory faculty." Mochizuki, "On the Scriptures Introducing the Prohibition of Meat and Alcohol by Dol Po Pa," 43.

Refraining from Meat

By Dolpopa Sherab Gyaltsen

Translated by Michael Sheehy

Om!
Praise to the gurus, buddhas, and bodhisattvas!

With devotion, I take refuge and pay homage
to all the victors and their spiritual children
who remain inseparable from the illustrious, sublime masters.

I pray that you always hold me
and all sentient beings who inhabit the three worlds with tremendous love.

To you, whose qualities of the two knowledges are without limit,
who relinquish every instinct toward the two obscurations
and with a great wave of effort unite the two accumulations—
to Buddha Śākyamuni and your spiritual heirs,
I bow!

Because the commitments are utterly pure,
and their meaning, to be taken into experience,
is aligned with the vast and profound teachings
that were so eloquently spoken in the words of the Buddha,
here, I dare to express only a few things
about the levels of observance.[136]

In accord with the extensive explanations of the Mahāyāna commitments, to benefit those who are feebleminded and to revitalize and keep me vigilant,

136. Dolpopa is referencing the codes of precepts to be observed (*bsrung bya'i rim pa*), based on the structure of his text: śrāvaka (*nyan thos*), bodhisattva (*byang chub sems dpa'*), inner secret mantra (*nang gsang sngags*).

I'll discuss a few different explanations of the commitments. The purpose is twofold: first, I'll discuss and extensively explain the faults of drinking alcohol; second, I'll discuss the faults of eating meat, which causes voracity toward the life and breath of sentient beings.

I. Refraining from Drinking Alcohol

[This section is not included in this translation.][137]

II. Refraining from Eating Meat

The faults of eating meat are threefold: the proscription found in the precepts of the (1) the śrāvaka, (2) the secret bodhisattva, and (3) the inner secret mantra.

Precepts of the Śrāvaka Vehicle

First, the precepts taught for the śrāvaka are: "It is permitted to simply avoid killing for the sake of selling meat in a market." This is what is stated, and it will be explained below.

Precepts of the Bodhisattva Vehicle

Second, according to the precepts of the bodhisattva, from the beginning, meat eating is not condoned. As it states in the *Mañjuśrī Pradarshana*:[138]

> The Muni[139] gave his own flesh,
> and did not take the flesh of others.
> Since he did not have an angry thought,
> in this life, be the Buddha!

The same text says:

137. The section on alcohol has been omitted, as the focus of this volume is on meat eating. For an English translation of this section, see Mochizuki, "On the Scriptures Introducing the Prohibition of Meat and Alcohol by Dol Po Pa."

138. *Teachings on Mañjuśrī's Own View* (Tib: *'Phags pa 'jam phal gyi rang gi lta ba'i 'dod pa mdor bstan pa yongs su brtag pa*).

139. Śākyamuni, the historical Buddha.

If you use material goods to buy fish meat,
is this not eating deceptively?

Likewise, the *Hastikakṣya Sūtra*,
Mahāmegha Sūtra, *Mahāparinivāṇa Sūtra*,
Aṅgulimālīya Sūtra, and *Laṅkāvatāra Sūtra* all read:
"I do not condone eating meat."

Whether you sever a life for the purpose of acquiring material things
or you pay a price [for someone else to kill] for your food,
in either case, you are a killer and will roast in the Crying Hell.[140]
Sentient beings are killed for the sake of material objects.
So if no material things are offered, there will be no killing.
For there to be an animal killer, there must always be a relationship
between a living being and an agent [who kills].

If there is no demerit when a householder
purchases fish with material goods,
then how could good merit come
from constructing statues and the like?

A stūpa is built by a specialist,
and a fish is killed by a fisherman.
Those who worship a stūpa did not build it,
and those who eat fish are not killers.

So if there is no one who committed wrongdoing
among those who eat the fish,
then there is no merit for those who build stūpas
for the sake of those who worship stūpas.

But we must distinguish
between the killer and the eater.
Killers lust for possessions.
Eaters do it for food.

140. One of the eight hot hells, where you are consumed by torturous moaning and crying, both your own and that of all the other hell denizens that cry there with you in pain.

Killers who lust for possessions
will boil for a hundred thousand kalpas.
Eaters who lust for meat
will boil for ten million kalpas.

A fisherman kills a fish
so that a śrāvaka[141] remains pure.
A barmaid makes alcohol
so that a brahman remains pure.
These are no different in being free from misdeeds.[142]

Those humans who eat meat
first fall into being a hungry ghost,
then eventually into the Crying Hell.

There is no compassion in eating meat,
no joy in drinking alcohol,
no counsel in taking another's woman,
and no even-mindedness in placing blame.

This is also included within the secret mantra. As it reads in the *Bodhisattva Sūtra*:[143]

> [*The Bodhisattva states*:] King, a wise person must not sever a life. [*The King asks*:] What is the reason for this? [*The Bodhisattva responds*:] Great King, those humans who sever the life of another person will shorten their lives, will be reborn as a hell being, in the realm of animals, and in the Lord of Death's domain. This is stated in these verses:
>
> Those who sever a life have short lives,
> numerous severe illnesses, and are reborn as a hell being
> [in a realm] where they are extremely unhappy.

141. An ordained monk.

142. Dolpopa's point here is that it is hypocritical to criticize a brahman for drinking alcohol (which he himself has not made), while saying that it is permissible for a monk to eat fish (because he himself has not caught it).

143. *The Sūtra on Engaging in the Conduct of a Bodhisattva* (Full Skt: *Bodhisattvagocaropāyaviṣayavikuvāṇanirdeśa Sūtra*; Tib: *Byang chub sems dpa'i spyod yul gyi thabs kyi yul rnam par 'phrul pa bstan pa'i mdo*).

Therefore those who are wise,
who seek happiness in this life
and seek not to suffer,
do not sever the life of another.
Protect animals like they are your own self.

And in the *Laṅkāvatāra Sūtra* it reads: "Mahāmati," the Buddha said, "bodhisattvas who embody compassion do not eat meat for innumerable reasons, only some of which I will explain. Mahāmati, it is not easy to find someone who was not once your father, mother, brother, sister, son, daughter, kinsman, friend, or the like at some point during the long ages of saṃsāra. Your friends and relatives in the past, they have now changed their form and become wild animals, domestic animals, and birds, whatever their karma dictates. Bodhisattvas and great beings aspire to the Buddha's Dharma, aspire to become like me. So how could they eat the meat that comes from living creatures? Mahāmati, even demons turn away from eating meat when they hear the wholesome Dharma of the tathāgatas, turning away from their demonic nature toward compassion. So what need is there to speak of those who aspire to the true Dharma? In that way, Mahāmati, bodhisattvas look on all beings of the here and now as the transformations of their previous relatives and friends. Therefore they cultivate looking on each of them as their only child. Because of this, bodhisattvas—the embodiment of compassion—do not eat any type of meat."

It also reads: "Therefore, Mahāmati, bodhisattvas do not eat any meat. Mahāmati, bodhisattvas who aspire to purity do not eat meat, as it comes from semen and blood. Not wanting to scare living beings, Mahāmati, bodhisattvas who possess the yoga of kindness do not eat any type of meat. It is the case, Mahāmati, that when a dog sees, even at a great distance, a butcher, outcast, fisherman, or anyone else that eats dog meat, it is thrown into a state of fear. Thinking, 'they will come and kill me,' the dog almost dies of fear! It is similar, Mahāmati, with those tiny beings that live in the air, on the earth, or in water. As soon as they see a distant meat eater, or when they detect one with their subtle sense of smell, then, fearing death, they quickly turn aside, just as a human might turn from a demon. Mahāmati, since bodhisattvas who abide in kindness do not want to cause fear, they do not eat meat."

It also reads: "Mahāmati, compassionate bodhisattvas do not eat meat in order to avoid scandalizing people so that they disparage my teachings. So it is, Mahāmati. There are some in the world who speak ill of my teachings, saying, 'Alas, what type of virtue do those people have? Though they say it is important to act purely, they have abandoned the food of their own previous sages. Wandering throughout this world, like carnivorous animals, they fill their bellies with meat, terrifying those small animals that live in the sky, on the earth, and in the water. Their virtuous practice has declined! They have stopped turning aside from evil! They do not have any Dharma and they do not have any discipline!' Thus these people use many critical comments to disparage the teachings. Therefore, Mahāmati, since they desire to avoid scandalizing people who would then disparage my teachings, bodhisattvas who embody compassion do not eat any type of meat."

And it also reads: "Mahāmati, in the future benighted beings will speculate about the Vinaya. Proposing many subtle distinctions, they will conclude that meat is acceptable food. But in truth this is because they are predisposed to eating meat and are attached to its taste.

"Mahāmati, I teach this for the sake of those great bodhisattvas who do the work of the buddhas of the past, who cultivate virtue, who have faith, and who are without conceptions. They are the children of Śākyamuni's lineage, my human sons and daughters who are not attached to body, life, or enjoyments. Unattached to sense pleasures, they are not greedy for tasty food. Endowed with compassion, they aspire to be like me. They cherish all beings as if they were their only child. I teach this for their sake."

And it also reads: "Mahāmati, in this present life Kangtra and his brothers have been born in the city of Kimdün, and they are very attached to meat, to the extent that they even eat forbidden meats. Because of this, in the future they will be born as hateful spirits that consume human flesh. Even after that life, their strong, ongoing attachment to meat will cause them to fall into exceptionally fierce birth states, such as lions, tigers, leopards, wolves, cats, foxes, owls, and other carnivorous animals. They will even be born as rākṣasa demons that eat a lot of meat. After such a fall, it will be hard for them to again achieve a human life, let alone achieve nirvāṇa! Mahāmati, these are the faults of eating meat."

And it reads: "If someone gives up meat, Mahāmati, then animals will not be killed. This is because innocent beings are usually killed for money; other reasons are rare."

And it reads: "Mahāmati, in the future there will be stupid people who are ordained in my tradition, who call themselves 'children of the Śākya,' and who bear aloft the saffron victory banner, but whose minds are spoiled by wrong views. Their ego-clinging will be vast, and they will lust for the taste of meat. Speculating on subtle distinctions in the Vinaya rules, they will find all kinds of justifications for eating meat. They will spread these justifications to others, so that people ridicule me, saying I am not pure."

And it reads: "In the past, I did not forbid the meat of animals that have died from natural causes. But now, in these times, I strongly forbid it to everyone, no matter what method they follow. Just so, Mahāmati, I do not condone meat eating by anyone. It is not condoned and will not become condoned. Mahāmati, I declare that the consumption of meat is unsuitable for anyone who has ordained as a monk.

"Mahāmati, foolish people whose past karmic defilement drives them to ridicule me by saying that even the Tathāgata ate meat will endure meaningless suffering for a long time, devoid of joy. Mahāmati, my noble śrāvakas do not eat ordinary, vulgar food, so what need is there to speak of unsuitable foods like meat and blood?"

And it reads:

> Bodhisattvas of strong mind,
> do not consume meat,
> alcohol, garlic, or onions.

And it also reads:

> Whether of confused animals or one's own friends,
> all meat comes from semen and blood.
> Yogis do not eat meat,
> as consuming it causes other beings to fear.
>
> All meats, garlic, onions,
> all types of alcohol,
> wild onions, and white garlic—
> yogis abandon all of these!

And it also reads:

> People pay money for meat,
> causing animals to be killed for profit.
> Both the killer and buyer own this sinful karma,
> and will roast in the Crying Hell.
>
> All those who go against the Buddha's words,
> and eat meat with an ignoble mind,
> destroy their lives, both now and in the future.
> So uphold the conduct found in the Śākya's teachings!

Those people endowed with sinful karma
go to hells that are thoroughly terrifying.
Those who eat meat will roast
in the ferocity of the Crying Hell.

And it also reads:

Beings that eat each other
take birth as carnivores.
Or they become madmen,
foul smelling with low reputations.
Again and again they are born
as outcasts, dog eaters, and dyers.
Or they are born as animal-headed gods,
or among flesh-eating demons.
After this present human life,
they come back as demons or cats.

And it also reads:

In just this way, meat and alcohol
are also obstacles to liberation.

In future times,
ignorant supporters of meat eating
will say that meat is sinless and suitable,
and will claim that I say the same.

This is taught repeatedly and wisely throughout the sūtras.

Moreover, according to the Vinaya, it is imperative that there are no circumstances in which meat is permissible. Even the pratyekabuddha teaches that it is not condoned in the Vinaya. Some may say, "it is condoned in the *Vinayasūtra*."[144] But because this is a Mūlasarvāstivāda text we must take a look at each of the four other schools as well.

144. *The Vinayasūtra* (Tib: *'Dul ba mdo*). Despite its name, the *Vinayasūtra* is not a sūtra spoken by the Buddha. Instead, it is an important treatise on the Vinaya written by the seventh-century Indian master Guṇaprabha. For more on this work, see the introduction to the translation from Karmapa Mikyö Dorjé's *Commentary on the Vinayasūtra* in chapter 6 of this volume.

Precepts of the Secret Mantra Vehicle

According to the precepts of the secret mantra, there is the literal and the nonliteral.

The Literal Meaning

Some say, "The Mahāyāna is not permitted in secret mantra." But this should be discussed. In this context, from the very beginning slaughtered meat is not condoned. The precedent for this was taught by the noble Mañjuśrī and is in the *Kālacakra Tantra*:

> In their next life, those who kill animals with their five limbs[145] will be reborn as lions, snakes, mongooses, tigers, ravens, etc. Kings will become three of the many kinds of beings.
>
> Monks who lack compassion continually partake in this criminal act [of killing]. Because of this, they thirst to have the tastes and flavors of meat on their tongues, and so they fall deep into the hells where they kill themselves and undergo other punishments.
>
> Novice and fully ordained monks are also taught to act like doctors toward injured monks, bleeding them severely.[146]
>
> Due to the crime of taking lives, they die by lightening, fire, and water, without ritual services or being directed to the other side. Nevertheless, they are taught that in this life they are not at fault for what they eat, regardless of all the reasoning.
>
> For many monks, meat possesses the ten powers. So this [meat eating] is no different than overcoming death.[147]
>
> The bodies of those who eat meat and the like will undoubtedly be obese and end up under the ground. The animals will for certain be reborn in the realm of the hungry ghosts.

145. The five limbs (*yan lag lnga*) refers to the the two arms, two legs, and head of a human.

146. This seems to be a medical practice for certain sicknesses and injuries.

147. These ten powers (*stobs bcu*) are understood to be inherent within buddhahood. The ten powers of a tathāgata are: (1) knowing what is possible and what is not possible; (2) knowing the results of actions; (3) knowing the aspirations of men; (4) knowing the elements; (5) knowing the higher and lower powers of men; (6) knowing the path that leads everywhere; (7) knowing the origin of upsetting emotions, which leads to meditation, liberation, samadhi, and equanimity; (8) knowing previous lives; (9) knowing transference and death; (10) knowing that the defilements are exhausted. Meat eating is linked with these ten powers in the *Kālacakra Tantra*.

And likewise, it also reads in the *Ādibuddha Tantra*:

> Eaters and killers are, nonetheless, both killers.

Since this is what it says, you might ask, "How are the five meats explained?"[148] Now, the five meats are not killed for the purpose of meat but have died naturally. These [five meats] are mixed with the juniper berry to make ambrosia pills[149] that yogis eat not merely out of lip service but for the sake of their tantric vows—they need to increase the strength of their body, abate various arrogances, and guide sentient beings. With this in mind, yogis who eat meat yet are incapable of guiding sentient beings should stop eating meat of any kind.

In the *Hevajra Tantra* it reads, "The wise should eat meat so that sentient beings remain under their influence." So it reads.

The Nonliteral Meaning

As for the definitive meaning: internally, while you abide within meditative equipoise, your eyes and other five sense faculties should not rush toward their sense objects.[150] As it reads in the *Kālacakra Tantra*:

> Internally, the five aggregates are the five ambrosias;[151]
> the five lamps are the five sense faculties, corresponding to sound and so forth.
>
> The practice of approach[152] is not to rely on these,
> but to completely relinquish lusts for your body and material things.

And as it states in the *Ḍākārṇava Tantra*:[153]

148. These five meats (*sha lnga*) are: (1) human meat (*mi'i sha*), (2) cow meat (*ba lang gi sha*), (3) dog meat (*khyi'i sha*), (4) elephant meat (*glang po che'i sha*), and (5) horse meat (*rtai' sha*).

149. This is a reference to an elixir that is prepared from the decoction of five plant essences (*bdud rtsi lnga lums*), including juniper.

150. This is a reference to the yoga of withdrawal (*pratyāhāra, so sor sdud pa*). See the introduction to this translation.

151. The five ambrosias (*bdud rtsi lnga*) are: (1) feces (*dri chen*), (2) urine (*dri chu*), (3) semen (*byang sems dkar po* or *rdo rje'i zil ba*), (4) blood (*byang sems dmar po* or *rak ta*), and (5) flesh (*mam sa* or *sha chen*), which can refer to human brain fluid.

152. This is a reference to the tantric practice of approaching and familiarizing oneself with the deity (*bsnyen pa*) via mantra, etc.

153. *The Ocean of Ḍākinīs Tantra* (Tib: *Mkha' 'gro rgya mtsho'i rgyud*).

Sense fields are all meats.
Incite this with your mind of bliss!

And in the commentary:[154]

A vajra-like lotus on a ship is said to be "cow meat."
It is taught that a cow is bound by the faculty of the ear.

The same text also states, "Supreme wisdom eats conceptualization." And it also states, "The meat of an elephant is said to be the faculty of the nose." And it also states, "All meat is Varāhi."[155] It is taught that, moreover, "this is the faculty of the tongue." And it also states, "The meat of a dog, horse, water buffalo, and so forth are perceived through taste, touch, and as objects of mind. To taste and feel the other sensations of pristine awareness is to taste the qualities of the secret seat.[156] The meaning of this is, 'To eat conceptuality.'" And it also states, "When you are in meditative equipoise on the qualities of the six types of sense consciousness, such as the eye and so on—give up eating concepts!" There are all kinds of similar teachings.

This is how it is further explained: To eat the five meats is to devour the five sense faculties of ordinary awareness that rush toward the five sense objects and to expand the powers of nonconceptuality. Without moving, reside in the center of the outer maṇḍala of the five energies. Eat all the meat of conceptuality that gives rise to the five upsetting emotions. Eating the five meats will expand the powers of pristine awareness.

Kye ma!

Those who lust for food deprecate the Victor.
Like a blind man searching for a jewel in the dark,
they do not see the sūtras and tantras, the sun and moon.

Kye ma!

154. Padmavajra's *Ḍākārṇavamahayoginitantrarajavahikatika* (*The Great Commentary on the Ḍākārṇava Tantra*; *Dpal mkha' 'gro rgya mtsho rnal 'byor ma'i rgyud kyi rgyal po chen po'i 'grel pa gru gzings*).

155. Varāhi here is a tantric deity, yet it also refers to a sow, an adult female pig (*phag mo*), signifying to the reader the tantric semiotics of both the ethics of refrain as well as the taste of pristine awareness.

156. The secret seat (*gsang ba'i gdan*) refers to the seat of nonconceptual pristine awareness.

Where is there a single safe place for beings?

Kye ma!
Even while what's called "Mahāyāna" is dead,
the lock of the six limits and four ways remains secure.[157]

The deluded conceit created by the possessions of the Mighty One[158]
is a different species than the instructions of the masters and Shambhala kings!

Even if you want to search for the key of the six limits and four ways,
divorced from the eye of wisdom, you'll be deprived of the hands of effort.

By licking beef, you think you can sit on the throne of sense desires.
By possessing a perverted mind, you think you can realize the meaning of the sūtras and tantras.

Divorced from the mind's perfect eye, would you not deceive yourself and others with numerous meaningless teachings? Would you not promote various unsuitable sayings as the "words of the Victor"? Or when you see a Dharmaholder, criticize them in public? While you would not purify yourself, you would create obstructions for others.

Kye ma! Kyi hung!
Renounce the sūtras and tantras, throw them out!

If you connect sūtra discourses with tantras,
you'll be a master of hypocrisy![159]

If you teach that emptiness is nothingness,
you'll be a chief among the bipedals!

157. The six limits (*mtha' drug*) are: (1) the provisional meaning (*drang don*), (2) the definitive meaning (*nges don*), (3) the intended meaning (*dgongs pa can*), (4) the meaning that is not intended (*dgongs pa can ma ying pa*), (5) the literal meaning (*sgra ji bzhin pa*), and (6) the nonliteral meaning (*sgra ji bzhin ma yin pa*). And the four ways (*tshul bzhi*) are: (1) the word (*tshig*), (2) general (*spyi*), (3) hidden (*sbas*), and (4) the ultimate (*mthar thug*).

158. This is a reference to theistic tendencies.

159. Synthesizing sūtras with tantras is a hallmark method of Dolpopa's. Hopkins, *Mountain Doctrine*, 7.

If you clearly distinguish the two truths,
you'll be a master of relativity!

Kye ma!
How do I realize the intent of the Victor?

This concludes the discussion.

Due to whatever roots of merit may be planted here,
may the entirety of sentient beings in the three realms
be free from the stains of emotional upset,
and may the stainless three trainings be protected!

This text was composed by the one endowed with the fourfold reliance [Dolpopa Sherab Gyaltsen] on the twenty-first day of the month of December during the female wood-ox year [1325] on the shore of the magnificent palace of the Nāga Anavatapta who lives in the neighboring region of the River Ganges. May this be of benefit to the teachings and sentient beings!

Sarva Mangalam!

Source Texts

Dolpopa Sherab Gyaltsan (Dol po pa Shes rab rgyal mtshan). n.d. *Sha chang bkag pa'i lung 'dren rnams* (*Refraining from Meat and Alcohol*). In *Kun mkhyen dol po pa shes rab rgyal mtshan gyi gsung 'bum*, vol. 6, 324–32. 'Dzam thang edition. BDRC: W21208.

———, 1992. *Sha chang bkag pa'i lung 'dren rnams* (*Refraining from Meat and Alcohol*). In *Kun mkhyen dol po pa shes rab rgyal mtshan gyi gsung 'bum*, vol. 5, 757–78. Delhi: Shedrup Books. BDRC: W4CZ45311.

———, 2011. *Sha chang bkag pa'i lung 'dren rnams* (*Refraining from Meat and Alcohol*). In *Jo nang kun mkhyen dol po pa shes rab rgyal mtshan gyi gsung 'bum*, vol. 7, 290–308. Dpal rtsegs bod yig dpe rnying zhib 'jug khang. BDRC: W1PD133157.

Other Tibetan Sources

Bod yig tshig gter rgya mtsho (*A Precious Ocean of Language*). 2012. Chengdu: Si khron mi rigs dpe skrun khang. BDRC: W1PD159382.

Dolpopa Sherab Gyaltsan (Dol po pa Shes rab rgyal mtshan). n.d. *Ri chos nges don rgya mtsho zhes bya ba mthar thug mong ma yin pa'i man ngag* (*Mountain Dharma*). In *Kun mkhyen dol po pa shes rab rgyal mtshan gsung 'bum*, vol. 3, 189–741. 'Dzam thang. BDRC: W21208.

Padmavajra (Pad ma rdo rje). 1982–1985. *Ḍākārṇavamahayoginitantrarajavahikatika* (*Dpal mkha' 'gro rgya mtsho rnal 'byor ma'i rgyud kyi rgyal po chen po'i 'grel pa gru gzings*). In *Sde dge bstan 'gyur*, vol. 20, 4–637. BDRC: W23703.

Shes bya'i gter mdzod (*Precious Treasury of Knowledge*). 1997. Chengdu: Si khron mi rigs dpe skrun khang. BDRC: W19837.

Secondary Sources

Arnold, Edward A., ed. *As Long as Space Endures: Essays on the Kalachakra Tantra in Honor of the Dalai Lama*. Ithaca, NY: Snow Lion Publications.

Henning, Edward. 2009. "The Six Vajra-Yogas of Kālacakra." In Arnold, *As Long as Space Endures*, 237–58.

Hopkins, Jeffrey. 2006. *Mountain Doctrine: Tibet's Fundamental Treatise on Other-Emptiness and the Buddha Matrix*. Ithaca, NY: Snow Lion Publications.

Kapstein, Matthew. 1992. *The 'Dzam-Thang Edition of the Collected Works of Kun-Khyen Dol-Po-Pa Shes-Rab Rgyal-Mtshan: Introduction and Catalogue.* Delhi: Shedrup Books.

Mochizuki, Kaie. 2009. "On the Scriptures Introducing the Prohibition of Meat and Alcohol by Dol Po Pa." *Acta Tibetica et Buddhica* 2: 25–64.

Shabkar [Tsogdruk Rangdrol]. 2004. *Food of Bodhisattvas: Buddhist Teachings on Abstaining from Meat*. Translated by Padmakara Translation Group. Boston: Shambhala.

Sheehy, Michael R. 2005. "Rangjung Dorjé's Variegations of Mind: Ordinary Awareness and Pristine Awareness in Tibetan Buddhist Literature." In *Buddhist Thought and Applied Psychological Research*, 105–28. London: Routledge.

———, 2009. "A Lineage History of Vajrayoga and Tantric Zhentong from the Jonang Kālacakra Practice Tradition." In Arnold, *As Long as Space Endures*, 219–36.

———, 2019. "The Dharma of the Perfect Eon: Dolpopa Sherab Gyaltsan's (1292–1361) Hermeneutics of Time and the Jonang Doxography of Zhentong Madhyamaka." In *The Other Emptiness: Rethinking the Zhentong Buddhist Discourse in Tibet*, edited by Michael R. Sheehy and Klaus Dieter-Mathes, n.p. Albany: State University of New York Press.

Stearns, Cyrus. 2010. *The Buddha from Dolpo: A Study of the Life and Thought of the Tibetan Master Dolpopa Sherab Gyaltsen*. Revised and expanded edition. Ithaca, NY: Snow Lion Publications.

Wallace, Vesna A. 2001. *The Inner Kālacakratantra: A Buddhist Tantric View of the Individual*. Oxford: Oxford University Press.

Wedemeyer, Christian K. 2012. *Making Sense of Tantric Buddhism: History, Semiology, and Transgression in the Indian Traditions*. New York: Columbia University Press.

3. Ngorchen Künga Sangpo on the Faults of Alcohol and Meat

*By Jörg Heimbel**

THE STRONG ADVOCATE of vegetarianism and tantric expert Ngorchen Künga Sangpo (1382–1456)[160] was one of the most outstanding and influential Sakya masters of fifteenth-century Tibet; not only was he a towering figure on the religious scene of his native Tsang Province in Central Tibet, but his sphere of influence stretched all the way from Far-Western Tibet (including Mustang) to Kham Province in the east.[161] Among his manifold influential activities, Ngorchen is most of all remembered for his founding, in 1429, of Ngor Ewam Chöden Monastery. Withdrawing from the worldly distractions of the bustling town of Sakya as well as from sectarian conflicts,[162] he left his traditional alma mater of Sakya Monastery and set up his new monastic seat in the remote Ngor valley, located about 30 kilometers

160. Tib: Ngor chen Kun dga' bzang po.

161. On the life of Ngorchen, see Heimbel, *Vajradhara in Human Form*.

162. For instance, Ngorchen became involved in a gradually intensifying religious dispute with the polemic-loving Khedrup Jé (1385–1438) on a variety of tantric topics; see Heimbel, *Vajradhara in Human Form*, 229–48; Heimbel, "The Dispute between mKhas grub rJe and Ngor chen." This dispute may also have been over the issue of meat eating, and Khedrup Jé's Vinaya-based defense of meat eating could thus be understood as a critical response to Ngorchen's prohibition of meat. Khedrup Jé presented his position in an undated work about the three vows that he wrote while living at the monastery of Riwo Dangchen in Nyangtö (Ri bo Mdangs can, Nyang stod) of Tsang Province. Following Jackson, "Rong ston bKa' bcu pa," 355, Khedrup Jé would have written this work between 1427 and 1431, and thus after Ngorchen had written his own work against meat eating in 1425. For Khedrup Jé's position on meat eating, see chapter 4 of this volume.

* I am very grateful to Khangsar Genla Jamyang Yeshe for discussing the sūtric passages from Ngorchen's *Epistle*. I would also like to thank Prof. Dr. Dorji Wangchuk for his valuable comments on several passages from the translation.

southwest of Samdruptse (present-day Shigatse) in Tsang Province, where, based on the observance of a strict monastic discipline, he hoped to go back to traditional Sakya teaching and practice in a more supportive environment. Immediately Ngor became a new center for tantric training within the monastic circles of the Sakya school. Ngorchen, as the leading tantric expert, trained a whole new generation of young students, producing some of the school's brightest minds. Grounded on his distinctive understanding of tantric ritual and practice, Ngorchen became the founding father of the Ngor tradition, which quickly developed into the most prominent subdivision of the Sakya school. At a crucial point in the history of that school, which had lost political power in the mid-fourteenth century with the collapse of the Yuan dynasty (1271–1368), Ngorchen was one of a few highly influential figures whose activities caused Sakya's influence on the religious sphere to not only continue flourishing but also strengthen. Furthermore, through his religious activities he was able to establish new bonds on the political stage with such powerful rulers as the kings of Mustang or the Phakmodrupa regime, the rulers of Tibet.

Like Tsongkhapa Losang Drakpa (1357–1419), the founder of the Geluk school, Ngorchen can be considered a religious reformer who tried to renew his own Sakya school from within. He made efforts to cleanse the Sakya teachings from elements he considered to be mistaken, aiming to return to the religious roots of his tradition by transmitting what he perceived to be the pure and untainted teachings of the early great Sakya founders. The consumption of alcohol and meat by monastics, and their use in tantric rituals, was but one of those elements he wanted to wipe out,[163] as is well illustrated by a verse from his pen:

> Hey! Followers of mine,
> give up the impure lifestyle of consuming meat, alcohol, and the like!
> Being the sole basis of all marvelous qualities,
> cherish the precious discipline more than your life![164]

This verse is found at the end of Ngorchen's well-known composition, *An Epistle Benefitting Students*, one of the longest Tibetan literary works of its kind, in which he urgently argues from both sūtric and tantric points of view

163. Ngorchen's positions were not undisputed within the Sakya school and were criticized, for instance, by adherents of the Dzong tradition. Regarding his discussion about utilizing meat within the tantric feast offering (*gaṇacakra, tshogs kyi 'khor lo*), Ngorchen was criticized by Gongkar Dorjé Denpa Künga Namgyal (1432–1496), the founder of Gongkar Monastery; see Heimbel, *Vajradhara in Human Form*, 403.

164. Ngorchen, *Spring yig slob ma la phan pa*, 658.1.

against the consumption and tantric use of alcohol and meat by monastics, and which he compiled in 1425 at age forty-three[165] when he was still based at Sakya Monastery.

As an introduction to my preliminary attempt in translating this *Epistle*, I shall at first discuss briefly what I was able to learn about Ngorchen's personal motives and reasons for compiling the *Epistle*, and then also address other outcomes of his stance against alcohol and meat and the influence this had on the religious tradition he established at Ngor Monastery.

To highlight Ngorchen's tough stance against eating meat, Sangye Phüntsok (1649–1705), the twenty-fifth abbot of Ngor, included in his biography of Ngorchen a small section on how his protagonist gave up eating meat. According to his presentation, Ngorchen himself related that he could not remember having eaten offal or raw meat as a child. When he grew older, from his sixth year on, by merely seeing meat or blood or others eating it, especially monastics, he is said to have lost his appetite for many days. Thinking that it was not the proper lifestyle for monastics to eat meat, and that the Buddha himself had not allowed eating it, he became a vegetarian at age twelve. Later, the smell of meat alone could reportedly harm his well-being.[166]

Ngorchen also adhered to a specific form of asceticism, the so-called ascetic discipline of the single mat with white (i.e., vegetarian) ingredients,[167]

165. The age has been given according to the Western system of counting. According to Tibetan tradition, a child is already one year old (or in his first year) at birth and advances one year in age at the Tibetan New Year.

166. See Sangye Phüntsok, *Rdo rje 'chang kun dga' bzang po'i rnam par thar pa*, 488.4–6, 489.1–2; Heimbel, *Vajradhara in Human Form*, 106. The Ngorchen biography by Sangye Phüntsok is a compilation of early Ngorchen biographies written by the latter's direct disciples. On Ngorchen's biographies, see Heimbel, *Vajradhara in Human Form*, 23–61.

167. The Tibetan term *denchik dokar* (*stan/gdan gcig rdor/sdor dkar*) or its variant *dokar denchik* (*rdor/sdor dkar stan/gdan gcig*) is made of two elements: *denchik* designating the single-mat practice, and *dokar* referring to white (i.e., pure or virtuous and thus vegetarian) food. Another variant of *dokar* that is attested in biographical works is the term *kardor* (*dkar rdor*), which Dungkar Losang Trinle describes in his dictionary as a general term for a vegetarian diet by monastics and devout laypeople who make use of cheese, vegetables, and fruits as ingredients (*rdor*) for their foodstuffs, which are not mixed with other foodstuffs such as meat, fat, eggs, and bones; see Dungkar Losang Trinle, *Dung dkar tshig mdzod chen mo*, 160. There exists also a homophone variant of *dor* (spelled *sdor*), which Zhang explains as nutritious ingredients such as meat or fat that are added to soup or broth; see Zhang, *Bod rgya tshig mdzod chen mo*, 1482. Similarly, Dobi Tsering Dorjé et al. give as an example for the use of *dor* (*sdor*) the word *thugdor* (*thug sdor*), which is explained as meat or bones that are put into a soup; see Dobi Tsering Dorjé et al., *Deng rabs bod skad tshig mdzod*, 975. In addition to meat and fat, Padma Dorjé et al. specify *dor* (*sdor*) also as vegetables and seasonings that can be added to soup or broth to make them nutritious and add flavor; see Padma Dorjé et al., *Bod kyi nyer mkho'i zas rigs tshig mdzod*,

which should be considered another of his influences. This single-mat discipline demanded that food was not eaten more than once per day, whereby a whole day's food was taken at a single sitting at noon. One finds this discipline included as the fifth among the Mahāyāna tradition of the "twelve qualities of a purified ascetic," as listed in the *Mahāvyutpatti*.[168] In the Indian Buddhist context, these were ascetic practices "the Buddha authorized monks to adopt voluntarily for the purpose of cultivating contentedness with little detachment, energy, and moderation. These austerities are not enjoined on monks and nuns by the Vinaya, but are rather optional practices that monastics were sanctioned to adopt for limited periods of time in order to foster sensory restraint."[169] As far as Ngorchen is concerned, he is known to have observed the single-mat practice since his monastic ordination at age eight, as well as what appears to have been an even stricter form of practice that was limited to a meatless diet.[170] Recent research has so far shown that in Tibet the single-mat practice, and also its stricter vegetarian form, were practiced by adherents of the Sakya school and of the Drigung branch of the Kagyü school, whereby the former inherited the practice most likely from the Vinaya tradition and related ordination lineages that the Kashmiri scholar Śākyaśrībhadra (1127–1225) introduced during his ten-year sojourn in Tibet (1204–1214) and from the four monastic communities that were founded in his tradition. It is also in this tradition that Ngorchen received full monastic ordination at age eighteen (or nineteen), and prior to that, most likely also his monastic ordination at age eight.[171]

96. Based on these explanations, I have translated *dor* (*rdor*/*sdor*) as "ingredients." We find both variants of *dor* already mentioned by Jäschke, who gives two meanings: (1) "Würze" (seasoning, condiment) and (2) "Gewürz" (spice). He illustrates the first meaning with the word *thugdor* (*thug sdor*), explaining, "was d. Suppe kräftig macht, Fleisch" (that which gives substance to soup—viz., meat); see Jäschke, *Handwörterbuch der Tibetischen Sprache*, 300. English translations according to Jäschke, *A Tibetan-English Dictionary*, 297. See also Heimbel, "The Jo gdan tshogs sde bzhi," 222n203; Heimbel, *Vajradhara in Human Form*, 106–107n206; Hou, "Some Remarks," 206.

168. For the twelve qualities of a purified ascetic (*dvādaśadhūtaguṇāḥ*, *sbyangs pa'i yon tan bcu gnyis*), including the single-mat practice (*aikāsanikaḥ*, *stan gcig pa*), see the *Mahāvyutpatti* (*Two Fascicle Lexicon*; Tib: *Sgra sbyor bam po gnyis pa*), 85–86, nos. 1127–32.

169. Buswell and Lopez, *The Princeton Dictionary of Buddhism*, 256.

170. See Müchen, *Snyigs dus kyi rdo rje 'chang chen po chos kyi rje kun dga' bzang po'i rnam par thar pa*, 468.2; Sangye Phüntsok, *Rdo rje 'chang kun dga' bzang po'i rnam par thar pa*, 554.5; Heimbel, *Vajradhara in Human Form*, 105–6.

171. On the Sakya relation and those four monastic communities (*tshogs sde bzhi* or *jo gdan tshogs sde bzhi*), see Heimbel, "The Jo gdan tshogs sde bzhi." On the Drigung relation, see Hou, "Some Remarks." On Ngorchen's ordinations, see Heimbel, *Vajradhara in Human Form*, 103–8.

In addition to his personal aversion and disgust for meat and his vegetarian single-mat practice, the adverse conditions at Sakya Monastery and worsening behavior of some of its monks may have finally prompted Ngorchen to write his *Epistle*. Such an understanding is based on the prelude to the foundation account of Ngor Monastery, in which Ngorchen's biographer introduces the reasons why Ngorchen separated himself geographically from his home monastery:

> Up to that point, Ngorchen performed in that way inconceivably great activities for the benefit of others in the domain of the Monastic Seat [i.e., Sakya]. Nevertheless, though his altruistic activities at the Monastic Seat were inconceivably great, the extremely numerous distractions and festivities existing at the Monastic Seat exerted a negative influence on the studies of the monks, resources were wasted, and a few monks—unable to overcome those temptations—were even spoiled. Thus Ngorchen thought that it would be of greater benefit for the teachings of the Buddha and for monks if teaching and studying were exerted while living at a remote place devoid of women selling alcohol.[172]

According to this description, Sakya Monastery, which had served as the government seat of Tibet during the Yuan dynasty, had by Ngorchen's time obviously developed into a bustling town, attracting all kinds of people and offering a variety of distractions and entertainments.[173] Ngorchen felt that this atmosphere exerted a negative influence on the education of the monastic community and that some monks succumbed to those temptations, losing their vows. I consider it thus possible that these developments were not only an important factor for Ngorchen founding Ngor Monastery but, prior to that, also motivated him to write his *Epistle*.

After its composition in early 1425, the *Epistle* became an important and influential work utilized for teaching and studying Ngorchen's instructions on abandoning the consumption and tantric usage of alcohol and meat by monastics, as its mention in biographies of early Sakya and Ngor masters suggests. Having taken all three types of ordination from Ngorchen himself,

172. Sangye Phüntsok, *Rdo rje 'chang kun dga' bzang po'i rnam par thar pa*, 524.2–4; Heimbel, *Vajradhara in Human Form*, 249.

173. In his 1475 study of Sakya Monastery, Tsang Jampa Dorjé Gyaltsen (1424–1498) lists not only religious structures of Sakya but, among the common ones of everyday life, also two taverns (*chang rwa*); see Tsang Jampa Dorjé Gyaltsen, *Sa skya 'khon gyi gdung rabs*, 72a5, 73a4.

Tsultrim Gyaltsen (d. 1476), for instance, studied the *Epistle* together with the *Laṅkāvatāra Sūtra*'s seventh chapter on abstaining from meat. As another example, the famous tenth abbot of Ngor, Könchok Lhündrup (1497–1557), received teachings on the *Epistle* from his ordaining preceptor after having received from him layman and novice-monk ordination at age twelve at Ngor.[174] Moreover, the *Epistle* was also utilized and referenced by other Tibetan scholars, as Gorampa Sönam Senge (1429–1489), the sixth abbot of Ngor, did in his brief section on abstaining from meat that he included in his commentary on Sakya Paṇḍita's *Distinguishing the Three Vows*.[175]

Four years after the compilation of the *Epistle*, Ngorchen institutionally incorporated his personal condemnation of alcohol and meat into the monastic code he established at his new monastic seat of Ngor. To counter those developments at Sakya, he enforced a strict monastic discipline, prohibiting the consumption of meat and alcohol, banning women from entering the monastic complex, and forbidding his monks to engage in any form of sectarian debates. Moreover, in the territories of his benefactors, he is said to have put restrictions on hunting wild animals and fishing, stopped meat and blood sacrifices, and banned meat and alcohol from monastic institutions.[176]

Two accounts suggest that the ban on meat was initially observed at Ngor and that vegetarianism was a customary practice of the early adherents of the Ngor tradition. The first account is found in the biography of Palden Dorjé (1411–1482), the fifth abbot of Ngor. Like Ngorchen, he observed the ascetic discipline of the single mat in its even stricter vegetarian form. While he had already observed this discipline during his sūtric studies at the monasteries of Sangden and Ngamring and during his tantric training at Sakya, his biographer informs us that it goes without saying that he also did so when he came to Ngor to pursue his training under Ngorchen. This narrative takes for granted that its readers are familiar with both Ngorchen's observance of a vegetarian single-mat practice and the strict monastic code that he had established at Ngor.[177] The second account is found in the biographies of two senior Sakya

174. See Lowo Khenchen Sönam Lhündrup, *Chos kyi rje tshul khrims rgyal mtshan gyi rnam par thar pa*, 9a3–6; Könchok Palden, *Rje btsun dkon mchog lhun grub kyi rnam thar*, 180.6–181.1; Heimbel, *Vajradhara in Human Form*, 253n181.

175. See Gorampa, *Sdom pa gsum gyi rab tu dbye ba'i rnam bshad*, 121.5. For the translation of Gorampa's passage, see chapter 5 of this volume.

176. See Sangye Phüntsok, *Rdo rje 'chang kun dga' bzang po'i rnam par thar pa*, 527.6–528.1, 541.6–542.1; Heimbel, *Vajradhara in Human Form*, 249. Ngorchen sent a letter to the Jumla king Bālirāja (r. 1404–1445) advising him to abandon in his domain the practice of sacrificing animals; see Heimbel, *Vajradhara in Human Form*, 328–29.

177. See Drakpa Dorjé, *Mtshungs med chos rje dpal ldan rdo rje'i rnam thar*, 596.5–6; Heimbel,

masters: Lowo Khenchen Sönam Lhündrup (1456–1532) and Sangye Gyaltsen (1542–1618). Both present the same account of a conversation in which the speaker emphasizes the importance of giving up the consumption of both meat and alcohol as a highly important practice for an adherent of Ngorchen's tradition:

> At the time when the Dharma Lord, the Great Vajradhara [i.e., Ngorchen], traveled to Ü [i.e., the eastern province of Central Tibet], he saw that all the great kalyāṇamitras of Ü were shamelessly enjoying all kinds of meat and thus he felt extremely sad. He then collected from the Sūtra section authoritative works that point out the faults of consuming meat and alcohol, and later on arranged them as a treatise. His composition is the *Epistle Benefitting Students*.[178] We Ngorpa followers should rely on the conscientious armor that does not transgress the prescribed rules taught in the *Epistle Benefitting Students*. The Lord, the Great Vajradhara, had never placed meat or alcohol on his tongue and had never touched women with his bare hands. Having investigated the activities of how he set an example of the Buddha's teachings, we must live up to his intentions, at least to a portion of those activities, because at the very end of the *Epistle Benefitting Students* he states:
>
> Hey! If you want to be followers of mine,
> give up the impure lifestyle of consuming meat, alcohol, and the like!
> Being the sole basis of all marvelous qualities,
> cherish the precious discipline more than your life!
>
> If one keeps only this versified Stages of the Path teaching, which is in accordance with the transmission of the Buddha's doctrine, it will be very meaningful. Since the root transgression of the prātimokṣa training is alcohol and the root transgression of the bodhisattva training is meat, the practice of renouncing both meat and alcohol is the best example to build up the Buddha's teachings from their foundation. . . . In short, this renunciation of meat and

Vajradhara in Human Form, 253–54.

178. As Ngorchen completed the *Epistle* on the fifth day of the first half of the first month of 1425 at Sakya, Tsang, the Ü sojourn refers to his first visit to that area from 1414 to 1417; see Heimbel, *Vajradhara in Human Form*, 212–18, 498n155.

> alcohol is one customary practice of us Ngorpa and must therefore be practiced painstakingly by all means.[179]

Emulating Ngorchen's example, many of his successors on the abbatial throne of Ngor are known to have either observed the ascetic discipline of the single mat in its vegetarian form or adhered to a meatless diet, though most took up this discipline at the time of their monastic ordination. Nevertheless, the biographies of some of those abbots make it very clear that a vegetarian diet was mandatory for the incumbent abbot of Ngor.[180] At one point, however, Ngorchen's prohibition of alcohol and meat was broken by members of the monastic community. Rinchen Migyur Gyaltsen (1717–1780), the thirty-seventh abbot of Ngor, complains that during his tenure there were only a few people left following Ngorchen's instructions. On top of that, by then the use of tobacco had become a huge problem as well, and so the Ngorpas were slowly losing the reputation they once enjoyed as adherents of a very strict monastic discipline.[181]

As an interesting aside, the life stories of these Ngorpa masters note that their protagonists became physically weak or emaciated because of adhering to a vegetarian diet. Ngorchen's biographers, for instance, report that his physical condition was always extremely weak since he began at age eight to observe the ascetic discipline of the single mat in its vegetarian form.[182] His biographer Sangye Phüntsok relates in his own autobiography that though he himself adopted a vegetarian diet at about age fifteen, because of his many obligations his body could not be sustained on such a diet alone. He thus later, at about age twenty-nine, had to break his pledge to eat vegetarian.[183]

179. Künga Drölchok, *Dpal ldan bla ma 'jam pa'i dbyangs kyi rnam par thar pa*, 319.6–321.1; Ame Shab, *Rje btsun mus pa chen po sangs rgyas rgyal mtshan gyi rnam par thar pa*, 157.2–158.4; Heimbel, *Vajradhara in Human Form*, 254–55.

180. For a list of references to those biographies, see Heimbel, *Vajradhara in Human Form*, 255n187.

181. See Guru Phel, *Rin chen mi 'gyur rgyal mtshan gyi rnam par thar pa*, 13b5–14a5; Palden Chökyong, *E waṃ pa'i gdan rabs rin chen phreng mdzes kyi kha skong*, 583.4–584.4; Heimbel, *Vajradhara in Human Form*, 255n187, 269–70.

182. See Müchen, *Snyigs dus kyi rdo rje 'chang chen po chos kyi rje kun dga' bzang po'i rnam par thar pa*, 468.2–5; Sangye Phüntsok, *Rdo rje 'chang kun dga' bzang po'i rnam par thar pa*, 554.5–555.2; Heimbel, *Vajradhara in Human Form*, 380.

183. See Sangye Phüntsok, *Bya bral ba sangs rgyas phun tshogs kyi myong ba brjod pa*, 192.5–6; Heimbel, *Vajradhara in Human Form*, 380.

Structure and Themes

After this brief excursus trying to shed some light on the possible genesis of the *Epistle*, a few remarks are due regarding its structure. Ngorchen arranged his work into three main parts:

1. Explaining the Faults of Consuming Alcohol
2. Explaining the Faults of Nourishing One's Body with the Meat of Slaughtered Animals
3. Explaining How the Two—Meat and Alcohol—Are Prohibited in the Secret Mantra[184]

The topics of each of the first two parts Norgchen discussed using a threefold progression: first the faults of consuming alcohol and meat are outlined in general, then the faults for adherents of the Śrāvakayāna are discussed as a second step, before progressing to the third and final step, the faults for followers of the Mahāyāna. His third main point on the prohibition in a tantric context is presented under two subsections:

1. Explaining That Mantrins Must Give Up Meat and Alcohol
2. Eliminating Objections about This[185]

However, since my knowledge of tantric Buddhism is insufficient to translate Ngorchen's third main part, and since tantric topics are not openly discussed within the Sakya school without having received the necessary empowerments, this portion of the *Epistle* has been omitted from the translation.

About the Translation

The *Epistle* as included in the revised Dergé blockprint edition of Ngorchen's collected works from 1894 is the only traditional recension that is available at present, and it has been published in three different reproductions.[186]

184. See Ngorchen, *Spring yig slob ma la phan pa*, 622.1–628.1, 628.1–640.4, 640.4–657.1.

185. Meaning that relying on meat and alcohol by those persons who have entered the Great Yoga—that is, the Niruttarayoga tantric system—is impermissible. See Ngorchen, *Spring yig slob ma la phan pa*, 640.4–643.3, 643.3–657.1.

186. On the three reproductions of the revised Dergé blockprint edition that include the *Epistle*, see Heimbel, *Vajradhara in Human Form*, 415–21, 459. Therein, the *Epistle* comprises

Moreover, the Dergé recension seemingly served as the basis not only for two new digital-input editions of Ngorchen's collected works containing the *Epistle* but also for two individual publications of it.[187] Since Ngorchen pieced his work together with numerous citations from the sūtras and tantras, it is highly important to identify these citations in their original canonical versions. But as those citations are rather fragmentary or selective—omitting parts that are otherwise found in the canonical versions, which appears to be a general practice of Tibetan authors—it is difficult at times to locate them in their originals. The additional difficulty with the Dergé blockprint edition is that some of its citations are corrupted to such an extent that it is hardly possible to understand them anymore, let alone translate them.[188] This is why I have translated all citations, as far as I succeeded in locating them, on the basis of their canonical versions, making use of the comparative editions of both Kangyur (K) and Tengyur (T) as prepared by the China Tibetology Research Center (CTRC), Beijing, China. For better readability, I have refrained (with few exceptions) from using brackets to supply any additional explanatory words or phrases that are implicit in the original works or clarified in their commentaries.

twenty-one folios in six lines (1b–2a, 21b only two lines). As catalogued by David Jackson in his handlist of Tibetan texts in the Bihar Research Society, Patna, another xylographic edition of the *Epistle* is housed there, which was "sponsored by Dpal Chu-mig bla-brang (an early Gtsang edition?)"; see Jackson, *The 'Miscellaneous Series' of Tibetan Texts in the Bihar Research Society*, 222, nos. 1502–3. It comprises eighteen folios in seven lines and was contained in volume 6 (*cha*) of a further unspecified collection.

187. On the two new digital-input editions of Ngorchen's collected works, see Heimbel, *Vajradhara in Human Form*, 459. The details of the two modern digital-input editions of the *Epistle* are as follows: Ngor chen Rdo rje 'chang Kun dga' bzang po, *Sha chang gi nyes dmigs bshad pa: Spring yig slob ma la phan pa* ([s.l.]: Ngor E waṃ chos ldan dgon, [s.d.]); Rgyal ba gnyis pa Ngor chen Kun dga' bzang po, *Springs yig slob ma la phan pa* (Dehradun: Sakya College Loving-kindness Vegetarian Committee, [2009]).

188. One explanation for these corruptions could be the faulty transmission history of the work, during which many such mistakes slipped into it while copying and recopying it. The fact that in one case the Dergé recension of the *Epistle* reads *rigs* (family, lineage) instead of *ri dwags* (wild game) suggests that the Dergé blockprint was originally based on a manuscript version in which *ri dwags* had been abbreviated as *rigs*, which the editors of the Dergé recension were unable to recognize as an abbreviation; see the *Mahāparinirvāṇa Sūtra*, 122.8; Ngorchen, *Spring yig slob ma la phan pa*, 631.4.

An Epistle Benefitting Students

By Ngorchen Künga Zangpo
Translated by Jörg Heimbel

Svasti prajabhyaḥ

General Advice for My Own Monks, Benefitting Students:

I pay homage to all buddhas and bodhisattvas.

With his insight, he opens the words of the Sugata,[189] like the rays of the sun open the lotus grove.
With his compassion, he outshines bad talk, like the moon outshines the stars.
Through his activities, which are as endless as the sky, he ripens infinite living beings.
With genuine faith, I take refuge at the feet of the second Munīndra, my lama.[190]

This precious human body equipped with the eight freedoms and ten endowments,[191]
which was accomplished from immeasurable virtuous merit accumulated in the past, and which has now been obtained once:
there is no possibility that it will last for a long period of time.
Thus apply your body and speech to virtue, my friends!

189. Sugata is an epithet for Buddha Śākyamuni meaning "well gone"; see Buswell and Lopez, *The Princeton Dictionary of Buddhism*, 865.

190. Ngorchen's lama can most likely be identified as Sharchen Yeshe Gyaltsen (1359–1406); see the colophon of this text at the end of the translation. "Munīndra," the Lord of Sages, is here used as an epithet for Buddha Śākyamuni.

191. The (eight) freedoms and (ten) endowments (*kṣaṇasampad*, *dal 'byor*) characterize a rebirth as a human being under circumstances allowing for the study of the Buddha's teachings; see Buswell and Lopez, *The Princeton Dictionary of Buddhism*, 445–46.

Cast far away the doctrinal system of the tīrthikas,[192] who propose heedless conduct as Dharma!
In line with what Munīndra, who benefits living beings, taught, it is reasonable to adhere to heedful conduct.

Therefore students who wish well for themselves,
and who are endowed with discernment and insight,
as for the way of studying the path that delights the Victorious One,
listen, because I will explain it as it originates from the stainless authoritative scriptures!

At this time when we have obtained the extraordinary support for practicing the holy Dharma—that is, the completely purified human body equipped with freedoms and endowments—in order to accomplish the precious unsurpassable awakening, by abiding properly in the correct view and pure conduct, the human bodily support equipped with freedoms and endowments must be nourished for a long time by a pure livelihood that is in line with the Dharma. People of an uneducated nature nourish their precious human body endowed with freedoms and endowments with alcohol that causes heedlessness and with the meat and blood of slaughtered sentient beings. Beyond this, they even formulate the argument: "In the Vinaya of the holy Dharma and Vajrayāna, they were taught as permissible to consume." This kind of conduct is improper. It is an evil course of action and a tenet that causes others to also apply it after one engaged in it oneself, just like a frog with sores infecting all other frogs in the frog pit. It causes departure from the conduct that delights the Victorious One. It causes its adoption by the nonvirtuous. And it produces great damage for oneself. For refuting this kind of conduct, there are thus three points:

1. Explaining the Faults of Consuming Alcohol
2. Explaining the Faults of Nourishing One's Body with the Meat of Slaughtered Animals
3. Explaining How the Two—Meat and Alcohol—Are Prohibited in the Secret Mantra

192. The general term *tīrthika* refers to followers of a non-Buddhist religion and is typically used for followers of non-Buddhist Indian schools; see Buswell and Lopez, *The Princeton Dictionary of Buddhism*, 915.

Explaining the Faults of Consuming Alcohol

This first point has three subpoints:

1.1 The Faults of Drinking Alcohol in General

In the *Nandika Sūtra*,[193] it is explained that alcohol, which possesses numerous faults, should not be drunk by human beings:

> People who enjoy drinking alcohol
> are not able to benefit themselves and please others.
> Since it is alcohol that makes one dull and leads to a bad complexion,
> it should not be drunk, just as black aconite poison should not be drunk.[194]

Its faults are also taught in that same sūtra:

> The Bhagavān taught: "Nandika, the thirty-five faults of alcohol made of fermented grains and of plant or fruit juices, which are the basis for heedlessness, should be understood as follows. If one asks what is the group of thirty-five faults, it is the following:
>
> 1. One's wealth will be consumed during this lifetime.
> 2. One's diseases will increase.
> 3. One will bring forth fighting and disputes.
> 4. One will care about meaningless things.
> 5. One's bad repute will spread everywhere.
> 6. One's insight will weaken.
> 7. One's possessions, obtained once, will not be obtained anymore.[195]
> 8. One's possessions, obtained once, will be consumed and exhausted altogether.
> 9. One will not be able to keep secrets anymore.

193. *Sūtra of Nandika* (Tib: *Dga' ba can gyi mdo*).

194. *Nandika Sūtra*, 776.10–13.

195. In this and many of the following examples, the nominalized main verb (plus *la don* particle) is followed by the auxiliary verb *'gyur*, which I have left untranslated here. This auxiliary verb emphasizes a dynamic process—that is, the main verb is going to happen, will turn out to happen, or will come to happen (or that one will become that kind of person who performs or undergoes the action of the main verb).

10. The limit of one's proper actions will be obscured completely.
11. One's power will decrease.
12. One will not honor one's own mother.
13. One will not honor one's own father.
14. One will not honor monastic renunciants [śramaṇa].
15. One will not honor brahmans.
16. One will not venerate the "head of the family."
17. One will not show respect for the Buddha.
18. One will not show respect for the Dharma.
19. One will not show respect for the Saṅgha.
20. One will not show respect for those who have properly undertaken the Training.[196]
21. One's discipline will degenerate.
22. One will not restrain one's senses.
23. One will go after women heedlessly.
24. One will be abandoned by kinsmen, relatives, friends, and ministers.
25. One will become repugnant to many people.
26. One will disagree with many people.
27. One will conduct oneself in a non-Dharmic way.
28. One will embrace what is non-Dharma.
29. One will abandon the holy Dharma altogether.
30. One will abandon one's sense of shame and embarrassment.
31. Though living with hostile people, one will not think to ask learned persons [for help?].
32. One will conduct oneself heedlessly and impulsively.
33. One will not at all abide in the words of the Tathāgata.
34. One will be further removed from nirvāṇa.
35. Since one created and accumulated the karma of a mad person, one's body will come to ruin, and after one has died, one will be born among the hell-beings of the lower realms of existence. Even if one passes away from there and is born here in this world as one who has the same fortune as human beings, wherever one is born, one will turn into a mad person and one's memory will be blurred.

196. The term "training" (*śikṣā, bslab pa*) is mainly used in two contexts: (1) the three trainings in higher discipline or morality, higher meditation, and higher insight, and (2) the Vinaya, where it refers to proper conduct; see Buswell and Lopez, *The Princeton Dictionary of Buddhism*, 819.

Nandika, the faults of alcohol made of fermented grains and alcohol made of plant or fruit juices, which are the basis of heedlessness, should be understood as this group of thirty-five."[197]

1.2 Drinking Alcohol by Those Who Have Entered the Śrāvakayāna Is Impermissible

In the *Vinayasūtra*,[198] it is taught:

> A sick person should not drink alcohol even with *kuśa* grass.[199]
> Everyone, including upāsakas,[200] should not pour it.[201]

And in its *Extensive Commentary*, it is explained:

> Everyone, including upāsakas, should not pour it.
> If poured, it was taught in the *Sūtra* that one will be born in the Wailing Hell.[202]

Therefore it was explained that it is impermissible that those who have entered the door of individual liberation drink alcohol, even so much as a drop taken with the tip of a blade of grass.

That is the case if the body abides in its natural state [i.e., free of any illness]. But if one wonders whether it is permissible to give alcohol to a sick person, it is not. As for the statement in the *Vinayasūtra* that "for a sick person there is

197. *Nandika Sūtra*, 774.10–775.20.

198. Guṇaprabha, *Vinayasūtra* (*Sūtra of Monastic Discipline*; Tib: *'Dul ba'i mdo*).

199. That is, even so much as a drop that was taken with the tip of *kuśa* grass.

200. An upāsaka is a male lay disciple who has taken refuge and upholds the five basic precepts (not to kill, steal, engage in sexual misconduct, lie, or use intoxicants); see Buswell and Lopez, *The Princeton Dictionary of Buddhism*, 941.

201. Guṇaprabha, *Vinayasūtra*, 1027.13–15.

202. Quotation from the *Extensive Commentary* (*'Grel pa*) unidentified. Dharmamitra explains that even all those who have not taken on the moral training (*śikṣā*, *bslab pa*) of Buddhism, including upāsakas, should not offer alcohol, and lists the selling of alcohol as one of the six activities upāsakas should not engage in; see Dharmamitra, *Vinayasūtraṭīkā* (*Commentary on the Sūtra of Monastic Discipline*; Tib: *'Dul ba'i mdo'i rgya cher 'grel pa*), vol. 91, 564.6–11. This is also stated by Guṇaprabha, *Vinayasūtravṛttyabhidhānasvavyākhyāna* (*Autocommentary on the Sūtra of Monastic Discipline*; Tib: *'Dul ba'i mdo'i 'grel pa mngon par brjod pa rang gi rnam par bshad pa*), 1169.4–10.

no downfall,"[203] it means that alcohol is merely smeared on the body and kept in the cheeks but is not swallowed internally:

> A sick person should drink alcohol mixed with melted butter and grain oil. If it has become nonalcohol, it has no faults. Nonalcohol is gained after boiling alcohol.[204]

In the *Commentary*, it is explained: "The mixture of alcohol with melted butter was boiled in three volume measures of butter and three volume measures of alcohol."[205]

In line with that, the mixture should only be smeared on the sick person's body but not allowed to be swallowed internally. In case it must be drunk internally because of an illness, its alcoholic strength is withdrawn by boiling the alcohol. Other liquids that are imbued with the smell of alcohol can be drunk because it is taught in the *Vinayasūtra*: "If the liquid is boiled, the alcohol vanishes from it."[206]

And because it is taught in the *Vinayasūtra*:

> In order to be freed from one's thirst for alcohol, one should drink a powder of dry medicine consisting of roots, stems, leaves, flowers, and fruits that is imbued with the smell of alcohol and mixed with water. The powder should be imbued by leaving it hanging in a vessel with alcohol. It should be prevented from touching the alcohol. Because of this, the vessel should not be full and the alcohol should be free of alcoholic strength.[207]

Therefore what is nowadays known to Tibetans as *changköl*[208] is permissible to be taken by a sick person if it does not possess either the taste or strength of

203. Guṇaprabha, *Vinayasūtra*, 953.12.

204. Guṇaprabha, *Vinayasūtra*, 1027.2–4. For an explanation of this passage, see Dharmamitra, *Vinayasūtraṭīkā*, vol. 91, 560.20–561.10; Guṇaprabha, *Vinayasūtravṛttyabhidhānasvavyākh yāna*, 1166.14–1167.2.

205. Quotation from the *Commentary* (*'Grel pa*) unidentified.

206. Guṇaprabha, *Vinayasūtra*, 953.6–7.

207. Guṇaprabha, *Vinayasūtra*,1027.7–11. The detailed process is outlined by Dharmamitra, *Vinayasūtraṭīkā*, vol. 91, 562.13–563.12; Guṇaprabha, *Vinayasūtravṛttyabhidhānasvavyākhyāna*, 1167.20–1168.13.

208. "Boiled alcohol"—that is, a boiled soup made of traditional Tibetan *chang* beer and roasted barley flour.

alcohol. But it is impermissible if the alcohol taste and strength have not vanished. Thus the meaning of *changköl* has been explained as not being alcohol.

But if a person is not sick, even keeping alcohol in the cheeks is impermissible because it is explained in the *Vinayasūtra*: "Keeping alcohol in the cheeks and smearing it on the body are similar to making use of it."[209]

Also, some say: "There is no fault if one drinks alcohol in moderation." But this is extremely inadmissible. As Ācārya Śākyaprabha explains:

> One may say, "Since the mind will not be deluded, it will not become a fault if one drinks in a controlled manner." It is not like that, because one does not know the right amount for becoming intoxicated and because one would overdo it greatly—and this is why people with such dispositions should completely abandon the drinking of alcohol. Therefore the drinking of alcohol was prohibited in every possible way. The Bhagavān[210] taught: "Bhikṣus,[211] those of you who take teachings from me, the Teacher, should neither give nor drink intoxicating liquids, not even the amount taken with the tip of *kuśa* grass."[212]

Because of that, in line with the statement: "Alcohol is the root of all faults and thus not even a grass tip's worth should be drunk,"[213] it has been prohibited

209. Guṇaprabha, *Vinayasūtra*, 953.11–12.

210. The term *bhagavān* is used here as an epithet for Buddha Śākyamuni, meaning "endowed with fortune" and generally given in English by terms such as "Blessed One"; see Buswell and Lopez, *The Princeton Dictionary of Buddhism*, 108.

211. The term *bhikṣu* refers to a fully ordained monk; see Buswell and Lopez, *The Princeton Dictionary of Buddhism*, 115.

212. Śākyaprabha, *Mūlasarvāstivādaśrāmaṇerakārikāvṛttiprabhāvatī* (*Commentary on the Stanzas of the Mūlasarvāstivāda Novice Vows, the Illuminator*; Tib: *Gzhi thams yod par smra ba'i dge tshul gyi tshig le'ur byas pa'i 'grel pa 'od ldan*), 355.13–20. Cf. Ngorchen, *Spring yig slob ma la phan pa*, 625.5–626.1: ". . . because one would overdo it greatly, and people with such dispositions, by merely drinking alcohol, will happen to experience a behavioral downfall. Therefore the Teacher taught: "Those who take teachings from me should neither give nor drink alcohol, not even with *kuśa* grass!"

213. Jikten Sumgön (1143–1217) locates the source of this quote as the "Vinaya of the holy Dharma" but gives a slightly different reading: ". . . and not even the amount taken with *kuśa* grass is thus drunk"; see BDRC (W3JT13348): *dam pa'i chos 'dul ba nas| chang ni nyes pa kun gyi rtsa ba ste| rtswa mchog gis kyang blangs te mi mthung ngo|| bgyi ba gsung|*. Similarly, Mangthö Ludrup Gyatso (1523–1596) locates the source of this quote in the "Vinaya" and gives the second part as: ". . . and not even the amount of a droplet on *kuśa* grass should thus be drunk"; see Mangthö Ludrup Gyatso, *Bsnyen gnas cho ga'i lag len gsal ba'i sgron me*, 267.4: *'dul bar| chang ni nyes pa kun gyi rtsa ba ste|| rtsa mchog zil pa tsam yang btung mi bya|| zhes bshad pa dang|*.

in every possible way. This is also the reason for what was explained by Ārya Upagupta: "Because it is the source of the five acts that bring immediate retribution, of the five types of downfalls, and of all faults."[214]

Ācārya Guṇaprabha explained the statement, "Drinking alcohol is solely an action that is objectionable in virtue of prohibition" as "the transgression of an action that is objectionable in virtue of its prohibition."[215] In the *Extensive Commentary*,[216] it is explained:

> [Some Vaibhāṣikas say: "It is an action that is by nature objectionable] because it was explained that it is faulty conduct just as killing and the like, because it was taught as the very cause for beings of the lower realms of existence, because it was explained as the basis of heedlessness, and because it does not allow one to stay focused single-pointedly."[217]

In short, since it is an extremely severe wrongdoing, the Teacher properly prohibited the drinking of alcohol in the scriptural collections of the śrāvakas.

214. The source for this quotation is most likely Śākyaprabha, *Mūlasarvāstivādiśrāmaṇerakārikāvṛttiprabhāvatī*, 358.6–11: *'phags pa nyer sbas kyis ni myos par 'gyur ba'i khu ba bcas pa'i kha na ma tho ba dang bcas pa yin yang shin tu smad pa yin te| rang bzhin gyis kha na ma tho ba dang bcas pa'i rgyu yin pa'i phyir dang| mtshams med pa bzhi po dag dang ltung ba ris* [= *rigs*] *lnga dag la rab tu 'jug par byed pa yin pa'i phyir dang| nyes pa thams cad kyi 'byung gnas yin pa'i phyir ro zhes gsungs so||*.

The five acts that bring immediate retribution (*pañcānantarya, mtshams med lnga*) are listed in Buswell and Lopez, *The Princeton Dictionary of Buddhism*, 615–16, as: "(1) patricide, (2) matricide, (3) killing an arhat, (4) spilling the blood of a buddha, and (5) causing schism in the monastic community." The five types of downfalls (*ltung ba'i rigs lnga*) are likewise enumerated (621–22, 752–53, 637, 665–66, 275–76) as: (1) "'defeat,' . . . those misdeeds that entail automatic . . . expulsion from the Saṃgha and reversion to laity" (*pārājika, phas pham pa*); (2) "'probationary offense'; a category of offences in the roster of monastic rules . . . that require penance and/or probation" (*saṃghāvaśeṣa, dge 'dun lhag ma*); (3) "'requiring expiation,' 'transgression to be confessed,' a lesser category of violations of the monastic code" than the former two, and "those that are expiated simply by being confessed to another monk" (*pāyattika, ltung byed*); (4) "'entailing acknowledgement' or 'disclosure'; a group of four ecclesiastical offenses related to the receiving and eating of food, which are to be disclosed to, or confessed before, another monk" (*pratideśanīya, so sor bshags par bya ba*); and (5) "'wrongdoing'; a general category for the least serious of ecclesiastical offenses" (*duṣkṛta, nyes byas*).

215. Both quotations unidentified.

216. *Extensive Commentary* (*Rgya cher 'grel pa*), that is, Jinaputra's *Bodhisattvaśīlaparivartaṭīkā* (*Commentary on the Chapter about the Bodhisattva Precepts*; Tib: *Byang chub sems dpa'i tshul khrims kyi le'u rgya cher 'grel pa*).

217. Jinaputra, *Bodhisattvaśīlaparivartaṭīkā*, 568.8–11. The beginning part supplied in brackets is as Ngorchen opens his citation; see Ngorchen, *Spring yig slob ma la phan pa*, 526.3.

1.3 Relying on Alcohol by Those Who Have Entered the Mahāyāna Is Impermissible

In the *Aṅgulimālīya Sūtra*,[218] it is taught:

> As for those sentient beings who have turned away from the tathāgatagarbha, having become mice and neuter, still drinking alcohol they will again turn into mice and neuter because of drinking something extremely impure.[219]

And in the *Saddharmānusmṛtyupasthāna*,[220] it is taught that one must give up drinking alcohol from the perspective of its infinite faults:

> People relying on alcohol
> are the axe of all Dharmas.
> The foremost among those engaging in shameless activities,
> they were taught as lacking self-control.
>
> That which produces an extremely dull mind and
> causes both worlds to come to ruin,[221]
> that which solely makes the Dharma of liberation burn, like a fire,
> is alcohol.[222]

And in that same sūtra, it is taught:

> As for always drinking alcohol,
> there are thirty-six faults.
> Thus the one who knows the faults
> should give up alcohol for good.

218. Tib: *Sor mo'i phreng ba la phan pa'i mdo.*

219. *Aṅgulimālīya Sūtra*, 408.17–19.

220. *Mindfulness of the the Excellent Doctrine* (Tib: *Dam pa'i chos dran pa nye bar gzhag pa*).

221. The inanimate outer world or habitat, and the animate world of sentient beings that live in the former.

222. *Saddharmānusmṛtyupasthāna*, vol. 68, 467.9–10, 467.14–16. The fourth metrical foot of the first verse is given differently by Ngorchen, *Spring yig slob ma la phan pa*, 627.2, which is, however, in line with a variant reading of that verse as included by Paltsek, *Gsung rab rin po che'i gtam rgyud dang shākya'i rabs rgyud*, 954.21–955.2, 1003, no. 955/1: "They were taught as what should be abandoned."

As for those of noble descent and scholars,
it will defile them greatly.
Human beings, just as *kasa* flowers,[223]
it will only make them unrestrained.

Deceived by the noose of craving,
whatever sin you have committed,
it will simmer fiercely in you.
What else is there for me to say?

As for those people who were distracted by alcohol,
though alive, they resemble the dead.
Whosoever wishes to always be alive
should completely give up alcohol for good.[224]

If not given up, great suffering will be encountered, and in the *Sūtra Discriminating between Virtuous and Sinful Karma*,[225] it is taught thus: Since one drinks a lot of alcohol in this life, one will be born in the Hell of Drinking Molten Copper.[226]

Not only that, even if one gives alcohol to others, that action will turn into a fault, because it is taught in the *Siṃhaparipṛcchā Sūtra*:[227] "If one gives alcohol, one will be born with crippled hands for five hundred births."[228]

And because in the *Ṛṣivyāsaparipṛchhā Sūtra*,[229] giving alcohol, poison, weapons, and the meat of slaughtered animals are explained as impure donations.[230] Hence it is explained in the *Saddharmānusmṛtyupasthāna*:

223. The *Saddharmānusmṛtyupasthāna*, vol. 69, 541.10, specifies the flower as *ka sa'i me tog*, whereas Ngorchen, *Spring yig slob ma la phan pa*, 627.2, gives it as a spring flower (*sos ka'i me tog*).

224. *Saddharmānusmṛtyupasthāna*, vol. 69, 541.8–9, 541.9–11; vol. 68, 450.2–4, 466.18–19.

225. In general, the convention of this volume has been to use Sanskrit titles for canonical works originally written in Sanskrit. Neither the translator nor the editor, however, have been able to identify a Sanskrit title for this work (*Dge ba dang mi dge ba'i las kyi rnam par smin pa bstan pa'i mdo*) so the title has been provided in English.

226. *Dge ba dang mi dge ba'i las kyi rnam par smin pa bstan pa'i mdo*, 604.8–9.

227. The title found in the text *Seng ges zhus pa* (*Questions of Siṃha*) refers most likely to the *Siṃhaparipṛcchā* (*Questions of Siṃha Sūtra*; Tib: *Seng ges zhus pa'i mdo*), though this identification is tentative.

228. Quotation unidentified.

229. *Questions of Sage Vyāsa Sūtra* (Tib: *Drang srong rgyas pas zhus pa'i mdo*).

230. *Ṛṣivyāsaparipṛchhā Sūtra*, 784.5–786.18.

> Those people who give up alcohol
> place their mind in the meditative equipoise of the nature of the Dharma.
> They go to those supreme holy places
> where there exists no death.[231]

In line with that, those who have entered the Bodhisattva Piṭaka should not drink alcohol and should study.

Now, the second main point shall be addressed:

2. Explaining the Faults of Nourishing One's Body with the Meat of Animals That Have Been Slaughtered

This has three subpoints:

2.1. The Faults of Eating Meat in General

In the noble *Laṅkāvatāra Sūtra*,[232] it is taught extensively:

> Mahāmati, once in the past, there was a king called Siṃhasaudāsa. He ate meat as food and relied on meat that is impermissible to eat.[233] Due to his strong craving and desire for its taste, he happened to eat even the flesh of humans. As a result, he was abandoned by the masses of his people, including his friends, ministers, relatives, and kinsmen, let alone his townsmen and countrymen. Since he had to discard his political power and country, he became utterly afflicted emotionally.
>
> Mahāmati, even Indra, having previously obtained dominion over the gods, took on the physical form of a hawk due to the fault of his karmic imprints of eating meat, and he greatly threatened Viśvakarmā, who had taken the form and appearance of a pigeon. The faultless King Śibi himself, who possessed loving affection for all living beings, had then to be weighed on a scale and forced to experience great suffering [to ransom the pigeon with his own

231. *Saddharmānusmṛtyupasthāna*, vol. 68, 467.16–17.

232. *Sūtra of the Descent into Laṅka* (Tib: *Lang kar gshegs pa'i mdo*).

233. See also Jñānavajra, *Tathāgatahṛdayālaṃkāra* (*Commentary on the Sūtra of the Descent into Laṅka, the Ornament of the Essence of the Tathāgata*; Tib: *Lang kar gshegs pa zhes bya ba theg pa chen po'i mdo'i 'grel pa de bzhin gshegs pa'i snying po'i rgyan*), 638.3–4.

flesh].[234] Mahāmati, having accustomed himself to the eating of meat over many lifetimes, even having become Indra, the lord of the gods, if he causes himself and others to experience faults in such a way, what need is there to speak of others?

Mahāmati, there was also another lord of men who was carried away by a strong horse and wandered about in the wilderness. To avert misfortune in his life, he united with a lioness and offspring were born as well. Because of his association with the lioness, the king's sons were called Speckled Feet and so on. Though they became the lords of men, they also ate meat due to their karmic imprints of the fault of having eaten meat in previous lifetimes. Mahāmati, if also in this present life in a village equipped with the Seven Households they extremely lust after meat and rely on meat that is impermissible to eat,[235] they will be born as malevolent, human-flesh-eating male and female *tramen* spirits.[236] Mahāmati, even after they have changed lives, that very attachment to the taste of meat will have them fall into the birth realm of creatures eating lots of meat, such as lions, tigers, leopards, wolves, jackals, cats, foxes, and owls, and also into the birth realm of extremely ferocious creatures, such as rakṣās who eat lots of meat. If, for those who have fallen there, it is difficult to obtain even a human realm of birth, what then of nirvāṇa! Mahāmati, if such as these are the faults of

234. The British Museum houses a panel depicting this scene (Zwalf, *A Catalogue of the Gandhāra Sculpture in the British Museum*, vol. 1, color plate v, vol. 2, plate 136), which is described by Zwalf, vol. 1, 142, as follows: "The theme . . . occurs, with variants, in different texts and tells how Indra tested the resolve of the Bodhisattva in his birth as King Śibi. Śibi, who had vowed to protect all creatures, ransomed a pigeon pursued by Indra disguised as a falcon, eagle, or sparrow-hawk, while the pigeon was really the god Viśvakarmā acting at Indra's behest. Śibi offered in his own flesh the equivalent of the pigeon's weight; parts of his body were successively cut off and heaped into a scale, but the pigeon proved still too heavy until the king, with what was left of himself, got into it. In this extremity he reaffirmed his joy at fulfilling the Bodhisattva vow and prayed, in token of his sincerity, to become whole again; and this then came about. The two gods resumed their own forms." On Buddhist and non-Buddhist textual sources of this tale, see Meisig, *König Śibi und die Taube*; Ohnuma, *Head, Eyes, Flesh, and Blood*, 275; Storm, *Head and Heart*, 116–19; Zwalf, *A Catalogue of the Gandhāra Sculpture in the British Museum*, vol. 1, 142n3. See also the explanation given by Jñānavajra, *Tathāgatahṛdayālaṃkāra*, 638.4–10.

235. In Jñānavajra, *Tathāgatahṛdayālaṃkāra*, 638.12–17, the Seven Households are enumerated as butcher, alcohol seller, prostitute, fowler, fisher, the royal palace, and either low castes, such as a hunter, or tīrthikas who hold a wrong view and like the act of sacrificing lives.

236. According to Jñānavajra, *Tathāgatahṛdayālaṃkāra*, 638.19–20, *phra men* are beings that belong to the class of *yakṣas*. Cf. Ngorchen, *Spring yig slob ma la phan pa*, 629.2, who has *ḍākas* and *ḍākinīs* instead.

> eating meat, what need is there to mention that people who devote themselves excessively to eating it will surely be born there. By turning away from it, there are a great many good qualities. Mahāmati, spiritually undeveloped ordinary beings do not thoroughly comprehend these qualities and faults, and others as well.[237]

And it is taught there:

> Also, in the *Hastikakṣya*, *Mahāmegha*,
> *Mahāparinirvāṇa*, *Aṅgulimālīya Sūtra*, and
> *Laṅkāvatāra Sūtra*,
> I condemned eating meat completely.[238]
>
> The buddhas, bodhisattvas,
> and śrāvakas condemned eating it.
> Someone eating it shamelessly
> will always be born as a mad person.
>
> Since one has given up meat and the like,
> in the brahman caste or as a yoga practitioner,
> as a wise or rich person—
> as those one will be born.[239]

As this says, the faults of eating meat were taught extensively in those five kinds of texts of the Sūtra section, such as the *Hastikakṣya Sūtra*. But fearing it would be too much here, I have not elaborated on them. In brief, those belonging to the human realm, such as those depending on the Seven Households, should know that the faults for consuming meat are infinite.

237. *Laṅkāvatāra Sūtra*, 382.2–383.10.

238. For the *Hastikakṣya Sūtra* (*Sūtra of the Elephant's Exertions*; Tib: *Glang po'i rtsal gyi mdo*), *Mahāmegha* (*The Great Cloud Sūtra*; Tib: *Sprin chen po'i mdo*), *Mahāparinirvāṇa Sūtra* (*Sūtra of the Great Nirvāṇa*; Tib: *Mya ngan las 'das pa chen po theg pa chen po'i mdo*), and *Aṅgulimālīya Sūtra*, see *Bka' 'gyur dpe bsdur ma* 225, 250, 138, 231, respectively. On these Mahāyāna sūtras from the fourth or fifth century and their arguments against meat eating, see Schmithausen, "Essen, ohne zu töten," 177–93. For a briefer discussion in English, see Schmithausen, "Meat-Eating and Nature," 190–94. According to Schmithausen, "My Scholarly Life," xxxii, he is working on a "full-fledged monograph" on meat eating and vegetarianism, which will include "critical editions and annotated translations of the pertinent chapters of the *Mahāyāna Mahā-parinirvāṇa-sūtra*, the *Aṅgulimālīya-sūtra* and the *Laṅkāvatāra-sūtra*."

239. *Laṅkāvatāra Sūtra*, 387.16–388.1.

2.2. Eating Meat by Those Who Have Entered the Śrāvakayāna Is Impermissible

In the noble *Laṅkāvatāra Sūtra*, meat is prohibited for śrāvakas:

> Mahāmati, I explained that food made of meat is impermissible for monastics. Mahāmati, whosoever thinks to denigrate me by saying, "Even the Tathāgata eats meat," that one, Mahāmati, is a foolish person abiding in the obscuration of his own karmic faults. Those kinds of people will bring about for themselves, for a long time, what has no benefit, what is harmful, and what is unpleasant. Mahāmati, if my noble śrāvakas do not even eat ordinary food, what need then to mention that food made of meat and blood is impermissible?[240]

Likewise, it is taught in the *Mahāparinirvāṇa Sūtra*:

> Son of the family, henceforth I will not permit my śrāvakas to eat meat. If one says, "The alms of the country are like the flesh of one's son," how could I permit eating meat? Eating meat will result in the great loving-kindness being cut off. Thus have I taught.[241]

Due to that, let alone eating meat by śrāvakas in its entirety, it is explained that even food mixed with meat is impermissible to eat because in that same sūtra it is explained:

> [A kinsman of Kāśyapa asked,] "Fully ordained monks or nuns, or laymen or laywomen who subsist on alms food given by others, as for plenty of food, the object of which was not investigated, how should they purify alms mixed with meat?"
>
> *Reply*: "Son of the family, in any case, without going against the Vinaya, they should eat the alms by washing them with water.[242] Thus have I taught.
>
> "As for such an object—namely, food and drink that appear to have for the most part been mixed with food made of meat—they should be given up. Food, the vessels of which touched each

240. *Laṅkāvatāra Sūtra*, 385.10–17.

241. *Mahāparinirvāṇa Sūtra* (shorter version), 118.20–119.2.

242. That is, washing out the meat contained within the alms.

> other but the actual food was not mixed,[243] has no fault.[244] Those foods that are adulterated by meat, fish, wild game, dried lizard,[245] or other contaminations of meat will turn into a downfall. Thus have I said."[246]

But what if one were to ask whether the two rules taught in the Vinaya scriptures contradict each other? [The two rules being:] "Food having come in one's begging bowl, such as meat and fish, that was offered by respectable people—if, after it was investigated by thinking 'Is it not prohibited meat, such as human flesh?' it is [found that it is] not, it should be eaten." And "One should not eat leftover meat that was eaten by a tiger and the meat of an animal that was specifically made [i.e., killed]." They do not contradict each other.[247] Their intended meaning by the Buddha refers to the spiritual sustainment of those who by simply having given up meat wrongly think to have a pure view, such as Devadatta, and of those who do not enter the Buddha's doctrine because they are attached to the taste of meat, like King Speckled Feet. The basis for the Buddha's thought is in regard to a fully ordained sick monk who relies on meat for medicine: A genuine, fully ordained monk, like Mati, who abides in great loving-kindness must rely on medicine made of meat. If he does not rely on it, he is going to die. If he dies, the holy Dharma is going to disappear in the world. For this kind of a person it is permissible to eat meat. The valid cognition damaging the explicit teaching [i.e., the contradiction of taking a provisional meaning literally] is taught in the *Mahāparinirvāṇa Sūtra*:

243. That is, one vessel containing food with meat touched another vessel with meatless food.

244. That is, to eat the meatless food.

245. The meaning of the Tibetan term *rmig pa skam po* (dry hoof) is unclear, as is the Sanskrit term that may be behind it. For some first speculative thoughts by Dorji Wangchuk, who suggests "dried shellfish," or Dan Martin, who proposes "lizard," see Wangchuk, "Rmig pa skam po."

246. *Mahāparinirvāṇa Sūtra* (shorter version), 122.1–10. On this passage, cf. Schmithausen, "Essen, ohne zu töten," 181–82.

247. The first passage draws on Śākyaprabha, *Mūlasarvāstivādiśrāmaṇerakārikā* (*Stanzas of the Mūlasarvāstivāda Novice Vows*; Tib: *Gzhi thams yod par smra ba'i dge tshul gyi tshig le'ur byas pa*), 187.12–15. For an explanation of this passage, see Śākyaprabha, *Mūlasarvāstivāda-śrāmaṇerakārikāvṛttiprabhāvatī*, 373.17–374.14. For the second passage, see Śākyaprabha, *Mūlasarvāstivādiśrāmaṇerakārikā*, 188.13–14. For an explanation of this second passage, see Śākyaprabha, *Mūlasarvāstivādaśrāmaṇerakārikāvṛttiprabhāvatī*, 381.12–383.10. For an explanation of both passages, see also Vinītadeva, *Triśatakārikāvyākhyāna* (*Exposition of the Three Hundred Stanzas*; Tib: *Tshig le'ur byas pa sum brgya pa'i rnam par bshad pa*), 646.8ff., 655.18ff., respectively.

> *Question*: "Bhagavān, how then did you permit eating meat that is pure from three angles?"[248]
>
> *Reply*: "I endorsed the eating of meat that is completely pure from three angles for the sake of gradually tightening the code of precepts. But these days I discarded that rule."
>
> *Question*: "Bhagavān, what were you thinking when you taught the ninefold purpose and ten kinds of meat that should be given up?"
>
> *Reply*: "I also decided on these regulations for the sake of tightening the precepts for not eating meat."
>
> *Question*: "Bhagavān, what were you thinking when you taught even meat and fish as fine foods?"[249]
>
> *Reply*: "I did not teach meat and fish as fine foods. But I taught sugarcane, *salu* rice, grains, wheat, barley, black legumes, green legumes, *ngarbag* sugar, white sugar, honey, butter, milk, and grain oil as fine foods."[250]

The explicit teaching on meat in the Vinaya was taught by the Teacher himself with an intended meaning. This is why Śāntideva, the son of the Victorious One, also clarified it in the *Śikṣāsamuccaya*,[251] along with a quotation:

> What was permitted in the Vinaya when it says, "If one eats meat with threefold purity, it will not become an obstacle that needs to be given up," is so that those who have completely given up eating meat eliminate their exaggerated pride of wrongly thinking that they are holding a pure view. And it is so that those who have a good karmic fortune but are attached to meat dispose of their

248. That is, one had not seen, heard, or suspected that the animal had been killed particularly for oneself. Monks could only accept meat that was "pure from three angles" (*trikoṭipariśuddha*, *mus gsum yongs su dag pa*)—that is, according to Schmithausen, "Meat-Eating and Nature," 188–89, "if the monk had not seen nor heard that the animal had been killed particularly for him, nor had any reason for suspecting so."

249. That is, types of food a monk was not allowed to request for himself explicitly but allowed to accept and eat if offered. According to Schmithausen, "Essen, ohne zu töten," 159, "in this context [i.e., of fine foods] it is not about the connection of meat and fish with animal killing, but about asceticism: the monks are not allowed to ask for delicious food because this does not behoove ascetics and would raise doubts about their seriousness in the eyes of the laity" [translated by Jörg Heimbel].

250. *Mahāparinirvāṇa Sūtra* (shorter version), 119.2–14. On this passage, see also Schmithausen, "Essen, ohne zu töten," 180–81.

251. *Compendium of Trainings* (Tib: *Bslab pa kun las btus pa*).

inability to enter the Buddha's doctrine. That was also taught in the *Laṅkāvatāra Sūtra*:[252] "The proclamation of my teachings and the code of precepts therein is set up in stages in the manner of how the rungs of a ladder connect. Establishing the rule of meat with threefold purity, I prohibited both meat that was specifically prepared for oneself, and later I even went so far as to prohibit the meat of animals that have died naturally from one of ten kinds of death.[253]

Hence the Buddha proclaimed in the *Laṅkāvatāra Sūtra*:

> Mahāmati, if I am endowed with the conception that all sentient beings are like my own child, how could I permit the śrāvakas to eat the flesh of my own child? How can we speak of I myself eating it? As for the statements, "I permitted it for the śrāvakas" and "I myself ate it," Mahāmati, they are without any basis.[254]

This proclamation is true. That being so, some contemporary upholders of the Vinaya state: "In the Vinaya Piṭaka, it was taught that 'meat was permitted' and that 'eating meat has no faults because it does not contradict the rules of any of the three vows.' Many hundreds of bhikṣus should loudly proclaim this everywhere." These developments were also prophesied by the Victorious One himself, and he taught in the *Mahāparinirvāṇa Sūtra*:

> Son of the family, when many hundreds of years will have passed after I have died, srotaāpannas [stream-enterers], sakṛdāgāmins [once-returners], anāgāmis [non-returners], and arhats [worthy ones] will have disappeared. At the time when the holy Dharma will have perished in perpetuity, bhikṣus will appear who imitate maintaining the Vinaya and Mātṛkā and who possess various discursive thoughts. They will nourish their own bodies,[255] cherish all kinds of meat, be tormented by sickness, hunger, and thirst. Their appearance will be very frightening, they will be like cowherds and fowlers who wear Dharma robes bearing colored patterns but exhibit the deliberate behavior of a cat.[256] They will claim, "I am

252. Cf. the *Laṅkāvatāra Sūtra*, 385.5–8.

253. Śāntideva, *Śikṣāsamuccaya*, 1184.16–1185.3.

254. *Laṅkāvatāra Sūtra*, 386.5–9.

255. By being attached to food.

256. Though wearing saffron-colored monk's cloth, they are like a hunter: with eyes lowered to

> an arhat," but will be afflicted by many kinds of sufferings. Their bodies will be tainted with their own urine and excrement. Outwardly they will model their dress in an excellent style just like a sage [or the Muni].[257] They will change into a śramaṇa-like person without actually being a śramaṇa. They will uphold fabricated texts that are similar to the holy Dharma. These people will destroy the Vinaya, rituals, and proper domains of conduct that I instituted, and they will destroy the texts of complete liberation from attachment to the impermissible and of the suchness of liberation. They will alter whatever they like from the Vinaya and individual Sūtra sections and teach it. They will say: "In this way, the Bhagavān taught in our Vinaya: 'The donation of meat nutriments is permissible.'" People pretending to be monastic renunciants [śramaṇa], sons of the Śākya, are going to appear, who will themselves make up teachings and make assertions that contradict my teachings.[258]

And the Buddha extensively taught in the *Laṅkāvatāra Sūtra*:

> Mahāmati, whatever [meat of threefold purity] one considers, the meat permitted for śrāvakas—that is, meat not specifically made for them, meat not requested to be made for them, and meat one did not examine [that was given by benefactors]—this meat is also impermissible [because directly or indirectly it harms sentient beings].[259] Mahāmati, in future times, foolish people, ordained into

the ground and walking slowly, they resemble a cat stalking a mouse.

257. But inwardly their mind is suppressed by jealousy and desire.

258. *Mahāparinirvāṇa Sūtra* (shorter version), 120.12–121.9. Cf. the respective passage in the enlarged *Mahāparinirvāṇa Sūtra* (longer version), vol. 52, 131.5–132.5, as translated into Tibetan from the Chinese translation of Dharmakṣema, which contains additional parts entirely missing in the Tibetan translation from Sanskrit done by Jinamitra, Jñānagarbha, and Devacandra. Cf. Blum, *The Nirvana Sutra*, 113, for the translation of the respective passage from Chinese. For the sake of clarification, some additional parts from the Tibetan translation of the Chinese version have been supplied in notes 255–57. On the different versions and translations of the *Mahāparinirvāṇa Sūtra*, see Buswell and Lopez, *The Princeton Dictionary of Buddhism*, 504–5.

259. The explanatory remarks in brackets are given according to Jñānavajra, *Tathāgatahṛdayālaṃkāra*, 639.5–10. Note that within this context the threefold purity of meat is formulated differently than outlined above. Jñānavajra explains it as: meat of an animal that was not killed by oneself, meat of an animal that one did not make someone else kill, and meat given by benefactors, the source of which one did not examine. In the versified summary at the end of the *Laṅkāvatāra Sūtra*, 387.9–11, another formulation of threefold purity is found as well: "As for

> my teachings and declaring "I am the son of Śākya," upholding the victory banner of saffron-colored robes, will have their minds corrupted by mistaken conceptual sophistry. They will think in manifold ways about the Vinaya, their advocated view of the transitory collection[260] will be comprehensive, and they will be attached to their lust for meat. They will teach all those pseudo reasons for eating meat, and I think they will also denigrate me by saying that I am not right. Investigating all those episodes when the matter of meat eating emerged in my discourses, they will say: "As for the emergence of this matter, in these episodes the Bhagavān allowed food made of meat and taught it as both permissible[261] and a delicacy. Even the Tathāgata himself ate meat." Mahāmati, nowhere in any of my sūtras did I permit the consumption of meat, and I also did not specify it as permissible among the delicacies.[262]

After that, it is taught in conclusion:

> In future times,
> those deluded propagators of meat eating will say:
> "The Buddha explained:
> 'Meat is without sin and permissible.'"
>
> Food, being like medicine,
> and meat, similar to the flesh of one's own son,
> the former eaten moderately and the latter given up with the notion of being unwholesome[263]—
> in such a manner the yogi should make use of food.

meat of threefold purity—that is, which was not examined, not begged for, and not requested—there is none. Therefore meat should not be eaten" (*rnam gsum dag pa'i sha rnams ni* || *ma brtags pa dang ma bslangs dang* || *ma bskul ba yang yod med pas* || *de bas sha ni mi bza'o* ||). For a discussion of these different formulations, see Gorampa, *Sdom pa gsum gyi rab tu dbye ba'i rnam bshad*, 119.4ff.

260. That is, the mistaken view of a self.

261. The *Laṅkāvatāra Sūtra*, 384.13–14 reads "as not permissible," which is very difficult to understand within this context. I have thus followed the version in Ngorchen, *Spring yig slob ma la phan pa*, 635.4, which has "as permissible." Such an understanding is also supported by the explanation given by Jñānavajra, *Tathāgatahṛdayālaṃkāra*, 639.20–640.1.

262. *Laṅkāvatāra Sūtra*, 384.3–16.

263. Translated according to the explanation given by Jñānavajra, *Tathāgatahṛdayālaṃkāra*, 642.16–18.

> Since meat eaters will be born as lions, tigers,
> foxes, and so on, and associate with their own kind,
> for those who abide in loving-kindness, I
> condemned eating meat always and in all aspects.[264]

Because of that, even if one is not able to practice properly, one should not set up a scriptural tradition that proposes "the consumption of meat has no faults," for doing so will badly harm the teachings of the Victorious One and will lead one's followers onto a mistaken path. That being so, formerly, in the land of Tibet, the adherents of the Old Mantra school [i.e., the Nyingma school] took the words of the tantras literally, such as of the *Sarvatathāgatatattvasaṃgraha* that says:[265] "Even though one would have killed all sentient beings, if it was for the benefit of sentient beings and for the purpose of the Buddha's doctrine, one would not have been tainted with sin."[266] And so ritual practices and a scriptural tradition emerged that propound liberation through killing as Dharma. That system and the tenet system that was established by contemporary upholders of the Vinaya appear to be the same! Thus, with the palms of my two hands put together, I supplicate in all directions: "Do not establish a scriptural tradition such as this!"

2.3 Presenting That Eating Meat by Those Who Have Entered the Mahāyāna Is Impermissible

In the noble *Laṅkāvatāra Sūtra*, it is taught at great length:

> Mahāmati, living beings have been cycling through saṃsāra for a long time. Whatever it may be, a sentient being who has not

264. *Laṅkāvatāra Sūtra*, 388.5–10. Jñānavajra, *Tathāgatahṛdayālaṃkāra*, 642.18–20, explains the first two metrical feet as: *wa la sogs dang 'grogs bya bas|| zhes pa ni de de dag tu skye zhing de'i rigs dang 'grogs pa'o||*, and my translation reflects this explanation. Moreover, since this and the other verses, as found at the end of the *Laṅkāvatāra Sūtra*, are a concise summary of points that were already explained in the preceding part in prose, the only fitting passage deals with meat eaters born in the birth realm of lions, tigers, and so on, as translated above. In addition, because the other occurrences of the verb *smad* (to condemn) in some preceding verses take meat eating as their object, it seems unlikely to me that the first two metrical feet should be taken as the object, and an alternative translation be: Those who band together with lions, tigers, foxes and so on, I, who abide in loving-kindness, condemned them always and in all aspects.

265. *Compendium of Realities* (Tib: *De kho na nyid bsdus pa*).

266. *Sarvatathāgatatattvasaṃgraha* (*Compendium of Reality of All the Tathāgatas*; Tib: *De bzhin gshegs pa thams cad kyi de kho na nyid bsdus pa*), 194.17–19.

been your father, mother, brother, sister, son, daughter, kinsmen, relative, or like a relative [i.e., a friend], there is no such type whatsoever that is easy to find. Those who were your relatives and friends changed their bodily form in another life and transformed into the birth realm of wild animals, livestock, and birds, whichever realm was karmically appropriate. A bodhisattva who is a mahāsattva desiring the Buddha's Dharma and desiring that all living creatures become just like his own self, how could he eat the flesh that originated from all those previously related beings who have now turned into other kinds of living beings? Mahāmati, even flesh-eating rākṣasa demons, after hearing the excellent inherent nature [dharmatā] of all phenomena [dharma] of the tathāgatas, they turn away from eating meat and, freed from their demonic nature, they become compassionate. If so, what need to speak of living beings desiring the Dharma? Under these circumstances, Mahāmati, with regard to all those beings who moved on in their succession of lives, in order to cultivate the notion that all sentient beings are like one's only son through the association that all sentient beings were once one's own kinsmen and relatives, a bodhisattva of compassionate nature should not eat any meat at all.

Mahāmati, since it is also impermissible and mistaken to eat meat, a bodhisattva who observes proper conduct should not eat any meat at all. Mahāmati, [tabooed or prohibited kinds of meat such as][267] the meat of donkeys, camels, dogs, elephants, humans, and so on is not eaten by worldly people.[268] For their profit, butchers say that these kinds of meat are permissible to eat and sell them in the middle of streets. For this reason as well, Mahāmati, a bodhisattva should not eat any meat at all.

Also, Mahāmati, because he desires to be pure, a bodhisattva should not eat meat, for meat originated from male semen and female blood.

Since it would also scare living creatures, Mahāmati, a yogi-bodhisattva desiring loving-kindness should not eat any meat at all. It is thus, Mahāmati, that even if dogs merely see people who eat dog meat from a distance—such as śvapākas [dog cookers], caṇḍālas,

267. See Schmithausen, "Essen, ohne zu töten," 163–70.

268. That is, eaten only by outcasts.

and fishermen—they bark at them out of fear, and some, thinking, "They come to kill us," almost die. Likewise, Mahāmati, also those other very small beings who live in the sky, upon the earth, and in the water, as soon as they see meat eaters from a distance or sense their smell with their sharp nose faculty, they quickly turn away just like humans do from flesh-eating rākṣasa demons, some even fearing to die. Therefore Mahāmati, since all those beings would get scared, a bodhisattva who abides in loving-kindness should not eat meat.

Mahāmati, by consuming meat a nonsuperior ordinary being is given a bad smell and infamy descends upon him. Since also a superior being [ārya] has completely given up consuming meat, a bodhisattva should not eat meat.

Mahāmati, a superior being eats the food of sages [*ṛṣi*]. Because he thus eats no blood and meat, this is also why a bodhisattva should not eat meat.

Mahāmati, in order to safeguard the mind of many beings, a bodhisattva of compassionate nature who desires that denigrating the Teachings be given up should not eat meat. It is as follows: Mahāmati, there are people in the world disparaging the Teachings, saying: "Oh my! What is the monastic renunciation of these people? Also, where could there be any practicing of purity among these people? After they discarded the food of the previous sages, their bellies filled with food of meat, just like carnivorous animals, they wander throughout these worlds, scaring small beings living in the sky, upon the earth, and in the water. Their monastic renunciation has degenerated. Their practice of giving up evil deeds has perished. Neither do they possess any Dharma nor discipline." Those holding a hostile mindset like that disparage the Teachings in various ways. Because of that, Mahāmati, in order to safeguard the mind of many beings, a bodhisattva of compassionate nature who desires that disparaging the Teachings be given up should not eat any meat at all.

Mahāmati, corpses of dead beings smell bad and unwholesome; meat is similar. This is also why a bodhisattva should not eat meat. Mahāmati, there is not any difference at all between the smell of the roasted flesh of a dead human and the roasted meat of another nonhuman being; both are equally bad-smelling. This is another reason why, Mahāmati, a yogi-bodhisattva desiring to be pure should not eat any meat at all.

> Mahāmati, eating meat obstructs practicing magical formulas and liberation for those who dwell in charnel grounds, for yogis who live in far-off places in the wilderness haunted by ghosts, for those who engage in yoga and abide in loving-kindness, for those upholding magical formulas, and for those wanting to accomplish magical formulas. Therefore a bodhisattva desiring to benefit his own body and that of others should not eat any meat at all upon perceiving that eating meat is going to cause hindrances for all those practicing yoga among the sons and daughters of the family who have entered the Mahāyāna.
>
> Since eating meat also generates attachment due to an awareness that focuses on matter, a bodhisattva having the compassionate nature that all living creatures were once he himself should not eat any meat at all.
>
> Mahāmati, in order that the gods give it up as well, a bodhisattva having a compassionate nature should not eat any meat at all.
>
> Mahāmati, because even in this very life his mouth will be bad-smelling, a bodhisattva should not eat any meat at all.[269]

Thus and so on it is taught at great length in the noble *Laṅkāvatāra Sūtra*. Therefore, for bodhisattvas who have entered the Mahāyāna, meat has been prohibited in every aspect.

Omitted from the translation:[270]

269. *Laṅkāvatāra Sūtra*, 377.10–380.16. For a discussion of the different arguments of the *Laṅkāvatāra Sūtra* against meat eating, see Schmithausen, "Essen, ohne zu töten," 186–91.

270. As mentioned in the introduction, I have not translated Ngorchen's discussion of the prohibition of meat and alcohol from a tantric point of view. My knowledge of tantric Buddhism is insufficient, and tantric topics are not openly discussed within the Sakya school without having previously received the related empowerments.

3. How the Two—Meat and Alcohol—Are Prohibited in the Secret Mantra

3.1 Explaining That Mantrins Must Give Up Meat and Alcohol

3.2 Eliminating Objections about This[271]

Concluding Verses

At this time when the completely purified human body equipped with freedoms and endowments has been obtained,
which is the extraordinary bodily support for practicing the holy Dharma,
and which is difficult to acquire through many hundreds of hardships,
adhere to a heedful conduct, insightful people!

All three levels of existence possess the nature of impermanence.
Also, the life of human beings, just like dew on the tip of grass,
is impermanent. Since one will certainly die quickly,
generate strong diligence, intelligent people!

Since present pleasure and pain, rising and falling, meeting and parting
follow after previously accumulated karma,
cause and result are without deceit and unobscured in their content.
Thus behave properly in line with what should be accepted and what rejected, insightful people!

All of saṃsāra possesses the nature of suffering.
Having understood that there is no chance for happiness,
one recalls the virtuous and fine qualities of liberation.
Engage thus in the conduct of a bodhisattva, intelligent people!

Infinite living beings, as one's father and mother
they acted and helped numerous times.

271. That is, relying on meat and alcohol by those persons who have entered the Great Yoga—that is, the Niruttarayoga tantric system—is impermissible.

For liberating them from the ocean of saṃsāra,
generate supreme bodhicitta, insightful people!

The Three Disciplines, the Six Perfections, and so forth:
the powerful conduct of the sons of the Victorious One,
constituting the roots of the unmistaken path of liberation—
uphold them properly and respectfully, intelligent people!

The various nets of conceiving a grasped object and a grasping subject
bind one to the great suffering of saṃsāra.
Train this agitated mind in calm-abiding and concentration!
One-pointedly engage in virtuous practice, insightful people!

Make yourself realize that all external and internal phenomena such as matter
are devoid of any self-nature from the very beginning.
With the firelight of the individually discriminating insight,
burn the firewood of ignorance, intelligent people!

Hey! Followers of mine,
give up the impure lifestyle of consuming meat, alcohol, and the like!
Being the sole basis of all marvelous qualities,
cherish the precious discipline more than your life!

The Mādhyamaka scriptural system, the essence of the Buddha word,
I ask you to study it correctly by means of hearing and contemplation.
The Vinaya scriptures and Bodhisattva Piṭaka,
by relying on them, comply with a heedful conduct!

Attending to a king and the like because of desiring gain and esteem,
give up all activities that impair your own benefit!
At remote, far-off places praised by the Victorious One,
cultivate the two types of bodhicitta and tame your mind!

When in that way through respect and diligence in application
the mind training of the common path has been completed,
enter the path of the profound Vajrayāna,
which is far superior than the other vehicles!

Making one practice on the nonvirtuous path,
distance yourself from a master who is of a demonic type!
With whomsoever one associates, he should be able to make one practice in virtue.
Wherever a qualified lama resides, rely on him!

Since the basis of the path is the lama,
please him, even as far as with your body and life,
with the conception that he is inseparable from one's own special practice deity,
and drink the nectar of the essential instructions of the Great Secret!

Discard this bad system of people pretending to be Mantrins
and of people reciting only arrangements of rituals and scriptures!
The Tantra sections that have been purified through the three kinds of analysis,
practice them properly by way of correct reasoning!

Understand the supreme root of all mantric siddhis
as the perfectly pure tantric samayas and vows!
According to the intent of the flawless scriptures,
practice and especially generate diligence!

Since the intent of the perfectly pure Tantra sections is inconceivable,
one does not find their tantric meaning in just one portion.
Study thus impartially the myriad mantric scriptures
of the four tantra classes together with the commentaries on their intent!

When hearing and contemplation have been concluded in such a way,
the yoga of the two stages together with its ancillary practices,
engage in its practice unceasingly and clearly,
like the current of a river and the tip of a butter lamp!

If done in such a way, you karmically fortunate ones will swiftly achieve
happiness or the status of Śākya, the Lord of Sages,
the Teacher who actualized the three bodies, the perfect buddha,
oh my supreme friends.

In order to benefit and show the excellent path of happiness
to my group of karmically fortunate students in such a way,
this profound epistle for urging you toward the Dharma,
I put this heartfelt advice into writing with a pure intention.

Though I merely happened to piece it together,
the other parts I recorded just as they originate
from the words of the Teacher, the treatises, and stainless tantras.
Thus accept this respectfully, just like the words of the Sage!

Having completely cleared away the dense darkness of sinful conduct
through the one-hundred-thousand-light-ray-possessing merit of compiling this epistle,
may the four continents of the Buddha's teachings be illuminated throughout
with the radiance of the light of the unmistaken Dharma.

This Epistle of General Advice for My Own Monks, Benefitting Students was compiled by me, Śākya bhikṣu Ngorchen Künga Sangpo—who respectfully took with the crown of my head the dust of the feet of the Venerable Lord, the Lord of Scholars, Yeshe Gyaltsen Palsangpo,[272] *who has traversed the ocean of our own and others' tenets, and from whom I received the kindness of granting me the three vows—on the fifth day of the first half of the first lunar month of 1425 at the great monastic university of Glorious Sakya, the source of numerous precious qualities. Shenyen Sangpo acted as scribe.*

And may this teaching be beneficial for all human beings![273]

272. On the life of Sharchen Yeshe Gyaltsen (1359–1406), one of Ngorchen's main teachers, see Heimbel, *Vajradhara in Human Form*, 111–38.

273. I would like to thank Prof. Kazuo Kano for suggesting this translation for the aspiration that is given in Tibetanized Sanskrit at the end of the text (Ngorchen, *Spring yig slob ma la phan pa*, 660.2): *idaṃ śāsanaś ca sarvasatvā hito bhavantu* [= *ayaṃ śāsanaś ca sarvasattvahito bhavatu*].

Kangyur (Canonical Scriptures)

Aṅgulimālīya Sūtra (*Sor mo'i phreng ba la phan pa'i mdo*). In *Bka' 'gyur dpe bsdur ma*, no. 231, mdo sde, vol. 62 (*tsha*), 347–549.

Bka' 'gyur dpe bsdur ma. 108 vols. Krung go'i bod rig pa zhib 'jug lte gnas kyi bka' bstan dpe sdur khang, ed. Beijing: Krung go'i bod rig pa dpe skrun khang, 2006–2008. BDRC: W1PD96682.

Dge ba dang mi dge ba'i las kyi rnam par smin pa bstan pa'i mdo. In *Bka' 'gyur dpe bsdur ma*, no. 375, mdo sde, vol. 76 (*aḥ*), 596–616.

Hastikakṣya Sūtra (*Glang po'i rtsal gyi mdo*). In *Bka' 'gyur dpe bsdur ma*, no. 225, mdo sde, vol. 62 (*tsha*), 254–92.

Laṅkāvatāra Sūtra (*Lang kar gshegs pa'i mdo*). In *Bka' 'gyur dpe bsdur ma*, no. 125, mdo sde, vol. 49 (*ca*), 141–506.

Mahāmegha Sūtra (*Sprin chen po'i mdo*). In *Bka' 'gyur dpe bsdur ma*, no. 250, mdo sde, vol. 64 (*wa*), 314–598.

Mahāparinirvāṇa Sūtra (*Mya ngan las 'das pa chen po'i mdo*; longer version translated from Sanskrit via Chinese). In *Bka' 'gyur dpe bsdur ma*, no. 137, mdo sde, vols. 52 (*nya*)–53 (*ta*).

Mahāparinirvāṇa Sūtra (*Mya ngan las 'das pa chen po theg pa chen po'i mdo*; shorter version translated from Sanskrit). In *Bka' 'gyur dpe bsdur ma*, no. 138, mdo sde, vol. 54 (*tha*), 3–376.

Nandika Sūtra (*Dga' ba can gyi mdo*). In *Bka' 'gyur dpe bsdur ma*, no. 352, mdo sde, vol. 72 (*sa*), 770–78.

Ṛṣivyāsaparipṛchhā Sūtra (*Drang srong rgyas pas zhus pa'i mdo*). In *Bka' 'gyur dpe bsdur ma*, no. 110, dkon brtsegs, vol. 44 (*cha*), 776–842.

Saddharmānusmṛtyupasthāna (*Dam pa'i chos dran pa nye bar gzhag pa*). In *Bka' 'gyur dpe bsdur ma*, no. 305, mdo sde, vols. 68 (*ya*, 238)–71 (*sha*, 603).

Sarvatathāgatatattvasaṃgraha (*De bzhin gshegs pa thams cad kyi de kho na nyid bsdus pa*). In *Bka' 'gyur dpe bsdur ma*, no. 504, rgyud 'bum, vol. 84 (*nya*), 3–432.

Siṃhaparipṛcchā Sūtra (*Seng ges zhus pa'i mdo*). In *Bka' 'gyur dpe bsdur ma*, no. 98, dkon brtsegs, vol. 44 (*cha*), 72–81.

Tengyur (Canonical Treatises)

Bstan 'gyur dpe bsdur ma. 124 vols. Krung go'i bod rig pa zhib 'jug lte gnas kyi bka' bstan dpe sdur khang, ed. Beijing: Krung go'i bod rig pa dpe skrun khang, 1994–2007. BDRC: W1PD95844.

Dharmamitra (Chos kyi bshes gnyen). *Vinayasūtraṭīkā* (*'Dul ba'i mdo'i rgya cher 'grel pa*). In *Bstan 'gyur dpe bsdur ma*, no. 3350, 'dul ba, vols. 90 (*'u*, 177)–91 (*yu*, 178).

Guṇaprabha (Yon tan 'od). *Vinayasūtra* (*'Dul ba'i mdo*). In *Bstan 'gyur dpe bsdur ma*, no. 3347, 'dul ba, vol. 88 (*wu*, 174), 837–1104.

———. *Vinayasūtravṛttyabhidhānasvavyākhyāna* (*'Dul ba'i mdo'i 'grel pa mngon par brjod pa rang gi rnam par bshad pa*). In *Bstan 'gyur dpe bsdur ma*, no. 3349, 'dul ba, vol. 89 (*zhu–zu*, 175–76).

Jinaputra (Dzi na mi tra). *Bodhisattvaśīlaparivartaṭīkā* (*Byang chub sems dpa'i tshul khrims *kyi le'u rgya cher 'grel pa*). In *Bstan 'gyur dpe bsdur ma*, no. 3275, sems tsam, vol. 75 (*'i*, 147), 526–606.

Jñānavajra (Dznyā na badzra). *Tathāgatahṛdayālaṃkāra* (*Lang kar gshegs pa zhes bya ba theg pa chen po'i mdo'i 'grel pa de bzhin gshegs pa'i snying po'i rgyan*). In *Bstan 'gyur dpe bsdur ma*, no. 3251, vol. 70 (*pi*, 137), 3–802.

Mahāvyutpatti (*Sgra sbyor bam po gnyis pa*). See Sakaki 1987.

Paltsek (dPal brtsegs). *Gsung rab rin po che'i gtam rgyud dang shākya'i rabs rgyud*. In *Bstan 'gyur dpe bsdur ma*, no. 3602, sna tshogs, vol. 115 (*co*, 219), 650–1006.

Śākyaprabha (Shākya pra bha). *Mūlasarvāstivādiśrāmaṇerakārikā* (*Gzhi thams cad yod par smra ba'i dge tshul gyi tshig le'ur byas pa*). In *Bstan 'gyur dpe bsdur ma*, no. 3354, 'dul ba, vol. 93 (*shu*, 181), 167–99.

———. *Mūlasarvāstivādaśrāmaṇerakārikāvṛttiprabhāvatī* (*Gzhi thams cad yod par smra ba'i dge tshul gyi tshig le'ur byas pa'i 'grel pa 'od ldan*). In *Bstan 'gyur dpe bsdur ma*, no. 3355, 'dul ba, vol. 93 (*shu*, 181), 200–443.

Śāntideva (Zhi ba lha). *Śikṣāsamuccaya* (*Bslab pa kun las btus pa*). In *Bstan 'gyur dpe bsdur ma*, no. 3170, dbu ma, vol. 64 (*khi*, 126), 1009–1519.

Vinītadeva (Dul ba lha). *Triśatakārikāvyākhyāna* (*Tshig le'ur byas pa sum brgya pa'i rnam par bshad pa*). In *Bstan 'gyur dpe bsdur ma*, no. 3356, 'dul ba, vol. 93 (*shu*, 181), 444–722.

Tibetan-Language Works

Ame Shab (A mes zhabs Ngag dbang kun dga' bsod nams, 1597–1659). 1974. *Mkhyen brtse nus pa'i mṅa' bdag rgyal ba sras daṅ slob mar bcas pa'i spyi gzugs dam pa dus gsum sgrib med du gzigs pa'i rje btsun mus pa chen po saṅs rgyas rgyal mtshan gyi rnam par thar pa byin rlabs kyi char 'bebs ṅo mtshar sarga gsum pa: The Biography of the Sixteenth-Century Sa-skya-pa Scholar and Saint Mus-chen Saṅs-rgyas-rgyal-mtshan*. Reproduced from a print from the Sde dge or Ṅor blocks at the order of H. H. the Sa-skya Khri-'dzin Rin-po-che. Dehra Dun, U.P.: Sakya Centre.

Dobi Tsering Dorjé (Rdo sbis Tshe ring rdo rje) et al., eds. 2016. *Deng rabs bod skad tshig mdzod*. Lhasa: Bod ljongs mi dmangs dpe skrun khang.

Drakpa Dorjé (Grags pa rdo rje, fl. 15th century). 2008. *Mtshungs med chos rje dpal ldan rdo rje'i rnam thar*. In *Path with the Fruit 2*, vol. 27 (*sha*), 559–608.

Dungkar Losang Trinle (Dung dkar Blo bzang 'phrin las, 1927–1997). 2002. *Mkhas dbang dung dkar blo bzang 'phrin las mchog gis mdzad pa'i bod rig pa'i tshig mdzod chen mo shes bya rab gsal*. Beijing: Krung go'i bod rig pa dpe skrun khang.

Gorampa (Go rams pa Bsod nams seng ge, 1429–1489). 1995. *Sdom pa gsum gyi rab tu dbye ba'i rnam bshad rgyal ba'i gsung rab kyi dgongs pa gsal ba*. In *Kun mkhyen go bo rab 'byams pa bsod nams seng ge'i bka' 'bum: The Collected Works of Kun-mkhyen Go-rams-pa Bsod-nams-seng-ge*, vol. 9 (*ta*), 1–323. 13 vols. Kangra, H.P.: Yashodhara Publications for Dzongsar Institute India.

Guru Phel (Gu ru 'phel, fl. 18th century). n.d. *Dpal shar pa mkhan rin po che rdo rje 'chang rin chen mi 'gyur rgyal mtshan gyi rnam par thar pa| smra ba'i seng ge'i gsung rdo rje sgra ma'i mchod pa rgyas par spros pa zhing khams rgya mtsho'i mchod sprin*. In *Dpal ldan shar pa mkhan chen rdo rje 'chang rin chen mi 'gyur rgyal mtshan gyi gsung 'bum*, 157a–254a. Degé blockprint. BDRC: W00EGS1016236.

Könchok Palden (Dkon mchog dpal ldan, 1526–1590). 2008. *Rje btsun dkon mchog lhun grub kyi|| rnam thar 'dod dgu'i dpal 'byung gi|| rnam bshad 'dod dgu'i chu gter mchog|| blo gsal ngang pa'i bsti gnas lags||*. In *Path with the Fruit* 2, vol. 28 (*sa*), 173–232.

Künga Drölchok (Kun dga 'grol mchog, 1507–1566). 2011. *Dpal ldan bla ma 'jam pa'i dbyangs kyi rnam par thar pa legs bshad khyad par gsum ldan*. In *Bod kyi lo rgyus rnam thar phyogs bsgrigs thengs gnyis pa*, edited by Dpal brtsegs bod yig dpe rnying zhib 'jug khang, vol. 56 (*li*), 213–351. 30 vols. (31–60). Xining: Mtsho sngon mi rigs dpe skrun khang.

Lowo Khenchen Sönam Lhündrup (Glo bo Mkhan chen Bsod nams lhun grub, 1456–1532). n.d. *Chos kyi rje tshul khrims rgyal mtshan gyi rnam par thar pa dgos 'dod kun 'byung*. In *Glo bo mkhan chen bsod nams lhun grub kyi gsung 'bum*, vol. 1 (*ka*), 148a–174b. 7 vols. BDRC: W00KG01660.

Mangthö Ludrup Gyatso (Mang thos Klu sgrub rgya mtsho, 1523–1596). 1999. *Bsnyen gnas cho ga'i lag len gsal ba'i sgron me*. In *Mang thos klu sgrub rgya mtsho'i gsung skor*, edited by the Sa skya rgyal yongs gsung rab slob gnyer khang, vol. 1 (*ka*), 251–79. 6 vols. Dehra Dun, U.P.: Sakya College.

Müchen Könchok Gyaltsen (Mus chen dKon mchog rgyal mtshan, 1388–1469). 1983. *Snyigs dus kyi rdo rje 'chang chen po chos kyi rje kun dga' bzang po'i rnam par thar pa mdor bsdus pa*. In *Path with the Fruit* 1, vol. 1 (*ka*), 432–73.

Ngorchen Künga Sangpo (Ngor chen Kun dga' bzang po, 1382–1456). 1993. *Spring yig slob ma la phan pa*. In *Ngor chen kun dga' bzang po'i bka' 'bum*, vol. 4 (*a*), 619–660.2. 4 vols. Dehra Dun, U.P.: Ngor Pal E-Wam Cho Dan. BDRC: W11577.

Padma Dorjé (Padma rdo rje) et al., eds. 2000. *Bod kyi nyer mkho'i zas rigs tshig mdzod*. Xining: Mtsho sngon mi rigs dpe skrun khang.

Palden Chökyong (Dpal ldan chos skyong, 1702–1760). 1985. *E waṃ pa'i gdan rabs rin chen phreng mdzes kyi kha skong rtogs brjod byin rlabs 'dod dgu'i dpal ster*. In *Lam 'bras Tshogs bśad: The Sa-skya-pa Teachings of the Path and the Fruit, according to the Ṅor-pa Transmission. As Arranged by 'Jam-dbyaṅs Blo-gter-dbaṅ-po and His Successors and Incorporating Other Texts Transmitting the Lineage through the Present Ṅor and Sa-skya Systems*, vol. 4, 495–593. 6 vols. Reproduced from prints from the Sde-dge blocks from the library of the Ven. Klu-sdiṅs Mkhan Rin-po-che of Ṅor. Sa-skya Lam 'bras Literature Series 22–27. Dehra Dun, U.P.: Sakya Centre.

Path with the Fruit 1. 1983–1985. *Lam 'bras slob bśad: The Sa-skya-pa Teachings of the Path and the Fruit, according to the Tshar-pa Transmission. As Arranged by 'Jam-dbyaṅs-blo-gter-dbaṅ-po and Supplemented by Texts Continuing the Lineage through Khaṅ-gsar Dam-pa and Sga-ston Ṅag-dbaṅ-legs-pa Rin-po-ches*. 21 vols. Reproduced from prints from the Sde-dge redaction from the library of the Ven. Klu-sdiṅs Mkhan Rin-po-che of Ṅor. Sa-skya Lam 'bras Literature Series 1–21. Dehra Dun, U.P.: Sakya Centre.

Path with the Fruit 2. 2008. *Gsung ngag lam 'bras tshogs bshad chen mo: The Great Collection of the Lamdre Tshogshe Teachings*. 5 vols. (vols. 27–42). Edited by Khenchen Ape Rinpoche Yöntan Sangpo (Mkhan chen A pad Rin po che Yon tan bzang po, 1927–2010). Kathmandu: Sachen International (Rgyal yongs sa chen).

Sangye Phüntsok (Sangs rgyas phun tshogs, 1649–1705). 1983. *Rdo rje 'chang kun dga' bzang po'i rnam par thar pa legs bshad chu bo 'dus pa'i rgya mtsho*. In *Path with the Fruit* 1, vol. 1 (*ka*), 475–585.

———. 2008. *Bya bral ba sangs rgyas phun tshogs kyi myong ba brjod pa nges 'byung gtam gyi rol mtsho*. In *Path with the Fruit* 2, vol. 29 (*ha*), 145–264.

Tsang Jampa Dorjé Gyaltsen (Gtsang Byams pa Rdo rje rgyal mtshan, 1424–1498). n.d.

[title on the title page illegible; incipit title:] *Sa skya 'khon gyi gdung rabs*. Dbu can manuscript, 90 fols. (incomplete, folio 91 missing). NGMCP (Reel no. L 591/4).

Zhang, Yisun, ed. 1993. *Bod rgya tshig mdzod chen mo*. 2 vols. Beijing: Mi rigs dpe skrun khang, 1993.

Non-Tibetan-Language Works

Blum, Mark L., trans. 2013. *The Nirvana Sutra* (*Mahāparinirvāṇa Sūtra*), vol. 1. (Taishō Volume 12, Number 374). Translated from the Chinese. BDK English Tripiṭaka Series. Berkeley, CA: Bukkyo Dendo Kyokai America, Inc.

Buswell, Robert E., Jr., and Donald S. Lopez, Jr., eds. 2014. *The Princeton Dictionary of Buddhism*. Princeton, NJ: Princeton University Press.

Heimbel, Jörg. 2013. "The Jo gdan tshogs sde bzhi: An Investigation into the History of the Four Monastic Communities in Śākyaśrībhadra's Vinaya Tradition." In *Nepalica-Tibetica: Festgabe for Christoph Cüppers*, edited by Franz-Karl Ehrhard and Petra Maurer, vol. 1, 187–242. *Beiträge zur Zentralasienforschung* 28.1–2. Andiast: International Institute for Tibetan and Buddhist Studies GmbH.

———. 2017. *Vajradhara in Human Form: The Life and Times of Ngor chen Kun dga' bzang po*. Lumbini: Lumbini International Research Institute.

———. 2017. "The Dispute between mKhas grub rJe and Ngor chen: Its Representation and Role in Tibetan Life-Writing." In *Fifteenth Century Tibet: Cultural Blossoming and Political Unrest*, edited by Volker Caumanns and Marta Sernesi, 249–89. Lumbini: Lumbini International Research Institute.

Hou, Haoran. 2015. "Some Remarks on the Transmission of the Ascetic Discipline of the 'Single Mat' within the 'Bri gung Bka' brgyud pa Tradition." In *The Illuminating Mirror: Tibetan Studies in Honour of Per K. Sørensen on the Occasion of his 65th Birthday*, edited by Olaf Czaja and Guntram Hazod, 205–18. Contributions to Tibetan Studies 12. Wiesbaden: Dr. Ludwig Reichert Verlag.

Jackson, David P. 1989. *The 'Miscellaneous Series' of Tibetan Texts in the Bihar Research Society, Patna: A Handlist*. Tibetan and Indo-Tibetan Studies 2. Stuttgart: Franz Steiner Verlag Wiesbaden GmbH.

———. 2007. "Rong ston bKa' bcu pa: Notes on the Title and Travels of a Great Tibetan Scholastic." In *Pramāṇakīrtiḥ: Papers Dedicated to Ernst Steinkellner on the Occasion of His 70th Birthday*, edited by Birgit Kellner et al., 345–60. Vienna: Arbeitskreis für Tibetische und Buddhistische Studien, Universität Wien.

Jäschke, H. A. 1871. *Handwörterbuch der Tibetischen Sprache*. Gnadau: Universitätsbuchhandlung.

———. 1881. *A Tibetan-English Dictionary. With Special Reference to the Prevailing Dialects, to Which Is Added an Englisch-Tibetan Vocabulary*. London: The Secretary of State for India in Council.

Meisig, Marion. 1995. *König Śibi und die Taube: Wandlung und Wanderung eines Erzählstoffes von Indien nach China*. Studies in Oriental Religion 35. Wiesbaden: Harrassowitz Verlag.

Ohnuma, Reiko. 2007. *Head, Eyes, Flesh, and Blood: Giving Away the Body in Indian Buddhist Literature*. New York: Columbia University Press.

Sakaki, Ryōzaburō, ed. 1987 [1916]. *Honyaku myōgi taishū (Mahāvyutpatti)*. 2 vols. Tokyo: Kokusho Kankōkai.

Schmithausen, Lambert. 2000. "Essen, ohne zu töten: Zur Frage von Fleischverzehr und Vegetarismus im Buddhismus." In *Die Religionen und das Essen*, edited by Perry Schmidt-Leukel, 145–202. Diederichs Gelbe Reihe 163. Munich: Heinrich Hugendubel Verlag.

———. 2005. "Meat-Eating and Nature: Buddhist Perspectives." *Buddhism and Nature* (*Bukkyō to shizen*). Supplement to the *Bulletin of the Research Institute of Bukko University*, Kyoto: 183–201.

———. 2016. "My Scholarly Life: A Brief Sketch Presented at the International College for Postgraduate Buddhist Studies (Tokyo) on November 28, 2012." In *Lambert Schmithausen: Collected Papers*, vol. 1, *1963–1977*, edited by Florin Deleanu et al., xxi–xxxiii. Studia Philologica Buddhica, Monograph Series 34a. Tokyo: The International Institute for Buddhist Studies.

Storm, Mary. 2013. *Head and Heart: Valour and Self-Sacrifice in the Art of India*. London: Routledge.

Wangchuk, Dorji. "Rmig pa skam po." *Philologia Tibetica*, November 17, 2017. http://philologia-tibetica.blogspot.de/2017/11/blog-post.html.

Zwalf, W. 1996. *A Catalogue of the Gandhāra Sculpture in the British Museum*. 2 vols. London: British Museum Press.

4. Khedrup Jé on Meat in the Monastery

By Anna Wolcott Johnson

KHEDRUP JÉ GELEK PALSANG (1385–1438)[274] was a monk and scholar in fifteenth-century Central Tibet. Khedrup studied with several prominent scholars of his time, from both the Sakya tradition and the emerging Geluk (Ganden) tradition, including Bodong Choklé Namgyal (1375–1451), Rendawa Shönnu Lodrö (1349–1412), and most famously, Tsongkhapa (1357–1419). His position as one of two primary disciples of Tsongkhapa would be established by the sixteenth century when he begins to be referred to within the epithet "The three: noble father and his sons,"[275] in which "noble father" refers to Tsongkhapa and "sons" refers to Khedrup and Gyaltsap Jé Darma Rinchen (1364–1432). Tsongkhapa was a prolific scholar and exegete whose work formed the basis for the philosophical and doctrinal positions of the Geluk sect.

During his lifetime, Khedrup played a central role in elucidating and defending the philosophical positions that would put Tsongkhapa at odds with Sakya orthodoxy. Khedrup wrote extensive commentaries, gave tantric initiations, taught philosophy and doctrine, founded monasteries, and served as abbot to several of those monasteries. Most notably, in 1432 Khedrup became the third abbot of Ganden monastery (after Tsongkhapa and Gyaltsap) and founded the first monastic college there.

Khedrup was born in Western Tsang to a government administrator. He became a novice monk at age seven and was fully ordained at age twenty-one by the Sakya scholar Rendawa Shönnu Lodrö. He met Tsongkhapa at age twenty-three, became abbot of Ganden at forty-seven, and passed away at the age of fifty-three. He is known for his biting polemics and his role in debates that determined the separation of the Geluk as a distinct sect from the Sakya tradition in which Khedrup and Tsongkhapa were originally educated. One of his most notable opponents was the Sakya scholar Ngorchen

274. Tib: Mkhas grub Rje Dge legs dpal bzang.

275. Tib: *rje yab sras gsum.*

Kunga Sangpo (1382–1456), whom he attacked personally, disagreed with on doctrinal points, and competed with for patronage.[276] Relevant to the discussion here, Ngorchen instituted a monastery-wide ban on meat eating at Ngor based on the *Laṅkāvatāra Sūtra* and other Mahāyāna texts (Ngorchen's primary work on meat, *An Epistle Benefitting Students*, is discussed and translated in chapter 3 of this volume). As a personal opponent of Ngorchen and a monastery administrator himself, Khedrup's discussion and defense of meat eating here may be understood as a counter to Ngor's ban.

Can Monks Eat Meat?

The following text is excerpted from Khedrup's treatise *Polishing the Jewel of the Sage's Teachings: A Brief and Conclusive Presentation on the Three Vows.*[277] In this text, the first three chapters focus respectively on the three sets of vows taken by Tibetan Buddhists: the prātimokṣa vows that determine conduct of body and speech and increase in number from lay vows to full ordination; the bodhisattva vow, or aspiration to become a buddha in order to then liberate all beings from the cycle of existence; and the secret mantra vows, which delineate a tantric practitioner's relationship and commitment to the guru, consort, and deity. The fourth chapter discusses how all three of these vow sets can be held by one person simultaneously.[278] Khedrup discusses meat eating in chapter 1, on prātimokṣa, under the subheading "How to Protect the Vows after You Have Taken Them."

Khedrup's discussion engages two seemingly contradictory textual traditions and puts them into conversation with each other. The first textual tradition is the Vinaya corpus of the early Buddhist canon that provides the code of conduct for monks and nuns and institutional guidelines for the administration of monasteries, along with narratives of Shakyamuni Buddha and his disciples for whom the rules and regulations were originally laid down. In referencing this textual tradition, Khedrup quotes canonical texts from the Vinaya, such as the *Vinaya Uttaragrantha* and *Vinaya Vibhaṅga*,[279] but largely

276. For more on Khedrup's critique of Ngorchen, see Bentor, "Did mKhas Grub Rje Challenge the Authenticity of the Sa Skya Lam 'bras Tradition?"; and Heimbel, "The Dispute between mKhas Grub rJe and Ngor Chen."

277. Tib: *Sdom pa gsum gyi rnam par bzhag pa mdor bsdus te gtan la dbab pa'i rab tu byed pa thub bstan rin po che'i byi dor.*

278. For more on the Tibetan three-vow genre, see Sobisch, *Three-Vow Theories in Tibetan Buddhism*; Dudjom Rinpoche, *Perfect Conduct*; and Sakya Paṇḍita Kunga Gyaltshen, *A Clear Differentiation of the Three Codes.*

279. *Great Vinaya Text* (Tib: *'Dul ba gzhung dam pa*) and *Exposition of the Vinaya* (Tib: *'Dul*

relies on Guṇaprabha's seventh-century work, the *Vinayasūtra*,[280] along with Dharmamitra's twelfth-century commentary[281] on that text. The second textual source that Khedrup analyzes is the *Laṅkāvatāra Sūtra*,[282] a Mahāyāna sūtra that is set up as a dialogue between Śākyamuni Buddha and a bodhisattva named Mahāmati, in which the Buddha forbids his disciples to eat meat. Khedrup's main discussion of this text is within the context of Śāntideva's eighth-century citation of the same excerpt in his *Śikṣāsamuccaya*;[283] this is evident in that Khedrup omits the same verses that Śāntideva does and in that Khedrup's lengthy citation of the *Laṅkāvatāra Sūtra* includes the immediately succeeding portion of the *Śikṣāsamuccaya*, including Śāntideva's own words as well as an additional scriptural citation.

Khedrup retains the authority of both textual traditions, one firmly within the Mahāyāna and one that he would have considered Hīnayāna, or related to the śrāvakas, disciples of the Buddha who were not, or not yet, taught the bodhisattva path toward full buddhahood. Khedrup navigates these two textual and soteriological categories to produce a nuanced analysis of the potential moral charge of meat eating in various scenarios. Khedrup's text could easily be quoted selectively to both defend meat eating and to condemn it, and later Tibetans have certainly done so.[284] However, when taken as a whole, his discussion does not offer a simple yes or no to the question of whether meat eating is ultimately a moral fault.

Khedrup begins his discussion by firmly establishing that at no point in the Vinaya does the Buddha prohibit meat eating. He argues that it is not found in any of the 253 rules for fully ordained monks in the *Prātimokṣa Sūtra* nor in any of the seventeen chapters of the canonical *Vinayavastu*.[285] He quotes textual sources that indicate that the Buddha specified certain types of animals

ba rnam 'byed).

280. *Vinayasūtra* (Tib: *'Dul ba'i mdo rtsa ba*). Despite its title, this is not a sūtra spoken by the Buddha; the Sanskrit word "sūtra" in this context is used in its more general sense to mean aphorisms or notes. For more on this text, see the introduction to Karmapa Mikyö Dorjé's *Great Commentary on the Vinayasūtra* in chapter 6 of this volume.

281. *Commentary on the Vinayasūtra* (Tib: *'Dul ba'i mdo'i rgya cher 'grel pa*).

282. *Descent onto Laṅkā Sūtra* (Tib: *Lang kar gshegs pa'i mdo*). For a translation of the relevant portions of this text and its role in Tibetan debates on meat eating, see chapter 1 of this volume.

283. *Compendium of Training* (Tib: *Bslab pa kun las btus pa*). For a full translation, see Goodman, *The Training Anthology of Śāntideva*.

284. For an extended passage in which the nineteenth-century Shabkar depicts Khedrup as almost entirely opposed to meat eating, see Shabkar, *Food of Bodhisattvas*, 87–90, 105–6, 112, 117–18.

285. *Vinaya Chapters* (Tib: *'Dul ba'i gzhi*).

whose flesh monks are not allowed to eat and then concludes that if meat were altogether prohibited, there would have been no need for the Buddha to single out certain ones that were specifically restricted. He lays out the specific circumstances under which Śākyamuni Buddha allowed his monastic disciples to eat meat, grounded in the concept of "threefold purity." That is, if a monk or group of monks are given meat on alms rounds and any of them hear, see, or suspect that the animal was killed with the intention that those particular monks eat it, then the meat is considered impure and they are not allowed to eat it. If all three of these factors are absent—that is, that the monks have not seen, heard, or suspected that the meat is from an animal killed for their own benefit—then that meat is said to have threefold purity. Monks are allowed to consume meat with threefold purity because it ensures that they are not karmically implicated in the killing of an animal in any way. It also ensures that monks on alms rounds do not ask for meat and thereby run the risk of diminishing the Buddhist community in the eyes of the laity on whom they rely for patronage.

Khedrup then pursues more closely the connection between killing and eating meat in terms of karmic actions and results. These arguments summarize a position set forth in Bhāviveka's sixth-century text, *Madhyamakahṛdaya Kārikā*, and his autocommentary, the *Tarkajvālā*.[286] Bhāviveka argues against those he identifies as non-Buddhist opponents who criticize the Buddhist practice of meat eating and claim that if there were no meat eaters, there would be no killing, and therefore the karmic result of killing accrues equally to the meat eater. Khedrup, summarizing and elaborating on Bhāviveka's verses, argues that if that were the case, all kinds of absurd consequences would follow, including that anyone who wore pearl, leather, silk, or wool would accrue the same karmic result as the manufacturers of those goods who had to kill animals in order to produce them. Further, anyone with any connection to the act of killing, even the animal to be killed, would accrue the same result. It would, he argues, entail the absurd claim that someone would experience the result of an action they did not commit.[287] Khedrup returns to this line of reasoning later in his discussion when he claims that those who defend vegetarianism

286. *Verses on the Heart of Madhyamaka* (Tib: *Dbu ma'i snying po'i tshig le'ur byas pa*) and *Blaze of Reasoning* (Tib: *Dbu ma'i snying po'i 'grel pa rtog ge 'bar ba*). For more on these texts, see Eckel, *Bhāviveka and His Buddhist Opponents*; Hoonaert, "An Annotated Translation of Madhyamakahṛdayakārikā/Tarkajvālā V.69-84"; and Hyoung Seok Ham, "Buddhist Critiques of the Veda and Vedic Sacrifice."

287. For more on Bhāviveka's arguments, including a translation of some of the relevant passages, see Catherine Hardie's translation of Khenpo Tsultrim Lodrö's *Clear Mirror* in chapter 12 of this volume.

with the argument "If there were no meat eaters, there would be no killers" by citing the *Kālacakra Tantra* and its commentary, the *Vimalaprabhā*, do not realize that it is the position of an opponent, and not the authors' own. For Khedrup, a meat eater is only at fault and only accrues the karmic result of killing if he pays a butcher to slaughter a live animal so that he can eat its flesh for the purposes of his own enjoyment.

Khedrup's next line of reasoning focuses on the *Laṅkāvatāra Sūtra*. Khedrup first rejects that the text can be read to determine proper conduct for a monk. He asserts that, rather, it is intended for bodhisattvas, whom he describes in relatively exalted terms, as being of the nature of compassion, having completely pure bodies, being recognized by others to be bodhisattvas, and accepting such praise. The problems associated with meat eating are centered around the fault of acting with craving and desire, and not with meat itself. Khedrup argues that doing anything out of desire is considered to be a misdeed for a bodhisattva, so by extension eating meat out of desire would also be a fault. He lists specific circumstances in which refraining from meat can be used as a practice for beginner bodhisattvas. The purpose of abstaining is to counteract craving and the deterioration of one's compassion. However, he makes a point of saying that these faults do not always necessarily arise from meat eating. And if they do not arise, there is no fault in eating meat. Khedrup even suggests that in some cases, eating meat might increase a bodhisattva's compassion, in which case it is certainly acceptable.

While Khedrup makes a point to show that the Vinaya materials and the Mahāyāna literature should be understood within their own distinct contexts, he also shows several places where they overlap. One commonality is that both scriptures privilege the mental state or intention of the meat eater over the act itself and offer instructions on how a practitioner should position his mind in order to reverse craving and attachment to food. While Khedrup states early in the discussion that "the permission for meat eating in the Vinaya is very clear and appears many times," he qualifies this statement later on by saying, "We absolutely never say that there is permission in the Vinaya to eat meat while influenced by craving for its taste," followed by his frequently quoted line, "Not even in a dream would I say there is no fault in something like this." He supports the claim that the Vinaya is also concerned with attitude and intention by citing Guṇaprabha's explanation of ten conceptions that produce a sense of aversion to food in general. Some of these conceptions are mere facts about the food, including that it will become your phlegm and bile, and some are imaginative notions to ponder in order to produce a sense of revulsion, such as that flour looks like ground up bones and rice porridge looks like worms. Yet in the Vinaya context, and in some cases in the bodhisattva context, these conceptions are meant to eliminate craving for the food but not to prevent the practitioner from eating it. Khedrup's frequent qualification of meat eating with the phrases "with craving for its taste" and "for one's own benefit" focus his discussion on the internal mental state of the practitioner and not on the mere act of meat eating.

Further nuancing the moral weight of meat eating, Khedrup asserts that not only does the *Laṅkāvatāra Sūtra*'s restriction on meat not apply to all monks, it does not even apply to all bodhisattvas. Khedrup insists that not all bodhisattvas who eat meat produce the possible obstacles of increasing their craving, inhibiting their loving-kindness and compassion, or inhibiting their ability to practice mantra spells. In fact, Khedrup says that these are only possible results, and that to say that meat eating always produces them would be like making the absurd claim that wherever there are barley seeds there are always also barley sprouts. A reader might assume that the relationship between a bodhisattva's compassion and the act of meat eating would be that if a bodhisattva has loving-kindness and compassion, he would naturally abstain from meat eating out of his care for the animals. However, Khedrup never makes this argument. In fact, quite the opposite argument is made: rather than compassion causing vegetarianism, vegetarianism is used as a tool in order to increase compassion. The primary reason for a bodhisattva to abstain from meat is that it reinforces his own selfish craving and inhibits loving-kindness and compassion. If a bodhisattva lacks craving and has loving-kindness, there is no fault in his meat eating.

Further, Khedrup's work conspicuously lacks any substantial discussion connecting a bodhisattva's altruism to restraint from harming animals. In fact, Khedrup directly dismisses any arguments for vegetarianism based on harming animals by asserting that only the evil Devadatta, the Buddha's cousin and nemesis, used such a claim as a reason to refrain from meat eating, whereas the Buddha himself never mentioned it. The closest this text comes to considering the value of the life of an animal is in the injunction for bodhisattvas to imagine meat to be the flesh of their mother and father or their only child. However, as mentioned above, this injunction, as well as the warning that meat eaters cause animals to be frightened, serves as a way to eradicate feelings of desire and craving and is a practice to be done while eating meat but not necessarily to prevent one from doing so.

A reason for this absence of direct statements of concern for animals could be that Khedrup is here primarily concerned with scriptural analysis and how the Buddha's seemingly contradictory teachings should be understood to delineate specific behavioral guidelines for monks in monasteries and for bodhisattvas. He interprets both the Vinaya and Mahāyāna sūtra literature to privilege the mind training or internal mental state of the practitioner rather than the life and experience of the animal. When external circumstances are considered, the potential for the karmic result of killing as it accrues to the practitioner is of greater concern than the very fact of killing. That is, a monk's karmic proximity to the act of butchering is of more importance than the fact of the animal's loss of life.

Potential social consequences of meat eating are of central importance in both Vinaya and Mahāyāna literature, which underscore the importance of the laity's perceptions of the Buddhist monastic community. However, Khedrup only rarely shifts his focus away from scriptural analysis to address his own contemporaneous monastic culture. He does not, for example, acknowledge that the rules laid out in the Vinaya and the entire conceptual framework of the threefold purity rule pertain to an Indian cultural sphere in which monks went on alms rounds, begging for food from the laity from house to house. Khedrup does not once address the fact that Tibetan monks do not go on alms rounds and that rules regarding food might be reinterpreted accordingly. Khedrup provides only one brief, and contentious, mention of the monastic culture of his own time. He asserts that meat, alcohol, and garlic are all prohibited equally in the Vinaya and asks his reader why the former would be prohibited when it is clear that monks partake of the latter two publicly and without criticism.

Khedrup's analysis of meat eating is most directly summarized in the section I have subtitled "When Is Meat Faultless?" Here he offers high praises to bodhisattvas who choose not to eat meat in order to reduce their craving and increase their compassion, which he earlier asserted to be the basic intention of the *Laṅkāvatāra Sūtra*. He then outlines two contexts in which eating meat is permitted—one specific to bodhisattvas and one specific to monks. For a bodhisattva, it is acceptable to eat meat if it is done for the benefit of others, if it is to cure an illness, if it does not produce in him a feeling of craving that then serves as an obstacle to loving-kindness and compassion, if it, instead, serves as an antidote to craving and increases his loving-kindness, if it supports his body so he can engage in vast activities for beings, and if he eats the meat while imagining that it is the flesh of his only child and is medicine. A monk, on the other hand, is permitted to eat meat when it has the threefold purity, when it is not from one of ten types of restricted animals, such as insects or single-hooved animals like horses, and, similar to the bodhisattva, while giving rise to certain conceptions and attitudes that restrict the arising of his craving and attachment for the taste of meat. He praises these two instances of meat eating by saying, "There is supreme beauty in the path free from the two extremes," by which he means the two behavioral extremes of asceticism and indulgence.

About the Translation

Khedrup's work is structured as a series of responses to others' potential arguments and claims. He sometimes answers these rhetorical questions and claims directly and at other times frames his responses by informing his reader how to respond if confronted with such claims. While this is a rhetorical style, I chose to translate it as direct speech using quotation marks around both the opponent's words and Khedrup's response.

Further, it proved most challenging to capture Khedrup's emotive style, which can range from gentle coercion, to frustrated indignation, to pure insult. He accuses his opponents of being idiots, biased, and grasped by the demon of jealousy. His sarcasm, in particular, is often difficult to render into English. This text's dialogical style forces the reader to pay close attention to emphasis and tone in order to discern Khedrup's own opinions. As in any Tibetan polemical work, just because a certain reason for a claim is attacked and seen to be internally faulty does not mean that a reader can conclude that the claim itself is seen by the author to be incorrect. Another reader and another translator could understand Khedrup's priorities and emphases differently and arrive at different conclusions about his own opinions and perspectives. Khedrup poses no single answer to the question of whether meat eating is a moral fault; his entire discussion is a complex attempt to frame the question with layers of nuance.

I consulted several editions of this text both in computer input and blockprint. The text is included in *Compendium of Indispensibles: The Writings of the Noble Father and His Sons*, a collection of Tibetan works on vows by Tsongkhapa and two of his students, Khedrup and Gyaltshap, published in Lanzhou in 1999 by the Gansu Cultural Publishing House.[288] I checked this work against other versions found in Khedrup's *Collected Works*, primarily the Zhol[289] and Kumbum Jampaling editions.[290]

Lama Tenpa Gyaltsen answered many of my questions during work on the first draft of this translation. At the time of polishing a final draft, I was fortunate to be able consult Geshé Damdül Namgyal's unpublished translation.[291]

288. *Rje yab sras kyi gsung rtsom nyer mkho phyogs bsgrigs*, 253–554.

289. Khedrup Jé, *Sdom pa gsum gyi rnam par bzhag pa mdor bsdus* (1980–1982).

290. Khedrup Jé, *Sdom pa gsum gyi rnam par bzhag pa mdor bsdus* (n.d.).

291. Forthcoming in the composite volume *The Ethics of the Three Codes*, The Library of Tibetan

While he and I differ in terms of style and terminological choices, I find that our understanding of the text is substantially similar. Hyoung Seok Ham was an invaluable resource for understanding Khedrup's references to Bhāviveka. Christopher Emms helped with quotes from Guṇaprabha's *Vinayasūtra* and Dharmamitra's commentary, and in particular with figuring out the technical terms for types of animals and meats prohibited in the Vinaya. Finally, Christopher Stagg, a highly skilled translator and my dear friend, offered invaluable comments and suggestions on a final draft. I dedicate this translation to his memory.

Classics, vol. 12 (Somerville, MA: Wisdom Publications in association with the Institute of Tibetan Classics), as Khedrup Jé's *Dusting Off the Precious Teaching of the Buddha* (*Thub bstan rin po che'i byi dor*).

Polishing the Jewel of the Sage's Teachings

By Khedrup Jé Gelek Palsang

Translated by Anna Wolcott Johnson

Meat Eating in the Monastic Vows[292]

Now I will investigate the question, Is meat permitted or prohibited for monks?[293] Someone might say, "No monk should eat meat. Since there are meat eaters, there are those who kill in order to sell meat to them; if there were no meat eaters, there would be no killers. Therefore meat eating is an extreme misdeed and a fault is incurred equivalent to taking life." You should ask that person this: "If the Vinaya prohibits meat eating for monks, then does a fully ordained monk incur an infraction if he eats meat?" If not, then this contradicts the assertion that the Vinaya prohibits meat eating for monks. If he claims that an infraction does occur, then it would absurdly follow that there would be 254 rules.[294] Ask him whether that infraction is in the cate-

292. I have added topical subheadings throughout this text. These are not found in Khedrup's Tibetan but are inserted in order to help orient the reader.

293. I have chosen to translate the Tibetan, *rabjung* (*rab byung*; Skt: *pravrajyā*), as "monk," and the Tibetan, *gelong* (*dge slong*; Skt: *bhikṣu*), as "fully ordained monk." While the latter is specifically male, the former is gender neutral. I have chosen to translate both using male-gendered terms because it is assumed that Khedrup's text is addressed to a male audience, and he only ever references canonical works on monastic conduct for monks. This is not to say that the general ideas would not have applied to female novice and pre-novice nuns in Tibet.

294. Here Khedrup asserts that if refraining from meat eating were a vow, there would be 254 vows for a fully ordained monk instead of 253. These numbers vary across different *vinayas*. While the *Mūlasarvāstivāda Vinaya* lists 262 rules, Tibetans list 253, omitting the *aniyatas* and *adhikaraṇaśamathas*. There are 4 *pārājikas*, or "defeats," which entail automatic expulsion. There are 13 *saṃghāvaśeṣas*, "probationary offenses," which require an open confession of the misdeed followed by penance or probation as punishment. There are 2 *aniyatas*, "indeterminates," which involve a monk's conduct with a woman and must be determined by the community to be either a *pārājika*, a *saṃghāvaśeṣa*, or a *pāyattika*. There are 30 *naiḥsargikapāyattikas*, "forfeiture offenses," which pertain to a monk's robes, bowl, or other possessions and require that the monk forfeit the relevant item. There are 90 *pāyattikas* (alternately referred to as *pātayantika* and *pāyantika*), "transgressions to be confessed," which require only that a monk confess the misdeed to another monk. There are 4 *pratideśanas*, "disclosures," all of which pertain to food

gory of *pārājika*, *saṃghāvaśeṣa*, *naiḥsargikapāyattika*, *pāyattika*, *pratideśana*, or *śaikṣadharma*. If it is the first, then there would be 5 *pārājikas* instead of 4. If it is in the second category, there would be 14 *saṃghāvaśeṣas*. If it is the third, there would be 31 *naiḥsargikapāyattikas*. If it is the fourth, there would be 91 *pāyattikas*. If it is the fifth, there would be 5 *pratideśanas*. If it is the sixth, there would be 113 *śaikṣadharmas*.

If someone were to say, "It is an infraction included in the chapters," then respond, "Where in the seventeen chapters is it explained?[295] Was a rule made or not, such as: 'The Bhagavat taught in the Vinaya's modes of discipline that fully ordained monks should not eat meat.'?" If such a rule was not made, that would contradict the statement that an infraction would occur from breaking such a rule. If the rule was made, then please provide the rule's background story, including, for example, at what place, at what time, and for what person it was made. I have not seen such a rule in the four parts of the Vinaya scriptures or their commentaries.[296]

Someone might say, "There is no direct prohibition, but it is prohibited by association. That is, killing was directly taught to be unacceptable and meat eating is prohibited by association since, in general, there would be no meat if there were no killing." Then respond by saying, "Well then, the leather sole of

and which require confession to another monk in specifically prescribed words. There are 112 *śaikṣadharmas*, "training qualities," which are rules of etiquette pertaining to food, dress, teaching, and toileting, and require confession. There are 7 *adhikaraṇaśamathadharmas*, "rules for settling disputes," which detail how to resolve conflicts that arise within the monastic community. For more on these infractions, see Prebish, *Buddhist Monastic Discipline*; Clarke, "Vinayas," 60–61. See also the entries for each category in Buswell and Lopez, *The Princeton Dictionary of Buddhism*.

295. This refers to the seventeen chapters (*vastus*) included within the *Vinayavastu* of the *Mūlasarvāstivāda Vinaya*. Each are devoted to a different disciplinary or institutional topic. They are: Ordination (*Rab tu byung ba'i gzhi, Pravajyāvastu*), Confession (*Gso sbyong gzhi, Poṣadhavastu*), Ending of Retreat (*Dgag dbye'i gzhi, Pravāraṇavastu*), Rains Retreat (*Dbyar gyi gzhi, Varṣāvastu*), Leather (*Ko lpags kyi gzhi, Carmavastu*), Medicine (*Sman gyi gzhi, Bhaiṣajyavastu*), Clothing (*Gos gyi gzhi, Cīvaravastu*), Distribution of Clothing (*Sra brkyang gi gzhi, Kaṭhinavastu*), Procedural Disagreements of Koshambi (*Ko sham bi'i gzhi, Kośambakuvastu*), Formal Procedures (*Las kyi gzhi, Karmavastu*), Amending Downfalls of Pāṇḍulohitaka (*Dmar ser can gyi gzhi, Pāṇḍulohitakavastu*), The Individual (*Gang zag gi gzhi, Pudgalavastu*), Demotion (*Spo ba'i gzhi, Pārivāsikavastu*), Suspension of Confession (*Gso sbyong gzhag pa'i gzhi, Poṣadhasthāpanavastu*), Dwellings (*Gnas lam gyi gzhi, Śayanāsanavastu*), Disputes (*Rtsod pa'i gzhi, Adhikaraṇavastu*), and Schisms in the Community (*Dge 'dun dbyen pa'i gzhi, Saṃghabedavastu*). See also Clarke, "Vinayas," 61–63.

296. Each rule established in the Vinaya is rooted in a story that narrates the particular situation in which the Buddha was compelled to create the rule based on the behavior of his disciples. These are called *nidāna* (*gleng gzhi*), translated here as "background story."

a shoe and the leg of a boot would then also be unacceptable, since, in general, they also would not exist if there were no killing. If you accept that these are also unacceptable, it disproves the foundation for the claim that they are acceptable." There are a great many other consequences similar to that.

The permission for meat eating in the Vinaya is very clear and appears many times. Guṇaprabha's *Vinayasūtra* says:

> Do not eat a tiger's kill.[297] Do not eat elephant, horse, or snake. Also, do not eat single-hooved animals, foxes, monkeys, woodpeckers, crows, vultures, water birds, dogs, hawks, owls, any other birds that eat human flesh, white birds, bats, lizards, earthworms, or insects.[298]

Dharmamitra's *Vinayasūtratīkā* says, "This applies to the statement, 'If you know that it is one of those meats, do not eat it.'"[299] Since the Buddha specified meats that are not acceptable to eat, such as the single-hooved, you know that it is acceptable to eat meats other than those. If you assert that all meat is prohibited, then it would have been sufficient for him to say, "It is prohibited in general." What need would there have been to prohibit each specific type of meat by name?

Furthermore, the *Vinayasūtra* says, "When meat is served by the laity, you should ask, 'Does this come from a prohibited animal or not?'"[300] The commentary says:

> When a benefactor makes a donation of meat to the monks, the eater should ask him, "Is this not a meat that is prohibited, a meat that is not acceptable to be eaten by a fully ordained monk, such as human flesh, a tiger's kill, horse, snake, single-hooved animals, and so on?" If it is not from among those, he should eat it. Those words are just an example; there is no fault if someone asks, "What meat is this?" without listing the others.[301]

297. This refers to a story in the *Vinayakṣudrakavastu* in which a group of monks bring the leftover remains of a tiger's kill from a forest back to the Buddhist community in Jetavana Grove. The tiger smells the carcass of his prey and follows the monks back to the monastery. See *Vinayakṣudrakavastu*, 393a5.

298. Guṇaprabha, *Vinayasūtra*, 77b1.

299. Dharmamitra, *Vinayasūtraṭīkā*, 223a6.

300. Guṇaprabha, *Vinayasūtra*, 77b2.

301. Dharmamitra, *Vinayasūtraṭīkā*, 223b4.

The statement in the *Vinayasūtra*, "If there are many, it is the first," means that if there are many eaters, the first one should ask. If there is a group of fully ordained monks, the elder of the community should ask. The statement, "If he forgets, by his junior," applies to the line from Dharmamitra's commentary, "When meat is served, ask." This means that if the first monk in line does not ask the question or forgets, then the monk junior to him should ask. When many monks are lined up and a donation of meat is given to everyone, if the first fully ordained monk forgets to ask, "Is this not human flesh, single-hooved, and so on?" then the second one should ask, and so on. It is directly stated that the meat should be eaten if it is other than those prohibited animals. The *Vinayasūtra* says:

> Roots, stems, leaves, flowers, fruit, cooked food, rice porridge, warm dough, porridge, meat, fried dough, milk, yogurt, butter, fish, and dried meat are not unacceptable.[302]

And the commentary clearly says:

> It is not unacceptable for fully ordained monks to eat roots, and so on; they are simply acceptable.[303]

And:

> Although these are mentioned in the context of their use as medicine by the sick, they are acceptable for others for mere sustenance.[304]

Although some unknowingly say, "In the Vinaya, the permission for meat is based on its being medicine for the sick," this very quote from the commentary specifies and negates that.

302. Guṇaprabha, *Vinayasūtra*, 79b7. The *Prātimokṣa Sūtra,* which lists vow infractions for fully ordained monks, and the *Vinaya Vibhaṅga,* one of the four parts of the Vinaya, both include the general category of "meat" in this list. They read: "fish, meat, and dried meat." Guṇaprabha and Dharmamitra both omit the word "meat."

303. Dharmamitra, *Vinayasūtraṭīkā*, 236a3.

304. Dharmamitra, *Vinayasūtraṭīkā*, 236a5.

Threefold Purity

Meat with threefold purity is allowed, whereas meat that does not have threefold purity is generally prohibited. The three aspects of purity are as follows. One, the eater himself directly hears that the meat is aimed at and intended for the benefit of that person who is the eater. Two, the eater hears from another person that the meat was intended for his benefit. Three, having examined the situation, the eater suspects, "Is it possible that an animal was killed for me?" If any one of these three is present, then the meat is not pure; if these three are all absent, then the meat has threefold purity. These points are also stated in the *Vinayasūtra* as follows, "If you know that the meat is intended for you, do not eat it."[305] Regarding this, the commentary clearly says:

> When a benefactor intends meat for the benefit of that eater, and that eater knows by means of seeing, hearing, or suspecting, he must not eat it. Therefore, monks are permitted to eat acceptable meat from a butcher or market that was obtained by a faithful lay person.[306]

"Acceptable meat" is meat that is devoid of the three explained above—seeing, hearing, and suspecting. Some fools say that meat that has been killed is necessarily meat that does not have threefold purity. This is complete nonsense stated by those who have not seen these words in Dharmamitra's commentary. If all meat from a killed animal were unacceptable, then think, how could you acquire acceptable meat from a market or butcher? Does this mean that a good butcher sells meat without killing an animal?

Someone might think, "Statements like this refer to sick people." If that were the case, it would then be reasonable to say, "by the sick," and it would be unacceptable to say, in general, "by monks." Even unacceptable intended meat is permitted for the sick. Dharmamitra's commentary directly says:

> There is no fault in unwholesome behavior that produces the benefit of curing an illness. For example, transgressions of rules such as, 'If you know that the meat is intended for you, do not eat it,' are exempted in the case of curing illness."[307]

305. Guṇaprabha, *Vinayasūtra*, 77a7.

306. Dharmamitra, *Vinayasūtraṭīkā*, 223b4.

307. Guṇaprabha, *Vinayasūtra*, 77a7; *Vinayasūtraṭīkā*, 209a5. The phrase "transgression of rules" (*pratikṣepaṇasāvadya, bcas pa'i kha na ma tho ba*) is a technical term meaning an act that

Therefore whoever says that the classification of meat—that is, if it has the threefold purity, it is acceptable, and if it does not, it is not acceptable—applies to the sick, they have not properly seen a mere word of the great scriptures, let alone understood their meaning. This is nothing but the confusion of a fool created by a wall of lies told by those who are in the clutches of the demon of needless jealousy.

Instances of Meat Eating in the Vinaya

Further, the *Vinaya Vibhaṅga*[308] includes a story about a householder in Rajagṛha who once offered food to the community of monks and found that he quickly became rich. Another householder thought, "That is a good way to get rich. I will do that, too." He boiled a soup of meat and ghee, and his guard invited the monks inside. The householder then filled the bowls of the monks who had come for alms with the meat soup. Another story states that the Buddha along with 1,250 monks were invited for a noon meal and the entire community enjoyed delicacies such as fish and pastry. Stories like these are told many times.

In the context of the infractions regarding asking for delicacies, the *Vinayasūtra* says, "Foods like milk, yogurt, butter, fish, and dried meat are delicacies."[309] The commentary says, "In the line 'Foods like milk, yogurt, butter, fish, and dried meat are delicacies,' the word 'like' has the meaning of the word 'type,'" and that identifies these foods as delicacies.[310] Then, in order to teach that it is an infraction to eat such delicacies when receiving alms from a householder who is not a relative, but it is not an infraction to eat such a food when receiving alms from a relative, Dharmamitra quotes the "Upāli Paripṛcchā" chapter of the *Vinaya Uttaragrantha*, which says:

> Upāli asked, "Venerable One, is there a case in which an infraction is not incurred when a healthy fully ordained monk acquires for

constitutes a misdeed because it breaks a rule or vow. This is opposed to a "natural transgression" (*prakṛtisāvadya, rang bzhin gyi kha na ma tho ba*), which is an act that is morally negative by its own nature, apart from whether or not there is a formal rule against it.

308. *Exposition of the Vinaya* (Tib: *'Dul ba rnam 'byed*). This is one of the four main divisions of the *Mūlasarvāstivāda Vinaya*, in addition to the *Vinaya Chapters* (*Vinayavastu, 'Dul ba'i gzhi*), *Vinaya Chapter on Miscellanea* (*Vinayakṣudrakavastu, 'Dul ba phran tshegs kyi gzhi*), and *Great Vinaya Text* (*Vinayottaragrantha, 'Dul ba gzhung dam pa*). I was not able to locate either of these stories in the *Vinaya Vibhaṅga*.

309. Guṇaprabha, *Vinayasūtra*, 226b3.

310. Dharmamitra, *Vinayasūtraṭīkā*, 326a2.

> himself, and then chews or eats, delicacies from a householder?" The Buddha answered, "There is. If he eats it having acquired it from a relative, there is no infraction."[311]

There are many other statements like this.

The Relationship between Killing Animals and Eating Meat

Bhāviveka's *Tarkajvālā* and *Madhyamakahṛdaya Kārikā*[312] state that the reasoning, "There would be no killers if there were no eaters," was made by non-Buddhist ascetics in order to indicate that meat eating is unacceptable.[313] If that reasoning were valid, then it would follow that if no one wore ornaments of pearls, for example, then no one would kill oysters that contain pearls in order to make jewelry. Those who wear pearl ornaments would then incur a fault equivalent to the one associated with meat. Also, if no one wore clothes, no one would remove skins, shear wool, and boil worms to make clothes. Therefore, anyone who wears wool, leather, or silk clothing would incur a fault equivalent to killing. If no one ate, there would be no farmers to produce food. So anyone who eats food would equally incur the fault of farmers who exploit slaves, cows, and others, forcing them into oppressive labor. They would also equally incur the fault of killing countless beings, since farmers drench with water countless animals who live on dry land, place on dry land countless animals that live in water, lift above ground animals who live underground, and bury underground animals who live above ground. If no one made purchases using measures of volume or weight, merchants would not deceive anyone with false measures of volume or weight. The buyer would incur equally the fault of the merchant who lied to him about the volume or weight of his purchase.

311. Dharmamitra, *Vinayasūtraṭīkā*, 326a4. This quote appears with slightly different terminology in: "Questions of Upāli" (*Upālipariprcchā, U pa li zhus pa*), in *Great Vinaya Text* (*Vinayottaragrantha, 'Dul ba gzhung dam pa*).

312. *Blaze of Reasoning* (Tib: *Dbu ma'i snying po'i 'grel pa rtog ge 'bar ba*) and *Verses on the Heart of Madhyamaka* (Tib: *Dbu ma'i snying po'i tshig le'ur byas pa*). For more on these texts, see Eckel, *Bhāviveka and His Buddhist Opponents*; Hoonaert, "An Annotated Translation of Madhyamakahṛdayakārikā/Tarkajvālā V.69–84"; and Watanabe, "A Translation of the *Madhyamakahṛdayakārikā* with the *Tarkajvālā* III. 137–46." For Bhāviveka's verses on meat eating, see Kawasaki, "Discrepancies in the Sanskrit and Tibetan Texts of Bhavya's *Madhyamaka-hṛdaya-Tarkajvālā*."

313. Bhāviveka, *Tarkajvālā*, 310a4; Bhāviveka, *Madhyamakahṛdayakārikā*, 38b1. Bhāviveka's opponents here are ascetic Brahmins whose main scriptural source is the epic *The Mahābhārata*.

To say, "There would be no killers if there were no eaters" is like saying that there would be no killers if there were nothing to be killed. There are many refutations to this, such as that it would then follow that both the killer and the sheep to be killed would incur the fault of killing sheep, without any difference between them. Bhāviveka teaches this in his *Madhyamakahṛdaya* in summarized verse such as, "Deceit in measure and weight . . . ," and explains it extensively in his commentary, *Tarkajvālā*.[314]

It is explained in the sūtras that when Devadatta created dissent in the community and added five trainings to his own group, he said, "The monk Gautama eats meat. We should not eat meat. If you ask why, it is because it causes harm to animals." However, there is no such prohibition by the Buddha in any of the Vinaya's modes of discipline.

Understanding the Laṅkāvatāra Sūtra

Śāntideva's *Śikṣāsamuccaya*[315] says:

> So indeed, you should protect the body with medicine at all times, but do not do so with meat or fish because they are prohibited in the *Laṅkāvatāra Sūtra*, which says, "The bodhisattva endowed with the nature of compassion does not eat meat at all."

The *Laṅkāvatāra Sūtra* also says:

> Whether of confused animals or one's own friends,
> all meat comes from semen and blood.
> Yogis do not eat meat,
> as consuming it causes other beings to fear.
>
> All meats, garlic, onions,
> all types of alcohol,
> wild onions, and white garlic—
> yogis abandon all of these.
>
> They relinquish rubbing with oil,
> and since small beings live in the

314. For more on Bhāviveka's arguments, including a translation of some of the relevant passages, see Catherine Hardie's translation of Khenpo Tsultrim Lodrö's *Clear Mirror* in chapter 12 of this volume.

315. *Compendium of Training* (Tib: *Slab pa kun las btus pa*).

open spaces inside mattresses,
yogis do not sleep on high beds.[316]

People pay money for meat,
causing animals to be killed for profit.
Both the killer and buyer own this sinful karma
and will boil in the Crying Hell.

All those who go against the Buddha's words,
and eat meat with an ignoble mind,
destroy their lives, both now and in the future.
They defile the conduct found in the Śākya's teachings.

Those people endowed with sinful karma
go to hells that are thoroughly terrifying.
Those who eat meat will be boiled
in the Crying Hell.

Meat that has threefold purity,
free of being considered, requested,
or coerced, does not exist.
So do not eat meat.

Yogis do not eat meat.
This is my teaching,
and that of all other buddhas.

Beings that eat each other
take birth as carnivores.
Or they become madmen,
foul smelling with low reputations.
Again and again they are born
as outcasts, dog eaters, and dyers.
Or they are born as ḍākinīs,[317]
or among flesh-eating demons.

316. The version of the *Laṅkāvatāra Sūtra* translated in chapter 1 of this volume includes two verses here that do not appear in Khedrup's work. Khedrup has extracted this *Laṇkāvatāra Sūtra* quote directly from Śāntideva's *Śikṣāsamuccaya* in which these two verses were originally omitted.

317. Both the Degé and Lhasa Tengyur editions of the *Laṅkāvatāra Sūtra* have the word "tramen" (*phra men*), or animal-headed demon here, while Śāntideva's *Śikṣāsamuccaya* and Khedrup's text both have "khandro" (*mkha' 'gro*), or *ḍākinī*, a cannibalistic female deity or female hell guardian. *Dākinīs* are exalted in tantric literature as deities who impart secret teachings to tantric practitioners.

After this present human life,
they come back as demons or cats.

This is why I teach that meat is utterly base,
in sūtras such as the *Hastikakṣya*,
Mahāmegha, *Parinirvāṇa*, and *Aṅgulimālīya*,
as well as this *Laṅkāvatāra Sūtra*.

Buddhas, bodhisattvas, and śrāvakas
all decry it as base.
This food, whose essence is turbulent,
always leads to birth as a madman.

Relinquishing meat, on the other hand,
leads to birth as a brahman or yogi,
or one endowed with wisdom and wealth.

Meat that you have seen, heard, or suspected:
all of it is utterly base.
But those born in meat-eating families
do not understand, despite their cleverness.
Desire creates an obstacle to liberation.
In just this way, meat and alcohol
are also obstacles to liberation.

In future times,
ignorant supporters of meat eating
will say that meat is sinless and suitable,
and will claim that I said the same.

Thinking of food as no different than medicine,
and of meat as the flesh of their own children,
yogis eat moderately,
without engaging in what is vile.[318]

I, who abide in love,
always and in every way reproach
associating with lions,
tigers, foxes, and the like.

318. In all editions of Khedrup's text I was able to consult, this line reads as it appears here, with the word "nganpa" (*ngan pa*), which I have translated as "vile." In both the Degé and Lhasa editions of the *Laṅkāvatāra Sūtra*, the line appears with the word "ranpa" (*ran pa*), meaning "appropriate or moderate." The *Laṅkāvatāra Sūtra* in this volume is translated based on the latter reading.

> Since it is in opposition to achieving liberation,
> and since it causes others to fear,
> do not eat meat.
> This is the noble banner of victory.

The *Jñānavatī* chapter of the *Samādhirāja Sūtra*[319] says that there is no fault for any meat eater who does so for the purpose of accomplishing great benefit:

> When this monk dies, even the word *samādhi*
> will completely disappear in Jambudvipa.
> Because he was cured, he obtained the samādhis.[320]

This is a case of effort made entirely toward great compassion. Eating meat has no fault because the intention does not lack loving-kindness.[321]

If you ask, "How should these passages be explained?" we would then ask you, "What is their purpose? Do these quotes from the *Śikśāsamuccaya* and the *Laṅkāvatāra Sūtra* teach behavior intended only for monks or not? If not, then think about whether these quotes make the claim that eating meat is unacceptable only for monks." Someone might respond, "It does teach behavior for monks." We would then ask, "Given that these statements in the *Śikṣāsamuccaya* are made in the context of describing the completely pure bodies of only bodhisattvas, then is it the case that if someone is a bodhisattva, he is necessarily a monk? Is a monk necessarily a bodhisattva? If not, then

319. *The King of Samādhi Sūtra* (Tib: *Ting nge 'dzin gyi rgyal po'i mdo*).

320. *Samādhirāja Sūtra*, 196a3–196a4. This refers to a story told by the Buddha as an example of a bodhisattva who is willing to give away the flesh of his own body to another bodhisattva if his health requires it. In the story, a very accomplished monk named Bhūtamati, who is a close friend and teacher to a king named Jñānabala, develops a boil on his leg. The king and the king's sixteen-year-old daughter both have the same prophetic dream in which a god declares that the monk will only live if he eats the cooked flesh of a human with pure mind, speech, and conduct and the boil is smeared with its blood. The king's daughter, named Jñānavatī, cuts off a piece of her own thigh, smears the monk's boil with her blood, and feeds him her flesh. The monk is cured and continues to teach the Dharma to many people. See Nalinākṣa Dutt, *Gilgit Manuscripts*, vol. 2, part 3, iv–v, and 481–82.

321. The *Śikṣāsamuccaya* quote ends here and includes both the quote from the *Laṅkāvatāra Sūtra* and from the *Jñānavatī* chapter of the *Samādhirāja Sūtra* (which Śāntideva refers to as the *Candrapradīpa Sūtra*). For a complete translation of Śāntideva's *Śikṣāsamuccaya*, see Goodman, *The Training Anthology of Śāntideva*.

think about whether these statements have any relevance to the claim that it is not acceptable for a monk to eat meat."

In general, how could it be said that the *Śikśāsamuccaya* establishes the disciplinary training of the prātimokṣa and proper conduct for only monks? These texts extensively explain the disciplinary training of bodhisattvas and the way they train in proper conduct. They are completely irrelevant for determining whether or not it is acceptable for monks to eat meat. Therefore this is a case of desperately citing a text that teaches that it is unacceptable for a Mahāyāna bodhisattva to eat meat in order to claim that it is unacceptable for all monks to eat meat. It is in no way different than citing the tantra that says, "Correctly hold the vajra, bell, and mudra" in order to claim that all monks should hold the bell and vajra.

The words "a bodhisattva who is of the nature of compassion" are stated at the beginning of that *Śikṣāsamuccaya* quote for that reason. This phrase thus indicates in general that it is unacceptable for bodhisattvas to eat meat. It is thus unacceptable for both householder and monastic bodhisattvas to eat meat. This applies to Mahāyāna monks, novices, kings, ministers, mayors, and village women who consider themselves bodhisattvas and accept it when others praise them and call them a bodhisattva. They should not eat meat if they are eliminating or wish to eliminate the obstacle that arises when they eat meat—that is, the production of intense craving for meat for their own benefit and the resultant deterioration of compassion. However, where does it say that eating meat is unacceptable for monks who merely accept devotion to the Mahāyāna but are not considered bodhisattvas and monks who do not know anything about accepting devotion to the Mahāyāna?

Some who have vowed to be a bodhisattva and generated Mahāyāna bodhicitta a hundred times do not even consider it unacceptable to intentionally and ceaselessly kill or cause the deaths of thousands of beings, so what is the point of talking about whether or not they eat meat? To say that someone who doesn't fulfill the qualifications for being considered a bodhisattva should not eat meat just because he is a monk is clearly the work of Īśvara.[322] This is what you should say.

322. What I have translated as "clearly the work of Īśvara" (*dbang phyug gi spyod pa*) is translated as "clearly [frivolous like that of a petulant] god" in Cabezon and Dargyay, *Freedom from Extremes*, 169, note 289. There, Gorampa uses the phrase to attack the views of Tsongkhapa, Khedrup's primary teacher. Cabezon points out that the phrase also appears in Dharmakīrti's *Pramāṇavarttika*. The phrase seems to originate in the ninth chapter of Bhāviveka's *Madhyamakahṛdayakārikā*, where he criticizes those who hold the view that a single god created the world. In verse 111, he points out that since the state of the world is ridiculous, it is absurd to assume that it was created by a perfect god: "The virtuous have short lives, the vile have long

Meat Eating and Karma

There are all kinds of other grounds for confusion regarding those words of the *Laṅkāvatāra Sūtra*, so I will briefly explain their meaning. In the above quote, the *Laṅkāvatāra Sūtra* says:

> People pay money for meat,
> causing animals to be killed for profit.
> Both the killer and buyer own this sinful karma.

This refers to a situation in which a person agrees to pay someone for meat and buys it so that he can eat it. In that case, the merchant, who wants to make a profit, kills an animal and brings him the meat because the buyer agreed to pay for it. When the buyer pays the money knowing that the animal was killed because he agreed to pay for it, both of them incur a fault equivalent to killing. However, there could be a situation in which a merchant who wants to make a profit kills an animal and then takes the meat to the market and sells it, and the one purchasing it does not think, "It's fine if this animal was killed because I agreed to pay for it." It is a denial of karma and its results to claim that in that situation, the buyer incurs the same fault as the one who killed the animal. The karma of someone who intentionally and without error kills someone is karma that is certain to ripen as experience and is known as karma that is done and accumulated.[323] Many sūtras and treatises teach that an act of killing can be done without a complete motivation. For example, someone might mistake a man for a scarecrow, throw a stone at him, hit him in the head, and kill him. This is known as karma that is done but not accumulated, and it is undetermined whether it will ripen as experience.[324] If it were the case that you would experience the ripening of killing a sentient being by merely hav-

lives, the generous are weak. [According to you,] this [ridiculous situation] is clearly the work of Īśvara." (Thanks to Hyoung Seok Ham for his unpublished translation from the Sanskrit and explanation through private correspondence.) Based on Bhāviveka's usage, I understand Khedrup's use of the phrase to be sarcastic in this same way. He points out an opponent's ridiculous position and retorts sarcastically, "Oh sure. That sounds like it was created by a perfect god." See Bhāviveka, *Madhyamakahṛdayakārikā*, 37a3, and *Tarkajvālā*, 302b4.

323. This differentiation between karma that is done (*kṛta*) and accumulated (*upacita*) is discussed in Vasubandhu's *Abhidharmakośabhāṣya*, chapter 4, verse 120. For an English translation of the complete text, see Pruden, *Abhidharmakośabhāṣyam of Vasubandhu*.

324. Determined (*niyata*) actions, which will definitely produce an experience as their effect, and undetermined (*aniyata*) actions, which may or may not, are explained in Vasubandhu's *Abhidharmakośbhāṣya*, chapter 4, verse 50.

ing bought meat in a market and eaten it, even though you were not compelled by the motivation to kill and have not committed the act of killing in any way at all, then it would absurdly follow that you could experience the ripening of an action you did not commit.

Clarifying Threefold Purity

In the above quote, the *Laṅkāvatāra Sūtra* says:

> All those who go against the Buddha's words,
> and eat meat with an ignoble mind,
> destroy their lives, both now and in the future,
> and defile the conduct found in the Śākya's teachings.

This passage refers to transgressing the Buddha's words, "Bodhisattvas should not eat meat." Eating unacceptable meat with the negative intention of disregarding the words of the Teacher defiles Mahāyāna conduct. This means that you should not consider that all teachings are the teachings of the śrāvakas nor that "conduct" refers to prātimokṣa conduct.

In the above quote, the *Laṅkāvatāra Sūtra* says:

> Meat that has threefold purity,
> free of being considered, requested,
> or coerced, does not exist.
> So do not eat meat.

The meaning is as follows. If someone were to ask, "Isn't it faultless to eat meat with threefold purity?" then say, "Bodhisattvas should not eat meat because for beginner bodhisattvas whose minds are influenced by a very strong habit of craving for meat, it is rare that there would exist meat with the threefold purity. That is, meat which you have not considered or thought, 'I will eat this,' out of craving and attachment to the taste of meat for your own benefit; which you have not directly requested from someone else due to craving for meat for your own benefit; or which, with that motivation, you have not coerced someone close to you to acquire for you." The three aspects stated here—not considered, not requested, and not coerced—are not the same as those known as "threefold purity." Rather, the three aspects that are known as "threefold purity" are identified later in the text.[325]

325. The three purities listed in the *Laṅkāvatāra Sūtra*'s discussion of threefold purity

The phrasing "śrāvakas decry" in the line "buddhas, bodhisattvas, and śrāvakas all decry it as base," does not mean "decried within the śrāvakas' own modes of discipline." Rather, it means that to relinquish compassion after having adopted bodhicitta, which is to regard all sentient beings like your only child, and to experience enjoyment through craving meat that has been killed so that you can eat it is denounced by everyone—buddhas, bodhisattvas, śrāvakas, and so on. Why must it be that if the decriers are śrāvakas, then the object that is decried pertains to the śrāvakas? The line "meat that you have seen, heard, or suspected: all of it is utterly base" identifies meat that does not have threefold purity. Since the three qualities are to see, hear, or suspect that meat has been killed for you, this is not different from what is taught in the Vinaya.

Further, when an animal is killed so that, for example, Devadatta can eat it, and Devadatta sees, hears, or suspects that it was killed for him, then this serves as eating meat with the threefold impurity.[326] This is like the statement in Dharmamitra's commentary on the *Vinayasūtra* in which he specifies the particular eater by saying that it is the eater who sees, hears, or suspects that the benefactor intended the meat for the benefit of that same eater. To say that something intended for the benefit of any eater at all would also be intended for a particular eater—for example, a monk named Devadatta[327]—and that therefore killed meat must necessarily be intended meat is the meaningless speech of idiots. If that were the case, you would have to accept many incredibly ridiculous things, like, for example, that anything donated to a community of monks would necessarily be donated to the monks of the Central Land of India. If that were the case, then when benefactors dedicate homages and offerings to the community of monks in Tibet, and when the community of monks in Tibet use them, they would actually be enjoying offerings that were intended for the community of monks of the Central Land of India.

In the above quote, the *Laṅkāvatāra Sūtra* says:

> In future times,
> ignorant supporters of meat eating
> will say that meat is sinless and suitable,
> and will claim that I say the same.

(considered, requested, and coerced) differ from the list given in the Vinaya, which Khedrup has already discussed (seen, heard, and suspected). Khedrup notes this difference here.

326. Here, the name Devadatta is used as an example of any monk, much like an "average Joe" in English.

327. This is discussed in Dharmamitra, *Vinayasūtraṭīkā*, 235b2.

Many say that this quote criticizes the great master, Guṇaprabha, and the author of the great commentary, Dharmamitra, who both said, "The Vinaya teaches that meat with threefold purity is allowed," as well as whoever said, "Śrāvakas may eat meat with threefold purity. Not to eat it is Devadatta's conduct."[328] However, the purpose of that quote is to criticize future monks who enjoy meat due to their own craving while claiming to be Mahāyāna practitioners. Even though the statements are in the context of the Mahāyāna, they reference the permission given in the Vinaya to say, "Since meat with threefold purity is permitted in the Vinaya, it is permissible for all monks to eat it." It is taught that an afflictive downfall occurs each time a bodhisattva enjoys any food, clothing, or shelter based on craving for his own benefit. So what need is there to speak of an infraction occurring when you enjoy meat while craving it for your own benefit and in opposition to great compassion?

The Three Stages of Restriction

However, the prohibition of meat for a bodhisattva is general. If you are unable to engage in vast activities for the benefit of the teachings and sentient beings without eating meat, but are able to persevere in that activity when you eat it, then since it restores health in your body, there is no fault. This was taught very clearly in the quotation above from the *Jñānavatī* chapter of the *Samādhirāja Sūtra* that was cited in the *Śikṣāsamuccaya*. Furthermore, the *Śikṣāsamuccaya* says:

> The Vinaya states that eating meat with threefold purity is not an obstacle to be relinquished. This permission eradicates the manifest pride of those who view themselves as pure because they have relinquished meat. It is also for the sake of those who are fortunate but cannot engage in the teachings due to attachment. The *Laṅkāvatāra Sūtra* also teaches this: "When I set forth this or that teaching, I created the modes of discipline in gradual stages, like the rungs of a ladder. I laid down a rule concerning threefold purity and prohibited meat that was prepared specifically for the eater.

328. This statement was made by Sakya Paṇḍita. See Sakya Paṇḍita Kunga Gyaltshen, *A Clear Differentiation of the Three Codes*, 66. Here the name Devadatta is used to mean the Buddha's cousin, disciple, and arch rival who attempted to start his own community of monks by giving them five rules not found in the Buddha's teaching, including the prohibition of meat. For more details on this passage, see the introduction to and translation of Gorampa's commentary on this verse in chapter 5 of this volume.

> Then I prohibited even meat from animals who died from the ten types of natural death."[329]

Some say, "The basic intention for permitting meat in the Vinaya is that it is for those who are unable to engage in the teachings because they are attached to meat. Therefore the permission to eat meat in the Vinaya is interpretable, and it is not appropriate to take it literally." This is nonsense for two reasons. First, if the Buddha taught that it is unacceptable to take literally the trainings of proscription, prescription, and permission of any of the three sets of vows, then those vows could not comprise the rules of what to adopt and reject. Even if the rules were known, you would doubt whether it is appropriate to understand them literally. You could not engage in what to adopt and reject in a straightforward manner according to the trainings as they were set forth. Therefore it is not possible that any of the rules of trainings of any of the three sets of vows are interpretable and not appropriate to be taken literally. Second, if the permission for meat given by the Buddha in the Vinaya scriptures were interpretable, then authoritative figures, such as Guṇaprabha and the author of the great commentary, Dharmamitra, would have explained in their commentaries on the scripture's meaning that it is interpretable and not to be taken literally, but they explained the words just as they were.

Therefore those words of the *Śikṣāsamuccaya* say that meat is permitted in the Vinaya and that permission is for a certain purpose. How could it be taught both for the purpose of permitting meat and at the same time taught as a topic that is open for interpretation? It takes great courage to comment on the meaning of the sūtras without even knowing the difference between a topic for interpretation and a definite purpose. If a rule can be taken as interpretable because the text says "restricted on the basis of a disciple such as this" and "restricted for a purpose such as this," then all of the 253 restrictions would be interpretable. None of the rules could be taken literally because each and every one of them say "restricted for a disciple such as this" and "restricted for a purpose such as this."

329. Śāntideva, *Śikṣāsamuccaya*, 76b2. There are several variations of this quote across Tibetan and Sanskrit manuscripts of the *Laṅkāvatāra Sūtra*. Here, Khedrup directly quotes Śāntideva, whose version of this line differs from the *Laṅkāvatāra Sūtra*'s Tibetan translations in both Degé and Lhasa editions of the canon, and hence in the English translation included in this volume. Jñānavajra's commentary on the *Laṅkāvatāra Sūtra* lists the ten types of natural death as divided into five outer and five inner conditions adverse to life. The five outer conditions are death from another living being or from one of the four elements—earth, air, fire, water. The five inner conditions are diseases of wind, bile, phlegm, and humors, and the natural end of a lifespan. See Jñānavajra, *Tathāgatahṛdayālaṃkāra*, 264b4.

The *Laṅkāvatāra Sūtra* says, "When I spoke this or that teaching, I arranged the modes of discipline in gradual stages, like the rungs of a ladder." The meaning of this line was explained by previous teachers as follows. These are the three rules. There are two stages set forth in the Vinaya. First, a rule is laid down that prohibits human meat and the meat of single-hooved animals, and so on. Second, the training is set forth that meat with threefold purity is permitted. Then, third, there is the general Mahāyāna training for bodhisattvas that prohibits all kinds of meat, including what has died naturally. Previous teachers have explained this. The prohibition of the ten types of meat from natural death is taught in the Mahāyāna, and the Vinaya permits meat from a killed animal that has the threefold purity. Thus there is no Hīnayāna or Mahāyāna training that allows eating meat from an animal that died a natural death but not meat from an animal that was killed and has threefold purity.

Consider what is taught in the *Laṅkāvatāra Sūtra*, as quoted above, which says, "all meats, garlic, onions; all types of alcohol," and "desire creates an obstacle to liberation. In just this way, meat and alcohol are also obstacles to liberation." It is clear that all three—meat, alcohol, and garlic—are prohibited without any difference. So why mention only meat and not alcohol and garlic? How many monks use alcohol and garlic without restraint? And this is not considered unacceptable even when it happens publicly. Ask yourself if this is not the mind being affected uncontrollably by the demon of intolerable jealousy.

The *Śikṣāsamuccaya* says:

> As for medicine that cures sickness, rely on the conduct of śrāvaka disciples for your own benefit and in order to remain in pure conduct. It is taught, "you can sell even the begging bowl or robes to protect the body," so what need is there to speak of the body of a bodhisattva that is the cause for completely protecting limitless beings?[330]

Therefore meat is permitted for all bodhisattvas for the purpose of health.

Reversing Craving and Other Antidotes

In the *Laṅkāvatāra Sūtra*, the bodhisattva Mahāmati supplicates the Bhagavat to teach on this topic:

> Then the great bodhisattva Mahāmati offered some verses and supplicated the Buddha, saying, "Bhagavān, Tathāgata, Arhat, Perfect

330. Śāntideva, *Śikṣāsamuccaya*, 76b4.

> Buddha, please explain how to view the faults of meat. Explain how I and other great bodhisattvas of the present and future can remove the desire for the taste of meat felt by those who are infused with a tendency toward eating the flesh of beings. Using what means can we eliminate their attachment to the taste of beings' flesh? Explain how, turning to the taste of Dharma, they may regard all beings as their own children, achieving a state of loving-kindness toward all of them. Explain how, having done this, they will train in the stages of the bodhisattva path and swiftly come to perfect, unsurpassed buddhahood. If not this, explain how, having rested at the level of śrāvakas and pratyekabuddhas, they will then attain the unsurpassed level of a buddha.[331]

It is very clear that the Bhagavat responded to that request in the *Laṅkāvatāra Sūtra* by teaching the extensive faults of meat eating. The following is a summary of the main points of the meaning of the entire teaching that is an extensive answer to Mahāmati's request.

Strong craving for meat in this life arises because the mind is affected by intense habitual patterns of meat eating. This obstructs the arising of a bodhisattva's great compassion and loving-kindness practice. Therefore these statements are primarily for beginners on the Mahāyāna path and anyone engaging in loving-kindness practice who must endeavor to eliminate their craving through mental engagement in the antidote. What antidotes should you mentally engage? The antidote to the desire that comes from being attached to beings is to conceive of them as ugly. Or conceive of yourself as sick, food as medicine, and all composite phenomena as adverse. Like that, you must eliminate craving for meat by becoming familiar with its faults and conceiving of it as adverse.

The way to conceive of what is adverse and unsuitable is as follows. Take such things as meat and blood, as well as rice, barley, milk, butter, and so on as examples. As soon as meat appears in front of you, if you conceive of it as food that is pleasing, pure, and very tasty, then your intense craving for it will expand and it will not be possible to stop it. Therefore, before you eat it, think that it is the uncleanliness that has arisen from its parents' semen and blood, and think that it is unsuitable. Think: "These beings have been my father and mother from beginningless time and should be seen as like my only child. Therefore it is unacceptable to crave for and eat the flesh of those who are like my children." For that reason, the *Laṅkāvatāra Sūtra* says:

331. *Laṅkāvatāra Sūtra*, 244b5.

> This food is unpleasant and unsuitable: it is food for the unwise. How could I permit my disciples to eat flesh and blood? Mahāmati, I say that eating the food of noble beings brings much virtue and gets rid of nonvirtue. Sages of the past delighted in foods like rice, barley, wheat, various large and small beans, butter, oil, honey, sugar, molasses, and sugarcane. These are delicacies and you should understand that I have permitted them. Mahāmati, in the future benighted beings will speculate about the Vinaya. Proposing many subtle distinctions, they will conclude that meat is acceptable food. But in truth this is because they are predisposed to eating meat and are attached to its taste. Mahāmati, I teach this for the sake of those great bodhisattvas who do the work of the buddhas of the past, who cultivate virtue, who have faith, and who are without conceptions. They are the children of Śākyamuni's lineage, my human sons and daughters who are not attached to body, life, or enjoyments. Unattached to sense pleasures, they are not greedy for tasty food. Endowed with compassion, they aspire to be like me. They cherish all beings, as if they were their only child. I teach this for their sake.[332]

The statement "this food is unpleasant and unsuitable: it is food for the unwise" is meant to teach a beginner bodhisattva how to train his mind. It does not contradict the Vinaya, which says, "milk, yogurt, butter, fish, and dried meat are delicacies . . ." It does not imply that these foods are unacceptable because eating them incurs a fault according to the Vinaya. Statements like that in the Vinaya do not state that monks view these foods as delicacies. Rather, lay householders find them delicious and supreme and strongly consider them to be delicacies. If a monk receives from a lay householder who is not a relative food that the householder highly values, there will be obstacles, such as the monk appearing greedy and unsatisfied and the householder losing faith. Therefore you incur the infraction of begging for delicacies when you receive and eat food from householders who are not relatives while knowing that those lay householders highly value that food. But there is no fault with respect to begging and food if you receive this type of food from a relative.

This is very different from the teaching in the *Laṅkāvatāra Sūtra* on the necessity of eliminating craving for meat and eliminating a bodhisattva's own conception of certain foods as superior delicacies. The way to cultivate conceptions of meat as adverse and unacceptable and to mentally engage the faults of craving for meat is as follows. Reflect on those extensive statements that have

332. *Laṅkāvatāra Sūtra*, 248a6.

been made about hunting wild game, fishing, and butchering. Reflect on what has been said about buying meat when agreeing to pay for it causes an animal to be killed and selling meat after killing animals for that purpose. Think about people like King Sengé Bangzang, who had such a habit and craving for meat that he killed and ate humans, and King Kangtra, and others.[333] Reflect on the fact that eating meat causes you to smell bad and to frighten many animals. Reflect on the fact that it is an obstacle to practicing many types of mantra spells, and that it obstructs the arising of great loving-kindness and great compassion. Since those faults arise from a craving for meat, they are the result of the fault of craving for meat. Some might assert that those faults necessarily arise whenever someone craves meat. But then you would have to also accept that smoke or sprouts must necessarily arise whenever there is fire or barley seeds, since smoke and barley sprouts are the results of fire and barley seeds. This is a fool's idea of liberation.

The *Laṅkāvatāra Sūtra* says:

> Mahāmati, in the future there will be stupid people who are ordained in my tradition, who call themselves "children of the Śākya," and who bear aloft the saffron victory banner, but whose minds are spoiled by wrong views. Their ego-clinging will be vast, and they will lust for the taste of meat. Speculating on subtle distinctions in the Vinaya rules, they will find all kinds of justifications for eating meat. They will spread these justifications to others, so that people ridicule me, saying I am not pure. They will examine the histories of the doctrine and will say, "In the relevant discourses, it is clear that the Buddha allowed the consumption of meat. Far from being unsuitable, it is a delicacy." They will even say, "The Tathagatha ate meat." But, Mahāmati, I have never permitted eating meat in any of my teachings. I have never said that it is suitable to consider it a delicacy.[334]

This means that no Hīnayāna or Mahāyāna sūtra grants permission to eat meat out of craving for the taste of meat. Even though it is considered a del-

333. The *Lāṅkāvatāra Sūtra* recounts the story of a king who impregnated a lioness, who bore a child that had a strong craving for meat. The child was known as Kangtra, or Spotted Feet, because he was half human and half lion. This child then became king but was so obsessed with eating meat that his own children were born as meat-eating demons. *Lāṅkāvatārasūtra*, 249a7.

334. *Laṅkāvatāra Sūtra*, 250a6.

icacy, it is not acceptable to eat meat with craving for the taste of meat. The *Laṅkāvatāra Sūtra* says:

> Mahāmati, I have forbidden eating any type of meat to all my sons and daughters who aspire to the Dharma and who follow any of the vehicles. This includes those who dwell in charnel grounds, those who abide in love, those who dwell in forests, yogis who have accomplished yogic feats, and those who think of all beings as their own children.[335]

Therefore we absolutely never say that there is permission in the Vinaya to eat meat while influenced by craving for its taste. Not even in a dream would I say there is no fault in something like that. However, it is acceptable to eat meat if it is for the benefit of others, or if a bodhisattva who diligently strives toward virtue eats meat for the specific purpose of healing his body. It is acceptable as an antidote to thoughts that are contrary to great compassion and as an antidote to the arising of craving. It is acceptable if he eats it while imagining that it is the same as the flesh of his only child, or that it is medicine to heal the body. This is what was said in the *Laṅkāvatāra Sūtra*, "Thinking of food as no different than medicine, and of meat as the flesh of their own children."[336]

The Vinaya also taught that it is unacceptable to eat meat or any food, like steamed rice and so on, because of a craving for its taste, and that it is necessary to conceive of such food as medicine. The *Vinayasūtra* says, "Conceive of yourself as sick and food as medicine,"[337] and the commentary says, "You should eat while conceiving of hunger and thirst as a sickness; you are a sick person when you are hungry or thirsty. Food is medicine because it sustains your life."[338] The *Vinayasūtra* teaches that you should eat after having closely considered the ten conceptions that cause us to feel averse to food. It says, "Consider food to be adverse by means of origin, similarity, becoming, enemies, concordance with its cause, its aspect of dependence, seeking, reliance on other, sickness, and individual considerations."[339]

335. *Laṅkāvatāra Sūtra*, 250b6.

336. *Laṅkāvatāra Sūtra*, 248a5.

337. Guṇaprabha, *Vinayasūtra*, 80a6.

338. Dharmamitra, *Vinayasūtraṭīkā*, 237b6.

339. In his autocommentary to the *Vinayasūtra*, Guṇaprabha explains these as ten things to think about when trying to eliminate attachment to food. "Origin" means that you should imagine that the food comes from filth and feces. "Similarity" means that you should imagine something similar to whatever you are eating but repugnant—for example, that rice porridge

The intention of the *Laṅkāvatāra Sūtra* is to completely prohibit the act of seeking out meat because of a craving for its taste and eating it with desire for its taste, regardless of what kind of meat it is, regardless of whether it has the threefold purity, and regardless of whether it came from an animal that was killed. It says:

> Just so, Mahāmati, I do not permit anyone to eat meat. It is not permitted and will not become permitted. Mahāmati, I declare that the consumption of meat is unsuitable for any monk.[340]

But how could it be taught that the Vinaya does not even permit meat that has threefold purity, that is eaten not because of a craving for its taste, and that is eaten with the conception that it is medicine to heal the body? It is extremely idiotic to say that having the desire to pursue eating meat with threefold purity is to have a craving for the taste. This is because while the desire to pursue and aspiration are mental factors with a definite object, since craving for the taste is desire, which is one of the mental factors that are the six primary afflictions, it is a different class of mental factor. This is also because, regarding desire, it was taught hundreds of times in the scriptures and sūtras that those who are free from desire still wish to seek out food, drink, medicine, clothes, and so on. This includes śrāvakas, pratyekabuddhas, arhats, and those who, based on a human body, have attained the mind of meditative stability that is the cause for the first level of meditative concentration (*dhyāna*) and beyond. The *Laṅkāvatāra Sūtra* also says:

is similar to worms and that flour is similar to ground up bones. "Becoming" means that you should imagine that after you eat, the food will become your phlegm, bile, and blood. "Enemies" means that you should imagine that the food is a cause for creating hostility between people and will cause fighting between mothers and children. "Concordance with its cause" means that you should imagine that the food is concordant, or the same as, whatever caused it, including very disgusting things like feces and urine. "Aspect of dependence" means that you should think about food in terms of dependent origination and imagine that the food depends on the farm and other things, and based on those, many other things come about, from craving to sickness. "Seeking" means that you should think about the intense labor involved in acquiring food. "Reliance on other" means that you should imagine that even if you go through the intense labor to plant, for example, barley seeds, you will get no crop if you do not have things like wind. In this way, you are always reliant on other things in order to acquire food. "Sickness" means that you should think about how all kinds of diseases, like infections, come about from bad digestion. "Individual considerations" includes four thoughts: first, that food is burned by the body's fire; second, that it becomes urine and feces; third, that worms eat it; and fourth, that it nourishes the body. Guṇaprabha, *Vinayasūtra*, 80a6, and Guṇaprabha, *Vinayasūtravṛttyabhid hānasvavyākhyāna*, 171b2.

340. *Laṅkāvatāra Sūtra*, 251a3.

> Mahāmati, foolish people whose past karmic defilement drives them to ridicule me by saying that even the Tathāgata ate meat will endure meaningless suffering for a long time, devoid of joy. Mahāmati, my noble śrāvakas do not eat ordinary food, so what need is there to speak of unsuitable foods like meat and blood? Mahāmati, my śrāvakas, pratyekabuddhas, and bodhisattvas all eat the food of Dharma, not worldly food. What need is there to speak of what the Tathāgata eats? Mahāmati, tathāgatas possess the body of Dharma and are sustained by the food of Dharma. They do not have a worldly body and do not sustain themselves with any type of worldly food. They have abandoned all inclination to seek after mundane existence and the affairs of the world, and do not have any inclination toward disturbing emotions. Their mind and insight have been completely liberated. They are all-knowing and all-seeing. They see all beings as the same as their only child and possess great compassion.[341]

To explain this well, you must refer to Asaṅga's *Abhidharmasamuccaya*,[342] which teaches that "worldly" means "afflicted."[343] Thus, to say that the Buddha has relinquished all latent tendencies of craving and seeking out worldly things is to say that the Buddha does not eat in a worldly way, out of craving for taste. It is utter nonsense to claim that it means that the Buddha does not appear to eat at all, not even in order to train the community of disciples. The text says, "eat the food of Dharma, not worldly food" in order to indicate that noble śrāvakas, pratyekabuddhas, and bodhisattvas do not eat food through craving for taste. Otherwise, the statement that they "do not eat ordinary food"[344] would mean that they do not even eat things like rice and butter. If that were the case, it would contradict the statement made just above, that they do eat foods such as rice.

341. *Laṅkāvatāra Sūtra*, 251a4.

342. *Compendium of Abhidharma* (Tib: *Chos mngon btus pa*).

343. Asanga, *Abhidharmasamuccaya*, 47b2. Asaṅga explains the word "worldly" (*zang zing, āmiṣa*) as a type of sensation that entails attachment to one's body (*zang zing dang bcas pa gang zhe na / lus la sred pa dang srungs par ldan pa*). For a complete translation of this text, see Walpola and Boin-Webb, *Abhidharmasamuccaya: The Compendium of the Higher Teaching (Philosophy) by Asaṅga*.

344. *Laṅkāvatāra Sūtra*, 251a6.

When Is Eating Meat Faultless?

It is a thing of great, supreme amazement when someone who has generated Mahāyāna bodhicitta becomes aware that when he eats meat, his great compassion declines, his mental strength deteriorates, and he craves the taste of meat for his own benefit. And in order to eliminate all of those obstacles, that bodhisattva does not eat any meat at all, regardless of whether it has threefold purity and whether it was from an animal that was killed or died naturally. However, there are some bodhisattvas for whom eating meat does not induce those obstacles in their minds. They eat meat for the purpose of sustaining their bodies in order to support acting with intense effort for the benefit of others while maintaining the conception that it is unsuitable, that it is the flesh of their child, and so on. Also, a monk who holds the prātimokṣa vows might eat meat that has the threefold purity, meaning that he has not seen, heard, or suspected that an animal was killed for him, and that is not a restricted type of meat, such as from a single-hooved animal, but is from an animal that was killed. He relies on recollection and awareness to ensure that the craving for the taste of the meat does not arise. He eats meat according to what is permitted in the Vinaya, conceiving of food as medicine and holding in his mind the ten recollections. There is no transgression whatsoever in either of these cases. Thus for intelligent ones who are not dependent on others whose minds are agitated by the demon of bias, there is supreme beauty in the path free from the two extremes.

The *Laṅkāvatāra Sūtra* also says that you should not eat meat because it is an obstacle that causes the teachings to be denigrated. If monks are seen eating meat in certain times and places, some might say that Buddhist practitioners are inferior to non-Buddhist naked ascetics and others who do not eat meat. This could cause them to lose faith in the teachings in general. However, this was not said regarding a specific instance in which some group denigrated another out of jealousy.

Meat in the Kālacakra Tantra

The *Vimalaprabhā*,[345] a commentary on the *Kālacakra Tantra*, says:

> The Tathāgata permitted yogis to eat food that is not eaten or sold by ordinary people in any country, the five meats of cow, dog, and

345. *Stainless Light* (Tib: *Dri ma med pa'i 'od*).

> so on,[346] animals who died because of their own actions, who died from bad actions in a fight or because of their own mistakes during a robbery, and so on. The Tathāgata did not allow them to eat meat endowed with certain characteristics—for example, it could not be purchased with money, the animal could not have been killed in a ritual for ancestors or as a sacrifice, and so on.[347]

The *Kālacakra* root tantra says:

> It is a transgression to desirously buy and eat the meat of harmless animals that were killed by evil ones who are difficult to tame, and who sell meat for the purpose of gods, their own fear, ancestors, or to accomplish their wishes. It is not a transgression to eat meat if it has fallen into your bowl without you having asked for it. It is best if many people eat the meat of one animal. One person should not eat the meat of many animals.[348]

Here, "meat endowed with certain characteristics" refers to meat from a killed animal having characteristics such as that the meat was purchased with one's own money and the animal was then killed so that the buyer could eat it, that it was killed as an animal sacrifice, and so on. The statement "it is a transgression to desirously buy and eat the meat of harmless animals" shows that it is a transgression to desirously purchase and eat meat from an animal that you know was killed in order for it to be sold to you. The statement "if it has fallen into your bowl without you having asked for it" indicates that it is not a transgression to eat meat that you have not asked for, that was not intended and killed for you, and that was offered to you by a benefactor. Thus this passage does not differ from our own assertions because it teaches that meat with threefold purity is faultless.

However, some people idiotically misunderstand the statement in the *Vimalaprabhā* "if there were no eaters, there would be no killers," because it was only stated in order to indicate an opponent's view.[349] That text says:

346. The text says, "goku, etc." The term "goku" here is short for *go ku da ha na*, an acronym for the five meats permitted in tantra literature in real, imagined, or figurative forms. These are cow (*go*), dog (*kukkura*), horse (*damya*), elephant (*hasti*), and human (*nara*), as explained in Sanderson, "The Śaiva Age: The Rise and Dominance of Śaivism during the Early Medieval Period," 217n493.

347. Puṇḍarīka, *Vimalaprabhā*, 118a4.

348. Puṇḍarīka, *Vimalaprabhā*, 118a6.

349. Puṇḍarīka, *Vimalaprabhā*, 118a2.

> Someone might say, "Well, the Bhagavat says that yogis in the Mantrayāna eat meat, but meat eating always arises from killing. If there were no killing, some animals would have longer lives. If there were no eaters, there would be no killers. For that reason, both eaters and killers engage in the act of taking a life. In this context, the Tathāgata also determined that each day the mantrin must engage in the four samayas."[350]

This is undeniably the opponent's view.

Closing Remarks: Human Flesh and Raw Meat

Thus meat with threefold purity is allowed for monks. However, human meat is not allowed even for the sick. Human flesh is prohibited for everyone. Dharmamitra's commentary says, "A heavy fault is incurred if you eat human flesh for any purpose, whether or not it is medicine."[351]

A heavy fault is incurred for eating raw red meat unless it is to cure an illness. This is because Guṇaprabha's *Vinayasūtra* says, "If for such a purpose, there is a fault,"[352] and Dharmamitra's commentary says, "If raw meat is eaten for a purpose other than medicine, such as to practice Secret Mantra, a heavy fault is incurred that is included within the *saṃghavaśeṣa* category of infractions, because it causes you to become a demon and thereby creates a schism in the community."[353]

This amount of detail is enough.

350. Puṇḍarīka, *Vimalaprabhā*, 117b7. This statement, the opponent's objections to the Buddhist practice of meat eating, appears in the *Vimalaprabhā* just before the quote from the same text that Khedrup cites just above. That is, this quote, which begins "Someone might say," presents the question or objection that leads into the text's own answer, found in the quote that begins, "The Tathāgata permits yogis." Thus Khedrup is pointing out that some people cite the non-Buddhist's objection and confuse it with the Buddhist's answer.

351. Dharmamitra, *Vinayasūtraṭīkā*, 222b7.

352. Guṇaprabha, *Vinayasūtra*, 77a7.

353. Dharmamitra, *Vinayasūtraṭīkā*, 222b6. See above, note 294, for an explanation of the category of monastic infractions called *saṃghavaśeṣas*, or "probationary offenses."

Source Texts

Rje yab sras kyi gsung rtsom nyer mkho phyogs bsgrigs (*Compendium of Indispensibles: The Writings of the Noble Father and His Sons*), 253–554. 1999. Kan su'u mi rigs dge skrun khang. BDRC: W30084.

Khedrup Jé Gelek Palsang (Mkhas grub rje Dge legs dpal bzang). n.d. *Sdom pa gsum gyi rnam par bzhag pa mdor bsdus te gtan la dbab pa'i rab tu byed pa thub bstan rin po che'i byi dor* (*Polishing the Jewel of the Sage's Teachings: A Brief and Conclusive Presentation on the Three Vows*). In *Collected Works*, Kumbum edition, vol. 2 (*kha*), 549–826. Sku 'bum byams pa gling par khang. BDRC: W23693.

———. 1980–1982. *Sdom pa gsum gyi rnam par bzhag pa mdor bsdus te gtan la dbab pa'i rab tu byed pa thub bstan rin po che'i byi dor* (*Polishing the Jewel of the Sage's Teachings: A Brief and Conclusive Presentation on the Three Vows*). In *Collected Works*, Zhol par ma edition, vol. 8 (*nya*), 175–446. New Delhi: Mongolian Lama Guru Deva. BDRC: W384.

Kangyur Sources

Laṅkāvatāra Sūtra (*Lang kar gshegs pa'i mdo*). In *Lha sa bka' 'gyur*, vol. 51, 87a–307b. BDRC: W26071.

Samādhirājasūtra (*Ting nge 'dzin gyi rgyal po'i mdo*). In *Lha sa bka' 'gyur*, vol. 55, 1a–269b. BDRC: W26071.

Vinayakṣudrakavastu (*'Dul ba phran tshegs kyi gzhi*). In *Lha sa bka' 'gyur*, vols. 10–11. BDRC: W26071.

Vinayavastu (*'Dul ba'i gzhi*). In *Lha sa bka' 'gyur*, vols. 1–4. BDRC: W26071.

Vinayavibhaṅga (*'Dul ba rnam 'byed*). In *Lha sa bka' 'gyur*, vols. 5–8. BDRC: W26071.

Vinayottaragrantha (*'Dul ba gzhung dam pa*). In *Lha sa bka' 'gyur*, vol. 13. BDRC: W26071.

Tengyur Sources

Asaṅga (Thogs med). *Abhidharmasamuccaya* (*Chos mngon pa kun las btus pa*). In *Sde dge bstan 'gyur*, vol. 236, 1a–77b. Toh 4049. BDRC: W23703.

Bhāviveka (Legs ldan 'byed). *Madhyamakahṛdayakārikā* (*Dbu ma'i snying po'i tshig le'ur byas pa*). In *Sde dge bstan 'gyur*, vol. 200, 1a–40a. Toh 3855. BDRC: W23703.

———. *Tarkajvālā* (*Dbu ma'i snying po'i 'grel pa rtog ge 'bar ba*). In *Sde dge bstan 'gyur*, vol. 200, 40a–329b. Toh 3856. BDRC: W23703.

Dharmamitra (Chos kyi bshes gnyen). *Vinayasūtraṭīkā* (*'Dul ba'i mdo rtsa ba rgya cher 'grel pa*). In *Sde dge bstan 'gyur*, vol. 264, 1a–364b. Toh 4120. BDRC: W23703.

Guṇaprabha (Yon tan 'od). *Vinayasūtra* (*'Dul ba'i mdo rtsa ba*). In *Sde dge bstan 'gyur*, vol. 261, 1a–100b. Toh 4117. BDRC: W23703.

Guṇaprabha (Yon tan 'od). *Vinayasūtravṛttyabhidhānasvavyākhyāna* (*'Dul ba'i mdo'i 'grel pa mngon par brjod pa rang gi rnam par bshad pa*). In *Sde dge bstan 'gyur*, vol. 263, 1a–274b. Toh 4119. BDRC: W23703.

Jñānavajra (Ye shes rdo rje). *Āryalaṅkāvatāranāmamahāyānasūtravṛttitathāgatahṛdayā laṃkāra* (*'Phags pa lang kar gshegs pa zhes bya ba theg pa chen po'i mdo'i 'grel pa de bzhin gshegs pa'i snying po'i rgyan*). In *Sde dge bstan 'gyur*, vol. 122, 1a–310b. Toh 4019. BDRC: W23703.

Śāntideva (Zhi ba lha). *Śikṣāsamuccaya* (*Bslab pa kun las btus pa*). In *Sde dge bstan 'gyur*, vol. 213, 3b–194a. Toh 3940. BDRC: W23703.

Puṇḍarīka (Padma dkar po). *Vimalaprabhā* (*Dri ma med pa'i 'od*). In *Sde dge bstan 'gyur*, vols. 11, 107b–277a, and 12, 1a–297b. Toh 1347. BDRC: W23703.

Secondary Sources

Bentor, Yael. 2017. "Did mKhas Grub Rje Challenge the Authenticity of the Sa Skya Lam 'bras Tradition?" In Caumanns and Sernesi, *Fifteenth-Century Tibet*, 227–48.

Buswell, Robert E., and Donald S. Lopez. 2013. *The Princeton Dictionary of Buddhism*. Princeton, NJ: Princeton University Press.

Cabezon, Jose Ignacio, and Geshé Lobsang Dargyay. 2007. *Freedom from Extremes: Gorampa's "Distinguishing the Views" and the Polemics of Emptiness*. Boston: Wisdom Publications.

Caumanns, Volker, and Marta Sernesi, eds. 2017. *Fifteenth-Century Tibet: Cultural Blossoming and Political Unrest*. Lumbini: Lumbini International Research Institute.

Clarke, Shayne Neil. 2015. "Vinayas." In *Encyclopedia of Buddhism*, 60–63. Leiden: Brill.

Dudjom Rinpoche. 1999. *Perfect Conduct: Ascertaining the Three Vows*. Translated by Gyurme Samdrup and Sangye Khandro. Boston: Wisdom Publications.

Eckel, Malcolm David. 2008. *Bhāviveka and His Buddhist Opponents: Chapters 4 and 5 of Bhāviveka's Madhyamakahṛdayakārikaḥ with Tarkajvālā Commentary*. Harvard Oriental Series 70. Cambridge: Harvard University Press.

Goodman, Charles, trans. 2016. *The Training Anthology of Śāntideva: A Translation of the Śikṣā-Samuccaya*. Oxford: Oxford University Press.

Heimbel, Jörg. 2017. "The Dispute between mKhas Grub rJe and Ngor Chen: Its Representation and Role in Tibetan Life-Writing." In Caumanns and Sernesi, *Fifteenth-Century Tibet*, 249–90.

Hoonaert, Paul. 2002. "An Annotated Translation of Madhyamakahṛdayakārikā/Tarkajvālā vv.69–84." *Studies and Essays. Behavioral Sciences and Philosophy* 22: 113–37.

Hyoung Seok Ham. 2016. "Buddhist Critiques of the Veda and Vedic Sacrifice: A Study of Bhāviveka's Mīmāṃsā Chapter of the Madhyamakahṛdayakārikā and Tarkajvālā." PhD dissertation, University of Michigan.

Kawasaki, Shinjō. 1992. "Discrepancies in the Sanskrit and Tibetan Texts of Bhavya's Madhyamaka-hṛdaya-Tarkajvālā (the IXth and Xth Chapters)." In *Tibetan Studies: Proceedings of the 5th Seminar of the International Association for Tibetan Studies*, edited by Ihara Shōren and Yamaguchi Zuihō, 131–44. Narita: Naritasan Shinshoji.

Nalinākṣa Dutt. 1954. *Gilgit Manuscripts*, vol. 2, part 3. New Delhi: Sri Satguru Publications.

Prebish, Charles S. 1974. *Buddhist Monastic Discipline: The Sanskrit Prātimokṣa Sūtras of the Mahāsāṃghikas and Mūlasarvāstivādins*. University Park: The Pennsylvania State University.

Pruden, Leo M., trans. 1991. *Abhidharmakośabhāṣyam of Vasubandhu*. Fremont, CA: Asian Humanities Press.

Rahula, Walpola, and Sarah Boin-Webb, trans. *Abhidharmasamuccaya: The Compendium of the Higher Teaching (Philosophy) by Asaṅga*. Fremont, CA: Asian Humanities Press, 2001.

Sakya Paṇḍita Kunga Gyaltshen. 2002. A *Clear Differentiation of the Three Codes: Essential Differentiations among the Individual Liberation, Great Vehicle, and Tantric Systems*. Translated by Jared Douglas Rhoton. New York: State University of New York Press.

Sanderson, Alexis. 2009. "The Śaiva Age: The Rise and Dominance of Śaivism during the Early Medieval Period." In *Genesis and Development of Tantrism,* edited by Shingo Einoo, 41–350. Tokyo: Institute of Oriental Culture, University of Tokyo.

Shabkar [Tsogdruk Rangdrol]. 2004. *Food of Bodhisattvas: Buddhist Teachings on Abstaining from Meat*. Translated by Padmakara Translation Group. Boston: Shambhala.

Sobisch, Jan-Ulrich. 2002. *Three-Vow Theories in Tibetan Buddhism*. Weisbaden: Dr. Ludwig Reichert Verlag.

Watanabe, Chikafumi. 1998. "A Translation of the Madhyamaka-hṛdaya-Tarkajvālā III. 137–46." *Journal of the International Association of Buddhist Studies* 21: 125–56.

5. Gorampa on Meat in the Three Vows

By Geoffrey Barstow

GORAMPA SÖNAM SENGÉ (1429–1489)[354] is one of the most prominent scholars of the Sakya lineage of Tibetan Buddhism. He was born in the eastern Tibetan region of Kham and traveled to Central Tibet at the age of nineteen, where he embarked on an extended program of study at the major Sakya institutions. By middle age Gorampa had established himself as a preeminent scholar and teacher, particularly known for his texts elucidating the view of the Madhyamaka school of Buddhist philosophy. Many of these texts were overtly polemical, particularly criticizing the Madhyamaka position of Tsonkhapa Losang Drakpa, founder of the Geluk lineage. Because of this criticism, his works were banned by the Fifth Dalai Lama in the late seventeenth century. This proscription remained in effect (at least in the Central Tibetan regions under the Dalai Lama's firm control) until 1905, when the Thirteenth Dalai Lama allowed the publication of his works.

In addition to his philosophical concerns, Gorampa had a keen interest in Buddhist ethics and monastic practice. It is likely that some of this concern stemmed from (or was at least influenced by) his relationship with Ngorchen Künga Sangpo. Gorampa met Ngorchen in 1453 and studied with him until Ngorchen's death in 1456. Ngorchen himself was a monastic reformer who had left Sakya monastery in 1429 in order to found his own monastery, Ngor Ewam Chöden, at least in part out of concern for the lax ethical standards at Sakya. Among Ngorchen's many concerns was meat eating among monastics, as clearly evidenced in the translation of his *Epistle Benefitting Students* in chapter 3 of this volume.[355] Gorampa maintained his connection with Ngor's tradition throughout the rest of his life, even serving as the sixth abbot of Ngor Ewam Chöden for the four years preceding his death in 1489. It is impossible to say if Gorampa's concern with meat eating predated his relationship with Ngorchen, but his writings on this issue clearly reflect a strong

354. Tib: Go rams pa Bsod nams seng ge.

355. For more detail on this remarkable figure, see Heimbel, *Vajradhara in Human Form*.

influence by Ngorchen and the vegetarian tradition he established at Ngor Ewam Chöden.[356]

Gorampa's Commentary on Distinguishing the Three Vows

The text translated here is a short extract from Gorampa's longer commentary on Sakya Paṇḍita's (1182–1251) *Distinguishing the Three Vows*.[357] Likely written in the 1230s, Sakya Paṇḍita's work is one of the most important Tibetan works on three-vow[358] theory. These three sets of vows include the vows of individual liberation,[359] the bodhisattva vow,[360] and the tantric samayas,[361] and are undertaken by almost all Tibetans who have a serious interest in Buddhist practice. Each set of vows approaches ethical questions from a distinct perspective, and while these perspectives often align well with one another, sometimes they do not. In those instances, a practitioner needs to decide which perspective—which set of vows—they will follow. One basic example of such differing perspectives is murder. According to the vows of individual liberation, all killing is prohibited, full stop. In the bodhisattva vow, on the other hand, while murder is generally forbidden, there could be situations where the greater good requires an individual to murder someone. Three-vow literature emerged, in part, as a way to guide practitioners through situations in which the vows seem to contradict each other.

Meat eating is another such situation. As Sakya Paṇḍita notes, the vows of individual liberation—as contained in the Vinaya—generally allow monks to eat meat as long as it has threefold purity. But in the bodhisattva vow, Sakya Paṇḍita claims, meat is completely forbidden. Like most other Tibetan authors, Sakya Paṇḍita argues that when different sets of vows contradict each other, the higher vow supersedes the lower.[362] Sakya Paṇḍita therefore argues that meat is generally forbidden for someone who has taken the bodhisattva vow.

356. This brief biography is largely based on Kassor, "Gorampa [go Rams Pa]."

357. For a full translation of this work, see Sakya Paṇḍita Kunga Gyaltshen, *A Clear Differentiation of the Three Codes*.

358. Tib: *sdom gsum*.

359. Skt: *prātimokṣa*; Tib: *so sor thar pa'i sdom pa*.

360. Skt: *bodhisattva-saṃvara*; Tib: *byang sems sdom pa*.

361. Skt: *samaya*; Tib: *dam tshig*.

362. Different scholars came to different conclusions regarding how, exactly, the three vows related to one another. For a detailed study of different approaches to this issue, see Sobisch, *Three-Vow Theories in Tibetan Buddhism*.

Not surprisingly, Gorampa follows Sakya Paṇḍita's lead in his commentary. What he adds, as commentaries generally do, is a wealth of detail. And it is in that detail that his work emerges as an original, and highly critical, take on the question of meat eating. He opens with a brief account of what he terms "the śrāvaka perspective," referring to those Buddhists who undertake only the vows of individual liberation but not the bodhisattva vow or tantric samayas. This is followed by a similarly brief account of meat eating as it should be understood from the Mahāyāna perspective of someone who has taken the bodhisattva vow. Both of these passages are composed largely of quotes from other sources, with Gorampa's own voice limited to summaries and explanations.

Following these brief introductions, Gorampa embarks on an extended discussion of what he terms the "actual (Tib: *dngos*) teachings of the Vinaya." In this section, he focuses on what, exactly, is connoted by the rule of threefold purity. As discussed in the introduction to this volume, several different understandings of what the "three" in "threefold purity" refers to have been current at different points in Tibetan history. Gorampa proceeds to examine and reject several of these, especially the enumeration found in the *Laṅkāvatāra Sūtra*. In the end, Gorampa adopts a canonical position, arguing that threefold purity refers to meat that you have not "seen, heard, or suspected was prepared for you." Having clarified this point, Gorampa then turns his attention to the troubling question of why the Buddha allowed meat with threefold purity to be eaten at all. Here he draws extensively on quotations from a variety of canonical sūtras and compositions by Indian masters to argue that this rule was only formulated in order to make entry into the Buddhist fold easier for beginners who are strongly attached to meat. "My own view," he concludes, "is that the Vinaya allows beginners to eat meat while they gradually practice the foundational discipline. Later, having perfected this foundational discipline and having studied the *Laṅkāvatāra Sūtra* and *Mahāparinirvāna Sūtra*, meat is forbidden, even to śrāvakas."

Finally, Gorampa turns his attention to distinguishing what is allowed and not allowed in the Mahāyāna and Hīnayāna Vehicles. In doing this, he looks specifically at Sakya Paṇḍita's root verses, which note that for śrāvakas and other Hīnayāna practitioners, flatly refusing meat "would be the conduct of Devadatta." Devadatta is, of course, the Buddha's wayward cousin, who tried repeatedly to kill the Buddha and who, when that didn't work, sought to undermine the Buddha's teachings by creating a rival order based on strict ascetic practices. Clearly, Devadatta is not a hero, but what, Gorampa asks, is the specific "conduct of Devadatta"? Again, Gorampa sets out to correct misperceptions, noting that some people claim that Devadatta's method is to seek liberation solely through strict vegetarianism. This cannot be true, he points out, as Devadatta himself enumerates more practices than mere vegetarianism. Further, Gorampa notes that Devadatta's method is not limited to the Hīnayāna, and that Mahāyāna practitioners can fall into this trap as well. Unfortunately, Gorampa's discussion ends abruptly at this point, leaving readers somewhat uncertain about what Devadatta's conduct is and why that distinction is important. My own sense is that Gorampa is suggesting that Devadatta's conduct is characterized by a broad austerity beyond mere vegetarianism. As such, in both the Hīnayāna and Mahāyāna contexts, practicing vegetarianism in and of itself is not the conduct of Devadatta and is not, therefore, an extreme austerity contrary to Buddhist values.

Overall, Gorampa's discussion in these pages provides a subtle and nuanced take on both the rule of threefold purity and the question of Devadatta's conduct. Unsurprisingly, he draws on the ideas taught by his teacher Ngorchen Künga Sangpo, citing this master's *Epistle* by name. But Gorampa's text is not simply a repetition of his esteemed teacher's work; rather, it breaks new ground on two of the most important questions in Tibetan debates over vegetarianism.

About the Translation

I have relied primarily on the edition of Gorampa's *Commentary* found in the fifteen-volume edition of his collected works published recently by Dzongsar Monastery in Kham. I was first introduced to the text by a Sakya monk near Nangchen in Tibet. I am withholding his name in order to preserve his anonymity, but nevertheless wish to extend my thanks.

This is a dense and difficult text (a fact reflected in my dense and perhaps obtuse translation). It contains several apparent misspellings, and some passages contain words that simply do not make sense in context. Further, many of the quotations differ significantly from the corresponding passages found in the actual source texts themselves. Throughout, I have done my best to render Gorampa's work in comprehensible English. Sometimes this has resulted in minor clarifications added to the text [in brackets] or extended footnotes. I want to thank Yangsi Rinpoché of Maitripa University and Khenpo Jorden of the International Buddhist Academy for their help clarifying some of these difficult passages. Despite my best efforts, I am certain that errors and mistranslations remain, and I wish to apologize in advance for these mistakes.

The Commentary on Distinguishing the Three Vows

By Gorampa Sönam Sengé

Translated by Geoffrey Barstow

> Śrāvakas may eat meat that has threefold purity.
> To refuse would be the conduct of Devadatta.
> In the Mahāyāna, meat is forbidden.
> Eating meat, it is taught, causes rebirth in the lower realms.
> —Sakya Paṇḍita, *Distinguishing the Three Vows*[363]

Third is an explanation of how to distinguish between what is permitted in the Greater and Lesser Vehicles. Pointing the śrāvakas[364] to the so-called three ways, the Buddha's method was to allow them to eat meat with threefold purity. In the Mahāyāna, his method was to forbid all meat. Here I will examine the intention behind these positions, analyzing and contextualizing the scriptures in granular detail. This discussion has four main points.

First, the Śrāvaka Perspective

The *Bhaiṣajya* chapter of the *Vinayavastu*[365] says, "The Blessed One said, 'I have said that meat that is not suitable by the three ways should not be eaten. What are these three? Meat that is seen to have been prepared for one's own sake. Meat that you have heard from trustworthy sources was prepared for your own sake. Meat that you think, based on suspicions that have arisen in your mind, has been prepared for your own sake.'" Thus, while meat that does not have threefold purity is explicitly forbidden, meat with threefold purity is implicitly

363. These are the two lines from Sakya Paṇḍita's *Distinguishing the Three Vows* that Gorampa is commenting on in the excerpt translated here. Sakya Paṇḍita, *Sdom pa gsum gyi rab tu dbye ba'i bstan bcos*, 34. For an alternate translation of this passage, see Sakya Paṇḍita Kunga Gyaltshen, *A Clear Differentiation of the Three Codes*, 66.

364. Sometimes termed "listeners," śrāvakas are Buddhists who adhere only to the Lower Vehicle and who reject (or at least do not practice) Mahāyāna teachings.

365. The *Chapter on Medicine* (Tib: *Sman gyi gzhi*). One of seventeen chapters in the *Vinayavastu* of the *Mūlasarvāstivāda Vinaya*.

allowed. Another scripture[366] says, "When a respectable person donates allowable fish, meat, or the like, monk[s] should ask themselves, 'Is this human flesh or other [forbidden meat]?' If it is not, they may eat." The *Tarkajvālā*[367] says, "According to the vehicle of the śrāvakas, those who eat meat with threefold purity do not accumulate any sin. Its essence becomes pure, so it is sinless, just like beggars' food."

Second, the Mahāyāna Perspective

The *Laṅkāvatāra Sūtra* explains this extensively:

> Mahāmati, in this present life Kangtra has been born among the people of Kimdün, and he is very attached to meat, to the extent that he even eats forbidden meat. Because of this, in the future he will be born as a malevolent ḍāka or ḍākinī[368] that consumes human flesh. Even after that life, Mahāmati, his strong, ongoing attachment to meat will cause him to fall into exceptionally fierce birth states, such as lions, tigers, leopards, wolves, cats, foxes, owls, and other carnivorous animals. He will even be born as a rākṣasa[369] demon that eats a lot of meat. After such a fall, it will be hard for him to again achieve a human life, let alone achieve nirvāṇa! Mahāmati, these are the faults of eating meat, and this is what happens to those who eat a lot of it! Relinquishing it, however, brings much virtue. Mahāmati, beings do not comprehend these virtues, faults, and so on.[370]

366. Gorampa does not name this text, and I have not been able to identify it based only on this short quote.

367. *Blaze of Reasoning* (Tib: *Rtogs ge 'bar ba*). Bhāviveka's autocommentary on his own *Madhyamakahṛdaya*, known mostly for its portrayal of Madhyamika philosophy.

368. Ḍākas and ḍākinīs are male and female deities of somewhat slippery and indeterminate nature. Often they are positive, assisting practitioners. But in other cases, as here, they are malevolent.

369. Sometimes translated as "cannibal demons," *rākṣasa* are a particular category of demon renowned for their ferocity and consumption of meat. See Buswell and Lopez, *Princeton Dictionary of Buddhism*, 695.

370. This section differs slightly from the corresponding passage in the translation of the *Laṅkāvatāra Sūtra* included in this volume. This is because the Tibetan text included in Gorampa's text differs somewhat from the edition used as a basis for the full translation of the *Laṅkāvatāra Sūtra*.

The *Laṅkāvatāra Sūtra* also says:

This is why I teach that meat is utterly base,
in sūtras such as the *Hastikakṣya*,
Mahāmega, *Parinirvāṇa*, and *Aṅgulimālīya*,
as well as this *Laṅkāvatāra Sūtra*.

Buddhas, bodhisattvas, and śrāvakas,
all decry it as base.
This food, whose essence is turbulent,
always leads to birth as a madman.

The *Mañjuśrī Pradarshana*[371] says, "Those who kill beings to earn a fee will be boiled for a hundred thousand eons. Those who, craving meat, eat it, will be boiled for ten million eons." The same text also says, "Whichever person eats meat will first be born as a ghost and then in the Crying Hell."

Further, the *Subāhuparipṛcchā Tantra*[372] says:

If ghost foods such as meat, alcohol, garlic,
bunched onion, leek, sesame oil, radishes, or other intoxicants
are mixed in with the offering torma[373] for the gods,
then the pure divinities will not eat the torma.

So it has been said.

Third, the Actual Teachings of the Vinaya

Allowing śrāvakas to eat meat with threefold purity is a teaching categorized as "interpretable meaning." One may wonder what the definitive meaning is. The two scholars Guṇaprabha and Śākyaprabha have explained that the actual teachings should be in accordance with a literal reading of the text.

371. *Teachings on Mañjuśrī's Own View* (Tib: *'Phags pa 'jam phal gyi rang gi lta ba'i 'dod pa mdor bstan pa yongs su brtag pa*). A philosophical text by Narendrakīrti.

372. *Dialogue with Subāhu Tantra* (Tib: *Dpung bzang gis zhus pa'i rgyud*), an important tantra with numerous details concerning ritual performance. Classified by Jamgön Kongtrül as a member of the Kriya (Action) class.

373. Torma (Tib: *gtor ma*) are offering cakes usually made of roasted barley flour and butter, but which sometimes include other ingredients.

Guṇaprabha's *Vinayasūtra*[374] says, "If you know meat was killed for you, don't eat it. Also, don't eat from tiger kills. And don't eat elephant, horse, or snake meat." The same text also says, "You should ask, 'Was this meat you are donating killed for me?' First find out the situation, then have the experience [i.e., eat the meat]."[375]

Śākyaprabha's *Śrāmaṇera Triśataka Kārikā*[376] explains eating meat that has been given to you as alms thusly: "When a respectable person donates fish or meat, monks remain attached to harm, unkindness, and flavor. They abandon the examined mind. Because of this, when they receive their begging bowl they root through it [for tasty food] and eat." Some say that this is eating allowable meat.

There is also the question of meat with threefold purity. Some say that threefold purity does not refer to everyday meat that you have not seen, heard, or suspected was killed specifically for you. But this is incorrect. The *Prabhāvatī*[377] says, "Do not eat meat or fish that has been produced for your sake. Meat that is produced for you, requested by you, or rejoiced in by you is forbidden, even if you approach it with a view that sees the three spheres of agent, action, and object as completely pure. This is forbidden because when it is produced for your sake and so on, then it creates unkindness and discord. Other than this it is not forbidden."

But those others explain threefold purity in accordance with this passage from the *Laṅkāvatāra Sūtra*:

> Meat that has threefold purity:
> free of being considered, requested,
> or coerced, does not exist.
> So do not eat meat![378]

374. *The Vinayasūtra* (Tib: *'Dul ba mdo*). Despite its title, this is not a sūtra spoken by the Buddha, but rather a key Vinaya treatise by the seventh-century Indian master Guṇaprabha. For more on this text, see the introduction to Karmapa Mikyö Dorjé's *Great Commentary on the Vinayasūtra* in chapter 6 of this collection.

375. Tib: *sha'i byin len stob pa la / bcad pa las byung ba nyid ma yin nam / zhes dri bar bya'o*. This is a relatively loose translation of a dense and difficult line. I wish to thank Yangsi Rinpoché for his help clarifying its meaning.

376. *Three Hundred Verses on the Noviciate* (Tib: *Phags pa gzhi thams cad yod par smra ba'i dge tshul gyi tshig le'ur byas pa*), by Śākyaprabha. A key source for Tibetan scholars of the monastic code, along with Guṇaprabha's *Vinayasūtra*.

377. *The Luminous* (Tib: *'Od ldan*). Śākyaprabha's own commentary on the *Śrāmaṇera Triśataka Kārikā*, his verses on the Vinaya quoted in the previous paragraph.

378. One figure who presented threefold purity in this way is Karma Chakmé, whose *Faults of*

But this is quite wrong! Threefold purity is taught in the Śrāvaka Vehicle. There, it says that eating meat that does not have threefold purity is not allowed. But this does not explain what threefold purity is according to the vehicle of the śrāvakas. Therefore we must look at the *Vinayakārikā*:[379] "Whoever sees, hears, or suspects the meat has been prepared for them should not eat it. This is taught for the sake of liberating and benefitting all." As this says, separate yourself from meat that you have seen, heard, or suspected was prepared for you. As for the phrase "prepared for you" in the previously mentioned *Bhaiṣajyavastu*, it refers to meat made for you when you are ill.[380] The master Śāntideva says that when the Vinaya allows meat with threefold purity, it is definitively a provisional teaching. In his *Śikṣāsamuccaya*,[381] he says:

> The Vinaya says, "Eating meat that is completely pure in the three ways should not become an obstacle to abandoning meat." So why allow it? Permitting meat with threefold purity clears away the manifest pride that sees oneself as pure because you gave up meat entirely. Further, permitting it allows those with good fortune to engage with the teachings, even if they are also attached to meat. This is explained in the *Laṅkāvatāra Sūtra*, "My various teachings are arranged in gradual stages, like the rungs of a ladder. I created rules such as threefold purity under this rubric. But now I also forbid the meat of animals that have died from the ten types of natural causes."

This passage explains things clearly.

Another intention here is that if a monk is sick, he can rely on meat as a form of medicine. The *Samādhirāja Sūtra*[382] says:

> There was a monk who taught samādhi to the world.
> If he had died, the roar of the teachings

Meat is translated in chatper 7 of this volume.

379. *Verses on the Vinaya* (Tib: *'Dul ba tshig le'ur byes pa*), by Viśākhadeva.

380. Tib: *sngar drangs pa'i sman gyi gzhi las bdag gi ched du shes gsungs pa ni nad pa'i dbang du dzes pa'o.* I wish to thank Yangsi Rinpoché for his suggestions in translating this difficult line. Even so, it remains somewhat out of place and seems to fit better with the quote from the *Samādhirāja Sūtra* provided after the next passage from Śāntideva.

381. *The Training Anthology* (Tib: *Bslab pa kun las btus pa*), by the famed eighth-century Indian monk Śāntideva. As in this passage, much of the text is composed of quotations from canonical Mahāyāna texts. It is also worth noting that the wording found in Gorampa's work differs significantly from the version of this text contained in the Tibetan canon.

382. *The King of Samādhi Sūtra* (Tib: *Ting nge 'dzin gyi rgyal po'i mdo*).

would fade forever for all beings.
By feeding him in this way, samādhi can still be obtained.

As this verse says, if there is a genuine monk who will die if he does not eat medicinal meat, and if his death will mean that the teachings on meditation will disappear from the world, then, in that instance, it is acceptable to eat meat. This is the intention behind allowing individuals to eat meat.

Devadatta and others require vegetarianism,[383] claiming that merely giving up meat will enable one to see clearly. Others, like Lord Indra, are so attached to meat that they cannot engage the teachings.[384] [The rule allowing meat] is meant to compassionately care for people like them, though it goes against the definitive meaning. The *Laṅkāvatāra Sūtra* says:

> Mahāmati, I declare that the consumption of meat is unsuitable for anyone who has ordained as a monk. Mahāmati, foolish people whose past karmic defilement drives them to ridicule me by saying that even the Tathāgata ate meat will endure meaningless suffering for a long time, devoid of joy. Mahāmati, my noble śrāvakas do not eat ordinary, vulgar food, so what need is there to speak of unsuitable foods like meat and blood?

The *Mahāparinirvāṇa Sūtra* says:

> Kāśyapa asked, "Bhagavān, why did you allow eating meat that is completely pure in the three ways?" The Bhagavān replied, "I have allowed meat that is completely pure in the three ways in order to restrain those at the beginning of the graded path. Thus I spoke that way at first. Child of my lineage, from that time on, I said that it is unsuitable for my śrāvakas to eat meat. When it comes to alms, I have allowed meat to be eaten if one sees it as the same as the flesh of one's own child."

My own teachers have only ever explained it in this way, such as in the *Epis-*

383. The Buddha's cousin and frequent foil. Devadatta once proposed that all monks be required to be vegetarians. Here Gorampa suggests that Devadatta believed that being vegetarian was, in and of itself, enough to attain liberation.

384. In a famous story cited in the *Laṅkāvatāra Sūtra*, Indra is driven by his desire for meat to take the form of a hawk. In that form he consumes many pigeons and other small birds. For a detailed discussion of this story, see chapter 3, note 234.

tle Benefitting Students. My view is that the Vinaya allows beginners to eat meat while they gradually practice the foundational discipline. Later, having perfected this foundational discipline and having studied the *Laṅkāvatāra Sūtra* and *Mahāparinirvāna Sūtra*, meat is forbidden, even to śrāvakas. As cited previously, the *Mahāparinirvāna Sūtra* says, "I have allowed meat that is completely pure in the three ways in order to restrain those at the beginning of the graded path. Thus I spoke that way at first. Child of my lineage, from that time on, I said that it is unsuitable for my śrāvakas to eat meat."[385] These are potent words. After thinking long and deep, I agree fully with these passages.

Fourth, Distinguishing What Is Allowed and Forbidden in the Mahāyāna and Hīnayāna

The Vinaya initially allows śrāvakas to eat meat with threefold purity while they practice the foundational disciplines. If at that time they think, "meat is not allowed," and they refuse to eat it, then this would be Devadatta's method. In the Mahāyāna, from the very beginning meat—with or without threefold purity—is forbidden. This is why eating it is said to be the cause of negative rebirths.

What is Devadatta's method? In some commentaries, people say Devadatta's method is to seek out pure liberation merely through the practice of not eating meat. But this explanation is not correct. Even Devadatta did not rely only a single method like this to seek pure liberation, since he is said to have also upheld four other practices.[386] Some say, "It is not correct that in our system the Buddha has forbidden meat. It is correct that this is Devadatta's method." Based on this, they say that Devadatta's method is merely to avoid meat. But those who speak like this are very wrong!

Sakya Paṇḍita's *Distinguishing the Three Vows* shows the difference between what is allowed and forbidden in the Hīnayāna and Mahāyāna. For śrāvakas, [avoiding meat] is Devadatta's method, but in the Mahāyāna it is not. You must understand this, lest the Mahāyāna also become Devadatta's method. So

385. Gorampa cites this exact same passage a few lines earlier. In this second instance, however, he leaves out a few phrases in the final line, leaving the passage somewhat unintelligible. I have reinserted the missing phrases into the translation, for the sake of clarity and consistency.

386. In addition to vegetarianism, Devadatta is said to have advocated a variety of other practices that the Buddha said were too extreme. Different texts enumerate these differently, but a few lines later Gorampa cites a passage from the *Purnamukhavadanasataka* that lays out four additional practices beyond mere vegetarianism: living alone (i.e., not in a monastic community), renouncing salt, renouncing dairy, and going naked. It seems likely that these are the four practices Gorampa is thinking of here.

what defines Devadatta's method? [Devadatta himself explains his method] in the *Purnamukhavadanasataka*:[387]

> While the ascetic Gotama [the Buddha] resides in a monastery, we reside near a village. Why is this? It is because when monks live in a monastery they have many faults. While the ascetic Gotama allows eating meat, we do not allow it. Why is this? It is because sentient beings are killed for it. While the ascetic Gotama allows eating salt, we do not allow it. Why is this? It is because it derives from evaporated ocean water.[388] While the ascetic Gotama drinks milk, we do not drink it. Why is this? It is because calves suffer for it. While the ascetic Gotama wears a set type of robes, we do not wear clothing. Why is this? It is because doing so wastes the people's labor.[389]

387. *One Hundred Stories* (Tib: *Gang po la sogs pa'i rtogs pa brjod pa brgya pa*). A collection of narratives contained in the Tibetan canon and attributed to the Buddha.

388. The Tibetan term here is *khu chu*, which usually means semen, though in this case it seems to refer to the process of boiling ocean water to create salt. Given the context, it seems likely that Devadatta's concern is that boiling ocean water for salt would kill the small creatures that live in the water.

389. This quote abruptly ends Gorampa's discussion of meat eating, without any further discussion or contextualization of this passage. My own reading is that Gorampa is noting that Devadatta's methods go well beyond simply rejecting meat: that is just one part of an ascetic regimen that is much more rigorous than the practices condoned by the Buddha. In the Mahāyāna context, Gorampa seems to imply that in order for it to be considered Devadatta's method (and therefore excessively extreme), one must practice *all* of these austerities, not just vegetarianism alone.

Source Texts

Gorampa (Go rams pa Bsod nams seng ge). 2004. *Sdom pa gsum gyi rab tu dbye ba'i rnam bshad rgyal ba'i gsung rab kyi dgongs pa gsal ba* (*Commentary on Distinguishing the Three Vows*). In *Kun mkhyen go bo rab 'byams pa bsod nams seng ge'i gsung 'bum*, vol. 9, 160–68. 15 vols. Rdzong sar khams bye'i slob gling. BDRC: W1PD1725.

Sakya Paṇḍita (Sakya paṇḍita Kun dga' rgyal btshan). 1999. *Sdom pa gsum gyi rab tu dbye ba'i bstan bcos* (*Distinguishing the Three Vows*). Dpal sa skya'i smon lam chen mo'i dran rten. BDRC: W1KG1686.

Secondary Sources

Buswell, Robert E., and Donald S. Lopez. 2013. *The Princeton Dictionary of Buddhism.* Princeton, NJ: Princeton University Press.

Heimbel, Jörg. 2017. *Vajradhara in Human Form: The Life and Times of Ngor chen Kun dga' bzang po*. Lumbini: Lumbini International Research Institute.

Kassor, Constance. 2017. "Gorampa [Go Rams Pa]." In *The Stanford Encyclopedia of Philosophy*, edited by Edward N. Zalta, https://plato.stanford.edu/archives/spr2017/entries/gorampa/.

Sakya Paṇḍita Kunga Gyaltshen. 2002. *A Clear Differentiation of the Three Codes: Essential Differentiations among the Individual Liberation, Great Vehicle, and Tantric Systems.* Translated by Jared Douglas Rhoton. Albany: State University of New York Press.

Sobisch, Jan-Ulrich. 2002. *Three-Vow Theories in Tibetan Buddhism*. Weisbaden: Dr. Ludwig Reichert Verlag.

Thakchoe, Sonam, and Jay L. Garfield. 2007. *The Two Truths Debate: Tsongkhapa and Gorampa on the Middle Way*. Boston: Wisdom Publications.

6. Karmapa Mikyö Dorjé's Critique of Meat in Tantric Ritual

By Geoffrey Barstow

MIKYÖ DORJÉ (1507–1554) was born in Kham in 1507.[390] There was some initial controversy over his selection, but in 1513 he was recognized and enthroned as the immediate reincarnation of Chödrak Gyatso, the Seventh Karmapa. As the head of the Karma Kagyü tradition, the position of Karmapa was one of the most prestigious incarnation lineages in Tibet. When Mikyö Dorjé was recognized as the Eighth Karmapa, therefore, he was immediately elevated to the highest levels of standing within the Tibetan tradition. As befitted his position as a high-level incarnation, Karmapa Mikyö Dorjé spent his youth immersed in the study of classical Buddhist texts and eventually became one of the most prolific authors in his lineage, with one recent edition of his collected works containing twenty-six volumes.[391] He was particularly known for his philosophical acumen, and his writings on Madhyamaka and Mahāmudrā have become staples in Karma Kagyü monastic education.[392] By the time he died in 1554, Mikyö Dorjé had become one of the most renowned and important religious figures of his day.

Mikyö Dorjé was a strong advocate for vegetarianism.[393] Nor was his critical stance on meat unusual in his lineage. Many of the Karmapas, in fact, were

390. Tib: Karma pa Mi bskyod rdo rje. The most extensive work on Mikyö Dorjé's life and times (and the source of these biographical details) is Rheingans, *The Eighth Karmapa's Life*.

391. Mikyö Dorjé, *Dpal rgyal ba karma pa sku 'phreng brgyad pa mi bskyod rdo rje'i gsung 'bum*, BDRC: W8039.

392. For an English translation of Mikyö Dorjé's commentary on Chandrakīrti's *Madyamakavatara*, see Chandrakirti and Mikyo Dorjé, *The Moon of Wisdom*.

393. It is worth noting that I have found no explicit, contemporary claims that Mikyö Dorjé was himself a vegetarian. Given his strong criticism of meat eating, however, it seems likely that he was.

either personally vegetarian or advocated it among their disciples.[394] In Mikyö Dorjé's case, this provegetarian stance can be seen in several of his written works, the longest of which is an obscure text that focuses entirely on vegetarianism and the faults of meat—*A Letter on the Unsuitability of Eating the Meat of Our Old Mothers.*[395] In addition to this stand-alone work, the Karmapa included critiques of meat in several other works of religious advice. Further, he banned meat eating at Tsurpu Monastery, the monastic seat of the Karmapa lineage. "Monks gathered here," Mikyö Dorjé wrote in his *Guidelines for Tsurpu*, "should, in particular, not consume meat or eggs."[396] It is impossible to know how strictly this rule was enforced, or for how long it was in place after Mikyö Dorjé's death, but it clearly demonstrates the degree to which the Eighth Karmapa felt that monks should not eat meat.

Meat in Tantric Ritual Offerings

The text translated here is a very short extract from a much longer work—Karmapa Mikyö Dorjé's *The Great Commentary on the Vinayasūtra*. The *Vinayasūtra* itself was written by the seventh-century Indian master Guṇaprabha.[397] In Tibet, the *Vinayasūtra* became a crucial reference for understanding the Vinaya, the formal rules for monks and nuns. Mikyö Dorjé's *Great Commentary on the Vinayasūtra*, therefore, was a presentation of how monastics should understand the rules governing their order. As the title suggests, Mikyö Dorjé's text is indeed "great." Written in 1532,[398] it fills almost three volumes of the Eighth Karmapa's collected works, providing a wealth of detail on how he felt monks and nuns should behave, both in general and with regard to innumerable specific topics.

394. It is often difficult to know whether a particular individual was personally vegetarian. With that said, there is good evidence to suggest that the Fourth, Sixth, and Seventh Karmapas were vegetarians. The Third and Eighth may also have been, though the evidence is less conclusive. And the current, Seventeenth Karmapa is both a personal vegetarian and one of the main driving forces behind the contemporary vegetarian movement among Tibetans.

395. Unfortunately, the only edition of this work that I know of is on microfilm and is quite difficult to read in many places. For this reason, it is not included in this volume. Those who read Tibetan can find the text in the archives of the Nepal-German Manuscript Preservation project (NGMPP Reel No. E 2943/4).

396. Mikyö Dorjé, *Dga' tshal karma gzhung lugs gling dang por sgar chen 'dzam gling rgyan du bzhugs dus kyi 'phral gyi bca' yig*, 709.

397. Guṇaprabha's dates are somewhat uncertain. For more on the complex issue of trying to date Guṇaprabha and his works, see Nietupski, "Guṇaprabha's Vinayasūtra Corpus."

398. Rheingans, *The Eighth Karmapa*, 101.

The extract translated below is only a couple pages of Mikyö Dorjé's longer work, but is nonetheless a good example of these patterns. Like other passages in the work as a whole, it explicitly focuses on how monks or nuns should understand a single issue—in this case the question of whether they should include meat in their offerings to protector deities. And it cuts straight to the heart of this question, among the most contentious issues in Tibetan debates over meat eating. Indeed, this brief extract has been included in this volume precisely because it provides such a clear and lucid account of this hotly debated topic.

As discussed in the general introduction to this volume, the question of meat in tantra was a fraught one for Tibetan proponents of vegetarianism. Several tantras[399] explicitly claim that practitioners must include the five meats[400] in their ritual offerings. It seems that many Tibetans took these commands to heart, frequently including not only the five meats but also everyday meats, such as yak and sheep, in their offerings, particularly when those offerings were made to wrathful deities. Despite the explicit sanction found in these tantras, however, many lamas seem to have been uncomfortable with this practice, developing a variety of strategies to either circumvent or minimize the use of meat in tantric ritual. Later in this volume, for instance, we will see that the seventeenth-century master Karma Chakmé argues that while meat is indeed required in tantric ritual, only the smallest amount possible—equivalent in size to the leg of an insect—should be used.[401] Other masters employed substitutes, arguing that representations of the five meats made out of dough served just as well as the real thing (particularly considering how difficult it could be to get the actual five meats).[402]

Karmapa Mikyö Dorjé takes a different approach, using debate-style logic to argue that meat simply should not be used in ritual offerings. He does this by first noting that the instructions to offer meat and alcohol are found only in the highest level of tantric practice—Unexcelled Mantra. Given that we are talking about Unexcelled Mantra rather than a lower form of tantric practice,

399. Tantras are texts that lay out the philosophies and practices of tantric Buddhism. Proponents generally assert that they were taught by the Buddha himself, though modern scholarship suggests that texts in this genre were composed between the sixth and twelfth centuries CE.

400. Usually the five meats are listed as human, cow, dog, horse, and elephant. These are all taboo meats in ancient India, so consuming them is deeply transgressive, lying well outside of the patterns of ordinary life. For a detailed study of the five meats in Indian Buddhist tantra, see Wedemeyer, *Making Sense of Tantric Buddhism*.

401. See the introduction to and translation of Karma Chakmé's *Faults of Meat* in chapter 7 of this volume.

402. For one example of this strategy, see Cantwell, "The Medicinal Accomplishment."

he points out that practitioners are, by definition, making offerings to enlightened, transcendent deities rather than to unenlightened, worldly deities. Therefore, the only appropriate offering is pure, divine nectar, not any kind of ordinary, worldly food. Mikyö Dorjé then notes that some people claim that meat and alcohol are the necessary ingredients for making this nectar. To rebut this claim he adopts a debating posture, asking if the meat and alcohol need to be transmuted—physically transformed into ambrosia through tantric ritual. If his opponent claims that they do not need to be transmuted, then Mikyö Dorjé points out that this means the meat and alcohol must already be divine. But this cannot be, he points out, since the meat and alcohol under consideration have a particular taste and smell, whereas divine ambrosia has no such worldly characteristics. So the meat and alcohol, Mikyö Dorjé argues, must need to be transmuted before they can be used as offerings. The problem here, he claims, is that a practitioner would need to be very advanced in order to actually make this transmutation happen. Most of us—and the Karmapa seems to include himself in this—are simply unable to do so. Thus the reader is left to understand that it is incorrect to offer meat, whether or not one thinks that it does not need to be transmuted.

Following this short but dense argument, Mikyö Dorjé proceeds to deal with a pair of objections. First, he summarily dismisses the idea that the smell of rotten meat and stale alcohol could, in and of itself, be divine ambrosia. Second, he argues that meat and alcohol are inappropriate offerings even for worldly deities. This is because, he argues, in the moment the offering is made, the deity in question should actually be visualized and treated as if they were a transcendent buddha rather than a mere worldly deity. Finally, Mikyö Dorjé concludes with the pithy statement, "When thinking about putting actual meat and alcohol in the torma, I say that since you are unable to truly transmute them into suchness, you should not use real meat or alcohol. This is my prayer."

In addition to the arguments themselves, Mikyö Dorjé's work is notable for the strength of his rhetoric. In the first paragraph, he makes the striking statement that those monks or nuns who include meat in their offerings "should go and live elsewhere, with other monastics." In the next paragraph, he turns the rhetorical heat up even higher, telling recalcitrant monks or nuns that if they offer meat, "Do not consider me your teacher. It is not suitable for you to be among my disciples. Do not treat me as your lama." Mikyö Dorjé was the Karmapa, the head of the Karma Kagyü lineage, and among the most important religious leaders in Tibet at the time. Every monastic in his tradition would have considered him their teacher, as would many others as well. Given this context, it is striking—almost shocking—to hear Mikyö Dorjé tell monks and nuns who offer meat to physically move elsewhere and to not take him as their teacher.

About the Translation

In preparing this translation, I have relied on the edition of Mikyö Dorjé's *Great Commentary on the Vinayasūtra* found in the twenty-six-volume edition of his collected works edited by Karma Delek and published in Lhasa in 2004. I first came across the text, however, by doing a keyword search in a digital edition of Mikyö Dorjé's works that was given to me by a monk in Kham, who wishes to remain anonymous. While this edition was riddled with typos and I did not rely on it for the actual translation, I want to thank this monk for his generosity, without which I would not have known about the text at all. I am also grateful to Lama Karma Drodhul of Karma Triyana Dharmachakra, who generously went over the text with me in July 2014.

The Great Commentary on the Vinayasūtra

By Mikyö Dorjé, the Eighth Karmapa

Translated by Geoffrey Barstow

Monks these days make offerings of blood and the like. They say they are making offerings to Mahākāla,[403] but they are actually creating an ongoing stream of sin. This is a sign of demonic blessings and corrupt teachings. In the Vinaya texts of the holy Dharma it says that this must be stopped, even if it is only the monks' servants who actually do it. If you are not able to stop it, then you should go and live elsewhere, with other monks. Since the Buddha said this, such practices should also be stopped in these present times. Therefore when I myself act like a lama and make offerings to the worldly deities, I offer appropriate tormas[404] made with pure flowers, medicinal fruits, rice, and similar ingredients. This is what the Vinaya teaches.

More specifically, do not include meat or alcohol in the particular torma used in the gutor[405] or similar rituals. If you do, then do not consider me your teacher. It is not suitable for you to be among my disciples. Do not treat me as your lama. Someone might argue with this, saying, "putting meat and alcohol in the gutor is the Buddha's tantric system." Ask them, "Where in the four sections of Tantra is this found? This tradition is not found in the three lower sections: it is only found in the Unexcelled Mantra."[406] In Unexcelled Mantra, is it appropriate to make offerings to worldly or to transcendent deities?[407]

403. Mahākāla (Tib: Nag po chen po) is one of the most common wrathful deities in the Tibetan pantheon, particularly in the Kagyü lineage that Mikyö Dorjé belonged to.

404. A torma (Tib: *gtor ma*) is an offering cake made of roasted barley flower, butter, and other ingredients. It is the contents of these tormas—and whether or not meat should be included—that are Mikyö Dorjé's immediate concern in this text.

405. A gutor (Tib: *dgu gtor*) is a specific offering ritual for the wrathful deity Mahākāla, often performed on the twenty-ninth day of the Tibetan lunar month.

406. "Unexcelled Mantra" (Tib: *Sngags bla med*) is a synonym for Anuttarayoga Tantra. The highest of the four classifications of tantra, according to the Sarma (New Translation) lineages.

407. In other words, deities that are not enlightened (worldly) as well as those that are enlightened (transcendent). The Karmapa's point seems to be that making offerings to worldly deities is inappropriate in the context of Unexcelled Mantra.

If you offer a torma, it should be a torma that has the nature of suchness:[408] an offering of the nectar of samaya[409] indivisibly united with the nectar of the wisdom of the nature of reality. In this context, the offering could not possibly be ordinary food!

Others might dispute this, saying, "Meat, alcohol, and so on are used to make the nectar of samaya!" So let's examine that meat and alcohol. Do the meat and alcohol that go into the nectar of samaya need to be transmuted or not?[410] If they do not need to be transmuted, then they are in contradiction with the nectar of samaya. This is because foods that already accord with suchness—and that are suitable locations for the nectar of samaya to enter wisdom nectar—have no particulars of smell or taste. Such foods do not appear before anyone other than yogis.[411] If they do need to be transmuted, then one must have achieved the path of preparation[412] in Unexcelled Mantra in order to have the ability to transmute them properly.

Someone might argue, "The disgusting smells of rotten meat and sour alcohol are themselves the nectar of samaya!" But really, why even respond to this? Someone else might say, "Meat and alcohol offered to the wisdom deities are indeed transmuted into the nectars of samaya and wisdom. But when offering to the worldly deities, actual meat and alcohol must be included because they are not able to consume the nectars of samaya and wisdom." If you are not well trained in the tantras, this is indeed true. But if I myself offer a torma to worldly deities, I engender that divinity as the supreme among worldly deities, grant them empowerment, and then visualize them as a wisdom deity. Then I make the offering. There is nothing wrong when you explain it like this.

In summary, when thinking about putting actual meat and alcohol in the torma, I say that since you are unable to truly transmute them into suchness, you should not use real meat or alcohol. This is my prayer.

408. That is, how things truly are.

409. "Nectar of samaya" connotes a pure, divine ambrosia, rhetorically connected to the purity of the practitioner's samaya commitments (the tantric vows taken by all who receive empowerment into a tantric Buddhist lineage). See the introduction to this volume for further discussion of the role of meat eating in maintaining one's samaya vows.

410. In other words, does it need to be transformed from an ordinary, worldly substance into divine nectar?

411. That is, advanced practitioners.

412. The second of five paths in some Mahāyāna depictions of the path. Here Mikyö Dorjé is emphasizing that only an accomplished practitioner is capable of actually transmuting ordinary meat and alcohol into divine nectar.

Source Text

Mikyö Dorjé (Mi bskyod rdo rje). 2004. *'Dul ba mdo rtsa ba'i rgya cher 'grel spyi'i don mtha' dpyad dang bsdus don sa bcad dang 'bru yi don mthar chags su gnyer ba bcas 'dzam bu'i gling gsal bar byed*. In *Dpal rgyal ba karma pa sku 'phreng brgyad pa mi bskyod rdo rje'i gsung 'bum*, vol. 7, 541–44. Lhasa. BDRC: W8039.

Other Tibetan Sources

Mikyö Dorjé (Mi bskyod rdo rje). 2004. *Dga' tshal karma gzhung lugs gling dang por sgar chen 'dzam gling rgyan du bzhugs dus kyi 'phral gyi bca' yig* (*Guidelines for Tsurpu*). In *Dpal rgyal ba karma pa sku 'phreng brgyad pa mi bskyod rdo rje'i gsung 'bum*, vol. 3, 700–715. BDRC: W8039.

———. n.d. *Gangs ri'i khrod na gnas pa gtso bor gyur pa skyabs med ma rgan tshogs la sha zar mi rung ba'i springs yig sogs* (*A Letter on the Unsuitability of Eating the Meat of Our Old Mothers*). NGMPP Reel No. E 2943/4.

Secondary Sources

Cantwell, Cathy. 2015. "The Medicinal Accomplishment (sman Sgrub) Practice in the Dudjom Meteoric Iron Razor (gnam Lcags Spu Gri) Tradition: Reflections on the Ritual and Meditative Practice at a Monastery in Southern Bhutan." *Journal of the Oxford Centre for Buddhist Studies* 8: 49–95.

Chandrakirti and Mikyo Dorjé. 2006. *The Moon of Wisdom: Chapter Six of Chandrakirti's Entering the Middle Way with Commentary from the Eighth Karmapa Mikyo Dorjé's Kagyü Siddhas*. Translated by Ari Goldfield, Jules Levinson, Jim Scott, and Birgit Scott. Ithaca, NY: Snow Lion Publications.

Nietupski, Paul. 2009. "Guṇaprabha's Vinayasūtra Corpus: Texts and Contexts." *Journal of the International Association of Tibetan Studies* 5: 1–19.

Rheingans, Jim. 2017. *The Eighth Karmapa's Life and His Interpretation of the Great Seal*. Hamburg: Numata Center for Buddhist Studies.

Wedemeyer, Christian K. 2012. *Making Sense of Tantric Buddhism: History, Semiology, and Transgression in the Indian Traditions*. New York: Columbia University Press.

7. Karma Chakmé's Comprehensive Critique of Meat

By Geoffrey Barstow

Karma Chakmé (1613–1678)[413] was a prominent scholar and prolific author who spent the majority of his life in the Kham region of eastern Tibet. Born in 1613, he received both novice and full ordination at the age of nineteen. He spent the rest of his life in and out of retreat, giving extensive teachings and composing numerous texts. Karma Chakmé is primarily associated with the Kagyü lineage, but he also received and transmitted many Nyingma teachings, positioning him as something of a forerunner of the *rimé*, or nonsectarian, movement that would emerge in Kham two centuries later. Among his most famous works, in fact, is *The Union of Mahāmudrā and Dzogchen*, a treatise that found common ground between the meditation instructions of the Kagyü and Nyingma lineages.[414] By the time of his death at the age of sixty-six, he had become one of the most important religious leaders of the region.

Among the most important of Karma Chakmé's students was Künzang Sherab (1636–1698), a Nyingma master who became the first throneholder of Pelyül Monastery when it was founded in 1665. Karma Chakmé was further connected to Pelyül through his relationship with the Nyingma tertön[415] Namchö Migyur Dorjé (1645–1667), whom he recognized, enthroned, and taught. The *Namchö*, or *Space Treasures*, Migyur Dorjé's primary revelation cycle, became the primary practice lineage at Pelyül. Thus while Karma

413. Tib: Karma chags med. This lama's name has been transliterated as Karma Chagme and Karma Chagmed, as well as variations with and without diacritics.

414. Tib: *Phyag rdzogs zung 'jug*. This text has received numerous English translations and commentaries. My personal preference is for Chökyi Nyima Rinpoché, *Union of Mahamudra and Dzogchen*; and Khenchen Thrangu, *Luminous Clarity*.

415. Tib: *gter ston*. Particularly associated with the Nyingma lineage, tertöns reveal special texts (*terma*; *gter ma*) that are usually said to have been composed by Guru Rinpoché during the Imperial period and then hidden, either physically or in the mindstream of a disciple. The tertön, usually identified as the reincarnation of one of these disciples, then reveals the text centuries later, at the most appropriate time.

Chakmé never personally served as an officer at Pelyül, he was deeply connected to the founding of the monastery and is often listed at the beginning of histories of this monastery.

Karma Chakmé's connection to Pelyül is important here because there is some evidence to suggest that vegetarianism was common at Pelyül for at least a few generations after its founding. Tsering Lama Jampal Sangpo's mid-twentieth-century *Garland of Immortal Wish-Fulfilling Trees*,[416] a lineage history of Pelyül, claims that both Künzang Sherab and Pema Lhundrup Gyatso (1659–1727; Künzang Sherab's successor to the abbacy of Pelyül) were both personally vegetarian and encouraged their disciples to give up meat. Tsering Lama Jampal Sangpo even claims that "thousands" of Pema Lhundrup Gyatso's students became vegetarian. This number is almost certainly inflated, as there were likely only a few hundred monks at Pelyül at that time, and it is worth noting that not all Pelyül lineage histories are as clear on this point as Tsering Lama Jampal Sangpo. Nevertheless, there is a good chance that Karma Chakmé's views on meat were broadly influential at the time and may have helped spark a broad movement toward vegetarianism among the monks of Pelyül.

Karma Chakmé on Meat Eating

This chapter contains translations of two works by Karma Chakmé. Both are found in volume 35 of his sixty-volume *Collected Works*. The full title of the first, much longer work is *Words of My Kind Lama: The Faults of Meat along with the Divisions of What to Accept and Reject*. This text, comprising twenty-five full folios in the Tibetan, is one of the most significant treatises on meat eating to be written by a Tibetan author.

Karma Chakmé opens with a general critique of meat, drawing on long quotations from the *Laṅkāvatāra Sūtra* but adding his own summaries and comments in his own voice. Having described the general faults of meat, Karma Chakmé proceeds to investigate several issues, all of which are discussed consistently throughout Tibetan works on meat eating and vegetarianism. The first of these is the uncomfortable question of why the Buddha allowed monks to eat meat. Drawing on the arguments found in the *Laṅkāvatāra Sūtra* and *Mahāparinirvāṇa Sūtra*, Karma Chakmé argues that this was simply a form of skillful means. The Buddha knew that if he mandated strict vegetarianism, some people who are deeply attached to meat would be driven away from the Buddha's teachings entirely. But, Karma Chakmé insists, this is only a provisional teaching. Once these people become more fully engaged

416. Tsering Lama Jampal Sangpo, *A Garland of Immortal Wish-Fulfilling Trees*.

in the Buddhist path, they—like all other Buddhists—should give up meat. Karma Chakmé next turns his attention to the question of meat eating in the Mahāyāna, claiming that in this vehicle, meat of any kind is simply unacceptable. He does note an important exception, however, allowing even Mahāyāna monks to eat meat if they are quite ill and if doing so would help them recover. In such a situation eating meat becomes the lesser evil, subordinated to the need to preserve the Dharma by preserving the practitioner's life.

The bulk of Karma Chakmé's text, however, is focused on the question of meat in tantric Buddhism. As should be clear by now, the question of meat consumption in tantra is one of the most fraught issues in Tibetan discussions of vegetarianism, and Karma Chakmé's comments on this front are among the subtlest in all of Tibetan literature.[417] Karma Chakmé opens this discussion by noting that not all tantras allow meat, and that the three lower tantric classes—Kriya, Charya, and Yoga—explicitly ask practitioners to be vegetarian. But Karma Chakmé then argues that meat is inappropriate even in the highest class of tantra, Anuttarayoga Tantra, whose texts do sometimes advocate eating meat. To do this, Karma Chakmé makes a fascinating argument, first noting that tantric masters are defined by their compassion and then quoting the famous *Mañjuśrī Pradarshana*[418] to suggest that eating meat is a marker of someone who lacks kindness. "Therefore," he concludes, "meat eating is not found among the defining traits of a master, and those who do so are not masters."

Karma Chakmé then embarks on an extended discussion of the use of meat in tantric ritual. He acknowledges that some tantric texts do require the ritual use of meat. But he takes care to differentiate this from the general, everyday consumption of meat. Even the latter is allowable, he admits, but only if the practitioner is truly able to either physically transform the meat into divine nectar or to physically transform their body into that of a meat-eating animal. Unless a practitioner is that advanced—and he clearly suggests that most of us are not—they should avoid consuming meat on a daily basis.[419] Further, the meat used in tantric ritual needs to be the true five meats, which are never slaughtered. Normal, everyday meat, on the other hand, does come from

417. For a longer discussion of the debates over meat in tantra, see the general introduction to this volume.

418. *Teachings on Mañjuśrī's Own View* (Tib: *Rang gi lta ba'i 'dod pa mdor bstan pa yongs su brtag pa*). A philosophical text by Narendrakīrti.

419. Interestingly, in his biography of Namchö Migyur Dorjé, Karma Chakmé repeatedly insists that Migyur Dorjé is just such a master, and that therefore it is OK that he ate meat. Karma Chagme, *The All-Pervading Melodious Sound of Thunder*, 85, 133, 161, 189.

slaughtered animals and is therefore not appropriate as an offering. Finally, Karma Chakmé addresses the question of how much meat is appropriate, making the somewhat surprising claim that ordinary practitioners should use only a miniscule amount of meat, equivalent in size to the leg of an ant! In conclusion, while entirely avoiding meat does violate tantric samayas, he is clear that normal practitioners must not get carried away with this, using only the five meats and only a miniscule amount of those meats. Karma Chakmé is clearly concerned about what he sees as the misuse of meat in tantric ritual. This is the single longest argument Karma Chakmé makes in this text, and he takes pains to support it with numerous quotations from a wide variety of tantras and commentaries.

In his conclusion, Karma Chakmé reiterates that practitioners should give up meat entirely. But he seems to recognize that this is a difficult thing for many of his readers to do, so he also suggests other practices that they can perform. While these are not as good as full vegetarianism, they are better than nothing. One step down from full vegetarianism, in his perspective, is giving up any meat that was killed for your sake, or, if you feel you must eat meat, to eat only a little bit. One step down from this, and what Karma Chakmé considers to be the minimal allowable commitment, is to say a prayer before eating meat, generating compassion for the animal whose remains you are consuming.

And this is precisely where the second text translated here comes in: *Eating Meat with Compassion: Oral Instructions on the Meaning, Combining Sūtras and Tantras* is a prayer to be recited before eating any meat. Perhaps not surprisingly, the prayer opens with an extended interlinear note describing the faults of eating meat and concluding that it is not acceptable. But if a practitioner must do so, Karma Chakmé suggests that they visualize themselves absorbing and purifying the animal's sin. Then, after again acknowledging that the animal in question was once their mother, the practitioner is encouraged to visualize the process of eating the meat as an inner fire-offering, as if the meat were being placed into a blazing fire as an offering to the deities. All of this is done while reciting appropriate mantras.

Composing a prayer such as this may seem strange, given the strength of Karma Chakmé's commitment to vegetarianism. But it actually fits nicely with his other work, as well as with the broader scope of the vegetarian movement in pre-Communist Tibet. Eating meat, Karma Chakmé makes clear, is morally problematic and should not be done. But many Tibetans, for a variety of reasons, felt that abstaining was very difficult. So Karma Chakmé tries to offer something to these people as well, a way to acknowledge that meat is problematic without actually having to give it up. Further, while simply reciting a prayer before eating meat may seem like an easy way to dodge the issue, it is worth noting that reciting this text takes a minute or two, even when done quickly. And doing so each time you eat meat continually reinforces the idea that doing so is wrong. Karma Chakmé might reasonably expect that someone who took this practice to heart might quickly find themselves uncomfortable with eating meat, perhaps reducing the amount they eat or even becoming vegetarian.

About the Translation

Both texts have been translated from versions found in the edition of Karma Chakmé's *Collected Works* published in sixty volumes at Nedo Sangngak Choling Monastery.

In preparing this translation, I am doubly grateful to Khenpo Karthar Rinpoché. First, for suggesting during a personal meeting in 2014 that I look through Karma Chakmé's works. And second for the oral teachings that he gave on *The Faults of Meat* in mid-March 2015. These teachings were delivered at Karma Triyana Dharmachakra in New York and orally translated by Lama Yeshe Gyamtso. Although I could not travel to New York, I was able to attend a live-stream of these teachings at Karma Thegsum Chöling in Columbus, Ohio. I had already prepared a working translation of the text, but Khenpo Karthar Rinpoché's teachings were invaluable for resolving several questions, and I am grateful for them, for Lama Yeshe Gyamtso's oral translation, and to KTC for making the teachings available via live-stream. I am also grateful to Khenpo Jorden of the International Buddhist Academy in Kathmandu, who generously helped me decipher several particularly thorny passages, and to Daniel McNamara, who helped to correct my rendering of the Sanskrit mantras in *Eating Meat with Compassion*.

Beyond the difficulty of some of the passages themselves, the *Faults of Meat* necessitated several difficult decisions for me as the translator. Perhaps most notable to readers was the decision to add section headings. Karma Chakmé's original text is long and does not have numbered sections, as some other works in this volume do. This means that it is not always clear when he changes direction or shifts topic. I decided, therefore, to include section headings with the hope of helping the reader understand which topic Karma Chakmé was discussing in any given passage. Karma Chakmé also twice quotes a passage from the *Laṅkāvatāra Sūtra* but says that it is from the *Saddharmasmṛtyupasthāna Sūtra*. I have tried, as much as possible, to translate the text as found in Karma Chakmé's Tibetan, while using footnotes and brackets to make the reader aware of these discrepancies. Finally, I should note that I have been unable to track down some of the tantric texts mentioned, though not quoted, in this work. I therefore have referenced only their Tibetan titles, as Karma Chakmé presents them.

As always, I apologize for any errors in these translations and hope that they are useful, despite their deficiencies.

The Faults of Meat

By Karma Chakmé

Translated by Geoffrey Barstow

Praise to Avalokiteśvara!
Having prostrated to this great treasure of compassion,
I will clarify when meat is permitted and when it is prohibited.

The General Faults of Meat

First, there are the general faults of meat. The *Laṅkāvatāra Sūtra* says:

People pay money for meat,
causing animals to be killed for profit.
Both the killer and buyer own this sinful karma,
and will lament vigorously.
. . .
Beings that eat each other
take birth as carnivores.
Or they become madmen,
foul smelling and base.
Again and again they are born
as outcasts, dog eaters, and dyers.
Or they are born as ḍākinīs,
or among flesh-eating demons.
After this present life,
they come back as cat-demons.
This is why I teach that meat should be utterly rejected,
in sūtras such as the *Hastikakṣya*,[420]
Mahāmega,[421] *Parinirvāṇa*,[422] and *Aṅgulimālīya*,[423]

420. *The Elephant's Power Sūtra* (Tib: *Glang po'i rtsal gyi mdo*).

421. *The Great Cloud Sūtra* (Tib: *Sprin chen po'i mdo*).

422. *The Great Nirvana Sūtra* (Tib: *Myang 'das chen po'i mdo*).

423. *The Angulimala Sūtra* (Tib: *Sor mo'i phreng ba la phan pa'i mdo*).

> as well as this *Laṅkāvatāra Sūtra*.
> Buddhas, bodhisattvas, and śrāvakas,
> all decry it as base.
> This food, whose essence is turbulent,
> always leads to birth as a madman.[424]

These are the faults of eating normal meat. It is said to be a hundred thousand times worse if you eat the meat of an animal killed the same day, meat that has been killed for your own sake, meat with the skin attached,[425] or the flesh of a being similar to humans! The *Mahāprajñāpāramitā Sūtra*[426] says, "If one eats one's own flesh, one will not be delivered from the eighteen hells." The same text also says, "In the hell of tiger cubs, lions, and so on, it is easy to see that meat with the skin on and so forth are a great fault."

The *Laṅkāvatāra Sūtra* says, "In the past there was a king named Sengé Bangzang. He ate meat, including types forbidden in the sūtras. He was so attached to the taste that he even ate human flesh! All those who lived in his cities and villages abandoned him, even his wife, his ministers, his relatives, and his friends. Thus abandoned, his suffering was very great!"

The *Laṅkāvatāra Sūtra* also says:

> At that time in the past, being accustomed to living with lions, Kangtra and the others were meat eaters. Because of these evil tendencies, Kangtra continued to eat meat over a succession of lives, even when he became a king of men. Mahāmati,[427] in this present life Kangtra has been born in the city of Kimdün, and he is very attached to meat and eats a lot of it. Because of this, in the future he will be born as a malevolent ḍākinī that consumes human flesh.

424. Alert readers will note that the *Laṅkāvatāra Sūtra* quotations in this text differ slightly from the corresponding passage in this volume's translation of the *Laṅkāvatāra Sūtra*. This is because the Tibetan text of Karma Chakmé's work differs slightly from the text of the *Laṅkāvatāra Sūtra* found in the Degé Kangyur. While consequential, these differences are far less significant than those found in Karma Chakmé's quotations from the *Mahāparinirvāna Sūtra*. For more on the errors in these citations, see the general introduction to this volume.

425. This is an unusual phrase (*rtsi sha* in Tibetan) and a tentative translation. If this is the correct reading, it seems to refer to meat that has not been processed or butchered.

426. *The Perfection of Wisdom in 100,000 Lines* (Tib: *Sher phyin 'bum*; here referred to as *Yab ryas pa*). The longest of the perfection of wisdom texts.

427. Mahāmati (Tib: Blo gros chen po; Karma Chakmé spells it Blon po chen po) is the one who initially requested the *Laṅkāvatāra Sūtra*. The entire sūtra is framed as a response to his questions.

> Even after that life, Mahāmati, his strong, ongoing attachment to meat will cause him to fall into exceptionally fierce birth states, such as lions, tigers, leopards, wolves, cats, foxes, owls, and other carnivorous animals. He will even be born as a cannibal demon that eats a lot of meat. After such a fall, it will be hard for him to again achieve a human life, let alone achieve nirvāṇa! Mahāmati, these are the faults of eating meat, and this is what happens to those who eat a lot of it! Giving it up, however, brings much virtue. Mahāmati, ordinary, childish beings do not comprehend these virtues, faults, and so on. Mahāmati, I have taught this so that bodhisattvas who embody compassion will see these virtues and faults and stop eating any kind of meat.

As for the specific issue of human flesh and so on, even outcasts, butchers, and others who eat worldly food refuse to eat it. As the *Laṅkāvatāra Sūtra* says, "Mahāmati, worldly people do not eat the meat of donkeys, camels, dogs, cows, or humans (even though butchers claim that it is wholesome and sell it on the streets in order to make some money)." The same sūtra also says, "When a dog sees a butcher, outcast, fisherman, or anyone else that eats dog meat, even at a great distance, it is thrown into a state of fear. Thinking, 'they will come and kill me,' the dog almost dies of fear! It is similar, Mahāmati, with those tiny beings that live in the air, on the earth, or in water. As soon as they see a distant meat eater, or when they detect one with their subtle sense of smell, then, fearing death, they quickly turn aside, just as a human might turn from a demon." Elsewhere, the *Laṅkāvatāra Sūtra* also says, "There is no difference between the smell of a roasting human corpse and the smell of the roasting flesh of some other kind of being. Both have the same disgusting smell." And again, the *Laṅkāvatāra Sūtra* explains that "even in this life, eating meat causes one's breath to stink, so bodhisattvas do not eat any meat." Thus the general faults of meat have been extensively explained.

In short, since there are no beings who have not been your mother or father in a past life, this is the flesh of your parents. Since there are none who have not been your kinsmen, this is the flesh of your child. Since animal bodies develop from semen and womb blood, their meat is a vile substance. Since it is similar to the vile taste of death, meat is also vile. This is why the gods abandon it! Meat makes the mouth smell foul. When sleeping, it causes painful dreams of death. If you are alone, nonhuman spirits will cause your radiance to fade, and you will be fearful and afraid. You cannot evaluate food and cannot digest it fully, so worms will grow in your belly. It is unhealthy, causing many diseases such as leprosy. For all these reasons, eating meat is a fault. But this is not widely known, so I have explained the faults of meat extensively.

Because of these faults, it brings great benefit when someone stops eating meat. As the *Laṅkāvatāra Sūtra* says:

> Abandoning meat, on the other hand,
> leads to birth as a brahman or yogi,
> or one endowed with wisdom and wealth.

In brief, for those born among the seven houses of the zodiac and their ilk, eating meat has limitless faults.

Why Is Meat Allowed in the Vinaya?

Because of its faults, even non-Buddhists refuse to eat meat. The noble Mahāyāna *Laṅkāvatāra Sūtra* explains, "The bodhisattva Mahāmati asked, 'Lord Buddha, even those extremists with wrong views of the Dharma—those who cling to the world, who uphold positions of either existence or nonexistence, or who are eternalists or nihilists—refuse to seek out meat. Even they do not seek it! But you are the protector of the world, and your teachings are indistinguishable from compassion. It is the teaching of all the perfect buddhas. Yet we Buddhists seek out meat. We have not put an end to seeking it.'"

On this point, the Buddha accepted those—such as King Kangtra[428]—whose attachment to meat would otherwise have prevented them from engaging with the teachings. Further, he allowed meat with threefold purity for the sake of Devadatta[429] and others like him who thought that they were pure buddhas simply because they gave up meat. This is why the Vinaya[430] says,

428. King Kangtra's story is found in the *Laṅkāvatāra Sūtra*. He was an Indian king who was so attached to meat that he would have been unwilling to even discuss Buddhism if vegetarianism had been required.

429. Devadatta was the Buddha's wayward cousin. Among other wrong ideas, he once proposed that all monks be required to be vegetarian, apparently in the belief that upholding such pure conduct was, in and of itself, sufficient to attain buddhahood. For an extended discussion of Devadatta's method, see the introduction to and translation of excerpts from Gorampa's *Commentary on Discerning the Three Vows* in chapter 5 of this volume.

430. The Vinaya is not a specific text, but rather the entire corpus (or basket, to use Buddhist terminology) of texts that lays out the monastic code, the rules that monks and nuns vow to uphold. In addition to the rules themselves, the Vinaya corpus contains the stories behind the rules. For more on the place of meat in the Vinaya, see the general introduction to this volume.

"Meat and fish that noble people have put in your bowl is pure. Having asked and ascertained that it is not human or another forbidden meat, it can be eaten." The Vinaya also says, "Do not eat meat if it was killed by tigers or killed for your own sake." This is the intention behind allowing meat with threefold purity in the Vinaya.

In the final perspective, on the other hand, Śāntideva[431] says that all meat is forbidden. The *Laṅkāvatāra Sūtra* explains, "In the past, I did not forbid the meat of animals that have died from the ten types of natural causes. But now, in these times, I strongly forbid it to everyone, no matter what method they follow. Just so, Mahāmati, I do not permit anyone who has ordained to eat meat." Further, the *Laṅkāvatāra Sūtra* says, "Mahāmati, my noble śrāvakas[432] do not eat ordinary, vulgar food, so what need is there to speak of unsuitable foods like meat and blood?" And, "I regard all beings as the same as my only child, and how could I permit the śrāvakas to eat the flesh of my child?"

Similarly, the noble *Mahāparinirvāna Sūtra*[433] says, "Child of my lineage, I have not allowed my śrāvakas to eat meat. If they receive it as alms from those who rule the land, they should think of it as if it were the flesh of their child. In this way, I have allowed eating meat." The same text also says, "[Kāśyapa asked], 'When meat is mixed in with other alms food, how should they cleanse it?' [The Buddha] replied, 'Child of my lineage, in order to not be in contradiction with the Vinaya, one must wash it with water before eating. This is my teaching. If, for instance, that place [the food in the bowl] is badly contaminated by large quantities of juicy meat, then abandon it. If the foods touch one another in the bowl but are not really mixed, there is no fault. [Eating] meat, fish meat, wild game, and dried lizard[434] is a fault for oneself and other noble beings. This is what I have said.'"

The *Mahāparinirvāna Sūtra* also explains, "Kāśyapa asked, 'Bhagavān, why did you previously allow eating meat that is completely pure from the three

431. Śāntideva was an eighth-century Indian monk and the author of the famed *Bodhicaryāvatāra, The Way of the Bodhisattva*.

432. Listeners: Buddhists who adhere only to the Hīnayāna path.

433. As with the texts by Ngorchen Künga Sangpo and Gorampa included in this volume, Karma Chakmé quotes the shorter of two versions of the *Mahāparinirvāna Sūtra* found in the Tibetan canon. This version differs from the passage translated in this present volume, which is derived from the longer version of the *Mahāparinirvāna Sūtra*, and this is why no precisely corresponding passage is found in that translation. See the introduction to the *Mahāparinirvāna Sūtra* in chapter 1 for more information on these differences.

434. Tib: *rmig pa skam po'i sha*; literally, "dried hoof meat." This is an obscure term of uncertain meaning. For a longer discussion of this term and its possible translations, see note 246 to Jörg Heimbel's translation of Ngorchen's *Epistle* in chapter 3 of this volume.

perspectives?'[435] [The Buddha] replied, 'I allowed meat that was completely pure from the three perspectives in order to restrain those at the beginning of the graded path. But now I set this aside.' [Kāśyapa] asked, 'Bhagavān, what was your intention when you taught that the ninefold purpose and ten types of meat should be abandoned?' [The Buddha] replied, 'I taught this teaching so that they would not eat meat.'"

The *Laṅkāvatāra Sūtra* explains:

All those who go against the Buddha's words,
and eat meat with an ignoble mind,
destroy their lives, both now and in the future,
and defile the conduct found in the Śākya's teachings!

Those people endowed with sinful karma,
go to hells that are thoroughly terrifying.
Those who eat meat will be boiled
in the Crying Hell.

The *Laṅkāvatāra Sūtra* also says:

Meat that you have seen, heard, or suspected—
all of it is utterly base.
But those born in meat-eating families,
do not understand, despite their cleverness.
Desire creates an obstacle to liberation.
In just this way, meat and alcohol
are also obstacles to liberation.

In future times,
ignorant supporters of meat eating
will say that meat is sinless and suitable,
and will claim that I say the same.

Again, the *Laṅkāvatāra Sūtra* says, "In the future, agitators will create their own scriptures that say eating meat is acceptable." There are many prophesies like this. These days, large numbers of bad monks eat like carnivores and yet say they are not in conflict with the three vows. This system is unaccept-

435. A slightly longer phrasing of "threefold purity."

able and must be vigorously stopped! Ngorchen Künga Sangpo[436] has also explained this.

Meat in the Mahāyāna

The Mahāyāna attitude is similar: all meat is unacceptable. The *Laṅkāvatāra Sūtra* says, "Bodhisattvas who possess the yoga[437] of kindness do not eat any type of meat." This has been stated many times. As for the meaning: there are no beings who have not been your father or mother.[438] Further, even demons give up meat after they hear the Dharma. How can a human who desires Dharma eat it? It also causes the fearful[439] to plant the seed of rejecting the teachings. For these reasons, not eating meat has been explained repeatedly. In brief, the *Laṅkāvatāra Sūtra* explains:[440]

> Whether of confused animals or one's own friends,
> all meat comes from semen and blood.
> Yogis do not eat meat,
> as consuming it causes other beings to fear.

In this way, meat is forbidden to those training as bodhisattvas.

436. Founder of the Ngor branch of the Sakya tradition and a committed advocate for vegetarianism. For more on Ngorchen and his views on meat eating, see Jörg Heimbel's introduction to and translation of his *Epistle Benefitting Students* in chapter 3 of this volume.

437. Contemporary readers should be aware that the term "yoga," as it is used here, does not refer exclusively or even primarily to contemplative practices that involved physical bodily positions. Instead, it carries its classical meaning, where it refers to spiritual practices in general, and sometimes connotes a sense of spiritual discernment.

438. Karma Chakmé does not spell out the rest of this argument, seeming to assume that his readers would understand that since all beings were once their parent, they should treat them kindly (by, for instance, not eating them).

439. It is unclear who, exactly, "the fearful" are. It could refer to animals who are afraid at the sight of meat eaters, but in his oral teachings on this text Khenpo Kartar Rinpoché explained that "the fearful" refers to non-Buddhist humans.

440. From the closing verses of the *Laṅkāvatāra Sūtra*; though Karma Chakmé (uncharacteristically) does not explicitly provide this attribution, I have added it for the sake of clarity.

A Mahāyāna Exception[441]

Meat is said to be without fault when someone eats it with the intention of converting those who lack kindness or compassion, or when a monk who propounds the Dharma is ill, or for the sake of someone who—having become endowed with great compassion—is practicing the accomplishment of the great meaning. The *Chapter on Yeshé Den*[442] says, "When the monk Chökyi Lodrö was ill, King Yeshé Ten offered him some meat. In this way he gained merit." Similarly, the *Śikṣāsamuccaya*[443] says, "There is no fault when meat is eaten for the sake of attaining the great meaning." What is the great meaning? The *Samādhirāja Sūtra*[444] explains:

> There was a monk who taught samādhi to the world.
> If he died, the roar of the teachings [would fade],
> and beings would always be acrimonious.
> By nourishing him in this way, samādhi can still be obtained.

Again, the *Śikṣāsamuccaya* says, "On this point, there is no fault if someone is truly striving for great compassion and has no unkind intention." Therefore there is no fault if a monk who propounds the Dharma eats meat, as long as it was not slaughtered for his sake. If this is not the situation, then meat is unacceptable and all the previously discussed faults are present.

441. Technically speaking, this section heading comes in the middle of a sentence. I have added it here, as Karma Chakmé abruptly changes direction but does not explicitly note this himself. In his oral teachings Khenpo Kartar Rinpoché insisted that the exceptions referred to in this section are very rare and emphasized that these were not normal, everyday occurances.

442. Tib: *Ye shes ldan gyi le'u*. I have consulted with several Tibetan scholars but have been unable to identify this text. From the title it seems to be a chapter from a longer work, but which work remains unclear. To add to the confusion, the name of the titular character is spelled differently in the title (*Ye shes ldan*) and in the quoted passage itself (*Ye shes brtan*). I have preserved this discrepancy in the transliterated names above, but my assumption is that both refer to the same person.

443. *Compendium of Training* (Tib: *Slab pa kun las btus pa*). An important Indian Buddhist treatise on ethics written in the eighth century by the acclaimed Indian master Śāntideva. For a full translation, see Goodman, *The Training Anthology of Śāntideva*.

444. *The King of Samādhi Sūtra* (Tib: *Ting nge 'dzin gyi rgyal po'i mdo*) is an important early Mahāyāna sūtra. Karma Chakmé does not identify the sūtra in his text, simply calling it "the sūtra." But this passage is from the *Samādhirāja Sūtra*, and I have added the attribution for the sake of clarity.

Meat in Tantric Ritual

Some people say that during the chöd[445] ritual feast,[446] when it comes time to distribute the corpse, it is necessary to eat a mouthful of human flesh and drink a sip of human blood. Through this, some think, all conceptions will become one-taste. In this way, they use horse meat, human flesh, and so on,[447] thinking of them as the authentic ritual feast substances. But this is very incorrect! The *Smṛtyupasthāna Sūtra*[448] says:

> Rather than associating with lions,
> tigers, foxes, or the like,
> I abide in kindness. Therefore,
> I always declare meat to be base.
> Since it is in contradiction with the Dharma of liberation,
> and because it makes people fearful,
> I have declared that it is not to be eaten.
> This is the noble banner of victory!

So it is taught. As for the meat that people fear, it is human flesh. Further, the *Yamārikṛṣṇa Tantra*[449] states:

> When a mantrin is worn out, they should eat food.
> Faultless food is easy to find:
> great meat,[450] horse, elephant,

445. Chöd (Tib: *gcod*), sometimes translated as "cutting" or "severance," is a tantric practice in which the practitioner visualizes offering their own body to a particular deity.

446. The feast ritual (Tib: *tshogs*) is a common feature of many tantric rituals in which sacralized substances are offered to the deities. Many tantric texts explicitly include the five meats (cow, dog, horse, elephant, and human) as part of the ritual feast offering.

447. Karma Chakmé is referring to the famous "five meats." These meats (cow, dog, horse, elephant, and human) were all taboo in India, where the tantras originated. Including them in the ritual was a means of forcing the practitioner to violate cultural norms. For more on the five meats in India, see Wedemeyer, *Making Sense of Tantric Buddhism*. For more on the five meats in Tibet, see Barstow, *Food of Sinful Demons*, 92–97.

448. *The Application of Mindfulness* (Tib: *Dran pa nyer bzhag*). An important early sūtra stressing the practice of mindfulness.

449. *The Tantra of Black Yamari* (Tib: *Gshin rje'i gshed nag po'i rgyud*). Full Sanskrit title: *Yamārikṛṣṇakarmasarvacakrasiddhikara*. A tantra of the Anuttarayoga (Highest Yoga) class. Karma Chakmé's text gives a very condensed version of this title (*Dgra nag gi rgyud*), and my identification of the quotation that follows this tantra remains tentative.

450. A euphemism referring to human flesh.

and especially, cow, dog,
donkey, camel, and jackal.

Someone might ask, Who is it that should nourish their body with these unslaughtered meats? The answer is that such a person must be able to either truly transform the meat into divine nectar or, if they do not transform it into divine nectar, they must be able to transform their body so that they appear as a burial-ground jackal, a tiger, a lion, or the like. After that they can eat. Other than that, if someone eats human flesh or the rest, then it is a violation of all three vows[451] at once! Because of this, the fault is a hundred thousand times worse than what was explained earlier! The *Vimalaprabhā*, the great commentary on the *Kālacakra Tantra*, explains that if you are unable to turn a tooth into a pearl, a skull-cup into a lotus, meat into sons' hair,[452] and blood into a heruka deity, then it is unacceptable to eat this. Even if they spend eons trying, ordinary people are unable perform such transformations. Therefore it is widely explained that they should not try to transform these substances into divine nectar by themselves.

Similarly, the *Saṃdhivyākaraṇa Tantra*[453] says:

If, because one is an ignorant being,
one eats fish, meat, and the like,
consumes beer, feces, urine, semen, and blood,
then one is a proponent of nihilism.

The same tantra also says:

Through the blessings of Mara,[454]
they seek minor yogic attainment,

451. As explained fully in the introduction to this volume, the three vows are the vows of individual liberation, the bodhisattva vow, and the tantric samayas. Karma Chakmé is here claiming that if one eats the five before one is fully qualified (and able to magically transform the meats), then it is a violation not only of the tantric samayas but of all three vows as well.

452. Tib: *pu tra ke sha*; Skt: *putrakeśa*. This is an obscure Sanskrit term whose meaning is not obvious. Vesna Wallace suggests that it may be a folk name for an herbal remedy (*The Inner Kālacakratantra*, 53). In the present context, it is clearly some type of pure substance that a yogi of exceptional ability would be able to transform meat into.

453. *The Tantra That Prophesies Realization* (Tib: *Dgongs pa lung bstan pa'i rgyud*). A tantra of the Anuttarayoga class, connected to the deity Guhyasamāja.

454. Sometimes described as the Buddhist Satan, Mara is the personification of negative mental attributes, including anger, ignorance, and desire. Being blessed by Mara is definitely not a good thing.

but in truth this makes them puffed with pride,
and they think, "I am like a great scholar!"[455]

As the master Smrtijnānakīrti[456] explains:

It is like one who, being ignorant of reality,
merely listens to the teachings,
and makes no effort at actually accumulating merit.
Such an inferior person is lost.
Some rely only on the mere words—
this leads to desire and conceptual mind,
which causes them to perform nonvirtue.
Such people go from bad to worse.

It is similar when non-Buddhists kill humans and water buffalos in order to offer them to Īśvara. They say that once it is offered, the dead creature is itself born among the gods and that Īśvara, Brahmā, Śiva, and Viṣṇu are pleased by the offering and bestow accomplishment. Thinking like this, non-Buddhists make red offerings. Ascetics and priests kill cows and yaks to be food for the wrathful deities. It is similar in some Tibetan areas, such as the Makung valley at Mount Tsari. There people say to give red offerings, so a lot of slaughtered meat is offered during ritual feasts. The result, they say, is that the animals attain signs of liberation, such as the uneaten parts dissolving into light. Here[457] also, animals are slaughtered for the hundred feasts and other rituals, and their meat placed in the offering cakes. This is unsuitable!

As Ācārya Śūra[458] says:

How could it be true that
killing a cow or other animal could be Dharma,
or that the animal will be born in the god-realm,
or that the gods are pleased by this killing?

455. This passage makes no direct reference to meat, but the implication seems to be that those who eat meat in the name of tantric practice are overly proud.

456. Tib: Slob dpon Ye shes grags pa. My identification of this figure with the Indian translator Smrtijnānakīrti is tentative.

457. This seems to be referring to Karma Chakmé's own community.

458. Tib: Slob dpon Dpa' bo. This identification is somewhat tentative.

It is false to think that it is Dharma
to kill an animal in order to send it to the higher realms,
through the power of mantra.

Who has ever achieved liberation through someone else's actions?
Their bad actions are not reversed by your mind,
and the cow or other animal killed for the offering
is definitely not creating good karma!
There is no ground for the animal itself to act,
so how can it attain a higher state?

The idea that the animals killed for an offering go to the higher realms—
If this is the Brahman's own Dharma,
then why does this method not appear anywhere in their own system?
So who could listen to these words?

The gods eat nectar offered by supreme goddesses,
which possesses a taste of unequaled potency.
So how could they rejoice
at the flesh and blood of slaughtered cows?

The *Rigyārali Tantra*[459] says:

Yogis who think they have attained faultlessness,
and thereby kill beings,
will not become accomplished.
Those who cultivate a mindset that protects beings,
will undoubtedly achieve accomplishment!

When the *Kālacakra Tantra*[460] says, "Eat great meat and other types that are not eaten or sold in this country," it is speaking to accomplished yogis. Even this meat is unsuitable for ordinary people, for the reasons explained earlier.

459. *The Tantra of Rigyārali* (Tib: *Ri gi A Ralli'i rgyud*). Another tantra classified in the Anuttarayoga class.

460. *The Wheel of Time Tantra* (Tib: *Dus kyi 'khor lo'i rgyud*). Among the most famous of the tantras. Notably for this volume, the *Kālacakra Tantra* includes several critiques of meat eating. For a good general introduction to this cycle of texts and practices, see Berzin, *Introduction to the Kalachakra Initiation*; Khendrup Norsang Gyatso, *Ornament of Stainless Light*.

Because it upsets the ḍākinīs, even meat from animals that were killed by someone else, meat that came from an animal that fell off a cliff, or meat from animals killed by a carnivore is unsuitable to be offered in the ritual feast. This is explained in the hundred texts on the feast offering found in the Dzokchen *Unimpeded Realization* cycle.[461] Elsewhere, it is said that offering meat from an animal that died naturally is acceptable, as long as it is not unwholesome, such as the meat of an animal that died of plague or after a long illness. The *Higher Commentary* on the *Cakrasaṃvara Tantra*[462] says, "Do not use flesh of those that died in anguish in battle or that had the evil karma of dying of illness." Others are acceptable.

If you tell someone, "If you bring it from the market and kill it, then I will buy it," this is "requested meat" whose slaughter was ordered. Even if you distribute it in feasts and other rituals, there is still killing. The animal is purchased and brought only because you said, "Bring meat for the feasts and other rituals." This is unsuitable. The commentary on the *Kālacakra Tantra* says, "Meat always comes from killing. If there was no killing, these beings would live longer lives. If there was no consumer, there would also be no butcher. For this reason, both the consumer and the butcher are both killers. So then what did the Buddha mean when he said, 'In this Mantrayāna Vehicle, yogis eat meat'? . . . He meant that you may eat it and offer it if you did not buy it, if your relatives did not buy it, and if it was not killed for the ritual. The Buddha did not say, 'Eat meat that is marked for you.'"[463]

The same text also says, "On the other hand, it is acceptable for a yogi who has attained accomplishment to eat meat, even if the animal was killed for his own sake. In short, meat with threefold purity is when you are not personally

461. Tib: *Dgongs pa zang thal.* Often know by its Tibetan name, *Gongpa Zangthal,* this is an important cycle of Dzokchen teachings, revealed in the late fourteenth century by Rigdzin Gödem.

462. *The Cycle of Supreme Bliss Tantra* (Tib: *'Khor lo bde mchog gi rgyud*). Another famous tantra of the Anuttarayoga class. For a translation and study of this tantra, see Gray, *The Cakrasamvara Tantra.*

463. This passage, as quoted by Karma Chakmé, is quite convoluted and condensed, with important sections of the original tantra missing. I have included only those lines cited by Karma Chakmé but have translated it in accordance with the meaning of the full passage, as found in the Degé Tengyur edition of the *Vimalaprabhā*. A further complication is a major difference between the text as quoted by Karma Chakmé and the original sūtra: In the final line, Karma Chakmé's version reads that the Buddha *does* allow this kind of meat (*bde bzhin gshegs pas gsungs*). The original text, on the other hand, includes the negating particle *ma*, making clear that the Buddha *did not* allow this meat (*bde bzhin gshegs pas ma gsungs*). Given that Karma Chakmé's language does not make sense in the overall sense of the passage, I have chosen to regard this as a typo and have translated according to the source text.

responsible for harming the animal." This is explained in Śāntideva's *Bodhicaryāvatāra*.[464] If meat is not fully dedicated for your benefit—meaning that it was killed for your own sake—and if you did not request it with awareness, and if you did not impel it by saying, "Bring me meat," knowing that this would cause the death of the animal—if all this is the case, then it is suitable to eat a little bit as the sacred substance during a feast ritual. To refuse this type of meat is unsuitable.

The *Saddharmasmṛtyupasthāna Sūtra*[465] [actually, the *Laṅkāvatāra Sūtra*][466] says:

> Meat that has threefold purity,
> free of being considered, requested,
> or coerced, does not exist.
> So do not eat meat!
> Yogis do not eat meat.
> This is my teaching,
> and that of all other buddhas.

If you do eat it, you will not attain accomplishment in mantra. As the *Laṅkāvatāra Sūtra* says, "Those who dwell in charnel grounds, who live in forest monasteries, who sleep in remote hermitages haunted by spirits, who engage in yoga, who abide in kindness, who are adepts accomplished in knowledge-mantras, or who aspire to accomplish knowledge-mantras all understand that eating meat is an obstacle to liberation. Therefore all those accomplished yogis who are my sons and daughters and who abide in the Mahāyāna do not eat any type of meat. They see it as an obstacle to benefitting themselves and others, so these bodhisattvas do not eat any type of meat."

Further, those who practice Anuttarayoga Tantra do not perform austerities. Some might say, "Through undertaking endless vows of austerity, you will torment your body and not attain accomplishment. But if you rely only on desirable enjoyments, you will swiftly become accomplished." But non-Buddhist ascetics do things like hanging on cliffs and stepping into fires. They

464. *The Way of the Bodhisattva* (Tib: *Byang chub sems dpa'i spyod pa la 'jug pa*).

465. *The Awareness of the True Dharmas Sūtra* (Tib: *Dam chos dran pa nye bzhag*). An important sūtra largely dealing with meditative practice. For a detailed study of this text, see Stuart, "A Less Traveled Path."

466. I have been unable to locate this passage in the *Saddharmasmṛtyupasthana*, though this exact wording is found in the *Laṅkāvatāra Sūtra*. It is likely—if somewhat surprising—that Karma Chakmé is misattributing this quote.

do not think of merely rejecting meat and alcohol as ascetic practice at all! As Chandrakīrti says, "Practices like hanging on cliffs and stepping into fires are horrible!"[467]

Ngorchen Kunga Sangpo explains it like this:[468] Although some say that it is acceptable to use ordinary, slaughtered meat as an offering or as samaya-substance,[469] this is not my intention. In rituals like the feast offering, you should use meat that has not been slaughtered and that has threefold purity. This is suitable to use in the torma[470] offered to the gods, as well as the samaya-substance consumed in the ritual feast. On this point there are two tantras from the Nyingma[471] tradition—the *Ekajaṭī Mahāyogeśvarī Tantra*[472] and *Durtrö Lhamo Nagpo*[473]—and two tantras from the Sarma[474] tradition—the *Gönpo Chakshipé Sunggyü Kragtso Kolma*[475] and *Yumtsa Jibmé Gyü Duklang*

467. The details of these practices are unclear to me, but Karma Chakmé's point here is that while Buddhists do, in fact, reject austerities, we should not understand vegetarianism as an austerity. Therefore rejecting austerities does not entail rejecting vegetarianism.

468. The text is not at all clear on whether this is a direct quote or simply a paraphrase. But this passage does not appear anywhere in Ngorchen's collected works, so I have interpreted it as a paraphrase rather than a direct quote.

469. Samayas are tantric vows or commitments. In many tantric systems, these vows include a pledge to consume the five meats and the five nectars. These are then known as samaya substances (Tib: *dam rdzas*).

470. For more on torma, see note 405 in chapter 6 of this volume.

471. The "Old Translation" lineage. One of the four main Buddhist lineages in Tibet, the Nyingma accept a collection of texts translated into Tibetan during the period of the first dissemination of Buddhism in Tibet, under the aegis of the Tibetan empire (roughly the seventh to ninth centuries).

472. *The Tantra of Ekajaṭī, Great Lord of Yogis* (Tib: *Rnal 'byor dbang phyug chen mo ral gcig ma'i rgyud*). Like other Nyingma tantras, this tantra is classified using a different system than Sarma tantras. In the Nyingma system of Mahāyoga, Anuyoga, and Atiyoga, this tantra is classified as Mahāyoga. I want to thank Ryan Damron for his help in identifying and transliterating the Sanskrit title for this and the following three texts.

473. *The Black Goddess of the Charnel Ground Tantra* (Tib: *Dur khrod lha mo nag mo'i rang rgyud*). Another Nyingma Mahāyoga tantra, found only in Nyingma tantric collections. I have used transliterated Tibetan, as found in Karma Chakmé's work.

474. In contrast to the Nyingma, the Sarma tradition includes the Kagyü, Sakya, and Geluk lineages and relies on translations done during the later dissemination of Buddhism in Tibet, from the late tenth century onward.

475. *The Ocean of Boiling Blood: A Tantra Spoken by Four-Armed Mahākāla* (Tib: *Mgon po phyag bzhi pa'i gsung rgyud khrag mtsho khol ma*). I have not found any texts with the specific title found in Karma Chakmé's text, either in the Kangyur, the standard Tibetan canon, or elsewhere. A close match, however, is the *Śrirutingadhisagarasarṇmahāghuhyatā Tantra* (Tib: *Khrag mtsho khol ma zhes bya ba mgon po gsang ba'i rgyud chen po*), a Sarma tantra associated

Kolma.[476] In all four of these tantras, it says to use meat and blood that were not slaughtered for the ritual as offering substances.

How Much Is Appropriate?

How should we eat this? During the feast ritual, when you consume meat with this kind of threefold purity, think of it as the flesh of your only child. Generate compassion for that animal and sow the blessings of mantras on its bones. Seal it with dedication prayers, and eat moderately, thinking of the meat as medicinal nourishment for the body. The *Saddharmasmṛtyupasthāna Sūtra* [actually the *Laṅkāvatāra Sūtra*][477] says:

> Thinking of food as no different than medicine,
> and of meat as the flesh of their own children,
> yogis eat moderately,
> not so much that they cannot digest it.

It is unsuitable to hoard meat from the ritual, eating it over and over again. Eat it quickly, without hoarding this substance of accomplishment. This is taught in the great accomplishment rituals. Beyond this, do not eat hungrily, but think about the quantity of feast dough, feast alcohol, and feast meat used. Be satisfied with what you eat and drink. So it is taught. If you eat too much, it cannot be digested, so eating like this is inappropriate. The *Kālacakra Tantra* says, "The point of any food is health. So do not eat more in a given day than you can digest in that day." The commentary on this says, "Eating food is similar. Now, the point of all types of food is health. Some eat only a little, and with that little, are healthy. For this reason, do not eat more than you can digest in a single day." What this says about food is certainly true. If you do not stuff your belly, you will not get indigestion. It is not suitable, therefore, for someone to eat more at one time than they can healthily digest.

During the ritual feast, it is not appropriate to consume more than a small

with the wrathful deity Mahākāla. As I am uncertain if this is the work Karma Chakmé references, however, I have used the Tibetan title in the above translation.

476. *Boiling Poison: A Tantra of Drawing up the Mother Channel* (Tib: *Yum rtsa 'jib ma'i rgyud*). I have found nothing along these lines in any of the resources I have access to, though one Tibetan scholar I consulted thought it might be related to the deity Cakrasaṃvara. Once again, in the absence of a Sanskrit title, I have been left to use a transliterated version of the Tibetan title.

477. Again, Karma Chakmé is misattributing a quote from the *Laṅkāvatāra Sūtra* to the *Saddharmasmṛtyupasthāna Sūtra*.

amount of meat, the equivalent of the leg of an insect. It is said that there is benefit from consuming an insect's-leg worth of the flesh of a seven-times-born brahman. So eating just this much is sufficient.

If you completely refuse to eat meat during the feast ritual, you will be committing the thirteenth root downfall. It is said that "samaya substances are suchness.[478] Not to rely on them is the thirteenth."[479] In his commentary on this, Jetsün Drakpa Gyaltsen[480] has explained the downfalls in this way, as has Rangjungpa.[481] Songtsen Gampo[482] has also said, "If you do not eat it during a feast ritual conducted at the time of taking one-day vows, then your samaya will be spoiled." Dombhipa[483] says, "If you eat while wrapped up with conceptual thoughts of purity, then you will be born in the Water Bubble Hell." This goes beyond just those who participate in the feast ritual. There is a story of a brahman who visited a feast ritual in the land of Orgyen.[484] The feast substances—meat and blood—nauseated him and disturbed his mind so much that his nose bled and he died. Orgyen Rinpoché[485] says, "Do not have doubts about this." Since he said this, do not have doubts! If you do have doubts about this, then you have the fault of committing the root downfall, and the ḍākinīs' punishment will occur.

Our own practice tradition is similar. There were always five hundred fully ordained monks in Lord Rolpé Dorjé's[486] entourage. It is said that they all

478. Meaning that they are primordially pure.

479. Meaning the thirteenth root downfall. In Sarma tantric systems, there are fourteen root downfalls that tantric practitioners must avoid in order to keep their tantric samayas. The thirteenth root downfall is to not observe the commitments, which in this case means to not consume the samaya substances. Karma Chakmé does not identify the text that this quote comes from.

480. Drakpa Gyaltsen (Tib: Grags pa rgyal mthsan) was an important early Sakya master (1147–1216).

481. I am unsure who Karma Chakmé is referring to by the name Rangjungpa (Tib: Rang byung pa), though I suspect it is Rangjung Dorjé (Tib: Rang byung rdo rje) the Third Karmapa, who was himself a staunch vegetarian.

482. In Tibetan accounts of the Tibetan empire, Songtsen Gampo (Tib: Srong btsan sgam po) is often credited with introducing Buddhism to Tibet. His birth date is somewhat uncertain, but he flourished in the early seventh century and died in 649.

483. I am uncertain, but believe Dombhipa (Tib: Dom bhi pa) refers to Dombhi Heruka (Tib: Dom bhi he ru ka), one of the famous eighty-four mahasiddas of Indian tantric Buddhism.

484. A Buddhist region in northwest India, often understood to be modern Pakistan.

485. Another term for Padmasambhava, the semimythical Indian tantric master who subdued the demons obstructing the establishment of Buddhism in Tibet. He is often said to be the "second Buddha," particularly by Nyingma practitioners.

486. The fourth Karmapa (1340–1383). Karmapa Rolpé Dorjé became a strict vegetarian at the time he took his monastic vows.

achieved complete liberation and never allowed meat in their presence, even pure meat or animal pelts. Lord Mikyö Dorjé[487] established firm rules about meat in Zur[488] and the other monasteries he founded. Even in those monastic centers that did not have rules about meat, he set it up so that those who had given up meat—known as "those who adhere to a white diet"—had their soup prepared separately from the others. Both father and sons[489] refused to allow meat into their presence, even white troma.[490] During feast rituals, on the other hand, all who otherwise reject meat consumed the feast meat. In order to not violate their samaya, both father and sons ate a little.

Conclusion

For all these reasons, the best option is to perform the holy act of relinquishing all meat. When you perform a ritual feast, use meat with threefold purity in order to guard your samaya. At that time, it is very important simply to not reject meat, alcohol, or dough. Eat only a little, however, an amount equivalent to the leg of an insect. The middle option is to give up meat that was slaughtered for your own sake, or, if you eat other meat, to eat only a little. The least option is to give up the meat of animals killed that day, the meat of animals of a similar species, and human meat. When you do eat it, bless it as divine nectar and consume it as an inner fire offering.[491] Then give rise to great compassion, purifying the animal's obscurations through prayers, mantras, and the names of buddhas. This distinction between meat and feast substances is taught in the sūtras, tantras, and ritual texts. This is the way it is done in the monasteries and great encampments.

487. The eighth Karmapa (1507–1554). Karmapa Mikyö Dorjé was a strong advocate for vegetarianism. For more on Karmapa Mikyö Dorjé's stance on meat, see the extracts from his *Great Commentary on the Vinayasūtra* translated in chapter 6 of this volume.

488. The identity of this monastery is unclear to me. It is possible that it refers to Tsurpu (Tib: Mtshur pu), the seat of the Karmapa lineage. Mikyö Dorjé wrote a guidebook for this monastery that banned meat. Despite the similar pronunciation, however, the Tibetan word *tsur* (*mtshur*; the first syllable in Tsurpu) is spelled quite differently from *zur* (*zur*), so this identification is speculative at best.

489. The "father and sons" here refers to the Karmapa and his followers.

490. Troma (Tib: *gro ma*) is a small wild sweet potato and was a common food in Tibet. It is not clear why the Karmapa and his retinue refused to eat it, though it is clearly presented as an even stricter version of vegetarianism. Perhaps they objected to the harvesting process, which involves digging in the ground and therefore runs the risk of killing insects?

491. During a fire-offering ritual, sanctified liquids are poured into a fire, causing it to blaze up. Karma Chakmé here suggests visualizing this process internally.

This was written by Arāgasa [Karma Chakmé], with apologies for any faults. May this virtue establish all who see or hear it in the training of the bodhisattvas, causing all beings to be led to Dewachen.

—Sarwa Mangalam

Eating Meat with Compassion

By Karma Chakmé

Translated by Geoffrey Barstow[492]

Praise Avalokiteśvara!

The Laṅkāvatāra Sūtra teaches to not eat meat except as samaya substances in the ritual feast, so do not do so. Naturally dead meat, dried meat, and meat from the bazaar: these three can be eaten without occurring a fault, according to the Vinaya. Slaughtered meat and meat dedicated for your consumption is a great fault.

On the other hand, meat can be eaten through the power of compassion. Meditate on the meat in front of you with immeasurable compassion and when you inhale, dissolve the sin and defilement of all beings, headed by the one you are about to eat, into yourself. Once all beings are free of that sin and suffering, exhale and dissolve your own collected virtues to all beings, headed by that one. Meditate that all beings have achieved happiness and enlightenment.

In that state, proclaim the names and recite: With **Praise**[493] **Bhagavan Tathāgata Kubera,** *purify the sin of killing. With* **Praise Tathāgata Śrībhadra,** *purify the sin of preparing the food. With* **Praise Tathāgata Abhijñā,**[494] *purify the sin of preparing the food. These three are the bodhisattva's confession, and [this passage] is a commentary on that.*

492. A note to the reader: The Tibetan original contains some phrases in a larger font and some smaller, as does this translation. The text in larger font is meant to be recited out loud. The smaller, italicized text is Karma Chakmé's interlinear instructions.

493. Tib: *phyag 'tshal lo*. This phrase literally means "prostrate to."

494. These three buddhas are all found among the thirty-five confession (or purification) buddhas. It is unclear to me (and to the Tibetan scholars I discussed this with) why Karma Chakmé selected these three specific buddhas from among the thirty-five. For more on the thirty-five confession buddhas, see Watt, "Thirty-Five Confession Buddhas."

Oṃ Ābhira Hūṃ Khecara Mūṃ[495] Svāhā[496]
Repeat [this mantra] seven times.[497]

Then, having offered the meat, eat it. There will be no fault, and the animal will be liberated from the lower realms. Lord Atiśa says that this is explained in the Kutagara Sūtra. This concludes the sūtra section.

As for the tantra section, recite: **Alas! This being, killed for the sake of meat, has been my old mother for many lifetimes and is worthy of compassion. So that you can complete the accumulations and purify your obscurations, I make this inner offering of clarified butter to the illusory gods.**

Engender the deity in this way, then say: **Āḥ. Instantaneously, I am Vajrasattva and the hot wind in my navel is the fire of wisdom. My tongue is a tongue of fire and my mouth is a furnace. In my hands the two types of ritual ladle[498] appear spontaneously. In the center of my heart are the forty-two peaceful buddhas. In my bone palace[499] there are the fifty-eight blood-drinkers. They are clear and the visualized deity is inseparable from the actual deity.**

Having clearly visualized the oven and the fire gods, the three syllables bless the fire-offering substances. Say:

Oṃ Āḥ Hūṃ.

Eating and drinking meat foods, offer amrita fire offerings. Thus the two obstructions of the being whose meat is consumed will be purified.

Oṃ Āḥ Hūṃ. Bhodhicitta Mahāsukhajñāna Dhātu Āḥ. Oṃ Rulu Rulu Hūṃ Byo Hūṃ. Māṃ Sajvāla Rāṃ Khāhi.

The sins and defilements of the being whose meat is food are Sarva Pāpaṃ Śāntiṃ Kuruye Svāhā. *Say this one time. Then eat. In order*

495. The Tibetan reads *Muṃ*, but this is likely to be a typographical error for the syllable *Huṃ*.

496. Throughout this prayer, I have done my best to render the mantras in accurate Sanskrit, with appropriate diacritical marks. Going from Tibetanized Sanskrit to actual Sanskrit, however, is not always clear, and I apologize for any mistakes. I also want to thank Daniel McNamara for his help transliterating these mantras.

497. Mantras are short Sanskrit phrases that embody the essence of the deity in question. They are an essential part of tantric Buddhism, and those who are unfamiliar with their use are encouraged to seek clarification on their meaning and import from a qualified teacher before undertaking practices such as the prayer translated here.

498. Two different types of ladles are used during a fire offering, known as gangsar (*dgangs gzar*) and lüsar (*blugs gzar*).

499. Another term for the skull.

to increase the mantras and dhāraṇīs,[500] *recite a mantra in your mind each time you take a mouthful.*

If abbreviated, say Oṃ Kaṃkani[501] *one time and Uṣṇiṣa*[502] *seven times.*

Having done this, say mantras and sprinkle water on the bones in a clean place.

In this way, I dedicate the merit of making these burnt offerings so that all beings can obtain enlightenment. By the virtue of this, may the being who I have eaten be swiftly born in Sukhāvatī.[503]

This was written between sessions by the tantrika A Rā Ga [Karma Chakmé].

500. Often more or less synonymous with mantras.

501. The *Kaṃkani* is the mantra of Buddha Akshobya, associated with purification.

502. The mantra of the Buddha Uṣṇiṣavijayā, one of a trinity of long-life buddhas.

503. The Land of Bliss (Tib: Bde ba can), the pure land of the Buddha Amitabha.

Source Texts

Karma Chakmé (Karma chags med). 2010. *Sha yi nyes dmigs dang gnang bkag gi sa mtshams dbye ba yul byang phyogs rgyud kyi paṇḍita 'jam dbyangs bla ma'i zhal lung* (*The Faults of Meat*). In *Mkhas grub karma chags med kyi gsung 'bum*, vol. 35, 451–76. Gnas mdo gsang sngags chos 'phel gling gi dpe rnying nyams gso khang. BDRC: W1KG8321.

———. 2010. *Sha ni snying rje can gyi bza' zhes pa'i don gyi man ngag mdo sngags bcud bsdus* (*Eating Meat with Compassion*). In *Mkhas grub karma chags med kyi gsung 'bum*, vol. 35, 477–79. Gnas mdo gsang sngags chos 'phel gling gi dpe rnying nyams gso khang. BDRC: W1KG8321.

Secondary Sources

Chökyi Nyima Rinpoché. 2004. *Union of Mahāmudrā and Dzogchen: A Commentary on The Quintessence of Spiritual Practice, The Direct Instructions of the Great Compassionate One by Karma Chagmey Rinpoche.* Translated from the Tibetan by Eric Pema Kunsang. Edited by Marcia B. Schmidt. Boudhanath: Rangjung Yeshe Publications.

Barstow, Geoffrey. 2018. *Food of Sinful Demons: Meat, Vegetarianism, and the Limits of Buddhism in Tibet.* New York: Columbia University Press.

Berzin, Alexander. 2011. *Introduction to the Kalachakra Initiation.* Ithaca, NY: Snow Lion Publications.

Goodman, Charles, trans. 2016. *The Training Anthology of Śāntideva: A Translation of the Śikṣā-Samuccaya.* Oxford: Oxford University Press.

Gray, David. 2007. *The Cakrasamvara Tantra.* New York: AIBS.

Karma Chagme Rinpoché. 2008. *The All-Pervading Melodious Sound of Thunder: The Outer Liberation Story of Terton Migyur Dorjé.* Translated by Lopon Sonam Tsewang and Judith Amtzis. Pharping: Palri Parkhang.

Khenchen Thrangu. 2016. *Luminous Clarity: A Commentary on Karma Chagme's Union of Mahamudra and Dzogchen.* Boulder, CO: Snow Lion Publications.

Khendrup Norsang Gyatso. 2001. *Ornament of Stainless Light: An Exposition of the Kalachakra Tantra.* Translated by Gavin Kilty. Boston: Wisdom Publications.

Shantideva. 1999. *The Way of the Bodhisattva.* Translated by Padmakara Translation Group. Boston: Shambhala.

Stuart, Daniel. 2013. "A Less Traveled Path: Meditation and Textual Practice in the Sad dharmasmṛtyupasthāna(sūtra)." PhD dissertation, University of California, Berkeley.

Tsering Lama Jampal Sangpo. 1988. *A Garland of Immortal Wish-Fulfilling Trees: The Pelyul Tradition of Nyingmapa.* Translated by Sangye Khandro. Ithaca, NY: Snow Lion Publications.

Wallace, Vesna A. 2001. *The Inner Kālacakratantra: A Buddhist Tantric View of the Individual.* Oxford: Oxford University Press.

Watt, Jeff. 2017. "Thirty-Five Confession Buddhas." 2017. Himalayanart.org. https://www.himalayanart.org/search/set.cfm?setID=660.

Wedemeyer, Christian K. 2012. *Making Sense of Tantric Buddhism: History, Semiology, and Transgression in the Indian Traditions.* New York: Columbia University Press.

8. Songs against Meat by the Yogi Shabkar

By Rachel H. Pang

SHABKAR TSOKDRUK RANGDRÖL (1781–1851)[504] was a meditation master and singer from the Amdo province of northeastern Tibet (contemporary Qinghai, PRC). After spending his youth among the lay tantric community[505] of the Rebgong valley, he was ordained as a monk by the prominent Geluk teacher Arik Geshé at the age of twenty. Shabkar then proceeded to the Lake Kokonor region, where he studied under his main teacher, the great Nyingma master Chögyel Ngakyi Wangpo. Following intense contemplation on Tsongkhapa's *Stages of the Path*, Shabkar was initiated into the tantric practice of the *Wish-Fulfilling Gem: Hayagriva and Varahi* (Tib: *Rta phag yid bzhin nor bu*) revealed by the tertön Kunzang Dechen Gyalpo (b. 1736). After many years spent in meditative retreat at sacred sites throughout the Amdo region, Shabkar would master this system of practice.

At the age of twenty-nine, adopting the lifestyle of an itinerant yogi, Shabkar embarked on a nearly two-decade-long pilgrimage to major sites across the Tibetan plateau, engaging in intense meditative retreats at renowned sacred sites in Tibet and Nepal, such as in Milarepa's Cave of Miracles at Mount Kailash. During this time, in addition to meditative retreats, teaching disciples, and performing religious rituals, Shabkar also learned and mastered the meditation practices of Mahāmudrā from the Kagyü tradition. It is truly an accomplishment for an individual to perfect the meditative practices within a single Tibetan Buddhist sect; to do so in two systems as Shabkar had done is a rare feat. In addition to this, Shabkar sought empowerments, transmissions, and instructions from masters from a wide range of sectarian affiliations. This impartial (Tib: *ris med*) attitude toward sectarian and religious diversity is one of the main themes in Shabkar's life and works.

504. Tib: Zhabs dkar Tshogs drug rang grol.

505. Tib: *sngags pa*. Like monks, mantrins—*ngakpa* in Tibetan—are professional Buddhist practitioners. Mantrins, however, do not take monastic vows and are free to marry and have children. They typically mark their status by wearing white robes and growing their hair long.

At the age of forty-seven, Shabkar journeyed back to the Amdo region, where he spent the rest of his life alternating between meditative retreats and serving his community through religious activities. A prolific writer, Shabkar left behind fourteen volumes of collected works. The most famous are his spiritual autobiography, songs and poems, and *Emanated Scriptures*.[506] The theme of vegetarianism is significant throughout Shabkar's writings.[507]

Arguments

Shabkar was renowned as a staunch vegetarian. Throughout his autobiography are descriptions of his numerous interactions with and acts of kindness toward animals. At the age of thirty, he became a committed vegetarian after he witnessed slaughtered sheep and goats on the circumambulation route around the temple housing the Jowo statue in Lhasa. Moved by unbearable compassion for all animals slaughtered for food, Shabkar vowed in front of the Jowo statue, "I will never again eat the sinful food that is the flesh of my parents." One of the songs associated with this event is preserved in his *Collected Songs* and is translated below (third song).

In the songs translated below, Shabkar uses vivid, powerful language that appeals directly to the emotions of his readers. For example, in the first poem, he describes animal suffering in graphic detail, noting the way in which slaughtered animals are "beheaded" and "disemboweled" after having their "mouths and snouts bound." In the third poem, alluding to the Buddhist belief that all beings were once our parents in previous lifetimes, he attempts to create a sense of guilt among butchers who "slaughter the flesh of their own parents" and monks who dwell "amidst heaps of flesh and bones from beings who were once our mothers." Finally, he notes his own emotional reaction to beings who kill animals and consume meat, noting the way in which his "tears spring forth" when he sees that they will eventually be "thrust unimpeded into hell's fiery pit" as a result of their actions. In this, Shabkar's writing is reminiscent of passages found in the works of other scholar-monks of his time, including Jigmé Lingpa, Patrül Rinpoché, and Nyala Pema Dündul. Together, their writings mark a shift in rhetoric that is used to support vegetarianism—they move away from scholastic language and toward emotional, affective rhetoric.

506. For more on Shabkar's *Emanated Scriptures*, see Pang, "Literature, Innovation, and Buddhist Philosophy."

507. For a detailed account of Shabkar's life, see Shabkar, *Life of Shabkar*; and Pang, "Dissipating Boundaries."

Admonitions to abstain from meat eating appear throughout Shabkar's *Collected Works*, but a few works in particular contain more sustained treatments of the topic. In a sermon that occurs in the second volume of his autobiography, Shabkar presents two main arguments for why one should abandon meat eating. First, he argues that killing animals results in negative karma that leads to rebirth in the lower realms and the hells in particular. Second, he argues that the consumption of meat hinders one's ability to generate genuine compassion. If one cannot generate compassion, then it follows that one will also not be able to generate the mind of awakening (Skt: *bodhicitta*). And because bodhicitta is the main cause of the state of awakening, one will not be able to attain enlightenment. An excerpt from this sermon is translated below, and the first song included here also provides an evocative rendering of these basic ideas in verse form.

Although Shakbar maintained a strict vegetarian diet and often preached the ills of killing and consuming animals, he does nevertheless offer his audiences a graded approach to adopting a vegetarian diet. For example, in the first song, he advises individuals who are not able to adopt a completely vegetarian diet to consume meat using the concept of the "threefold purity," in addition to meditating on compassion and reciting mantras for the benefit of the dead animal. His attitude toward monastic communities that consume meat, however, is markedly less lenient. The second song presents a passionate criticism of a group of monks from Drepung Monastery who had purchased meat at the monastery.

Shabkar is also the only author in this volume who makes an appeal to authorities to implement laws about meat eating and the killing of animals. Although many traditions of Buddhism encourage its adherents to adopt a vegetarian diet, the decision to do so is ultimately up to the individual. In these poems, however, Shabkar indicates that the religious and political leadership of Lhasa have established "Dharmic laws" that prohibit the hunting of wild animals;[508] he further encourages them to expand these laws so that it would be illegal for butchers to kill animals and for monks to consume meat. Thus, in addition to persuading individuals to adopt a vegetarian diet for moral reasons, Shabkar also advocates for the implementation of laws that prohibit the killing of animals in general and the consumption of meat among monks in particular. By implementing such laws, the decision to abstain from eating meat would shift from an individual choice to an externally imposed restriction.

508. For more on laws that "sealed" areas against hunting, see Huber, "The Chase and the Dharma."

There are several texts in Shabkar's *Collected Works* that discuss the sins of consuming meat, all of which are too long to include in this anthology.[509] These texts present the same general argument for vegetarianism, but are more detailed in their treatment of the topic and provide extensive citations from the Tibetan Buddhist canon that support the author's claims. The three songs from Shabkar's *Collected Works* translated in this chapter provide a pithy summary of many of Shabkar's main arguments and subarguments for vegetarianism found in these longer works, in a form that is aesthetically compelling. They belong to the "songs of spiritual realization" (Tib: *mgur*) genre and are believed to express the essence of the singer's experience of enlightenment. Shabkar was particularly renowned as a singer of spiritual songs, and it is fitting to introduce him through his songs.

About the Translation

The translations are based on passages from Shabkar's *Collected Songs* and the second volume of his autobiography. I used the 2003 Shechen edition of Shabkar's *Collected Works,* which is based on the original block prints and is the most reliable edition of Shabkar's works. While the passages that I worked with were generally easy to understand, I consulted Lama Tashi Dondup to ensure that I rendered certain ideas correctly, as I am not a native speaker of Tibetan. I have also chosen these particular passages because the second volume of Shabkar's autobiography and the majority of his *Collected Songs* are not yet available in English translation.

509. These texts are the *Emanated Scripture of Compassion*, *Dharma Discourse: The Altruistic Sun*, *Nectar of Immortality*, and sections from *Wondrous Emanated Scripture* (Ricard, *Writings of Shabkar*, 10, 11, 13, 16). While the first two texts remains untranslated, the latter two have been translated into English by the Padmakara Translation Group, in Shabkar, *Food of Bodhisattvas.*

Translations

From the Autobiography:[510]

One day, the monk Lodrö, a faithful, diligent, wise, and compassionate disciple who dwelled in mountain retreats, asked, "You always speak about the faults of meat. What is your intention behind repeatedly instructing Dharma practitioners and worldly people not to eat meat?"

"Well in my opinion," I replied, "generally speaking, it causes rebirth in the lower realms. More specifically, taking life is the main cause for rebirth in the hells. The main reason why people take life is for meat. Even more specifically, the state of omniscience arises from bodhicitta,[511] which arises from compassion as its root. The greatest hindrance to generating great compassion in one's mind is craving meat. Because of this, if one is able to abandon meat, then one blocks the many doors to negative action, and in turn, wouldn't this benefit the teachings and beings directly and indirectly? That's the reasoning behind my words."

From the Collected Songs:[512]

To the omniscient Longchenpa,[513]
who is the second victor Padmasambhava[514]
once again in human form—
I pray you grant your blessings.

The faults of eating meat are severe.
Benevolent deities are frightened by those
who eat meat and drink blood,
making it difficult to protect them.

510. Shabkar, *Rang rnam*, 2: 488.1–488.4.

511. *Bodhicitta* roughly translates as "the mind of enlightenment" (Tib: *byang chub kyi sems*) and is the mental drive to attain enlightenment for the benefit of all beings. Cultivating it is a foundational practice in Mahāyāna and tantric Buddhism.

512. Shabkar, *Mgur 'bum*, 4: 73.5–80.1. Excerpted from a longer song.

513. Longchenpa (Klong chen pa, 1308–1364) was a seminal Nyingma scholar and practitioner, responsible for systematizing much of Nyingma tantric practice, particularly Dzokchen.

514. Padmasambhava, known widely in Tibet as Guru Rinpoché, was an eighth-century Indian tantric master who, according to Tibetan historical narratives, was largely responsible for establishing Buddhism in Tibet.

If for the sake of consuming flesh, blood, and broth,
one kills many yaks, goats, and sheep,
one will have a short life tormented by many illnesses;
at death one will be reborn in hell.
Even if one is born as a human, it will be as a butcher
performing negative deeds in the land of the Mongols.

If those who constantly thirst for flesh and blood,
and find thrill in killing animals,
are able to give up meat, the benefits are immense.
Benevolent deities will surround them like clouds,
constantly guarding and protecting them.
They will enjoy a long life, good health, and physical and mental ease.
In the next life, they will be reborn as gods and humans.

For those with minimal attachment to meat,
no craving arises when they see a plump animal.
Subsisting on the three whites and three sweets,[515]
they are not cloaked in the faults of eating meat.
There is no doubt that such individuals
will go from joy to joy in all their lives.
Thus try to give up meat!

If you are not able to give it up completely,
then eat it in the faultless way
that involves threefold purity[516]—
that is, without seeing, hearing, or cognizing.
When you eat the meat, it is beneficial to
say whatever dhāraṇīs and mantras
you know, such as *Kaṃkani*[517] and so forth,
and then blow on the meat, and eat.
Meditate with compassion on that being.

515. The three whites are usually said to be milk, yogurt, and butter, while the three sweets are honey, sugar, and molasses. As Shabkar and others use this phrase, however, it is roughly synonymous with vegetarian foods.

516. Threefold purity refers to meat that the consumer has not seen, heard, or suspected was killed specifically for them to eat.

517. The *Kaṃkani* is the mantra of the Buddha Aksobya and is recited for purification.

After eating it, recite many *Oṃ maṇis.*[518]
Then it's good to make dedication prayers.

Otherwise, those killers of goats and sheep,
who in autumn intentionally
tackle goats, sheep, and yaks,
and murder them by binding their mouths and snouts,[519]
and all those who eat the flesh and drink the broth,
especially the leaders who command, "Kill!"
in the future will be reborn in hell,
and experience suffering for a long time.
Afterward, they will be reborn as yaks, goats, and sheep,
and will likewise experience being killed a hundred times
by having their mouths and snouts bound.
In this way, beheaded and disemboweled,
their life force will be severed.
In the future, they will be killed a hundred times in this way. . . .

This was also said by Tsokdruk Rangdröl.

From the Collected Songs:[520]

To the bodhisattvas of the tenth bhumi—
the Dalai Lama, the Panchen Lama, and the Regent, the Great Tutor,
 the Ganden Throneholder, and so forth,
and all the lamas, chant masters, and those exhorting virtue—
I present this supplication to your ears.

Once again, you have taken up the burden of serving beings,
establishing Dharmic laws prohibiting all—high and low—
from hunting wild animals in the hills and valleys
of Central Tibet, this pure realm—how kind!

Still, in the monasteries that are the foundations for the teachings,
the monks buy and consume our parents' flesh:

518. This refers to the recitation of Avalokiteśvara's six-syllable mantra, *Oṃ maṇi padme hūṃ*, which practice is widespread in Tibet. Avalokiteśvara is the bodhisattva of compassion.

519. Tibetans often slaughter animals by binding their snouts with tight cord until they suffocate.

520. Shabkar, *Mgur 'bum*, 5: 239.5–240.6.

hundreds and thousands of goats and sheep slaughtered by butchers.
The Sage spoke of the great faults of this.

If there were no eaters, there would be no killers.
Likewise, with many eaters, there are many killers.
Thus if all monks eat meat,
there is no opportunity for the goats, sheep, and yaks to escape.

Although monks are said to be precious, they are not rare—
Drepung alone has some seven thousand.
Look at the many monks on earth!

In order not to take the lives of our parents,
I beg you to teach Dharma and establish laws
that encourage all monks to rely on the three whites and sweets,
and that prohibit male and female butchers to kill.
Please consider this fervent cry for mercy!

When visiting Drepung Monastery one day, upon witnessing many monks carrying a lot of meat that they bought within the confines of the monastery, the renunciant Tsokdruk Rangdröl sang this song.

From the Collected Songs:[521]

It is unbearable to see the suffering of beings
who will be thrust unimpeded into hell's fiery pit.
Please dispel the suffering of these wretched, protectorless beings!
I pay homage to the victors of the three times.

Tears spring forth, upon witnessing these wretched beings.
I substitute my life for theirs without hesitation.
I pay respects to all bodhisattvas
who espouse loving-kindness, compassion, and bodhicitta.

In the degenerate age, the Buddha's teachings have deteriorated.
Outsiders have no need to come to Tibet:

521. Shabkar, *Mgur 'bum*, 5: 236.4–239.4.

slaughterers have covered the iron mountain of monasteries and temples
that surround us with crimson flesh and blood;
buddhas and bodhisattvas have left for other pure realms.

All those high and low who witness these sinners
slaughtering the flesh of their own parents gulp their saliva.
They show the fault of lacking loving-kindness and compassion.
It is suitable for them to go to the land of ogres southwest of Oḍḍiyāna.[522]

Ogres who crave the flesh of beings whose life-wind had been severed
and who were once their mothers have appeared in Tibet.
It's unacceptable for me not to speak out.
Alas! I suffer on behalf of sentient beings without protectors.
Though I cannot bear seeing this, I am utterly helpless.
I exhort the *bhūmi*[523]-dwelling bodhisattvas
such as the Dalai Lama, the Panchen Lama, and so forth!

The great impartial friend of beings, the Buddha,
turned the Dharma wheel for the benefit of beings.
To summarize, the Dharma includes both abandoning negative deeds and doing positive deeds—
this is said to be the teachings of the Buddha.
These days, in the monasteries and temples that surround us,
sinful slaughterers hang *thangkas*[524] of meat,
display offerings of lungs, hearts, and entrails,
and explicate their worth—who displays such things?
Amidst heaps of flesh and bones from beings who were once our mothers,
the monks, wielding knives, stuff their gaping mouths.

522. Oḍḍiyāna was a region in northwest India (now Pakistan), especially renowned for its association with tantric Buddhism.

523. The *bhūmis* (Tib: *sa*) refer to the ten levels of attainment of the bodhisattva.

524. A *thangka* is a traditional Tibetan scroll painting that features sacred subject matter such as buddhas, bodhisattvas, and other saintly Buddhist figures. Here Shabkar is comparing meat carcasses hung in a monastery storeroom to these religious paintings hung in a temple. For a description of s similar scene in Kumbum monastery in the early 1980s, see the interview with Arjia Rinpoché in chapter 11 of this volume.

Alas! If Buddhists dare do this to beings,
let's not speak of non-Buddhists!

The Buddha, the refuge-teacher, has gone to the pure realms,
and though it would be unacceptable for the Dharma, the place of refuge,
to disappear,
alas, due to India's lack of merit,
even the Dharma did not stay, but went to Tushita Heaven.
Although the Buddha Tsongkhapa has left for the buddhafields,
the Buddha's teachings are still here.
But alas, looking at the behavior of Tibetans,
it is as if the Dharma has gone to Tushita Heaven as well.

The non-Buddhists of India have spread darkness;
sinful butchers render Tibet red.
Alas! What to do for such wretched beings?
I sing this sorrowful lament in the four directions.

Hearing this sorrowful lament, the bodhisattvas who are here do nothing whatsoever for beings.
It would be good for the innumerable victors of the countless buddhafields
to come here and work for the sake of beings.
These children—wretched sentient beings who were once our mothers—
are entrapped in the suffering of a fiery pit.
By the power of praying to the buddhas and bodhisattvas on behalf of my parents, may they swiftly journey to the blissful bhūmis.

Each day, the butchers of Lhasa kill hundreds of their parents—goats, sheep, and yaks—and pile them up on the outer circumambulation route of the Jokhang to sell. Seeing this, I thought, "Wouldn't it be beneficial if the bhūmi-dwelling bodhisattvas—such as the refuge of all beings, the Dalai Lama, the Panchen Lama, the sublime Regent, and the Throneholder of Ganden, the Dalai Lama's Tutor, and so forth—taught the Dharma and established laws against killing?" The renunciant Tsokdruk Rangdröl said this with altruistic motivation.

Source Texts

Shabkar (Zhabs dkar tshogs drug rang grol). 2003a. *Snyigs dus 'gro ba yongs kyi skyabs mgon zhabs dkar rdo rje 'chang chen po'i rnam par thar pa rgyas par bshad pa skal bzang gdul bya thar 'dod rnams kyi re ba skong ba'i yid bzhin gyi nor bu bsam 'phel dbang gi rgyal po* (*Rang rnam*; *The Life of Shabkar*). In *Zhabs dkar tshogs drug rang grol kyi bka' 'bum*, vols. 1–2. New Delhi: Shechen Publications.

———. 2003b. *Bya btang tshogs drug rang grol gyis phyogs med ri khrod 'grims pa'i tshe rang gzhan chos la bskul phyir glu dbyangs dga' ston 'gyed pa rnams kyi stod cha* (*Mgur 'bum*; *Shabkar's Collected Songs*). In *Zhabs dkar tshogs drug rang grol kyi bka' 'bum*, vols. 3–5. New Delhi: Shechen Publications.

Secondary Sources

Huber, Toni. 2003. "The Chase and the Dharma: The Legal Protection of Wild Animals in Pre-Modern Tibet." In *Wildlife in Asia: Cultural Perspectives*, edited by John Knight, 36–55. Man and Nature in Asia 5. London: Routledge.

Ricard, Matthieu. 2003. *Writings of Shabkar: A Descriptive Catalogue*. New Delhi: Shechen Publications.

Pang, Rachel Hua-Wei. 2011. "Dissipating Boundaries: The 'Life,' Song-Poems, and Non-Sectarian Paradigm of Shabkar Tsokdruk Rangdrol (1781–1851)." PhD dissertation, University of Virginia.

———. 2017. "Literature, Innovation, and Buddhist Philosophy: Shabkar's *Nine Emanated Scriptures*." *Numen* 64.4: 371–93.

Shabkar Tsokdruk Rangdrol. 2001. *The Life of Shabkar: The Autobiography of a Tibetan Yogin*. Translated by Matthieu Ricard. Ithaca, NY: Snow Lion Publications.

Shabkar [Tsokdruk Rangdrol]. 2004. *Food of Bodhisattvas: Buddhist Teachings on Abstaining from Meat*. Translated by Padmakara Translation Group. Boston: Shambhala.

9. Nyala Pema Dündul's Inferno

By Adam Pearcey

THE NYARONG LAMA—OR Nyala for short—Pema Dündul (1816–1872)[525] was a visionary yogi renowned for his austere training, poetic songs of advice, and, above all, the unusual circumstances of his death. Born in Nyarong, eastern Tibet, in 1816 to a family of some wealth, he faced a series of unfortunate events during childhood, including the deaths of his father and two younger brothers. He also contracted smallpox and was compelled to live in isolation for a period and to beg and steal in order to survive. Shortly afterward, he began to devote himself wholeheartedly to the study and practice of the Buddhist teachings. Already as an infant he had been identified as an incarnation of the prominent treasure-revealer of Katok, Rigdzin Longsel Nyingpo (1625–1692), and received a number of instructions from his uncle and other lamas, but from the age of fifteen he approached the Dharma with great urgency and diligence.

When fighting broke out in Nyarong, Pema Dündul was forced to flee his homeland. He met the unconventional treasure-revealer Do Khyentsé Yeshé Dorjé (1800–1866), who had the role of mediator in the conflict. In the years that followed he met many other eminent masters from different traditions, received teachings and transmissions, and spent time meditating in isolation. For nine years he remained in retreat at the White Rock of Lhanglhang. When he deciphered a scroll that he had discovered years earlier, he found that it contained instructions on *chülen* (*bcud len*), the practice of extracting the vital essence or nutrients from rocks and minerals in the form of pills. Through this, he subsisted on little more than water and pills for several years while in retreat—on account of which he sometimes refers to himself as the "stone-eating yogi" (*rnal 'byor rdo zan*) in later compositions.

In 1860 Pema Dündul established the monastery of Kelzang Sangye Chöling beneath White Rock. This became his main seat, but he traveled throughout the Nyarong region, teaching and granting empowerments. To a

525. Tib: Nyag bla Padma bdud 'dul.

close circle of disciples in particular, he imparted instructions on tantric yoga and Dzokchen, as well as his own treasure revelations, most notably the collection known as *Self-Liberation Equal to Space* (*Mkha' mnyam rang grol*).[526]

In the early summer of 1872 he gathered his disciples for a final teaching in the Nyin valley in the lower Tromkhok region of Kham. At the end he recited prayers and instructed his followers to sew up the door of his tent and not to approach for seven days. Some reports say that it rained heavily throughout the following week and that rainbows appeared in the sky; others mention a triple earthquake on the seventh day accompanied by mysterious lights and music. When the disciples finally opened the tent, they found only clothing, hair, and nails. Their teacher's body had vanished, seemingly transformed into rainbow light as a mark of his attainment in Dzokchen practice. Contemporary masters regarded this example of the "rainbow body" as historically significant. For Dza Patrul Rinpoché it was evidence of the enduring strength of the Dharma, while Jamgön Mipham Rinpoché defended its authenticity in an essay addressed to those who had expressed doubts.[527]

Song of Advice for Giving Up Meat

Pema Dündul's compositions and revelations fill five volumes. They include a series of spiritual songs,[528] many of which exhibit an uncompromising commitment to meditative practice and the austere life of an itinerant yogi. In one song, for instance, Pema Dündul exhorts his followers to remain in isolated retreat. He contrasts this vocation not only with the mundane busyness of towns and villages but also with life in a monastic community. So staunchly does he endorse solitude that he portrays even the smallest encampment of just "two yak-hair tents" as a potential threat to tranquility.

A recurrent theme in Pema Dündul's songs and other works is abstinence. He discourages the consumption of meat, alcohol, and tobacco (in the form of snuff) and warns against sexual misconduct. For the latter, he employs what might be called an anti-Oedipal argument: since all beings have been one's mothers in previous existences, intercourse with anyone is tantamount to incest. These calls for ethical restraint follow a similar pattern as assertions build into a fuller thesis. What distinguishes the song of advice on giving up

526. For more on Nyala Pema Dündul's life, see Yeshe Dorjé, *The Cloud of Nectar*.

527. See Kapstein, "The Strange Death of Pema the Demon Tamer."

528. Several of these songs have been translated into English; see Kapstein, "The Strange Death of Pema the Demon Tamer"; Nyagla Padma Dündul, *Songs of Experience*; and Nyagla Padma Dündul, *The Song of Energy*.

meat (translated below) is that its arguments derive from a vision and are presented in the voice of Avalokiteśvara, the bodhisattva of compassion.

Pema Dündul tells us that one day he was meditating on the Great Compassionate One (following a text of his own revelation) when his entire perception suddenly transformed. Noble Avalokiteśvara appeared directly and the lower realms of saṃsāra became clearly visible. He witnessed the Reviving Hell in particular—one of eighteen hells according to Buddhist cosmology and the destiny of meat eaters and practitioners of so-called red offerings. Thus it would seem that the song's references to "the suffering that meat eating brings" concern the infernal torment of those responsible for animals' deaths rather than the pain of the animals themselves. It could be that the suffering involved in slaughter is too obvious to warrant commentary, whereas its karmic consequences, which are not directly apparent, require explanation. In any case, Pema Dündul appeals to his audience's compassion in other ways, such as when he argues that murder is no way to repay the kindness of beings who were one's mothers in previous lifetimes. More than once he highlights the hypocrisy of lecturing others about the law of cause and effect while failing to adhere to its principles. Meat eaters suffer in future lives, he says, but even in their current lifetime they will be plagued by illness and tormented by negative emotions and nonhuman spirits. In fact, they are just like demons themselves and find it impossible to develop genuine altruism. Vegetarians, by contrast, are widely revered, benefit from divine assistance, and easily cultivate the love and compassion that aid progress along the path. Thus the text is concerned not so much with the rules surrounding the consumption of flesh as with its consequences—both the negative effects of meat eating and the positive effects of abstention. Moreover, these karmic results are not proposed as theory or set out merely on the basis of scripture; they are reported as firsthand testimony that includes the authoritative voice of Avalokiteśvara.

The song concludes with a confession of past misdeeds and a pledge to abstain from meat eating in the future. Although Pema Dündul employs the first person here, the faults he lists apply to meat eaters in general. Thus there can be little doubt that readers are also encouraged to share in the author's declaration and make a similar commitment of their own. Effectively, the text captures a moment of conversion and invites others to reenact it.

About the Translation

What follows is a substantially revised version of a translation completed in 2004 (and published on lotsawahouse.org). Ringu Tulku Rinpoché kindly clarified several difficult words and passages at that time. Two editions of the

Tibetan have been consulted: a xylographic edition in *The Collected Revelations of Nyala Pema Dündul*[529] and a modern printed edition in *The Life and Songs of Nyala Pema Dündul*.[530] There are few differences between the editions, mostly variations in orthography, and only one that had a bearing on the translation.

529. Nyala Pema Dündul, *Grub chen nyi zla kun mdzes kyi gsung 'bum las/ nyams mgur skor skal bzang thar lam 'god pa'i phrin las*, vol. 4, 193–98.

530. Nyala Pema Dündul, *Sha za spong ba la gdams pa*, 161–65.

Song of Advice for Giving Up Meat

By Nyala Pema Dündul

Translated by Adam Pearcey

When I think of the suffering that meat eating brings,
I cannot bear the pain and anguish I feel within my heart.

Oṃ maṇi padme hūṃ hrīḥ

From a state of emptiness and compassion, you guide beings—
noble Avalokiteśvara, to you I pay homage.

Without having trained in love and compassion myself,
I ate the flesh of my mothers while lecturing others about cause and effect.
Without realizing the absolute, I wandered along the path of empty words.
I, the parrot-like beggar of White Rock,
was practicing austerities and "extracting the essence,"[531]
when, one day, while meditating on Lord Avalokiteśvara,
according to the union of stages from *Self-Liberation Equal to Space*,
my own body and everything around me suddenly disappeared
and transformed into a luminous body like that of the Great Compassionate One,
seemingly floating in space.

As I looked around, while experiencing luminous awareness,
I saw the inconceivable miseries of the lower realms
and, in particular, the vast sufferings of the Reviving Hell.
One of its quarters, I saw, was filled
with men and women, naked and helpless, before each of whom
stood throngs of evil-looking servants with heads

531. Tib: *bcud len*. Extracting the vital essence or nutrients from rocks and minerals in the form of pills.

like birds, wild and domesticated animals, and ferocious beasts.
Many of the servants held sharp weapons in their hands,
with which to slice apart and devour the flesh of their victims.
Time and again they cut, and time and again flesh grew back.
Victims did not expire until their karma was fully exhausted,
and habitual tendencies did not diminish, but only increased.
For those who had performed "red offerings" it was even worse.
Loudly, they all screamed in terrible pain and agony.
When I saw this external manifestation of my own perception,
I wondered what might be done to stop such suffering.

And in that very instant, in the sky before me,
the Great Compassionate One appeared, and said:
"*E ma!* My son, who has been close to me throughout many lives,
listen well now, you who are diligent and determined!
You have gained stability in the generation stage of deity yoga,
and have even developed a few qualities,
but the root of Dharma lies in loving-kindness and compassion.
Do you have real love and compassion within yourself?
How could anyone trained in compassion ever eat flesh?
Just look at how eating meat brings such suffering!
The results of our own actions will ripen on us alone;
there is nothing the buddhas of the three times may do.
Eating meat has no virtue whatsoever, but entails many faults.
It is the source of 400 forms of disease and 80,000 obstructing forces,
and it naturally brings about the 84,000 afflictive emotions.
Other than as part of the fearless conduct of benefitting all one encounters,
or as a medicine or sacred substance of the supreme Secret Mantra,
consumption of flesh involves not the tiniest trace of virtue.
Eating flesh is a sign of being either a māra or rākṣasa demon.
It causes discipline to degenerate and negative emotions to increase.
Without the cause, which is altruistic love and compassion,
you will find it hard to gain the fruit, the essence of awakening.

Meat eaters are not accompanied by the wisdom deities.
They lack blessings, accomplishment, auspiciousness, and activity.
The substance of altruism does not develop in eaters of flesh,
whom gods, nāgas, and others regard as demons.
Meat eaters are plagued by gandharvas, rākṣasas, māras,

yamas, ghosts, spirits, gyalpo, gongpo, and samaya-breaking demons.
The result of eating meat is rebirth in the hells,
or as a bird, jackal, cannibal demon, or the like.
Meat eating thus brings suffering beyond measure.
But by renouncing it, you are freed from all such faults,
and will always be revered by nonhuman beings,
who will see you as a pure, authentic brahman or god.
All the buddhas and bodhisattvas, together with their retinues, throughout the ten directions,
gurus, yidam deities, and ḍākinīs will gather around you like clouds,
and you will be accompanied by male and female bodhisattvas.
Quite naturally, you will possess the cause of loving-kindness and compassion,
and swiftly reach the fruit, which is the essence of awakening.
These are just some of the inconceivable virtues to be gained."

Thus he spoke; and then, once my own perception had returned,
I felt as if I had awoken from a lucid dream.
My body and mind were tormented as if by poison,
and I shook with fear and panic.
Just thinking of the terrible sufferings of the Reviving Hell,
I wished only to exchange my happiness for others' pain.
So utterly overwhelmed was my mind, I wept profusely.
And I felt intense, unbearable compassion.
Then, to take upon myself the sufferings of others,
and to purify their faults and obscurations caused by eating meat,
for every mother sentient being, as infinite in number as space is vast,
I made the following vow, true according to the two levels of reality:

A ho! Mighty sage Śākyamuni and all buddhas and bodhisattvas throughout the whole of space and time,
have compassion for this child who knew nothing of cause and effect!
Hosts of gracious root and lineage masters, care for me!
Have compassion for this child who knew nothing of cause and effect!
Supreme yidam deity, mighty Avalokiteśvara, care for me!
Have compassion for this child who knew nothing of cause and effect!

Overwhelmed by ignorance and the two obscurations,
I have often spoken of how all infinite beings have been our parents,
and, while living off their flesh, lectured about cause and effect.

I had no idea that the suffering involved was so great!
Often have I heard it said that eating meat with threefold purity[532]
is sanctioned by the Buddha and does not count as sin.
But this applies only to saints who benefit all they encounter,
like pure lotus flowers, unstained by negative emotions,
and to practitioners of the profound path of Secret Mantra.

For my part, I have no instruction more profound
than altruistic love and compassion,
and the infallibility of cause and effect.
To purify all the faults and obscurations of eating flesh
among all sentient beings, who extend throughout the whole of space,
from this moment on, I completely renounce the eating of flesh.
This is my unfailing commitment, which I shall never forsake.
Even if all the animals upon this earth were to be devoured,
there would still be no satisfaction; hunger would only continue to increase.

Deprived of food or drink for just a few days,
we feel as if we have never tasted even so much as a single morsel or drop before.
Now is the time to escape this demon, hunger.
What, after all, is the cause of flesh?
It springs only from self-clinging and attachment.
Merely to think of it makes me weary, nauseated.
This utterly unappetizing mound of mess and filth,
bound up with the thirty-six impure substances,
a body of habitual patterns and aggregates, is the basis for all suffering.

Each animal has its own negative actions,
and whoever eats the flesh of such beings will find it hard to win liberation.
Meat and alcohol are impure substances,
and to offer them does not qualify as generosity, the Buddha said.
Who, therefore, would eat this food of the afflictions?
Pretas must live for many thousands of human years

532. This means that you have not seen or heard anything to indicate that the meat has been butchered specifically for you, and not only that, you do not even have any doubt that this might be the case.

without seeing food or drink, enduring only suffering.
But we human beings gladly drink even ice-cold water
and have plenty to sustain us besides meat and alcohol.
If we are still not satisfied with such delights,
how could we repay past kindnesses so unfairly?

Throughout the course of countless eons past,
in every world within this universe so vast,[533]
there's not a single being who has not been our mother;
all the milk we drank from maternal breasts would fill a billion seas.
I abandon all pretence; let the Three Jewels be my witness!
In the past, under the sway of ignorance and habit,
I ate my parents' flesh and did not remorsefully confess.
Now, with pure motivation and the four powers complete,
as in the saying, "I was not, am not, and will not be attached,"
henceforth, may the thought of eating meat never even cross my
mind.
Should I ever fail, let the Three Jewels send their punishment.
May the protectors and guardians constantly keep watch.
Were I now to eat the flesh of my past mothers,
there would be no greater transgressor in all the three realms!

The Buddha said that harming others even slightly impairs one's vows.
So what need is there to mention flesh eating that involves taking life?
In the *Parinirvāṇa Sūtra*, *Laṅkāvatāra*, and elsewhere, it says
that eating meat is tantamount to killing.[534]
It is forbidden in both the Greater and Lesser Vehicles,
but is particularly unacceptable for bodhisattvas.
Our Teacher himself, when appearing as a partridge's young,
and as a ferocious beast[535] in the wild, did not eat meat.
How then could we, his followers, ever do so?
In accordance with the guidance of the Victorious One,
there were many great masters in India and Tibet who gave up meat.
As all this shows, the faults of meat eating are unimaginably vast.

533. Literally, "in all seven worlds" (*'jig rten bdun po*), meaning the six classes of beings (hell, preta, animal, human, asura, and deva) plus the bardo realm.

534. See the translations of these texts in this volume.

535. These are references to the Buddha's previous lives, as recounted in the so-called *Birth Stories*, or *Jātaka*.

Not cultivating negativity is itself genuine Dharma.
So may I always comply with the authentic teaching!

Having seen the boundless faults that come from eating meat,
even the thought of it is as nauseating as poison.
And so, I, the great beggar with the name of Dündul,
composed these words of advice to encourage my own renunciation
in the Sky Fortress hermitage of White Rock.
As the result of this virtue, may all sentient beings
purify all the faults and obscurations that come from eating meat,
so that they may see the thousand buddhas face to face!

Source Texts

Nyala Pema Dündul (Nyag bla Padma bdud 'dul). n.d. *Grub chen nyi zla kun mdzes kyi gsung 'bum las/ nyams mgur skor skal bzang thar lam 'god pa'i phrin las* (*Songs of Realization That Establish the Path to Liberation*). In *Nyag bla padma bdud 'dul gyi gter chos skor* (*The Collected Revelations of Nyala Pema Dündul*), vol. 4, 193–98. BDRC: W23695.

———. 1998. *Sha za spong ba la gdams pa* (*Song of Advice for Giving Up Meat*). In *Nyag bla padma bdud 'dul gyi rnam thar dang mgur 'bum* (*The Life and Songs of Nyala Pema Dündul*), 161–65. Chengdu: Si khron mi rigs dpe skrun khang. BDRC: W21701.

Secondary Sources

Kapstein, Matthew T. 2004. "The Strange Death of Pema the Demon Tamer." In *The Presence of Light: Divine Radiance and Religious Experience*, edited by Matthew T. Kapstein, 119–56. Chicago: University of Chicago Press.

Nyagla Padma Dündul. 1997. *The Song of Energy*. Translated by Andy Lukianowicz, Namkhai Norbu Rinpoche, and Enrico Dell'Angelo. Arcidosso: Shang Shung Publications.

———. n.d. *Songs of Experience*. Translated by Adriano Clemente and Andy Lukianowicz. Arcidosso: Shang Shung Publications.

Yeshe Dorjé. 2013. *The Cloud of Nectar: The Life and Liberation of Nyagla Pema Dündul.* Translated by Oriol Aguilar. Arcidosso: Shang Shung Publications.

10. A Necessary Evil: Shardza Tashi Gyaltsen on the Faults of—and Need for—Meat

By Geoffrey Barstow

UNLIKE EVERY OTHER AUTHOR included in this volume, Shardza Tashi Gyaltsen (1859–1933)[536] was not a Buddhist. Instead, he was a member of the Bön tradition. Bön has its roots in Tibet's pre-Buddhist age, but soon after the introduction of Buddhism it began to acquire many of the same forms and practices adopted by Buddhists, including formal monasticism, scholastic study, and tantric ritual, though it always maintained its self-identity as a separate, non-Buddhist lineage.[537] Shardza was born in 1859 into an eastern Tibetan family with deep roots in this monastic form of the Bön tradition. He was ordained as a monk at the age of twenty and quickly developed a reputation for strict adherence to the rules of the Vinaya, the monastic code. By the time of his death in 1935, he was the most influential Bön scholar of his generation.[538]

Among the many interesting facets of Bön is a longstanding tradition of vegetarianism, particularly among monastics. In the text translated here, Shardza cites the antimeat opinions of Metön Sherab Özer (1058–1132), one of the founding figures of Bön monasticism. Metön Sherab Özer's opinions were echoed in the Vinaya commentaries written by Nyamé Sherab Gyaltsen (1356–1415) and in the monastic rulebook for Menri Monastery written by Kudün Sönam Lodrö in 1810. Menri is the most important monastery in Bön, and Kudün Sönam Lodrö's guidebook explicitly forbids monks from eating meat. Shardza built on this tradition. When he took his monastic vows he also gave up alcohol, onions, afternoon eating, and consuming any meat that came

536. Tib: Shar rdza Bkra shis rgyal mtshan.

537. There have been quite a few academic works written about Bön. Some of my favorites include Samten Karmay, "A General Introduction to the History and Doctrine of Bon"; Millard, "Bon Religion in Reb Kong"; and Karmay, *The Treasury of Good Sayings*.

538. Shardza's biography has been translated in full in Gorvine, *Envisioning a Tibetan Luminary*.

from an animal that had been slaughtered.[539] Perhaps more important than his personal vegetarianism, he also promoted it among his many followers.

In addition to drawing on his own Bön tradition, Shardza's critical stance on meat also intersects with a broader vegetarian movement that was gaining force in his home region of Kham. Shardza was active in the late nineteenth and early twentieth centuries, precisely at the high point of the so-called *rimé*, or nonsectarian movement.[540] This movement was centered around several charismatic lamas of the Nyingma, Kagyü, and Sakya lineages who held one another in mutual respect and who actively taught that all of their respective lineages were valuable and worth supporting. Shardza himself maintained cordial relationships with many of these scholars, helping to insert Bön teachings into this largely Buddhist movement. Interestingly, many of those active in the rimé movement also either practiced or promoted vegetarianism. This includes Shabkar and Nyala Pema Dündul, both of whom are represented in this volume, as well as Patrül Rinpoché (1808–1887), Rigdzin Garwang (1858–1930), Sera Khandro (1892–1940), Ngawang Lekpa (1864–1941), and other masters whose works on meat eating have not been included here. When we add Shardza to this list, it becomes clear that the rimé period was not only a time of impressive nonsectarianism but also one of the high points in the history of vegetarianism in Tibet.[541]

Shardza's Faults of Eating Meat

The text translated here is a short, untitled work written at the behest of a small group of students. Like many other texts included in this volume, it approaches the question of meat eating from a variety of perspectives. Among these, two arguments stand out for their originality. The first is Shardza's treatment of the karmic repercussions of meat eating. Like others, Shardza believed that eating meat created negative karma. In one memorable image, he quotes a Bön scripture that asserts that meat eating leads to birth in hell, "where worms will claim their karmic debts."

Shardza, however, decides to delve into the details of this argument, presenting two different examples of killing an animal and then demonstrating

539. Shardza, *Shar rdza pa chen po bkra shis rgyal mtshan dpal bzang po'i rnam par thar pa ngo mtshar nor bu'i phreng ba thar 'dod mkhas pa'i mgul rgyun*, 91.

540. For more on the rimé movement, see Smith, "'Jam Mgon Kong Sprul and the Nonsectarian Movement"; Gayley and Schapiro, *A Gathering of Brilliant Moons*.

541. For a more thorough discussion of vegetarianism in the rimé movement, see the general introduction to this volume and Barstow, *Food of Sinful Demons*, 36–40.

that each is a fully complete karmic action, with all four elements present. These four elements are (1) the ground element, referring to an accurate knowledge of the situation; (2) the intention element, meaning that the agent actually intends to perform the action; (3) the application element, which is the actual performance of the action; and (4) the completion element, which means that the agent is pleased with, and does not regret, their action. Only if all four of these actions are complete will a particular action reap its full karmic result. If, for instance, someone kills an animal without knowing they are doing it, or if they regret their action after the fact, then the four elements will not be complete. In that case, while the action will produce a karmic result, that result will not be as strong as if the four elements were complete. Shardza demonstrates that for his two examples—one focused on killing a louse and the other on the slaughter of a yak for meat—the four elements are indeed complete. Someone who consumes meat casually, therefore, should expect the full karmic repercussions of their conduct in a future life.

The second argument I wish to highlight here is even more unique and interesting. Shardza spends the bulk of his work criticizing meat. He calls meat "nauseating" and argues at length that eating it is sinful and leads to birth in hell. But then, on the final page of his treatise, Shardza abruptly reverses his position and claims that people *must* eat meat. Without it, he claims, the body will become weak, feeble, and, crucially, unable to practice religion. And practicing religion is a rare opportunity, available only when one achieves a human birth with all of the freedoms and riches intact. But Shardza's advocacy of meat eating does not negate his earlier concerns. Instead, he is claiming that people should eat meat despite the fact that it is sinful. Further, he proposes that, in order to minimize the negative karma of meat eating, people should eat "suitable" meat. But what kind of meat is suitable? To this Shardza gives two examples: the meat of animals that have died naturally and meat purchased in a market. The first involves no act of killing, so is karmically pure. Shardza himself followed just such a diet, eating only the meat of animals that died naturally. Meat purchased in the market is more problematic, and Shardza clearly sees it as an inferior option. But he does include it, seeming to reflect the idea that meat purchased in the market is more distant from the act of killing than when someone either personally kills the animal or specifically asks someone else to do it for them.

In the end, Shardza's text is one of the more nuanced works in this volume. He makes the faults of meat clear, driving home his point with emotional and evocative language. But at the same time he recognizes the difficulty and health impact of adopting full vegetarianism. He tries, therefore, to come up with a system that reflects the negative aspects of meat eating while also allowing individuals to nourish their bodies in ways that many Tibetans felt were necessary.

About the Translation

This translation was based primarily on the text contained in the seventeen-volume edition of Shardza's *Collected Works* published in Chengdu in 2011. I have also occasionally consulted the version of this text found in a recent (but undated) edition of his collected works published in Chamdo. The text itself is untitled in both editions. I have adapted the title here, *The Faults of Eating Meat*, from the colophon, where Shardza claims to have "described the faults of eating meat."

The canonical texts Shardza cites do not have titles in Sanskrit. They do, however, have titles in Zhangzhung, the canonical language of Bön. I considered, therefore, using the Zhangzhung titles in the translation. In the end, however, I decided to translate the titles into English, reasoning that while many readers will be familiar with the Sanskrit titles of canonical texts, the same is unlikely to be true of Zhangzhung titles. I hope this deviation from the normal conventions of this volume will help the reader rather than confuse them.

I consulted with several Bön scholars in preparing this translation, and I am grateful for their help. In particular, I am grateful to two geshés at Shardza Ritrö in Kham, who went over the text with me in detail, but who asked to remain anonymous. I am also grateful to Geshé Lodoe Wosal of Triten Norbutse in Kathmandu, both for his help with the text and for granting me access to that monastery's wonderful library.

Finally, it is worth noting that this translation has been previously published in *A Gathering of Brilliant Moons*, a collection of religious advice literature from rimé masters edited by Holly Gayley and Joshua Shapiro. This present version has been reedited and slightly modified, but these changes are minor, and I am grateful to Wisdom Publications for granting permission to use the translation in this volume.

The Faults of Eating Meat

By Shardza Tashi Gyaltsen

Translated by Geoffrey Barstow

Possessing twofold purity, your body is that of a sugata,
  your speech the vast and profound realization of Bön.
Possessing twofold knowledge and liberation,
  your mind is that of a bodhisattva.
Lord, you unite the three jewels into one.

Possessing twofold wisdom and compassion,
  gracious guru, you are a glorious wish-fulfilling jewel.
Possessing twofold devotion,
  I continually praise you with fierce longing.
Care for me with compassion!

A SŪTRA[542] SAYS, "The activity of the teachings is compassion. Use compassion to guard beings!" Compassion is the essence of all the Buddha's teachings.[543] Become completely absorbed with this, so that you guard beings with great compassion, steadfast and immeasurable. Motivate yourself with the aim of establishing all beings in both temporary and ultimate happiness! With this as your intention, perform positive actions of body and speech. Exert yourself in this to the best of your ability, as everything is contained in this.

One who practices in this way is renowned as a follower of the Buddha. Some other people, however, act only out of desire for their own benefit,

542. Like many of the unattributed quotations in this text, I have been unable to identify which specific sūtra this line comes from, though it is presumably from the Bön canon.

543. This is a Bön, rather than Buddhist, text. It is at least a little surprising, therefore, to find Shardza invoking the Buddha. In comments on a previous version of this translation, some colleagues suggested that I change this reference to "Tönpa Shenrab's teachings," in reference to the buddha who founded Bön. But Shardza's text clearly uses the normal Tibetan term for buddha (*sangs rgyas*), and does not specify if he is referring to Tönpa Shenrab or the buddha known to Buddhists. After consulting with several Bön monks and scholars, I have elected to preserve the ambiguity present in Shardza's work.

bringing harm to other beings. Such people might call themselves "followers of the Buddha," but is it really appropriate to call them this?

If someone is motivated by desire to eat the flesh of beings, then butchers will seize yaks, sheep, and other animals and sever their minds from their bodies. How can those who consume meat and blood as food be followers of the Buddha? Such people pridefully consider themselves to be benefitting beings and protecting the weak, but their actions contradict the precepts! Meat is nothing but the cause of amassing terrifying sins.

It would be impossible to eat meat if beings were not killed. As it says in a sūtra,[544] "This food called 'meat' comes from the killing of animals." As for the karmic results of that killing, a scripture[545] says, "Among the ten kinds of nonvirtue, killing is the worst." Killing, therefore, has the worst karma of the nonvirtuous sins. Even if you kill just one being, you will have to repay this karmic debt with your life five hundred times. Moreover, killing a being is especially severe if the four elements of a complete action are present.[546] Looking at the specific issue of meat, we see that it is derived from killing. Therefore it contains all four elements and produces the karma of a complete act of killing.

Further, the severity of the intention determines which lower realm one is born in. Acting through hatred leads to hell, desire leads to the realm of hungry ghosts, and ignorance leads to birth in the animal realm. As an example, take the killing of a louse. When a louse is feeding on someone's body, that person knows that the louse is eating them. This knowledge is the ground element of a complete act. Seeing the louse on his arm, the killer is motivated by anger. This is the intention element. He places a fingernail on top of the louse and begins to press down, applying the means to kill the louse. This is the application element. Afterward, the bloody louse is removed from the top of the nail with a cry of triumph, completing the act of killing. This is the completion element. Killing in this way, motivated by hatred, brings karma that impels one to hell. The sūtras explain that the karma of anger will ripen like a burning flame, and you will be born in a hot or a cold hell.

As another example, take the killing of a yak. First, one thinks, "If I kill this yak, there will be lots of meat." This is the ground element, the knowledge that the object to be killed is a yak. Then, thinking, "Those yaks are a

544. I have been unable to identify the specific source of this quote.

545. Again, the source of this quote eludes me.

546. For an act to be complete and reap its full karmic result, it has to have four elements: (1) the ground element of accurate knowledge of the situation, (2) the intention element of voluntarily deciding on a course of action, (3) the application element of actually performing the action, and (4) the completion element of rejoicing in and not regretting the action.

herd of wealth," either you or someone else strings a rope around the animal's neck.[547] This is the intention element, the thought to kill the yak. Continuing from this, the yak is led into the butcher's corral, its limbs are bound, it is turned upside down, and its muzzle is wrapped with cord.[548] This is the application element, when the actual killing is done. Then the yak's breath is cut off and its mind is severed from its body. When its eyes bulge and its life force has been completely destroyed, this is the completion element. Killing in this way, motivated by desire, brings the karma that impels one to the realm of hungry ghosts. The sūtras explain that the karma of desire will ripen like boiling water, and you will wander through the realm of hungry ghosts, always hungry and thirsty.

Moreover, some non-Buddhists believe killing is a virtue that will benefit them after death, so they slaughter animals. This is certainly ignorance, and the sūtras explain it to be the cause for being impelled into a birth as a draft animal.[549]

Eating meat is motivated by desire, so it is a cause of birth as a hungry ghost. At the same time, however, it also definitely impels one toward hell. *The Stainless*[550] says:

> Meat is a sinful transgression.
> Through it you will be born
> in the hell of being boiled and burned,
> where worms will claim their karmic debts.

Therefore meat—this food that harms beings—is a very heavy fault.

Speaking generally, this thing called "meat" arises from a father's semen and a mother's blood, so it is made from unclean substances. *The Compendium of the Vinaya*[551] says:

547. The Tibetan word for wealth, *nor*, is also often used to refer to the animals in one's herd. Thus someone with many animals has a lot of wealth, or nor.

548. In Tibet, animals are often slaughtered by wrapping a cord around their muzzles until they suffocate. Killing an animal in this way preserves the blood in the meat.

549. Each of the last three paragraphs has been dedicated to one of the three poisons: anger, desire, and ignorance.

550. Tib: *Mdo dri med gzi brjid*. The longest, most extensive version of the biography of Tönpa Shenrab, the founder of Bön. *Bön Kangyur*, vols. 14–26.

551. Tib: *'Dul ba kun las bstus*. A commentary on the Vinaya by Metön Sherab Özer (1058–1132), a foundational figure in the development of Bön monasticism. I have not been able to locate a complete copy of this text.

The causes and conditions of meat
are the white and red conjugal substances of both a father and mother.
If you saw this with your eyes, you would tremble with fear.
How pitiful it would be to take it in your hands!
Just smelling it brings on nausea.
Once it is tasted by the tongue, how can it be kept down?

Similarly, since the beings of the three worlds have all been our fathers and mothers, there is not a shred of difference between our parents and our food. *The Stainless* says:

Of all the beings of the six realms,
not one has not been your father or mother.
There is no difference between the flesh of one's kind parents
and whatever meat one desires to eat.

Those who eat meat have not even a trace of compassion or kindness. As Jetsun Jangpa[552] says, "Meat eaters have no compassion." Meat eaters are no different than demons who eat their own flesh. A sūtra[553] says:

All who eat meat are demons
whose karma is to eat the flesh of their own body.
They have no shame about nonvirtuous activity
and cannot be distinguished from the sons of demons.

Those who enjoy the flesh and blood taken from other beings cannot stand it if a thorn pierces their own body. Asking such people to be the refuge and protector of beings is no different from thinking of a flesh-eating demon as an object of offerings. The *Nail Hole*[554] says:

If even a single thorn pierces our body, it is completely unbearable.
Some say that we need to eat the meat of many slaughtered beings.
Whoever says this is a demon.

By killing a single being for meat, the lives of innumerable tiny beings

552. Even after consulting several Bön scholars, I have not been able to identify this individual.

553. I have not been able to identify this particular quote, likely from a Bön sūtra.

554. Tib: *Mdo gzer mig*. The middle-length biography of Tönpa Shenrab, the buddha who founded Bön. *Bön Kangyur*, vols. 28–29.

are damaged.[555] Therefore the karmic retribution for the sin of eating meat is immeasurable. *The Vinaya Transmission*[556] says, "For each animal that is killed, innumerable tiny beings die." Through eating meat one will become more vital, but it also causes one's suffering and negative emotions to increase. *The Stainless* says:

> Therefore, when one engages with meat and blood,
> the roots of the five poisons are present.

The same text also says:

> Meat gives rise to the causes of all five poisons,
> so all evil will arise from that meat.

In the future, the karmic consequences of eating meat will ripen in one's own flesh and blood. As *The Sūtra Separating Causes and Effects*[557] says:

> Karmic debts incurred in the past pursue you now.
> Karmic debts incurred today will pursue you in the future.

It is certain that consuming the meat and blood of beings out of desire will result in being flung to the lower realms. For this reason, it is important to abandon meat forever.

At the same time, however, the Buddha is the extraordinary support for practice, and this free and favored human life is difficult to obtain. Eating meat supports long life, making it necessary for obtaining the supreme objective. If you do not eat it, your bodily strength will be feeble, you will not be able to perform virtue, and your life force will be weak, as if you had a wind disorder.[558] If you do not rely on a skillful method like this, you are throwing away your body. It is said to be a fault similar to tearing down the four supporting

555. While the concept of "bacteria" was unknown in Tibet, there was an awareness that innumerable small creatures lived in and depended on the bodies of larger beings.

556. Tib: *'Dul rgyud*. I have not been able to positively trace this quote, but it is likely from one of the *Six Transmissions of the Vinaya* (Tib: *'Dul ba rgyud drug*), a series of Bön texts on the Vinaya.

557. Tib: *Rgyu 'bras rnam par 'byed pa'i mdo*. Likely refers to chapter 23 of *The Stainless*, which carries this title, rather than an independent text. *Bön Kangyur*, vol. 18, 333–448.

558. In Tibetan medicine, the three humors—wind, phlegm, and bile—must be kept in balance for optimal health. If there is too much wind, the body is said to become thin, weak, and jittery.

pillars in a temple. It is important to nourish your body with suitable meat and other foods so that you can practice virtue.

If you ask, "What meat is suitable?" the answer is, "When you buy it, the meat must be free of having been seen, heard, or suspected."[559] This also applies to meat purchased for you by others. For example, meat from animals that have died naturally is suitable. The Vinaya says, "Abandon your desire for meat and, for the sake of nourishing the body, eat meat that has died naturally at the end of its time or that was purchased in the market."

A ho!
The precious Bön is the three trainings of the Lord's teachings.
In order to benefit beings, I have composed in accordance
with the Great Vehicle of the renunciant bodhisattvas
who skillfully bring beings to definitive goodness and the fulfillment of all desires.

I have clarified this according to the tradition
of the texts spoken by Mé,[560] who collected the best teachings
that aligned with the precepts of the hundred supreme protectors
renowned in the three worlds as the protectors of gods and men.

Having brought all beings to certainty in this way,
their minds have been tamed by gentle thoughts
without causing harm to one another.
May all be liberated into the space of equality.

Here I have briefly explained the faults of religious people eating meat. Following requests by the Supreme Incarnation Yungdrung, Namkha Öser—a pure monk of Gongyel Monastery—and Yungdrung Tri Ö—the meditator of Nyakrong—this was written in an isolated mountain range by the mad vagabond of the rocks with the name Manga Wershi.[561]

May it be virtuous!

559. In other words, it must have threefold purity.

560. Scholars at Shardza Ritrö in Kham told me this referred to Yorpo Mepal (1134–69).

561. Jean Luc Achard identifies Manga Wershi (Tib: Mangga wer zhi) as Shardza's name in Zhangzhung, the canonical language of Bön. See Achard, *Enlightened Rainbows*, xxix.

Source Texts

Bön Kangyur. 1999. *Theg chen g.yung drung bon gyi bka' 'gyur*. Khreng 'du: Si khron zhing chen par khrun lte gnas par 'debs khang. BDRC: W21872.

Shardza (Shar rdza bkra shis rgyal mtshan). 2011. *Sha'i nyes dmigs mdor bsdus* (*The Faults of Meat*). In *Kun mkhyen shar rdza pa bskra shis rgyal mtshan gyi gsung 'bum*, vol. 15, 148–54. Khreng tu'u: Si khron dpe skrun tshogs pa and Si khron mi rigs dpe skrun khang. BDRC: W1PD133161.

———. 2011. *Shar rdza pa chen po bkra shis rgyal mtshan dpal bzang po'i rnam par thar pa ngo mtshar nor bu'i phreng ba thar 'dod mkhas pa'i mgul rgyun* (*A Rosary of Jewels: The Life of Shardza Tashi Gyaltsen*). In *Kun mkhyen shar rdza pa bskra shis rgyal mtshan gyi gsung 'bum*, vol 1. Khreng tu'u: Si khron dpe skrun tshogs pa and Si khron mi rigs dpe skrun khang. BDRC: W1PD133161.

———. n.d. *Sha'i nyes dmigs mdor bsdus* (*The Faults of Meat*). In *Gsung 'bum*, vol. 13, 327–33. Amdo. Undated computer typescript.

Secondary Sources

Achard, Jean-Luc. 2008. *Enlightened Rainbows: The Life and Works of Shardza Tashi Gyeltsen*. Leiden: Brill.

Barstow, Geoffrey. 2017. "Bold Judgements on Eating Meat." In Holly and Schapiro, *A Gathering of Brilliant Moons*, 97–108.

———. 2018. *Food of Sinful Demons: Meat, Vegetarianism, and the Limits of Buddhism in Tibet*. New York: Columbia University Press.

Galey, Holly, and Schapiro, Joshua, eds. 2017. *A Gathering of Brilliant Moons: Practice Advice from the Rimé Masters of Tibet*. Somerville, MA: Wisdom Publications.

Gorvine, William M. 2019. *Envisioning a Tibetan Luminary: The Life of a Modern Bönpo Saint*. New York: Oxford University Press.

Karmay, Samten. 1998. "A General Introduction to the History and Doctrine of Bon." In *The Arrow and the Spindle: Studies in History, Myths, Rituals and Beliefs in Tibet*, 104–57. Kathmandu: Mandala Book Point.

———, trans. 1972. *The Treasury of Good Sayings: A Tibetan History of Bon*. Oxford: Oxford University Press.

Millard, Colin. 2013. "Bon Religion in Reb Kong." In *Monastic and Lay Traditions in North-Eastern Tibet*, edited by Yangdon Dhondrup, Ulrich Pagel, and Geoffrey Samuel, 141–63. Brill's Tibetan Studies Library 33. Leiden: Brill.

Smith, E. Gene. 2001. "'Jam Mgon Kong Sprul and the Nonsectarian Movement." In *Among Tibetan Texts: History and Literature of the Himalayan Plateau*, edited by Kurtis R. Schaeffer, 235–72. Boston: Wisdom.

11. Arjia Rinpoché on Giving Up Meat

By Sangseraima Ujeed

THE EIGHTH ARJIA RINPOCHÉ, Lobsang Tubten Jigme Gyatso,[562] was born in 1950 to ethnically Mongolian parents in Olonuur, eastern Tibet—today's Xining. At age two he was recognized by the Tenth Panchen Lama as the eighth in the line of Arjia incarnations, and thus one of the most senior individuals at Kumbum Monastery.[563] Barely two years old at the time, Arjia Rinpoché was enthroned as the Gomdag Abbot[564] of Kumbum Monastery, making him one of the highest-ranking Tibetan lamas of ethnic Mongolian descent. In 1958 the Communist regime denounced Arjia Rinpoché as a member of the "exploiting class," along with most other high lamas and religious leaders. Eventually, he and the entire monastic community were forced to disrobe and attend a Chinese school, though Rinpoché continued to receive Buddhist teachings when he could. By 1964 the political situation had worsened even more, and—like many other members of the monastic community—Rinpoché spent the next thirteen years performing hard labor in the fields.

In 1979, following the death of Mao,[565] China began a process of political liberalization that included relaxing restrictions on the practice of religion.

562. Tib: A rgya Rin po che Blo bzang thub bstan 'jigs med rgya mtsho. Rinpoché (Tib: Rin po che), literally "precious one," is a title accorded to very high-ranking religious leaders in the Tibetan tradition.

563. The Arjia Rinpoché reincarnation line originates from Jé Tsongkhapa's father, Lumbum Gye and is closely associated with Kumbum Monastery, which was founded in 1560 at the birthplace of Tsongkhapa in Amdo. Since its founding, Kumbum has become one of the largest and most important Geluk monasteries in Amdo. To the best of my knowledge, a comprehensive history of Kumbum Monastery has not yet been written in English. For a concise presentation, see Buswell and Lopez, *The Princeton Dictionary of Buddhism*, 829.

564. The title of Gomdag Abbot signifies that the Arjia Rinpoché reincarnation line is considered the highest in Kumbum Monastery and is the abbot of the three large sections of the monastery.

565. Mao died in 1976, after which his successors quickly began to dismantle the most extreme aspects of his rule, including the ban on religious practice.

At that time, Rinpoché was reinstated as the abbot of Kumbum Monastery and began the process of reviving the monastery to its prior glory. He was also appointed to a position on a government committee supervising religious practice. Rinpoché hoped that by working with the Chinese government, he would protect and help preserve and revive Tibetan Buddhism and Tibetan and Mongolian tradition and culture, and he quickly rose through the ranks of the government bureaucracy.

The situation changed in 1998, when Rinpoché was asked to become the tutor of the Eleventh Panchen Lama who had been chosen by the Chinese government[566] and was also nominated to be the leader of the Chinese National Buddhist Association. Convinced that fulfilling these demands would go against his principles, he decided to leave his homeland for good. Accordingly, Arjia Rinpoché came to America in 1998, settling in Mill Valley, California. In 2005 he was asked by His Holiness the Dalai Lama to become the director of the Tibetan Mongolian Buddhist Cultural Center in Bloomington, Indiana. Rinpoché moved there in 2006 and has since renovated and revitalized the center as a place from which to disseminate Buddhist teachings and promote Tibetan and Mongolian cultural events through regular teachings, retreats, and festivals.

Arjia Rinpoché on Vegetarianism

Arjia Rinpoché became a vegetarian on the Tibetan lunar new year of 1994. This decision, and his stance on meat eating in general, is grounded in the understanding that Buddhists should not kill animals and, on the contrary, should actively work to save animal lives whenever possible. Building on this basic assumption, and taking into consideration his own experiences at Kumbum, where large numbers of animals were slaughtered that would not otherwise be killed or donated to feed the monastic population, Rinpoché came to believe that eating meat should be avoided.

In addition to the animals themselves, Rinpoché also became concerned with the image of the Tibetan and Mongolian monastic community. He particularly highlights the fact that most Chinese Buddhist monks are vegetarian. When these monks performed ceremonies with members of the

566. After the death of the Tenth Panchen Lama in 1989, the Dalai Lama recognized a young boy, Gendun Chökyi Nyima, as his reincarnation. Rather than accept this child, however, the Chinese government selected another child, Gyaincain Norbu, as the Eleventh Panchen Lama. It is this latter figure, whose legitimacy is widely dismissed by Tibetans, that Arjia Rinpoché was asked to tutor.

Tibeto-Mongolian sangha, the latter would eat at a special table so they could be served meat. Because of this, Rinpoché recalls, the Chinese monks looked down on the Tibetans and Mongolians. Meat eating, he decided, caused animals to suffer and also harmed the social standing of Tibeto-Mongolian Buddhism. He therefore decided to personally adopt a vegetarian diet and to encourage this practice among his followers.

As the story of his conversion to vegetarianism suggests, Rinpoché prioritizes his personal experience—particularly the observed reality that monastic meat eating causes animals to be slaughtered—over abstract reflection on the Vinaya or other formal rules. This is particularly clear in his stance on the rule of threefold purity.[567] Rather than parse the intricacies of the Vinaya, Rinpoché suggests that this rule should be interpreted in the light of contemporary cultural practices. The rule of threefold purity, he notes, originated in a context in which monks and nuns begged for their daily food during alms rounds outside the monastery, meaning that they truly were not responsible for the death of any animals even if they ate meat. These days, however, monks and nuns no longer beg, so threefold purity, says Rinpoché, "is now really a loophole in the system rather than the rule's real meaning. In my opinion, we as Buddhists are using this idea, which is no longer necessary in our social and cultural context, as an excuse to keep eating meat without facing the ethical consequences." Arjia Rinpoché is a scholar and never dismisses the importance of textual analysis. But this analysis, he asserts, must take into consideration changes in an issue's broader context.

In line with this overall approach, while Arjia Rinpoché himself is usually a strict vegetarian, he approaches this question with a degree of flexibility, depending on the particular circumstances. Rinpoché himself notes that in some contexts, he relaxes his vegetarianism for social reasons. In particular, he is concerned about overly inconveniencing others in places like Japan, where finding pure vegetarian food is quite difficult. Rinpoché applies a similar flexibility to his discussion of nomads and vegetarianism. While he maintains that vegetarianism is good, he also recognizes the loss of nomadic culture that universal vegetarianism would entail. "Given this context," he admits, "vegetarianism is a sensitive issue, and I cannot say which way is wrong or which is right." As other authors in this volume also suggest, vegetarianism here is not an all-or-nothing proposition but is an ideal that needs to be balanced against social and culture realities.

567. Threefold purity is the Vinaya rule that allows meat to be eaten as long as the consumer has not seen, has not heard, and does not even suspect that the animal may have been killed specifically for his consumption.

Overall, Arjia Rinpoché's critique of meat eating is grounded in his belief that Buddhists should actively practice compassion toward animals and in his own experience administering a large Tibeto-Mongolian Buddhist monastery. His support for vegetarianism, however, is coupled with an awareness of the social and cultural contexts in which an individual's decision to eat meat is being made.

About the Interview

Unlike other texts in this volume, the following is not a translation from a Tibetan text but is based, rather, on an interview conducted on November 22, 2018, during Rinpoché's stay in Los Angeles after a teaching visit to Japan. I conducted this interview primarily in English with some recourse to Mongolian and Tibetan. The interview was recorded, then transcribed and edited to fit the structure of this volume. Certain points that needed more discussion were later clarified and some colloquialisms were replaced with standard English expressions. Rinpoché was consulted in making these edits and additions and gave his full consent for the final version that is found here.

Thoughts on Vegetarianism

By Arjia Rinpoché

Interview by Sangseraima Ujeed

I became vegetarian twenty-five years ago, for a number of reasons. After the Maoist period ended, monasteries were allowed to open their doors and revive the performance of religious ceremonies, rituals, and festivals. My main seat was at Kumbum Monastery in Kokonur, where I held the position of Gomdag Abbot. When we restarted the religious festivities and ceremonies, they quickly attracted many pilgrims and devotees. During these large events, the people would donate food and supplies such as meat, butter, money, and so on. In theory, the monastery would use these during the ceremonies and festivities. The money and the butter, we used a lot. But I found that we used only very little of the meat we were offered for the ceremony. Most of it was stored and used to feed the monastic community in its day-to-day life.[568] The thought occurred to me that this seemed inappropriate for our ideals as a monastery and as monastics. I thought, "As Buddhists, we avoid killing animals, avoid taking life. But we are still indirectly contributing to or encouraging the killing of animals. If we do not eat meat, why would animals need to be killed or donated?" I contemplated this issue quite often.

One day, some visitors on pilgrimage came to Kumbum. This was just after Kumbum had opened again, so it was sometime in early 1979. This particular group consisted of a large number of nomads. They went from temple to temple, paying homage to the religious supports[569] and so on. They came to our institution, where there was a big temple with a great hall. This particular hall was empty; it had been empty for a long time even before the Cultural Revolution. Our monastery had been using this hall to hang meat from ropes. We didn't have fridges or freezers back then, and winter was coming so the meat had been hung there to dry. When the pilgrims came across the temple, they thought it was an active temple with Buddha statues and they went inside. They came out and said, "There were no buddhas or bodhisattvas, but there

568. For an extensive discussion of monastic economies, permissible and impermissible donations, and the rules that surrounded such practices, see Jansen, *The Monastery Rules*, esp. 85–114.

569. Meaning the statues, paintings, and other items that serve as a support for religious practice.

were masses of meat hanging from ceiling to the floor." I thought then that this looked very bad for the monastery and the monks. This made me think a lot about everything. Our monastery at that time had around five hundred monks, but in the past there had been thousands. In those days, during the eighties, we had reopened our doors, we had restarted the festivals and ceremonies, and the number of monks at the monastery was also growing. If we suppose that the number was around five hundred and that a monk eats at least one sheep a year, then one monastery consumes five hundred sheep a year and ten monasteries of that size would consume at least five thousand sheep a year. I thought, "This is crazy! We should find a way to change this." It was the beginning of the journey that lead to my vegetarian lifestyle.

My resolve to be vegetarian was also strengthened by thinking about how we appeared in the eyes of Chinese Buddhists. I thought, "Socially, the Chinese Buddhist tradition requires and promotes vegetarianism. But Mongolians and Tibetans eat meat. If Mongolian or Tibetan monks go to Chinese monasteries for a festival or for an event, the Chinese monks have to prepare a special table for the Mongolians and Tibetans—a meat-eating table. As a consequence, the Chinese monks look down on us and think we are doing something inappropriate." For all of these reasons I stopped eating meat. I have always continued to think it was a good decision, and I have always remained proud of it. We are saving lives, and this very much fits the ethics of Buddhism.

When we think ethically, we think about the ten nonvirtuous actions. And when we think of the ten nonvirtuous actions, we should not only think of avoiding nonvirtue but also of practicing virtue. Instead of simply not killing, we should also be consciously trying to save lives. The texts, however, do not always clearly describe what we should do. Most don't directly say don't eat meat, so people make excuses and say the texts do not tell us not to, so we can. The rule of threefold purity is like this. In the past—by which I am really referring to the time of the Buddha in India when the ideal was first formulated—if someone was begging for food on the streets or going from door to door for alms, they might be offered a meal with meat. Eating this meat was OK. In those days, the monks had to go begging for alms and there were no huge monasteries. The monks had to make do with whatever food they were given and had to eat it right away. There were no occasions where monks had to prepare big feasts for the gathered masses, prepare ceremonial foods, or build huge kitchens to feed thousands of monks.

But this is not how monasticism functions today. Nowadays—and also in the past in Tibet and Mongolia—we can often find butchers right outside the main gates of many big monasteries. They are there to supply meat to the monks. Although the animals are not being slaughtered there, these shops only exist to serve the monastery. Because the monks eat meat, these businesses can survive and thrive. Kumbum had big butcher shops on either side of the main gate. I used to watch the monks going in and out of these butcher shops daily. In and out, all day long, buying meat. Not only were people donating meat to the monasteries, but due to the growing number of Buddhist ceremonies and festivals, the amount of meat the monasteries themselves bought from the butchers was also on the rise.

People may feel this meat had threefold purity, thinking, as long as we are not killing the animal, or it is not being killed for us, or we did not see the meat being killed for us, or we did not hear the animal dying, and so on, then it is OK. But I am not convinced by this attitude. We should find more meaning in the texts, analyze them in the context of our contemporary society and our ethics today. People say, this meat has threefold purity, but this is now really a loophole in the system rather than the rule's real meaning. In my opinion, we as Buddhists are using this idea, which is no longer necessary in our social and cultural context, as an excuse to keep eating meat without facing the ethical consequences.

Making such an excuse is also much easier in today's society, as the meat we buy is totally impersonal. It is perfectly packaged in little boxes in supermarkets next to the tofu—how do we even tell which is which? The farmers themselves no longer have to kill their own animals, and even the butchers have machines. The act of killing has become all too impersonal today. This new social reality needs more ethical analysis from our part.

In ancient times in Tibet and Mongolia, there was no popular movement comparable to today's vegetarianism. There were not even sufficient vegetables or other food for everyday individuals to keep a vegetarian diet. Of course, there were the exceptions, there were great masters of the past who were vegetarian, but it was not the norm. The living conditions, the weather, and lifestyle were tough, and meat and other animal products were the basis of most people's livelihood. So back then, in that context, it is understandable that people ate meat. However, in those earlier times, although we do not find pure vegetarianism so often, people actually ate much less meat than they do today. Why is this? In the fall, people would slaughter some animals, but only as much as they needed to last them the winter. As the temperature got colder, they could keep the meat in larders or dry it and eat it throughout the winter. However, in the summer, they were actually pretty much fully vegetarians. In the spring, the animals are just starting to reproduce. They graze on the new vegetation and start to produce milk. In the summer, the herds are really at the peak of their fattening period, and the young animals from that year are still reliant on their mothers. In those seasons there was plenty of dairy to supplement the dietary needs of the people. Therefore livestock were not slaughtered during the spring and summer seasons. During these seasons there was also plenty of wild vegetables, fruits, shoots, roots, and so on that people gathered for food. Along with dairy production, this was sufficient. Sometimes families might go hunting and then there might be a little bit of meat, but this did not apply to the majority. So meat was really only for the winter when there was nothing to gather and the animals had stopped producing milk. Compare this to today, when we no longer rely on seasonal foods, and when more and more people live in the cities and so no longer rely on traditional methods. This is why people were much healthier in the past.

Now that people eat more meat, they are overweight and develop lots of health problems. Also, due to today's capitalist attitudes, people chase business-oriented lives. This means that the general attitude is to try and make money from animals. People sell animals and meat products for the sake of profit without paying any attention to the actual health-related factors of human genetic makeup—needless to mention saving animal lives. People say today, Tibetans and Mongolians have it inbuilt in their DNA to love meat. But really, in the past, eating meat was a necessity rather than something that was done out of love or enjoyment of meat. Nowadays, when compared with the past, people are eating more meat than before, even though they have access to more vegetables, fruits, and vegetarian protein sources than ever before.

But there has been development in these attitudes. In 2006, in Mongolia, there were hardly any vegetarian restaurants or restaurants with simple vegetarian options. But by 2016 there were high numbers of vegetarian restaurants opening up and lots of young people were becoming vegetarian, and some even vegan. Among these young people, some are Buddhists and are doing it for Buddhist reasons. Some are becoming vegetarian because of new-age religions. Some for the preservation of life, animals, the environment, and so on—this is especially true for those who are becoming vegan.

Since I stopped eating meat, I have observed many benefits. I feel great, it has not affected my life in a negative way, and it has been very positive. It has been positive for others as well. For instance, when I was at Kumbum I was the Gomdag Abbot—one of the highest-ranking positions at the monastery. When there was a big gathering or ceremony, out of respect for my position, those preparing the ceremonies often decided that there would be only vegetarian food. Before I turned vegetarian, there were hardly any vegetarian ceremonies at Kumbum. But afterward, there were many days when only vegetarian food would be served in the monastery. This also was true for other monasteries where I performed ceremonies, rituals, and so forth.

Furthermore, because of my decision some of my students and followers also stopped eating meat. I have consciously been encouraging them to do so, as it is good for health, good for the animals, and good for the environment. When I have the opportunity, I also discuss this issue with other teachers, always encouraging them to stop eating meat. If people are influenced by me, or follow me, I hope that has some effect on their decision to eat or not eat meat. So either directly or indirectly, I believe it is making some difference, however big or small.

But there is also a cultural element to consider. Today some monks, teachers, and laity criticize Tibetans and Mongolians who eat meat, telling them to stop. Some other teachers, monks, and geshés,[570] however, criticize those who call for vegetarianism. These people say, You high lamas, geshés, and rinpochés, you eat what you want, you get offerings and have access to any foods and products in abundance. But you encourage poor and everyday Tibetans and Mongolians to become vegetarian and stop killing. If they do, then all the animals will be gone, and the lands the animals graze will be taken by the government. If there is no need to eat meat anymore, then there will no longer be a reason to support the nomadic lifestyle. The traditional Mongolian and Tibetan ways of life and culture will disappear.[571] In this way, they argue that to stop eating all meat is not compassionate. On the one hand, you are saving the animals, but on the other hand, the Tibetan way of life—its culture and traditions—could completely disappear as a result. It is already proving difficult for Tibetans and Inner Mongolians to preserve their culture in today's China. People who have lived like this for thousands of years and who are now struggling to preserve their way of life would lose their land and their culture and would dissolve into the Chinese world. So, given this context, vegetarianism is a sensitive issue, and I cannot say which way is wrong or which is right. Personally, I know my reasons for why I am vegetarian and why I can sustain such a lifestyle and why I am encouraging others to give up meat. But with the cultural element involved, it can be very difficult to make blanket conclusions.

Difficulties can also emerge with increasing globalization and multicultural societies. I sometimes go to places where there is no vegetarian food or vegetarian restaurants. In Japan, for instance, it is very difficult to find a purely vegetarian restaurant. They don't eat much red meat, but their diet is heavy with seafood products and we find seafood or seafood derivatives everywhere. Even the soup or broth has fish products. It can be inconvenient to be purely

570. Geshé (Tib: Dge shes) is a title awarded after fifteen to twenty-five years of scholastic study in a monastery. It is roughly the equivalent of a PhD.

571. For an analysis of one Tibetan intellectual's critique of pro-vegetarian lamas, see Buffetrille, "A Controversy on Vegetarianism."

vegetarian when traveling in Japan. If people want to invite me for a meal, or to conduct meetings, and so on, or if followers or students are hosting us, it is difficult. Our schedule when traveling is extremely tight, and we are often running from place to place to finalize contracts, perform ceremonies, and so forth. For that reason, when I find myself in such a situation, I make an exception. In Taiwan there is a saying that generally translates as "pot-side vegetarian." The basic idea is that when one cooks a meal with meat and vegetables, those who are vegetarian can eat the vegetables from the pot and not the meat. When we are traveling in places with few vegetarian options, we make this exception. If the sauce or the meal has meat in, then we just eat the vegetables from these and not the meat, and this is considered OK—but strictly in this context and not otherwise. If we are traveling and we really cannot find vegetarian food, if we have meetings that are important, and if the schedule is very tight, then we do make this exception.

Secondary Sources

Arjia Rinpoché. 2010. *Surviving the Dragon: A Tibetan Lama's Account of 40 Years under Chinese Rule*. New York: Rodale.

Buffetrille, Katia. 2014. "A Controversy on Vegetarianism." In *Trails of the Tibetan Tradition: Papers for Elliot Sperling*, edited by Roberto Vitali, 113–27. Dharamsala: Amye Machen Institute.

Buswell, Robert E., and Donald S. Lopez. 2013. *The Princeton Dictionary of Buddhism*. Princeton, NJ: Princeton University Press.

Jansen, Berthe. 2018. *The Monastery Rules: Buddhist Monastic Organization in Pre-Modern Tibet*. Oakland: University of California Press.

12. Khenpo Tsultrim Lodrö's Appeal to Contemporary Tibetans to Abandon Meat and Practice Nonkilling

By Catherine Hardie

THE VENERABLE Khenpo Tsultrim Lodrö (1962–)[572] is an eminent contemporary Nyingma scholar, practitioner, educator, and public intellectual based at the Larung Five Sciences Buddhist Academy (more commonly referred to as Larung Gar) in Serta County in Sichuan Province's Kardze Tibetan Autonomous Prefecture. He currently serves as a vice principal of the Academy and is one of the main spiritual heirs of its founder, the renowned late Nyingma and Rimé master Khenpo Jigmé Phunstok Rinpoché (1933–2004). From 1991 to 2013, Khenpo Tsultrim Lodrö served as Larung Gar's Dean of Education,[573] playing a leading role in the Academy's institutional development over the course of those two decades. The khenpo[574] is also widely active beyond his immediate seat and is well-known and respected for his civic engagement in eastern Tibetan regions as well as his cross-cultural religious outreach. He is particularly prominent in the Tibetan cultural world for his longstanding work in the preservation and development of Tibetan language and culture; his committed advocacy of nonkilling, vegetarianism, and the humane treatment of animals; and his efforts to uphold the centrality of religious ethics and values in rapidly changing Tibetan cultural worlds.[575] Fluent in Chinese, he is also a high-profile and influential teacher of Tibetan Buddhism among Sinophone Buddhist circles in mainland China and abroad. His extensive publications in Tibetan and Chinese and his active embracing

572. Tib: Mkhan po Tshul khrims blo gros.

573. Tib: Slob don khang gi gtso 'gan pa.

574. Khenpo (Tib: *mkhan po*) is an academic title awarded to those who complete a rigorous (often ten years or more) course of philosophical study.

575. For more on the contemporary vegetarian movement, see Buffetrille, "A Controversy on Vegetarianism"; Gaerrang, "Tibetan Identity and Tibetan Buddhism in Trans-Regional Connection"; and Gayley, "The Compassionate Treatment of Animals."

of online and digital media have seen his written works, teachings, and social commentary circulate widely among both domestic and global audiences.

Clear Mirror of Advice

The *Clear Mirror of Advice on the Rules on Eating Meat* is Khenpo Tsultrim Lodrö's earliest work on vegetarianism and was written only one year after Larung Gar—a saṅgha of almost ten thousand people—voted overwhelmingly to implement an institution-wide meat-free policy. Unprecedented on such a scale in the Tibetan Buddhist world, this development largely took place at the khenpo's instigation and should be seen as the genesis of the contemporary vegetarianism movement that has emanated from the Larung Academy. Prior to this, a strong ethic of compassion for animals was already pronounced in the broader Larung culture, with Khenpo Jigmé Phunstok opposing the practice of selling livestock for slaughter and encouraging his disciples to undertake life liberation widely. While Khenpo Jigmé Phuntsok's root guru, Thubga Rinpoché (1886–1956), had been vegetarian, due to a scarcity of alternative food sources, the remote Larung encampment had always followed the rule of threefold purity, which permits meat eating so long as the meat is not specifically killed for its eater. It was not until Khenpo Tsultrim Lodrö, who had embraced vegetarianism in the late 1990s, galvanized his fellow khenpos into action by showing them gruesome footage of killing scenes he had filmed in nearby slaughterhouses that a collective impetus for institution-wide change took hold. *Clear Mirror of Advice* was written in 2001, very soon after Larung Gar's transition to a meat-free policy, and signals the beginning of a campaign to push vegetarian reform outward by lobbying monastic institutions in Tibetan areas to prohibit meat. First printed and disseminated in 2001, *Clear Mirror* was officially published in 2006 in an edited collection by Khenpo Tsultrim Lodrö titled *Faults of Eating Meat and Benefits of Life Liberation*.[576] With a focus on antislaughter advocacy and life liberation as well as vegetarianism, the essays in this volume reveal the early years of the new millennium at Larung Gar to have been a period of particular activity with respect to ethical interventions in human-animal relations.

Clear Mirror sets forth a clear, reasoned, and scripturally grounded case for the normativity of a pro-vegetarian stance in the Tibetan Buddhist tradition. Geared to discredit the customary practice of meat eating on the part of Tibetan monastics, it seeks to draw a clear line between the cultural practice of eating meat in Tibet and the normative standpoint on meat eating of the

576. Tib: *Sha'i nyes dmigs dang srog blu'i phan yon*.

Tibetan Buddhist tradition. Its purpose is stated upfront: to explain the rules about eating meat for monastics and bodhisattvas as they are set out in the Vinaya and discourses of the Buddha, and to thereby acquaint the ethically minded reader with the boundary between what is prohibited and permitted. This exercise is necessary, the khenpo maintains, as a corrective to the frequent misconception that meat eating is condoned in the Tibetan Buddhist tradition and, especially, in the Vajrayāna. Pointedly, he contrasts the indifference of Tibetan practitioners toward meat eating with the positive example of Chinese Mahāyānists, who, he affirms, admirably perpetuate the sūtric vegetarian tradition. He also acknowledges the contemporary practice of the Śrāvaka school, whose adherents observe the rules on eating meat laid down in the Vinaya. Just where, he tacitly asks, does the Tibetan Buddhist tradition stand in relation to these other major lineages of Buddhism on the issue of eating meat?

With this introduction, *Clear Mirror* sets about describing the normative position on meat eating in the Buddhist patrimony of Tibet—a Mahāyāna tradition comprised of both exoteric *and* esoteric systems. What follows is a systematic presentation of authoritative excerpts from the Buddha's words and commentarial sources organized into three subsections that correspond with the standpoints of the three vows: the Vinaya, Mahāyāna, and Vajrayāna. The inevitable conclusion they build to is that the sūtric Mahāyāna prohibition on eating any meat is shared by the Vajrayāna, such that Tibetan practitioners who eat meat do so in contravention of all precepts.

Attending first to the Vinaya standpoint, Khenpo Tsultrim Lodrö makes clear that the fundamental restriction on eating meat in the Vinaya precepts pertains to meat that has been killed "for one's own sake." He begins with the *Bhaiṣajya*[577] chapter of the *Vinayavastu*[578] in order to establish the rule of threefold purity as the authoritative formula for determining the suitability of meat to be eaten. This rule clearly spells out, he says, that meat that has been seen, heard, or suspected to have been killed by someone for one's own sake is unsuitable to be eaten. He notes that this rule is also expressed in certain Vinaya sources as a prohibition on eating meat that has been "dedicated" for oneself. He emphasizes that this does not entail a prohibition on eating meat that has been killed for the sake of general consumption, as is the case with meat from butchers, which is permitted to be eaten according to the threefold-purity rule.

Moving on to the Mahāyāna standpoint, the khenpo goes about demonstrating conclusively that earlier permissions on eating meat, including the

577. *The Chapter on Medicine* (Tib: *Sman gyi gzhi*). One of seventeen chapters in the *Vinayavastu* of the *Mūlasarvāstivāda Vinaya*.

578. *Vinaya Chapters* (Tib: *'Dul ba'i gzhi*).

threefold-purity rule, were superseded and discarded by the teachings of the Bodhisattva Vehicle, which prohibits meat eating outright. With two full excerpts of the Buddha's discourses on the faults of meat from the *Laṅkāvatāra* and *Mahāparinirvāna Sūtras*,[579] this is the longest section of *Clear Mirror*. These authoritative excerpts are followed by a passage from the *Śikṣāsamuccaya*[580] in which Śāntideva cites approvingly the *Laṅkāvatāra Sūtra*'s prohibition on eating meat for the compassionate bodhisattva and reiterates the *Laṅkāvatāra*'s characterization of the training precepts on restricting meat as put in place gradually, like the rungs of a ladder. Rather than presenting a picture of complete unanimity in Mahāyāna commentarial sources, however, Khenpo Tsultrim Lodrö follows with a lengthy excerpt from the *Tarkajvālā*[581] in which Bhāviveka, the sixth-century Buddhist Madhyamaka philosopher, rejects a stance of complete vegetarianism in favor of the threefold-purity rule. The crux of his reasoning is that at the time that meat is actually consumed, the animal has already died and therefore eating its flesh does not constitute an act of direct harm on a living being. Bhāviveka therefore rejects the claim that eating meat is tantamount to killing, contending instead that no wrongdoing exists in consuming meat that was not killed specifically for oneself.[582]

While acknowledging the existence of Mahāyāna scholars like Bhāviveka who espoused the rule of threefold purity rather than accept the *Laṅkāvatāra Sūtra*'s teaching, Khenpo Tsultrim Lodrö rebuts the validity of this stance. Emphasizing that the Mahāyāna scriptures are unequivocal in their outright prohibition on eating meat, he draws attention to passages in the *Laṅkāvatāra* and *Mahāparinirvāna Sūtras* where this is stated in plain terms. In particular, he underlines the Buddha's insistence that meat with threefold purity does not exist, for even if one does not explicitly order meat to be killed for oneself, one still causes the killing indirectly as a general consequence of eating meat. He also underlines the *Mahāparinirvāna Sūtra*'s pronouncement that threefold purity was set forth as a temporary precept only and was later withdrawn, at which point the prohibition on eating any meat became applicable to both śrāvakas and bodhisattvas.

Progressing to the Vajrayāna standpoint, the khenpo draws both on earlier

579. The relevant portions of these texts have been translated in chapter 1 of this volume.

580. *Compendium of Training* (Tib: *Slab pa kun las btus pa*). For a full translation, see Goodman, *The Training Anthology of Śāntideva.*

581. *Blaze of Reasoning* (Tib: *Rtogs ge 'bar ba*).

582. For more on Bhāviveka and his stance on meat, see Eckel, *Bhāviveka and His Buddhist Opponents*; Hoornaert, "An Annotated Translation of Madhyamakahṛdayakārikā/Tarkajvālā V.69–84"; and Hyoung Seok Ham, "Buddhist Critiques of the Veda and Vedic Sacrifice."

and later tantric scriptures to reveal a consistent opposition to meat eating in the foundational texts of the Nyingma as well as in those of other lineages. He refers to a short excerpt from the *Vimalaprabhā*,[583] the commentary on the *Kālacakra Tantra*,[584] that decries eating and desiring to eat meat as well as the act of killing. Further excerpts from Kālacakra sources emphasize the dire karmic consequences of meat eating and note that while practitioners who are ill may need to eat meat to recover from an illness, as far as possible they should eat meat that has not been killed for consumption. The khenpo then moves on to address the key issue of meat consumption in the context of the ritual feast offering[585]—the very reason, he says in the essay's introduction, that the Vajrayāna tradition is often misunderstood to condone ordinary meat eating. By highlighting scriptural sources that emphasize significant restrictions that apply to the use of meat as a samaya substance, the khenpo demonstrates that accepting meat in the context of the ritual feast is fundamentally different to ordinary meat consumption.

He quotes a source from the *Unimpeded Realization*[586] terma cycle that recommends novice practitioners consume only "the mere scent" of the five types of amrita medicine and condemns heedless indulgence in blood, flesh, and alcohol. He cites another text from the same cycle that proscribes meat from an animal that has been killed by humans (or has died in a number of other improper ways) for use as a ritual feast offering. He also includes an excerpt from the *Vimalaprabhā* that explicitly addresses the tension between the requirement that yogis accept meat as a samaya substance and the reality that meat originates in the sinful act of killing. Endorsing the statement that without a meat eater there would not be a killer, the *Vimalaprabhā* stipulates that yogis should only consume faultless samaya substances that derive from animals that have died in a karmically neutral way or otherwise just consume samaya pills.

Changing tone, the khenpo concludes his analysis of the Vajrayana standpoint with two vivid and persuasive works on the faults of meat by Nyala Pema Dündul and Götsang Natsok Rangdröl, both eminent Tibetan yogis. The insertion of these pieces at this point in the essay would seem to be directed at making a broader point about the presence of a long legacy of great vegetarian

583. *Stainless Light* (Tib: *Dri ma med pa'i 'od*). The most important commentary on the *Kālacakra* cycle.

584. *The Wheel of Time* (Tib: *Dus kyi 'khor lo'i rgyud*).

585. Tib: *tsok*; Skt: *ganachakra*. For more on the feast offering, as well as a translation of an alternate take on the use of meat in this ritual, see chapter 6 of this volume.

586. A terma cycle revealed by Rigdzin Gödem and often known to English-language audiences by its Tibetan name, *Gongpa Zangthal* (Tib: *Dgongs pa zang thal*).

practitioners in the Tibetan Buddhist tradition. By highlighting this fact, the khenpo is able to counter misconceptions that all Tibetan Vajrayāna adepts have always eaten meat as well as counter detractors apt to dismiss Tibetan Buddhist vegetarianism as a modern, and perhaps Sinicized, innovation. Both Nyala Pema Dündul's *Song of Advice for Giving up Meat* and Götsang Natsok Rangdröl's untitled work demonstrate the existence of extraordinarily realized masters—practitioners typically viewed to be qualified to deliver dead beings through their acts of consumption—who are moved to renouncing meat by awakening to the terrifying karmic consequences of its consumption. In Götsang Natsok Rangdröl's sinister dream episode, he finds himself in the hands of a carnivorous monk executioner whose vocation is to sentence to death hypocritical meat-eating monastics in ways that mirror their own past methods of killing and eating their fellow mother sentient beings.

This graphic vignette of karmic retribution is a fitting lead to the conclusion of *Clear Mirror*, which until now has featured very little in the way of first-person commentary by the khenpo himself. Having allowed the scriptural evidence, skillfully presented, to speak for itself, the khenpo's own voice now comes to the fore. Reconfirming the principle that the Vajrayāna tradition permits neither meat that has been killed for consumption to be eaten nor its use in the ritual feast, he denounces those who use tantra as a pretext to wantonly indulge in blood, flesh, and alcohol. The karmic result of this sinful behavior, he assures the reader, is reincarnation as a carnivorous animal, resulting in continuous rebirth in the lower realms for eons to come. Only now does he address the contemporary situation in Tibetan areas, drawing into focus the issue of monasteries that kill animals for the sake of the sustenance of their monastic communities. The hypocrisy and cruelty inherent in this terrifying practice, he argues, is an ongoing cause of slander and wrong views about the Secret Mantrāyana. Presumably, the khenpo is referring here to critical opinion about meat eating by Tibetan monastics, primarily on the part of ethnic others—Chinese, Western, South Asian, and so on—whose presence and voices in Tibetan cultural worlds, both religious and secular, have increased dramatically since the mid-twentieth century.

Describing modern slaughterhouses as like "hell on earth" with regard to the large-scale suffering they inflict on sentient beings on a daily basis, the khenpo forcefully asserts that without meat eaters to purchase meat from butchers none of this atrocity would occur. He reinforces this point by quoting verses from the *Mañjuśrī Pradarshana*[587] that uphold the view that meat

587. *Teachings on Mañjuśrī's Own View* (Tib: *'Phags pa 'jam phal gyi rang gi lta ba'i 'dod pa mdor bstan pa yongs su brtag pa*).

eaters and animal killers are both guilty of grave karmic wrongdoing. While acknowledging that the ruinous conduct of buying and killing meat has been taking place since time immemorial, the khenpo laments that in modern times matters have significantly deteriorated. Highlighting improved transport conditions in Tibetan areas and a wider availability of meat-based processed foodstuffs from other parts of China, he warns against what may be described as an obscuration of the ethical relationship between the consumption and production of meat. To the degree that meat-based food comes at the cost of other beings' suffering, he concludes, it should never be an "object of free and unreflective enjoyment."

The two short texts that follow from *Clear Mirror* were also published in *Faults of Eating Meat and Benefits of Life Liberation*. Together they represent two personal appeals by Khenpo Tsultrim Lodrö to monastic and lay Tibetan audiences that center on the suffering of animals condemned to slaughter. The first text, *Request in the Presence of the Noble Dharma Holders*, entreats lamas and monks to give their wholehearted support to opposing the sale of livestock into slaughter in Tibetan regions. Notable here is the khenpo's declaration that protecting the environment and animals is particularly incumbent on members of the monastic saṅgha. The second text, *Appeal Not to Cruelly Slaughter Farm Animals*, is primarily addressed to rural lay Tibetans, urging them, in the event that killing simply cannot be avoided, to employ humane methods of slaughter to minimize the suffering to which animals are subjected. Taken together, *Clear Mirror* and the two appeals form part of an evolving religious-based campaign by Khenpo Tsultrim Lodrö to galvanize monastic and lay sectors of Tibetan society into ethical reform of the human-animal interface by abandoning meat, killing, and cruelty.

About the Translation

I would like to thank Lama Jabb and Lama Drimed Lodrö for their kindness in helping me to work through language and content in the following translations. I would also like to thank Khenpo Tsultrim Lodrö for clarifying a number of difficult points. Since *Clear Mirror* cites a wide variety of original texts, I have been fortunate in places to be able to directly use or consult existing translations, and in such cases I have acknowledged my colleagues' work or assistance. In spite of this generous help, all mistakes in the following translation naturally remain my own.

Clear Mirror of Advice on the Rules on Eating Meat[588]

By Khenpo Tsultrim Lodrö

Translated by Catherine Hardie

Namo Guru Manjushri!

To the kin of suffering beings and compassionate treasure
of the world arrayed with moon-crystal snow mountains,
who by the music of the three secrets' magical display
bestows the splendor of benefit and ease—
to you, Padmapani,[589] I bow down with reverence.

With this supplication, this essay will briefly describe the advice on the rules about eating meat for monastics and bodhisattvas as they are presented in the Vinaya and general discourses of Śākyamuni Buddha and the way in which this advice should be interpreted. In modern times it seems that adherents of the Śrāvaka school in southern countries do not proscribe meat; they practice in accordance with what is set forth in the Śrāvaka Vinaya. Chinese Mahāyānists follow what is taught in the Great Vehicle sūtras and for a long time have placed great emphasis on not eating meat. That this custom has continued until today is a cause of admiration. Our own region for the most part appears indifferent to meat eating. While some think this is due to the spread of Vajrayāna Buddhism, it will be explained that Vajrayāna samaya substances have no connection whatsoever with ordinary meat eating. Thus I have no criticism of great bodhisattvas who embody compassion and mighty siddhas who have reached the pinnacle of realization. Not only this, but I am also unqualified in the skillful activity of taming beings. Yet for ordinary people who wish to conduct themselves ethically it is important that they first be acquainted with the boundary between what is prohibited and what is allowed.

To this end, this essay will consist of two sections: the teachings of the

588. Tib: *Sha'i kha zas gnang bkag gi bslab bya blang dor gsal ba'i me long zhes bya ba bzhugs so.*

589. "Lotus-holder" (Tib: *Phyag na pad mo*), a popular epithet of Avalokiteśvara, bodhisattva of compassion.

Hīnayāna Vinaya and the teachings of the sūtras of the Mahāyāna Bodhisattva Pitaka.

The Vinaya Standpoint

First, I will begin with the standpoint of the Hīnayāna Vinaya, which consists of the teachings of the Buddha's discourses and those of the commentaries.

In the *Bhaiṣajya* chapter of the *Vinayavastu*, it says:

> The Buddha was staying in a multistory house by the Monkey Pond in Vaiśālī. In Vaiśālī there lived a chieftain named Sengé, and whenever the people living nearby brought him meat, he ate it. One day he learned from the Buddha what was true and did not eat meat anymore. Meat was still brought to him, but he offered it to the monks, who ate it. Some non-Buddhists condemned those monks who had eaten the food, denigrating and slandering them, saying, "Knowledgeable ones, the chieftain Sengé does not eat the meat that is prepared for him, so it is given to the monks of the son of the Śākyas. And the monks of the son of the Śākyas eat the meat that was prepared for chieftain Sengé."
>
> When the monks heard this, they asked the Buddha, who replied, "I have said that meat that is not suitable in three respects should not be eaten. What are those three? Meat that has been seen to have been prepared for one's own sake is unsuitable to be eaten. Meat that you have heard from trustworthy sources to have been prepared for your own sake is unsuitable to be eaten. Meat that you think, based on suspicions that have arisen in your mind, to have been prepared for your own sake, is unsuitable to be eaten. Monks, I have said that meat that is suitable in three respects can be eaten. What are those three? Meat that has not been seen to have been prepared for one's own sake is suitable to be eaten. Meat that you have not heard from trustworthy sources to have been prepared for your own sake is suitable to be eaten. Meat that you do not think, based on suspicion that has arisen in your mind, to have been prepared for your own sake, is suitable to be eaten."

Second, the *Vinayasūtra* says, "Furthermore, the essence of meat taken as medicine is permissible. It should all be obtained from a butcher. [In case of illness] this should be done," and, "Meat that is known to have been dedicated should not be eaten. Tigers' remnants should not be eaten. Elephants, horses, and nāgas should not be eaten. Animals with undivided hooves, foxes, monkeys, woodpeckers, crows, vultures, water fowl, dogs, hawks, owls, and other carrion birds, gray ducks, bats, snow lizards, worms, and insects should also not be eaten."

The *Vinayasūtraṭīkā*[590] says:

> The root text says, "If one knows that meat has been dedicated for oneself it should not be eaten." This meant that, if a donor dedicates meat for the sake of the eater and the eater learns of this by means of seeing, hearing, or suspecting, that meat should not be eaten. It is therefore permitted for monastics to eat meat that is suitable to be eaten and that has been obtained from a butcher or a market by a faithful layperson.

Therefore, according to this approach, the difference between meat that is dedicated and meat that is not should be determined based on whether one has seen, heard, or suspected that the meat has been killed by someone else for one's own sake. If these factors are absent, then apart from those kinds that are prohibited, meat is permitted to be eaten. Some scholars in the past spoke of "meat with threefold purity." Others spoke of an "absence of seeing, hearing, or suspecting [that meat] has been killed for one's own sake." To read these as saying, "Generally, any meat that is for consumption is prohibited" is incorrect.

In the *Prabhāvatī*[591] it says:

> Meat and fish meat that are killed for one's own sake should not be eaten. Even if one is innocent of the threefold acts of killing, causing to be killed, and rejoicing in the killing, because eating meat that is killed for one's own sake will lead one to become uncompassionate and because it is improper, it is prohibited. Apart from this kind, other meat is not forbidden.

In the śrāvaka tradition, it is spelled out extremely clearly in the *Bhaiṣajya* chapter of the *Vinayavastu* that the distinction between meat with threefold purity and meat without threefold purity is based on whether one sees, hears, or suspects the meat is killed by someone for one's own sake. The *Vinayasūtra* and its great commentary say that in terms of eating meat that is obtained

590. *Great Commentary on the Vinayasūtra* (Tib: *'Dul ba'i mdo rtsa ba rgya cher 'grel pa*). Dharmamitra's commentary on Guṇaprabha's *Vinayasūtra*.

591. *The Luminous* (Tib: *'Od ldan*). A Vinaya commentary by Śākyaprabha.

from a butcher, because it is generally for eating there is no question about whether it has been killed for one's own sake.

According to the *Prabhāvatī*, in the case of meat that has been killed for the sake of a monk by a hunter or the like, even if the monk is innocent of the threefold acts of committing the act of killing himself, causing the hunter to kill, or rejoicing in the killing of a wild animal, eating meat that has been killed for one's own sake is uncompassionate and improper.

To continue the above quotation from the *Prabhāvatī*:

> When the monk Chema-gyé was laid up with an illness, the Buddha instructed that raw meat be given to him. The monk asked, "From where should it be obtained?" The Buddha replied, "From the five major meat sellers in the neighboring community. What are these five? The butcher, duck seller, bird seller, pig seller, and the stall that sells the meat of wild-animal hunters. Monk, you ask who should obtain it and who should give it? A faithful layperson from the neighboring community should do so." The specification that a faithful layperson do so is to show there is no doubt about whether it was killed specifically for the monk's sake.

The Mahāyāna Standpoint

In the Mahāyāna there are the two traditions of the Sūtra and Mantra Vehicles. Turning first to the Buddha's words and commentaries of the Sūtra Vehicle, the *Laṅkāvatāra Sūtra*[592] says:

> "Mahāmati," the Buddha said, "bodhisattvas who embody compassion do not eat meat for innumerable reasons, only some of which I will explain. Mahāmati, it is not easy to find someone who was not once your father, mother, brother, sister, son, daughter, kinsman, friend, or the like at some point during the long ages of samsara. Your friends and relatives in the past, they have now changed their form and become wild animals, domestic animals, and birds, whatever their karma dictates. Bodhisattvas and great beings aspire to the Buddha's Dharma, aspire to become like me. So how could they eat the meat that comes from these beings, now born as animals? Mahāmati, even demons turn away from eating meat when

592. I would like to thank Geoffrey Barstow for permission to use his translation of the following excerpt from the *Laṅkāvatāra Sūtra*.

they hear the wholesome Dharma of the tathāgatas, turning away from their demonic nature toward compassion. So what need is there to speak of those who aspire to the true Dharma? In that way, Mahāmati, bodhisattvas look on all beings of the here and now as the transformation of their previous relatives and friends. Therefore they cultivate looking on each of them as their only child. Because of this, bodhisattvas—the embodiment of compassion—do not eat any type of meat.

"Mahāmati, it is mistaken and unsuitable for engaged bodhisattvas to eat meat, so they should not eat any type of meat. Mahāmati, worldly people do not eat the meat of donkeys, camels, dogs, cows, or humans (even though butchers claim that it is wholesome and sell it on the streets in order to make some money). Therefore, Mahāmati, bodhisattvas do not eat any meat. Mahāmati, bodhisattvas who aspire to purity do not eat meat, as it comes from semen and blood.

"Not wanting to scare living beings, Mahāmati, bodhisattvas who possess the yoga of kindness do not eat any type of meat. It is the case, Mahāmati, that when a dog sees, even at a great distance, a butcher, outcast, fisherman, or anyone else that eats dog meat, it is thrown into a state of fear. Thinking, 'they will come and kill me,' the dog almost dies of fear! It is similar, Mahāmati, with those tiny beings that live in the air, on the earth, or in water. As soon as they see a distant meat eater, or when they detect one with their subtle sense of smell, then, fearing death, they quickly turn aside, just as a human might turn from a demon. Mahāmati, since bodhisattvas who abide in kindness do not want to cause fear, they do not eat meat. Mahāmati, eating meat gives ordinary, non-noble beings a foul and disagreeable smell that makes them repulsive. Noble beings abandon this, and so bodhisattvas should not eat meat. Mahāmati, noble beings eat the food of sages, without meat or blood. Therefore bodhisattvas should also not eat meat.

"Mahāmati, compassionate bodhisattvas do not eat meat in order to avoid scandalizing people so that they disparage my teachings. So it is, Mahāmati. There are some in the world who speak ill of my teachings, saying, 'Alas, what type of virtue do those people have? Though they say it is important to act purely, they have abandoned the food of their own previous sages. Wandering throughout this world, like carnivorous animals, they fill their bellies with meat, terrifying those small animals that live in the sky, on the earth, and in the water. Their virtuous practice has declined! They have stopped turning aside from evil! They do not have any Dharma and they do not have any discipline!' Thus these people use many critical comments to disparage the teachings. Therefore, Mahāmati, since they desire to avoid scandalizing people who would then disparage my teachings, bodhisattvas who embody compassion do not eat any type of meat.

"Mahāmati, the smell of corpses is foul and disagreeable. Meat is no different, so bodhisattvas should not eat meat. Mahāmati, there is no difference between the smell of a roasting human corpse and the smell of the roasting flesh of some other kind of being. Both have the same disgusting smell. This is another reason, Mahāmati, that bodhisattvas who possess yoga and aspire to purity do not eat any type of meat. Mahāmati, yogis who dwell in charnel grounds, who live in forest monasteries, who sleep in remote hermitages haunted by spirits, who engage in yoga, who abide in kindness, who are **adepts accomplished in knowledge-mantras, or who aspire to accomplish knowledge-mantras** [1][593] all understand that eating meat is an obstacle to liberation. Therefore, all those accomplished yogis who are my sons and daughters and who abide in the Mahāyāna do not eat any type of meat. They see it as an obstacle to benefitting themselves and others, so these bodhisattvas do not eat any type of meat.

"Attachment arises based on the awareness of having a body, so that this body becomes identified with a being's self identity. This is why bodhisattvas who embody compassion do not eat any type of meat. Mahāmati, even the gods abandon it, so bodhisattvas who embody affectionate kindness do not eat any type of meat. Even in this life, Mahāmati, eating meat causes one's breath to stink, so bodhisattvas do not eat any meat.

"Meat eaters suffer when they are asleep and suffer when they are awake. They have dark dreams: you can see the hairs rise on their bodies. Dwelling in empty houses or alone in isolated places, they are haunted by spirits that steal their life force. Sometimes they get angry or have sudden feelings of fear and dread. They eat gluttonously, without a sense of proportion. They cannot digest the

593. Khenpo Tsultrim Lodrö follows this extract from the *Laṅkāvatāra Sūtra* with a glossary discussing key words and phrases. For the convenience of readers who wish to refer back and forth between the full passage and this glossary, these phrases have been put in bold and numbers have been added.

nourishment in their food, drink, and other sustenance. Worms grow in their stomachs, and they are prone to leprosy and many other illnesses. Despite such unpleasant experiences, they do not understand the cause.

"I have explained that food can be medicinal or as unwholesome as the flesh of children [2]. Mahāmati, ordinary, non-noble beings eat meat. Noble beings give it up. Meat causes the accumulation of much nonvirtue and the relinquishment of much virtue. This food is unpleasant and unsuitable: it is food for the unwise. How could I permit my disciples to eat flesh and blood? Mahāmati, I say that eating the food of noble beings brings much virtue and gets rid of nonvirtue. Sages of the past delighted in foods like rice, barley, wheat, various large and small beans, butter, oil, honey, sugar, molasses, and sugarcane. These are wholesome foods, and it should be understood that I have permitted them. Mahāmati, in the future benighted beings will speculate about the Vinaya. Proposing many subtle distinctions, they will conclude that meat is acceptable food. But in truth this is because they are predisposed to eating meat and are attached to its taste.

"Mahāmati, I teach this for the sake of those great bodhisattvas who do the work of the buddhas of the past, who cultivate virtue, who have faith, and who are without conceptions. They are the children of Śākyamuni's lineage, my human sons and daughters who are not attached to body, life, or enjoyments. Unattached to sense pleasures, they are not greedy for tasty food. Endowed with compassion, they aspire to be like me. They cherish all beings, as if they were their only child. I teach this for their sake.

"Mahāmati, in the past there was a king named Sengé Bangzang. He ate meat, including types that are normally forbidden. He was so attached to the taste that he even ate human flesh! All those who lived in his cities and villages abandoned him, even his wife, his ministers, his relatives, and his friends. Thus abandoned, his suffering was very great!

"Mahāmati, at the time when Indra had become king of the gods, even he had strong tendencies toward eating meat [3]. Because of this fault, he sometimes took the form of a hawk and tormented pigeons and small birds, clutching them in his talons. As a hawk, he even forced the blameless and compassionate king Shidan to put his flesh on the scales in order to ransom a dove, causing the king great pain. Thus, Mahāmati, the tendency toward eating meat that has built up over many lifetimes is the source of problems for both yourself and others. This is true even if you are born as Indra, king of the gods, let alone as a lesser being!

"Mahāmati, there was once another king of men. One day this king was carried off by a powerful horse into a wild and unruly forest. After wandering for long time, **he began living with a lioness in order to survive [4]**. Eventually they had sons, one of whom was named Kangtra. At that time in the past, being accustomed to living with lions, Kangtra and the others were meat eaters. Because of these evil tendencies, Kangtra continued to eat meat over a succession of lives, even when he became a king of men. Mahāmati, in this present life Kangtra has been born in **the city of Kimdün [5]**, and he is very attached to meat, to the extent that he even eats forbidden meats. Because of this, in the future he will be born as **a malevolent male or female animal-headed spirit that consumes human flesh [6]**. Even after that life, Mahāmati, his strong, ongoing attachment to meat will cause him to fall into exceptionally fierce birth-states, such as lions, tigers, leopards, wolves, cats, foxes, owls, and other carnivorous animals. He will even be born as a cannibal demon that eats a lot of meat. After such a fall, it will be hard for him to again achieve a human life, let alone achieve nirvāṇa!

"Mahāmati, these are the faults of eating meat, and this is what happens to those who eat a lot of it! Giving it up, however, brings much virtue. Mahāmati, ordinary, childish beings do not comprehend these virtues, faults, and so on. Mahāmati, I have taught this so that bodhisattvas who embody compassion will see these virtues and faults and stop eating any kind of meat.

"If someone gives up meat, Mahāmati, then animals will not be killed. This is because innocent beings are usually killed for money; other reasons are rare. Craving the taste of meat can be terribly overwhelming, Mahāmati, and **can even lead people to [7]** eat human flesh, let alone the flesh of wild animals, domestic animals, birds, and other animals. Mahāmati, those tormented by a craving for the taste of meat create all manner of nets and traps. Using these, hunters, butchers, and fishermen kill all sorts of innocent animals that live in the sky, on the earth, and in the water. Such people, Mahāmati, endowed with fierce hunters' minds, are devoid of compassion, just like rākṣasa demons. Anyone who recognizes that a being is alive and yet kills and eats it anyway can never develop compassion.

"**All meat is unsuitable** [8], Mahāmati, whether it is the type that I have allowed my dear śrāvakas to eat, the type I have **not allowed** [9], or **so-called unexamined** [10] meat. Mahāmati, in the future there will be stupid people who are ordained in my tradition, who call themselves 'children of the Śākya,' and who bear aloft the saffron victory banner, but whose minds are spoiled by wrong views. Their ego-clinging will be vast, and they will lust for the taste of meat. **Speculating on subtle distinctions in the Vinaya rules** [11], they will find all kinds of justifications for eating meat. They will spread these justifications to others, so that people ridicule me, saying I am not pure. They will examine the histories of the doctrine and will say, 'In these history books, it is clear that the Buddha allowed the consumption of meat. Far from being unsuitable, it is a wholesome food!' They will even say that I myself ate it! But, Mahāmati, in none of my teachings have I ever permitted eating meat. I have never said that it is wholesome or permitted.

"Mahāmati, some may think that I have permitted it, or that I have allowed it in order to appease my śrāvaka disciples. But I have forbidden eating any type of meat for those yogis who abide with love, and for all my sons and daughters who are on the pure path of the Mahāyāna. I have forbidden it so that they can practice seeing all beings as their only child. Mahāmati, I have forbidden eating any type of meat to all my sons and daughters who aspire to the Dharma and who follow any of the vehicles. This includes those who dwell in charnel grounds, those who abide in love, those who dwell in forests, and those who practice yoga. Indeed, I have forbidden eating any type of meat to anyone who does contemplative practice and who thinks of all beings as their own children.

"**When I spoke this or that teaching** [12], **I arranged the precepts in gradual stages** [13], like the rungs of a ladder. I created rules such as threefold purity with this in mind. This is why, in the past, I did not forbid the meat of **animals that have died from the ten types of natural causes** [14]. But now, **in these times, I strongly forbid it to everyone** [15], no matter what method they follow. Just so, Mahāmati, I do not permit anyone to eat meat. It is not permitted and will not become permitted. Mahāmati, I declare that the consumption of meat is unsuitable for anyone who has ordained as a monk.

"Mahāmati, foolish people whose past karmic defilement drives them to ridicule me by saying that even the Tathāgata ate meat will endure meaningless suffering for a long time, devoid of joy. Mahāmati, my noble śrāvakas do not eat ordinary, vulgar food, so what need is there to speak of unsuitable foods like meat and blood? Mahāmati, my śrāvakas, pratyekabuddhas, and bodhisattvas all eat the food of Dharma, not worldly food. What need is there to speak of what the Tathagata eats? Mahāmati, tathagātas possess the body of Dharma and are sustained by the food of Dharma. They do not have a worldly body and do not sustain themselves with any type of worldly food. They have abandoned all inclination to seek after mundane existence and the affairs of the world, and they do not have any inclination toward disturbing emotions. Their mind and insight have been completely liberated. They are all-knowing and all-seeing. They see all beings as the same as their only child and possess great compassion. In just this way, Mahāmati, I regard all beings as the same as my only child, and how could I permit the śrāvakas to eat the flesh of my child? What need is there to speak of my own food? Mahāmati, it is wrong to say that I have allowed my śrāvakas to eat meat or that I have eaten it myself. Thus have I spoken."

Bodhisattvas of strong mind,
do not consume meat,
alcohol, garlic, or onions.
The Victor, supreme among all, has taught this.
Because they lack noble kindness,
others consume such disgusting fare.

Meat is a food for carnivorous animals;
the Great Sage has declared it to be unsuitable.
You should bear in mind, Mahāmati,
the faults of eating meat,
and the virtues of giving it up—
remember everything that comes from eating meat.

Whether of confused animals or one's own friends,
all meat comes from semen and blood.
Yogis do not eat meat,
as consuming it causes other beings to fear.

All meats, garlic, onions,
all types of alcohol,
wild onions, and white garlic—
yogis abandon all of these!

They abandon rubbing with oil,
and since small beings live in the
open spaces inside mattresses,
yogis do not sleep on beds.

Food gives rise to pride in oneself,
and from this conceptual pride,
desirous cravings arise with force.
So do not eat such foods!

Desire arises from concepts,
and desire leads to mental confusion.
Confusion then transforms into a body,
and the birth process is not liberated.

People pay money for meat,
causing animals to be killed for profit.
Both the killer and buyer own this sinful karma
and will boil in the Crying Hell.

All those who go against the Buddha's words,
and eat meat with an ignoble mind,
destroy their **lives, both now and in the future,** [16]
and defile the conduct found in the Śākya's teachings!

Those people endowed with sinful karma,
go to hells that are thoroughly terrifying.
Those who eat meat will be boiled
in the Crying Hell.

Meat that has threefold purity,
free of being considered, requested,
or coerced, [17] **does not exist.** [18]
So do not eat meat!

Yogis do not eat meat.
This is my teaching,
and that of all other buddhas.

Beings that eat each other,
take birth as carnivores.
Or they become madmen,
foul smelling with low reputations.
Again and again they are born

as outcasts, dog eaters, and dyers.
Or they are born as animal-headed gods,
or among flesh-eating demons.
After this present human life,
they come back as demons or cats.

This is why I teach that meat is utterly base,
in sūtras such as the *Hastikakṣya*,
Mahāmega, *Parinirvāṇa*, and *Aṅgulimālīya*,
as well as this *Laṅkāvatāra Sūtra*.

Buddhas, bodhisattvas, and śrāvakas,
all decry it as base.
This food, whose essence is turbulent,
always leads to birth as a madman.

Abandoning meat, on the other hand,
leads to birth as a brahman or yogi,
or one endowed with wisdom and wealth.

Meat that you have seen, heard, or suspected:
all of it is utterly base.
But those born in meat-eating families
do not understand, despite their cleverness.
Desire creates an obstacle to liberation.
In just this way, meat and alcohol
are also obstacles to liberation.

In future times,
ignorant supporters of meat eating,
will say that meat is sinless and suitable,
and will claim that I say the same.

Thinking of food as no different than medicine,
and of meat as the flesh of their own children,
yogis **eat moderately,** [19]
not so much that they cannot digest it.

I, who abide in love,
always and in every way reproach
those who **associate with lions,**
tigers, foxes, and the like. [20]

Since it is in opposition to achieving liberation,

and since it causes others to fear,
do not eat meat.
This is the **noble banner of victory! [21]**

If I might briefly comment on some of the meanings above:

1. "Adepts accomplished in knowledge-mantras, or who aspire to accomplish knowledge-mantras," refers to mantric adepts who follow in the practice of action tantra and so on, or who aspire to accomplish dhāraṇī mantras and so on.
2. "I have explained that food can be medicinal or as unwholesome as the flesh of children" means that meat foods are like the flesh of children and that rice gruel and so on—the food of sages—is like beneficial medicine.
3. "When Indra had become king of the gods": Indra is said to have taken the form of a hawk to test the virtue of King Shidan. When a dove flew to the king seeking refuge, the hawk said, "That's my food, without it I will die." So the king paid the hawk in his own flesh equal to the weight of the dove.
4. "He began living with a lioness in order to survive," is saying that if the king did not do this he would have been killed.
5. "The city of Kimdün' [lit. Seven Families]" refers to the seven families that novice adherents of the teachings should not visit—namely, butchers, wine sellers, prostitutes, bird catchers, fishermen, the royal palace, as well as hunters and so on and other low castes. Alternatively, it is said to be the city of the seven families who delight in making offerings to non-Buddhists with wrong views.
6. "Malevolent male or female animal-headed spirit" refers to yakṣa (harm-bringers).
7. "Can even lead people to" means it is needless to say that a vice that is constantly engaged in will grow more serious.
8. "All meat is unsuitable" refers to all meat whatsoever, including meat with threefold purity.
9. This meat is "not allowed" because it directly or indirectly harms sentient beings.
10. "So-called unexamined" refers to meat that was neither considered nor suspected.
11. "Speculating on subtle distinctions in the Vinaya rules." This sentence and the lines that follow refer to people who would later claim

that eating meat is permitted since the Buddha told Ānanda that minor rules could be relaxed. While untrue, their claims would give the appearance of being logical.

12. "When I spoke this or that teaching" refers to the teachings of the Buddha from the turning of the Dharma wheel of the four noble truths up to and including the Vidyādhara Piṭaka.
13. "Arranged the teachings in three gradual stages" refers to the vows of individual liberation, the bodhisattva and the vidyādhara bases of training. In Khedrup Jé's *Polishing the Jewel of the Sage's Teachings*,[594] it says that the Vinaya teachings first prohibited eating the meat of humans and animals with noncloven hooves and later made a rule permitting meat with threefold purity. The Vinaya training precepts thus contained two stages. In the Mahāyāna, generally all meat, including that which comes from animals that have died naturally, is prohibited for bodhisattvas. The training precepts thus have three stages, as lamas in the past have explained.
14. "Animals that have died from ten natural causes." These include death as a result of the adverse external condition of a fatal encounter with another animal and the four nonanimal-related adverse conditions of earth, water, fire, and wind. In addition to these five are the internal adverse conditions of the four diseases linked to wind, bile, and phlegm, as well as the death of an animal at the end of its life due to a lack of favorable conditions. The meat of animals that have died in any of these ways should not be eaten.
15. "In these times, I strongly forbid it to everyone" means that everyone should avoid eating the meat of any animals at all times and should cultivate grains in order to distance themselves from directly or indirectly harming sentient beings.

From the verses:

16. "Lives, both now and in the future" refers to those of the killer and buyer jointly.
17. "Free of being considered" refers to meat that has not been considered, requested, or coerced.
18. "Does not exist" means that although one might not actually coerce

594. Tib: *Thub bstan rin po che'i byi dor zhes bya ba bzhugs so*, by Khedrup Jé Gelek Palzang (1385–1438). The portions of this text that discuss meat have been translated by Anna Johnson in chapter 4 of this volume.

the killing, one is still indirectly responsible as a general consequence of the fault of eating meat.

19. "Eat moderately" refers to Buddhist sages of the past, who ate their food in moderation and who, by virtue of understanding that meat was unsuitable, abandoned meat eating.
20. "Associate with lions, tigers, foxes, and the like" means to take birth as and keep company with these animals.
21. "Noble banner of victory" refers to an ornament of ethical discipline and the banner of victory over Māra.

In the translation of the *Laṅkāvatāra Sūtra* accompanied by the Chinese ācārya Wenhui's commentary,[595] it reads:

> Moreover, Mahāmati, in this regard, since those who take lives desire to attain profit, they kill and trade. Any fools that eat meat buy it with money.
>
> Those who do the killing desire profit, so they kill animals that fly in the sky, live in the water, and walk on the earth—and in many different ways, with hooks and nets—thus seeking profit. Mahāmati, since there is no such thing as meat that is not requested, sought, or perceived, you should not eat meat. Mahāmati, in the past I proscribed eating five and ten kinds of meat, but now, in this present sūtra, I cease all skillful permissions on eating certain kinds of meat at certain times.

It also reads:

> As there is no absence of "requesting, seeking and perceiving," there is also no meat with threefold purity. Since causeless karma does not exist, you should refrain from eating meat.

In a quotation from the *Laṅkāvatāra Sūtra* found in the *Śikṣāsamuccaya*, this is expressed with slightly different wording:

595. This a reference to the second and shorter Tibetan translation of the *Laṅkāvatāra Sūtra* that is found in the Kangyur (Tib: *Lang kar gshegs pa rin po che'i mdo las sangs rgyas tham cad kyi gsung gyi nying po zhes bya ba'i le'u*, Degé Kangyur, vol. 49, 192a–284b), which is a translation of Gunabahadra's Chinese version. The translated sūtra is accompanied by a commentary by the Chinese ācārya Wenhui that was probably written in the mid-ninth century. For more on this translation and its commentary, see Shanshan Jia, "Laṅkāvatārasūtra," 139; Suzuki, *Studies in the Lankavatara Sutra*, 13–15.

Meat that is endowed with threefold purity,
free of being considered, requested,
or coerced, does not exist.
So do not eat meat!

In the *Mahāparinirvāna Sūtra*, it says:

Then Kāśyapa asked, "If it is very important to engage in not eating meat, would it not then be wrong to give meat to eat to those who do not eat meat?"

"Very good!" the Bhagavān answered Kāśyapa. "You understand my purpose very well. One who guards the authentic Dharma should be like this. Child of my lineage, from now on I do not allow my śrāvakas to eat meat. If I have said that one should view the country's alms food as the flesh of one's son, how could I allow the eating of meat? I teach that the eating of meat severs great loving-kindness."

"Bhagavān, why did you allow eating meat that was pure in three respects?"

The Bhagavān replied, "I allowed threefold purity for the sake of gradually restricting the training precepts; I now discard it."

"Bhagavān, what was your intention behind teaching the ninefold benefit and ten types of meat that should be abandoned?"

"Those pronouncements were also made in order to restrict the precepts on eating meat."

"Bhagavān," the bodhisattva Kāśyapa asked, "why did you declare that meat and fish were wholesome foods?" The Bhagavān replied, "I did not say that meat and fish were wholesome foods! Sugarcane, winter rice, ordinary rice, wheat, barley, green lentils, black lentils, molasses, sugar, honey, butter, milk, and sesame oil: I have said that these are wholesome foods. If I have taught that even the various garments for covering one's body should be dyed an unsightly color, what need is there to speak of condoning attachment to the taste of meat?"

"Tathāgata," Kāśyapa said, "in that case, would it not then be fitting to forbid other things, such as the five milk products, sesame, sesame oil, sugarcane sap, conch shell, silk, and so forth?"

The Bhagavān replied, "Don't grasp at the views of the naked ascetics! I impose the precepts upon you with a different intention: I declare that you should not even eat meat that is pure in the three ways. Even those meats other than the ten previously forbidden kinds should be abandoned. The meat of animals that have died naturally should also be abandoned.

"No matter what they are doing—be it moving or resting—meat eaters terrify any animal that can smell them. If a person eats asafetida or garlic, everybody else feels uncomfortable and disagreeable—whether in a crowd of many people or in the midst of many creatures, they all know what the person has consumed. Similarly, all creatures can recognize a person who eats meat, and when they perceive the smell, they are frightened by the terror of death. Wherever that person travels, sentient beings in water, on dry land, or in the sky are frightened. Thinking, 'This person has come to kill us!' they faint and even die. For these reasons, great bodhisattvas do not eat meat. For the sake of those to be tamed, they may manifest the appearance of eating meat, but since they do not even eat ordinary food, what need is there to speak of meat?

"Child of my lineage, after I have passed into final nirvāṇa, when many hundreds of years have passed, there will be no stream-enterers, once-returners, non-returners, or arhats. In the age of the Dharma's decline, there will be monks who appear to uphold the Vinaya and Abidharma; who hold a multitude of dualistic concepts; who nourish their bodies and cherish various kinds of meat; who are afflicted by sickness, hunger, and thirst, whose clothing looks a fright; who are like cowherders and bird catchers; who wear the mark of saffron robes but behave like cats; who claim to be arhats; who are pained by many hurts; who are sullied with their own excrement and urine; who dress themselves finely as though they were sages; who contrive to be like śramaṇas even though they are not; and who hold fabricated writings to be the authentic Dharma. These people will destroy what I have set in place—the Vinaya, rituals, and proper domains of conduct, as well as the scriptures, which are meant solely for freeing and liberating one from attachment to what is improper. They will select passages from individual Vinaya texts and sūtras and expound on them according to their own inclinations. Thus there will appear śramaṇas, sons of Śākyamuni, who will claim that 'according to our Vinaya, the Buddha has said that offerings of the nourishment of meat are acceptable,' and who will make false assertions and contradict my teachings.

"Moreover, child of my lineage, there will also be those who accept unsuitable raw cereals and meat and fish, who do their own cooking and store pots of sesame oil, who make parasols and shoes, who are close to royalty, who keep divination texts, and who exert themselves in medicinal healing. These monks will have male and female servants and keep gold and silver, as well as corals, conches, crystals, and necklaces of pearls, and they will accept fruits. Some will study the arts, and there will be those who become painters, ceramists, and cultivators of plants, and some who will practice sorcery, compound medicine, and play childish games. They will learn to perform theater, do magic tricks, cast spells to control others, sing and dance, adorn themselves with flower garlands and tooth paint, and infuse butter with medicinal concentrates. They will keep incense and ointments, learn to walk affectedly, and exert themselves in sensuous activities. But the person I call a monk is one who abandons those things."

Then Kāśyapa again spoke to the Bhagavān, asking, "Bhagavān, what should be done by monks and nuns, as well as male and female laypeople, who depend on what is offered to them, to purify alms food they receive that is mixed with meat in locations where the food has not been examined?"

"Child of my lineage, I have taught that it does not contradict the Vinaya in any way if the meat is taken out and the other food is washed with water. Then they can eat it. This is my teaching. If it seems in such places that the food is substantially mixed with meat, it should be rejected. There is no fault if one food touches another in a bowl but is not actually mixed together. I say that noble ones who consume meat, fish, game, dried hooves, and even scraps of meat left over by others commit a transgression. Previously I taught this in cases that arose from the needs of the situation. Now, on this occasion, I teach the harm arising from meat eating. As the time has come for me to enter final nirvāṇa, I have spoken comprehensively. This, then, is what is called 'an answer provided by virtue of a question.'"

Second, turning to the viewpoint of the commentaries, Śāntideva's *Śikṣāsamuccaya* says:

In this way, you should protect the body with everyday medicinal food. But not with fish or meat, because that is forbidden in the *Laṅkāvatāra Sūtra*, in which it says: "I say that a bodhisattva who embodies compassion should not eat any meat. . . ."

Śāntideva continues his quotation from the *Laṅkāvatāra Sūtra* from the line, "Whether of confused animals or one's own friends, all meat comes from semen and blood" all the way to "This is the noble banner of victory!"[596] Śāntideva then resumes his commentary:

> In the chapter of Jñānavatī, it is taught if the eating of meat enables one to accomplish great objectives, there is no wrongdoing. It says:
>
> > "If this monk had died, even the word 'samādhi' would have perished from the world, and sentient beings would have gone into perpetual decline. By nourishing himself with this meat, he has attained samādhi. He is obviously intent on great compassion, and since there is also no doubt that he has loving-kindness, there is no wrongdoing."
> >
> > The *Ārya Ratnamegha Sūtra*[597] says, "A charnel-ground practitioner should not be involved with meat," which means that such a practitioner's nature is different from that above. Also, in the Vinaya, the permission that says, "If one eats meat that has threefold purity, no obstacle that needs to be abandoned will arise," the intention is to dispel the excessive pride of those attached to views about purity, and also so that those with karmic fortune, but who are attached to meat, will be able to enter the teachings. For the *Laṅkāvatāra Sūtra* says, "When the teachings were given, the training precepts were put in place gradually, like the rungs of a ladder. At first, meat that was impure in one of the three respects was forbidden. Later on, even the ten types of meat from animals that have died naturally were forbidden."

Bhāviveka's *Tarkajvālā*[598] says:

> On this topic, if you say: "Buddhists, while thinking 'we abide in the Dharma' and criticizing and disparaging others, are renowned

596. Śāntideva's original quotation includes most of the verse section of the *Laṅkāvatāra Sūtra* passage on meat eating. Khenpo Tsultrim Lodrö, having just quoted this entire passage himself, here abridges his quotation from the *Śikṣāsamuccaya*, eliding the *Laṅkāvatāra Sūtra* passage itself and skipping straight to Śāntideva's commentary.

597. *The Noble Cloud of Jewels Sūtra* (Tib: *'Phags pa dkon mchog sprin gyi mdo*).

598. I would like to express my gratitude to Hyoung Seok Ham for generously sharing with me his draft translation of this excerpt from *Tarkajvālā*, which has served as the foundation for the translation in this essay.

themselves for being greatly intent on eating meat. As they are devoid of compassion, and since one cannot obtain meat without taking the lives of sentient beings, they, like hunters of wild animals, commit sin."

To this, it should be said: How could the Lord Buddha, endowed with great compassion, who views all sentient beings like his only child and possesses love from the depths of his bones and feet, permit the eating of meat?

In the Mahāyāna sūtras, the Lord Buddha simply forbids it. In sūtras such as the *Hastikakṣya,* the *Mahāmegha*, the *Laṅkāvatāra*, and the *Aṅgulimālīya*, and so on, any form of meat eating is prohibited. In the scriptures of the Śravakayāna, however, eating meat that is pure in three ways does not constitute a wrongdoing. Since it will turn into semen and so forth, just like begged food, eating it is without wrongdoing. Such a teaching is found. Therefore if one has not seen, heard, or suspected that a living being has been killed for one's own sake, since one is devoid of an unvirtuous mind, eating such meat in order to cure an illness and so forth is not to be considered a sin. Since such food will only become semen, urine, vomit, and so forth, just like begged food eaten by beggars, eating it does not constitute a sin.

Furthermore, eating meat does not become a cause of evil, since it is merely the cause for counteracting hunger, just like food that is offered. "Meat" is dharmin, and "eating it does not become a cause of sin" is dharma.[599] This is because eating meat is a cause for counteracting and pacifying hunger, just like offerings of food and drink that are received at mealtime.

If you argue that meat should not be eaten since it is not fit for eating, then think about the body, which is supported by seeds [of semen and blood that unite to form an embryo], just like impure minute worms living in filth. If you argue: "Meat, just like excrement, should not be eaten," then think about these bodies of ours.

This body—consisting of the thirty-six impure substances of head hair, nails, body hair, skin, hide, flesh, sinew, blood, bone, marrow, kidney, heart, windpipe, liver, spleen, lungs, small intestine, large intestine, colon, urine, excrement, saliva, sweat, fat, phlegm, tears, pus, bile, mucus, body oil, drainage, odor, brain,

599. This sentence follows a typical syllogism in Indian philosophy whereby a thing or entity (*dharmin*) is identified on the basis of the properties (*dharma*) by which it is known.

cerebrum, eye sediment, and ear wax, which constantly leak from the nine wound openings—arises from the impure seeds of blood and semen.

When we consider that this body, which is fully supported by semen, covered with fluids of excrement and vomit, and originated in the womb, is as extremely impure as minute worms living in filth, how much more impure could it become by eating meat? Thus, the eating of meat is nothing at all.

If you also argue: "Though it is [only according to] the opinion of good people, fish meat should not be eaten because it originates in semen and blood, just like the meat of cows and donkeys."

To this, the following should be said: If you revile the eating of fish meat since it originates in semen and so forth, that reasoning would be inconclusive because of substances such as butter, milk, and so forth.

Are you saying that since it originates in semen and blood, fish meat, like cow meat, is not to be eaten? Or are you saying that since it originates in semen and blood, it is to be eaten, like butter and milk? Your reasoning is doubtful and therefore inconclusive.

If you argue: "If there were no meat eater, there would be no killer. Therefore the killer and the meat eater are both guilty of killing. For the sake of his sustenance and for the sake of consuming meat, the eater as good as causes the act of killing."

To this, I answer: If you say, on this basis, that eating meat is tantamount to killing a living being, then your reasoning would be inconclusive due to counter examples such as wearing leather. If there were no ascetics wearing leather, there would be no killing of animals like the sarabha.[600]

Thus, is it that eating meat, on this basis, constitutes an act of killing, just like someone who causes others to kill for meat? Or is it that meat eating, as in the case of wearing leather, does not constitute an act of killing? Your reasoning, accordingly, is inconclusive.

Should one attempt to comprehend [the opposing argument] merely on the face of reason, it turns out to have many other weaknesses and absurd implications . . .[601]

600. The sarabha is a part-lion and part-bird beast in Hindu mythology that has been variously described as an eight-legged creature more powerful than a lion or an elephant and an eight-legged deer. Ancient Indian medical texts list sarabha meat as an edible meat.

601. For the purposes of this translation, Khenpo Tsultrim Lodrö chose to omit a verse section

Furthermore, there is no fault in eating meat, since when one does so, one inflicts no harm on living beings, just as when one uses pearls, peacock feathers, rice, water, and so forth.

If pain arose in the body of an animal when one ate meat, it would be wrong to eat it. However, when one eats meat, since the flesh of the animal's body has no sentience, suffering does not arise. Therefore, how can it be a sin? For example, when one makes use of oysters, fish, the fruit of elephant pearls, peacock feathers, yak tails, teeth, bones, and hide, the animals in question do not experience even the slightest suffering. Just as there is no harming any being when one enjoys fruits and water, there is no harm done when one eats meat, and thus eating meat is without fault. If there were fault in doing so, it would also be sinful to cremate a corpse.

If you still contest this topic, saying: "Even so, meat should not be eaten because it gives rise to desire in the eater. This is because when one eats meat, strength arises, and from that strength, desire and so forth arise."

To this, I answer: Because desire arises from discriminating thought, meat eating is not its cause. Desire arises even in the absence of meat eating, as in the case of grass-eating animals such as cows and so forth. The root of desire, aversion, and ignorance is not eating meat. Since desire originates in discriminating thought, if you recognized this as the root of desire and therefore refrained from engaging in discriminating thought, desire would not arise in you. Statements such as this are found. Grass-eating animals such as cows and donkeys are afflicted by desirous minds at all times—but do they eat any meat?

Therefore one accrues no sin from eating meat that is pure in the three ways. Accordingly, one should not eat meat that one knows by means of seeing, hearing, or suspecting to have been killed for oneself. Apart from this kind, other meat can be eaten. After renouncing a craving for its taste, killing, and an attitude that is devoid of compassion, even though one may eat meat, there is no fault, and it is accordingly the most excellent food. Teachings of this kind are found.

here that was included in his original essay. In those verses, Bhāviveka elaborates on what he deems to be the logically absurd consequences of holding the eater of meat guilty of killing the animal.

Thus, as for the difference in the Mahāyāna tradition between meat that is suitable and meat that is not, rather than follow the *Laṅkāvatāra Sūtra* some scholars follow the tradition that "all meat that is seen, heard, or suspected is condemned," which, in accepting meat with threefold purity, is no different from the Vinaya. They hold that whether meat has been killed for the eater's sake depends on the presence of the factors of seeing, hearing, or suspecting. They cite the *Vinayakārikā*,[602] where it says: "Meat that has been killed for a purpose, if seen, heard, or suspected, should not be eaten; this was taught with concern for the benefit of all beings," and "Meat that is for consumption should be free from seeing, hearing, or suspecting."

In my opinion, as stated earlier, in the Vinaya tradition it is clear that meat that is killed for one's own sake is to be ascertained according to the presence or absence of the factors of seeing, hearing, or suspecting. In the Mahāyāna tradition, however, consuming any meat at all is unsuitable. The *Laṅkāvatāra Sūtra* states:

> All meat is unsuitable, Mahāmati, whether it is the type that I have allowed my śrāvakas to eat, the type I have not allowed, or so-called unexamined meat. / /
>
> Meat that has threefold purity, free of being considered, requested, or coerced, does not exist. So do not eat meat! / /
>
> Mahāmati, since there is no such thing as meat that is not requested, sought, or perceived, you should not eat meat. / /
>
> As there is no absence of requesting, seeking, and perceiving, there is also no meat with threefold purity. Since causeless karma does not exist, you should refrain from eating meat. / /

Notwithstanding that śrāvakas were granted permission to consume meat with so-called threefold purity, the above teachings hold that meat that is not considered by oneself or requested or coerced from others does not exist. Even if one does not do these things explicitly, because one still does them indirectly or in actuality, meat with threefold purity is held to be unsuitable. Thus what was earlier deemed suitable for śrāvakas is here declared unsuitable.

When looking at this level of rule, some scholars in the past held that bodhisattvas were not permitted to eat meat and that meat with threefold purity was allowed only for monks of the Hīnayāna tradition. Others taught that since what was earlier permitted for śrāvakas was later forbidden, the prohibition on all meat pertained not only to bodhisattvas but to śrāvakas, too.

602. *Verses on the Vinaya* (Tib: *'Dul ba tshig le'ur byes pa*), a Vinaya commentary by Viśākhadeva.

In respect of this, it is true that the Vinaya teachings allow eating meat with threefold purity. The learned scholars such as Guṇaprabha, Śākyaprabha, and Dharmamitra have taught only this rule, basing themselves on the previously cited passage from the *Bhaiṣajya* chapter of the *Vinayavastu* ("Monks, I have said that meat that is suitable in three respects can be eaten. What are those three?"), the many narrative discourses in which monks accept meat, and the fact that earlier and later statements on the unsuitability of meat with threefold purity do not appear anywhere in the Vinaya itself.

However, if we consider the plain words and meaning of the *Laṅkāvatāra Sūtra* and *Mahāparinirvāṇa Sūtra*, it is clear that later on it was taught that eating any meat was also prohibited for śrāvakas.

The *Laṅkāvatāra Sūtra* says: "When I spoke this or that teaching, I arranged the precepts in gradual stages, like the rungs of a ladder. I created rules such as threefold purity with this in mind." It also says, "Just so, Mahāmati, I do not permit anyone to eat meat. It is not permitted and will not become permitted. Mahāmati, I declare that the consumption of meat is unsuitable for anyone who has ordained as a monk."

The *Mahāparinirvāṇa Sūtra* says: "Child of my lineage, from now on I do not allow my śrāvakas to eat meat." And, "I stipulated threefold purity as a provisional basis of training; I now discard it." And also, "I have set in place the bases of training for you with a different intention: I stipulate that you should not even eat meat that is pure in the three ways." And also, "I say that consuming meat, fish, game, dried hooves, and even scraps of meat left over by others is committing an infraction."

Therefore, as the *Śikṣāsamuccaya* states, I believe that the Vinaya permitted eating meat with threefold purity by virtue of the need for a temporary teaching. Ultimately, the training level that says śrāvakas and bodhisattvas both eat no meat whatsoever was set in place like a rung in a ladder, and the earlier teaching that permitted meat with threefold purity was discarded. I believe that from that time on, it was taught that whosoever ate meat would fall to the lower realms.

The Vajrayāna Standpoint

Third, the standpoint of the Vajrayāna also consists of the teachings in the canonical scriptures and their commentaries. To begin with, the *Vimalaprabhā*, the great commentary on the *Kālacakra Tantra*, says:

> For the sake of gods and feared ancestors,
> and for accomplishing desires and doing trade,

> sinners who are difficult to subdue
> kill harmless sentient beings.
> Buying this meat and
> desiring to eat it are grave wrongdoings.
> Should it fall into one's vessel by chance,
> then there is no grave wrongdoing.
> The flesh of one animal
> would be better eaten by many people.
> Whereas the flesh of many animals
> should not be eaten by one person.

In the *Kālacakra Tantra Hṛdaya*,[603] it says:

> Buddhists should refrain from eating any meat at all,
> and from keeping it for themselves.
> Having the thought of killing and proceeding to do so
> while knowing that animals are living beings
> leads to degeneration.

The same text also says:

> Devoid of compassion, monks who search after
> tastes of meat to bring to their tongues,
> whether they are fully ordained or novices,
> they will bear themselves the sin of killing and so forth,
> and be damned to hell.

And:

> If one eats meat and so forth,
> one will surely reap the suffering
> beneath the earth
> of large-bodied beings.

603. *The Subsequent Heart Essence Kālacakra Tantra* (Tib: *Dus kyi 'khor lo'i rgyud phyi ma rgyud kyi snying po zhe pa*). A short canonical addendum to the *Kālacakra Tantra*, said to have been taught by King Yashas of Shambhala. This is the same king who taught the *Kālacakra Laghu Tantra*, which, in the absence of the lost *Kālacakra Mula Tantra*, is the primary text in the *Kālacakra* cycle. See Newman, "A Brief History of the Kalachakra," 63.

While someone who is ill may need to eat meat to recuperate from an illness, if there is meat available that has not been killed, they should eat that. The *Kālacakra Tantra Hṛdaya* also says:

> Even though a sick monk may be advised by a doctor to eat meat, meat that has been killed by hawks or for the sake of one's ancestors or for religious worship, or that comes from an animal that has died from harm incurred by water, fire, or indigestion should not be eaten. Whenever these connections are absent it can be eaten. Because such meat for monks possesses ten powers, it is for curing illness but not for deceiving death.[604]

The Secret Pith Instructions of the Ḍākinī Sequence from the Dharma cycle of *The Unimpeded Realization of Samantabhadra*[605] says:

> While Secret Mantra samaya substances are substances to be accepted, unless one has realized the absence of concepts of "purity" and "impurity" and "accepting" and "rejecting," one should renounce careless indulgence in blood, flesh, and alcohol and accept only the mere scent of the five types of amrita medicine.

and:

> Heedless consumers of blood, flesh, and alcohol,
> these foods of sinful beings are the demons of Dharma.

Second, I will turn to what is said in the commentaries. *A Compendium of Feast Offerings of Garab Dorjé, A Spontaneously Present Enlightened Activity of the Peaceful and Wrathful Deities* from the Dharma cycle of *The Unimpeded Realization of Samantabhadra*[606] says:

> First, for the feast offering: The one hundred foods replete with

604. Khenpo Tsultrim Lodrö adds a footnote here that reads: "In another version of this text, the preceding sentence reads 'because it possesses ten powers it is to prevent death but nothing else.'"

605. Tib: *Kun bsang dgongs pa zang thal mkha 'gro'i las rim gsang ba'i man ngag*. From the Dzokchen teachings of the *Gongpa Zangthal* revealed by the tertön Rigdzin Gödem.

606. Tib: *Kun bsang dgong pa zang thal zhi khro lhun grub kyi 'phrin las dga rab rdo rjes btus ba'i tsogs 'khor.* Also from the Dzokchen teachings of the *Gongpa Zangthal* revealed by the tertön Rigdzin Gödem.

> six tastes and materials should be perfectly arranged. Of these, the most praiseworthy are meat and alcohol. The meat should not come from a long-diseased animal or have been killed by a human or wild animal. [Meat from animals that have died of] various causes of abnormal death and bear meat should not be used. Only the meat of animals whose lives have been exhausted by their own conditions is praiseworthy. [The meat should come from an animal with] intact faculties. Flesh and blood that has been slaughtered with a knife is an offering for yakṣas.[607]
>
> For use as samaya substances: Meat from animals with undivided hooves or with leprosy or plague, contaminated meat, and unwholesome substances and spoiled items that do not delight ḍākinīs are unsuitable as samaya substances.

The *Vimalaprabhā*, the great commentary on the *Kālacakra*, says:

> The Buddha said that yogis of the Mantrāyāna would eat meat, but that meat itself always derives from killing. If there were no killing, the lives of animals would remain unharmed. If there were no meat eater, there would be no killer.
>
> Meanwhile, practitioners of the Secret Mantra must observe daily the fourth samaya. This was surely the Buddha's instruction. This being so, because consuming meat that has marks[608] or has grave wrongdoing is tantamount to killing, therefore the Buddha taught that yogis should eat cow meat[609] and so forth that is without marks and without grave wrongdoing. This meat is not whatever kind is eaten or sold by ordinary people in a certain place, but meat from an animal that has died as a result of its own karma. The Buddha taught that meat that comes from animals that have died in battle as a result of negative karma or that have been killed by robbers or bandits through their own fault can be eaten by yogis. It should not be purchased with money or slaughtered for the sake of

607. A broad class of deities, sometimes benevolent, but often, as in this case, seen as bloodthirsty and demonic.

608. The meat of marked animals refers to animals that are marked for sacrifice—that is, ritually slaughtered.

609. Since the slaughter of cattle was widely prohibited in ancient India, cow meat is recommended here as a type of meat that (putatively) derives from animals that have died as a result of their own karma, whose consumption is therefore free from the karmic sin of killing.

> one's ancestors or as a ritual offering. The Buddha did not teach that meat with marks could be eaten. Because the samaya rites are to be observed each day, five types of faultless substances like cow meat and so forth and five amrita pills the size of a small seed like pills of Vairochana and so forth should be consumed for this purpose.
>
> In this regard, should others say, "If there were no meat eater, there would be no animal killer; therefore they are both guilty of killing," one would answer, "This is true." It is for this reason that one should not use money to buy meat that is killed for consumption or eat meat that is marked with signs and killed for the sake of ancestors or killed as a ritual offering. Yogis should only consume meat from animals that have died as a result of their own karma or from animals, such as cows, that are not slaughtered in certain places, or otherwise they should just consume samaya pills.

Furthermore, in his *Song of Advice for Giving up Meat*,[610] the mighty siddha Pema Dündul says:

> When I think of the suffering that meat eating brings,
> I cannot bear the pain and anguish I feel within my heart.
>
> *Oṃ maṇi padme hūṃ hrīḥ*
> From a state of emptiness and compassion, you guide beings—
> noble Avalokiteśvara, to you I pay homage.
>
> Without having trained in love and compassion myself,
> I ate the flesh of my mothers while lecturing others about cause and effect.
> Without realizing the absolute, I wandered along the path of empty words.
> I, the parrot-like beggar of White Rock,
> was practicing austerities and "extracting the essence,"[611]
> when, one day, while meditating on Lord Avalokiteśvara,
> according to the union of stages from *Self-Liberation Equal to Space*,
> my own body and everything around me suddenly disappeared

610. I am grateful for Adam Pearcey's permission to use his translation of this song, which appears in chapter 9 of this volume.

611. Tib: *bcud len*. Extracting the vital essence or nutrients from rocks and minerals in the form of pills.

and transformed into a luminous body like that of the Great Compassionate One,
seemingly floating in space.

As I looked around, while experiencing luminous awareness,
I saw the inconceivable miseries of the lower realms
and, in particular, the vast sufferings of the Reviving Hell.
One of its quarters, I saw, was filled
with men and women, naked and helpless, before each of whom
stood throngs of evil-looking servants with heads
like birds, wild and domesticated animals, and ferocious beasts.
Many of the servants held sharp weapons in their hands,
with which to slice apart and devour the flesh of their victims.
Time and again they cut, and time and again flesh grew back.
Victims did not expire until their karma was fully exhausted,
and habitual tendencies did not diminish, but only increased.
For those who had performed "red offerings" it was even worse.
Loudly, they all screamed in terrible pain and agony.
When I saw this external manifestation of my own perception,
I wondered what might be done to stop such suffering.

And in that very instant, in the sky before me,
the Great Compassionate One appeared, and said:
"*E ma!* My son, who has been close to me throughout many lives,
listen well now, you who are diligent and determined!
You have gained stability in the generation stage of deity yoga,
and have even developed a few qualities,
but the root of Dharma lies in loving-kindness and compassion.
Do you have real love and compassion within yourself?
How could anyone trained in compassion ever eat flesh?
Just look at how eating meat brings such suffering!
The results of our own actions will ripen on us alone;
there is nothing the buddhas of the three times may do.
Eating meat has no virtue whatsoever, but entails many faults.
It is the source of 400 forms of disease and 80,000 obstructing forces,
and it naturally brings about the 84,000 afflictive emotions.
Other than as part of the fearless conduct of benefitting all one encounters,
or as a medicine or sacred substance of the supreme Secret Mantra,
consumption of flesh involves not the tiniest trace of virtue.

Eating flesh is a sign of being either a māra or rākṣasa demon.
It causes discipline to degenerate and negative emotions to increase.
Without the cause, which is altruistic love and compassion,
you will find it hard to gain the fruit, the essence of awakening.

"Meat eaters are not accompanied by the wisdom deities.
They lack blessings, accomplishment, auspiciousness, and activity.
The substance of altruism does not develop in eaters of flesh,
whom gods, nāgas, and others regard as demons.
Meat eaters are plagued by gandharvas, rākṣasas, māras,
yamas, ghosts, spirits, gyalpo, gongpo, and samaya-breaking demons.
The result of eating meat is rebirth in the hells,
or as a bird, jackal, cannibal demon, or the like.
Meat eating thus brings suffering beyond measure.
But by renouncing it, you are freed from all such faults,
and will always be revered by nonhuman beings,
who will see you as a pure, authentic brahman or god.
All the buddhas and bodhisattvas, together with their retinues, throughout the ten directions,
gurus, yidam deities, and ḍākinīs will gather around you like clouds,
and you will be accompanied by male and female bodhisattvas.
Quite naturally, you will possess the cause of loving-kindness and compassion,
and swiftly reach the fruit, which is the essence of awakening.
These are just some of the inconceivable virtues to be gained."

Thus he spoke; and then, once my own perception had returned,
I felt as if I had awoken from a lucid dream.
My body and mind were tormented as if by poison,
and I shook with fear and panic.
Just thinking of the terrible sufferings of the Reviving Hell,
I wished only to exchange my happiness for others' pain.
So utterly overwhelmed was my mind, I wept profusely.
And I felt intense, unbearable compassion.
Then, to take upon myself the sufferings of others,
and to purify their faults and obscurations caused by eating meat,
for every mother sentient being, as infinite in number as space is vast,
I made the following vow, true according to the two levels of reality:

A ho! Mighty sage Śākyamuni and all buddhas and bodhisattvas
throughout the whole of space and time,
have compassion for this child who knew nothing of cause and effect!
Hosts of gracious root and lineage masters, care for me!
Have compassion for this child who knew nothing of cause and effect!
Supreme yidam deity, mighty Avalokiteśvara, care for me!
Have compassion for this child who knew nothing of cause and effect!

Overwhelmed by ignorance and the two obscurations,
I have often spoken of how all infinite beings have been our parents,
and, while living off their flesh, lectured about cause and effect.
I had no idea that the suffering involved was so great!
Often have I heard it said that eating meat with threefold purity[612]
is sanctioned by the Buddha and does not count as sin.
But this applies only to saints who benefit all they encounter,
like pure lotus flowers, unstained by negative emotions,
and to practitioners of the profound path of Secret Mantra.

For my part, I have no instruction more profound
than altruistic love and compassion,
and the infallibility of cause and effect.
To purify all the faults and obscurations of eating flesh
among all sentient beings, who extend throughout the whole of space,
from this moment on, I completely renounce the eating of flesh.
This is my unfailing commitment, which I shall never forsake.
Even if all the animals upon this earth were to be devoured,
there would still be no satisfaction; hunger would only continue to
increase.

Deprived of food or drink for just a few days,
we feel as if we have never tasted even so much as a single morsel or
drop before.
Now is the time to escape this demon, hunger.
What, after all, is the cause of flesh?
It springs only from self-clinging and attachment.
Merely to think of it makes me weary, nauseated.

612. This means that you have not seen or heard anything to indicate that the meat has been butchered specifically for you, and not only that, you do not even have any doubt that this might be the case.

This utterly unappetizing mound of mess and filth,
bound up with the thirty-six impure substances,
a body of habitual patterns and aggregates, is the basis for all
suffering.

Each animal has its own negative actions,
and whoever eats the flesh of such beings will find it hard to win
liberation.
Meat and alcohol are impure substances,
and to offer them does not qualify as generosity, the Buddha said.
Who, therefore, would eat this food of the afflictions?
Pretas must live for many thousands of human years
without seeing food or drink, enduring only suffering.
But we human beings gladly drink even ice-cold water
and have plenty to sustain us besides meat and alcohol.
If we are still not satisfied with such delights,
how could we repay past kindnesses so unfairly?

Throughout the course of countless eons past,
in every world within this universe so vast,[613]
there's not a single being who has not been our mother;
all the milk we drank from maternal breasts would fill a billion seas.
I abandon all pretence; let the Three Jewels be my witness!
In the past, under the sway of ignorance and habit,
I ate my parents' flesh and did not remorsefully confess.
Now, with pure motivation and the four powers complete,
as in the saying, "I was not, am not, and will not be attached,"
henceforth, may the thought of eating meat never even cross my mind.
Should I ever fail, let the Three Jewels send their punishment.
May the protectors and guardians constantly keep watch.
Were I now to eat the flesh of my past mothers,
there would be no greater transgressor in all the three realms!

The Buddha said that harming others even slightly impairs one's
vows.
So what need is there to mention flesh eating that involves taking life?
In the *Parinirvāṇa Sūtra*, *Laṅkāvatāra*, and elsewhere, it says

613. Literally, "in all seven worlds" (*'jig rten bdun po*), meaning the six classes of beings (hell, preta, animal, human, asura, and deva) plus the bardo realm.

that eating meat is tantamount to killing.[614]
It is forbidden in both the Greater and Lesser Vehicles,
but is particularly unacceptable for bodhisattvas.
Our Teacher himself, when appearing as a partridge's young,
and as a ferocious beast[615] in the wild, did not eat meat.
How then could we, his followers, ever do so?
In accordance with the guidance of the Victorious One,
there were many great masters in India and Tibet who gave up meat.
As all this shows, the faults of meat eating are unimaginably vast.
Not cultivating negativity is itself genuine Dharma.
So may I always comply with the authentic teaching!"

Having seen the boundless faults that come from eating meat,
even the thought of it is as nauseating as poison.
And so, I, the great beggar with the name of Dündul,
composed these words of advice to encourage my own renunciation
in the Sky Fortress hermitage of White Rock.
As the result of this virtue, may all sentient beings
purify all the faults and obscurations that come from eating meat,
so that they may see the thousand buddhas face to face!

Je Götsang Natsok Rangdröl[616] says:

After falling asleep, in the illusion of my dream I found myself with several of our old monks who died long ago, including a few who regularly performed village rituals and a couple of deceased head caretakers. Reluctantly and powerlessly, I went with them. The place was called "Flesh Is Allowed to Be Eaten." In a narrow ravine blanketed by dark gloom was a person with a hideous dark complexion, dressed as a monk in robes made of blackish-green brocade, and about as tall as a two-story house. In the retinue of this terrifying being was a barbarous old monk roughly three times the height of a person, wearing religious garb and possessed of a repul-

614. See the translations of these texts in this volume.

615. These are references to the Buddha's previous lives, as recounted in the so-called *Birth Stories*, or *Jātaka*.

616. Götsang Natsok Rangdröl (Tib: Rgod tshang na tshogs rang grol) was also known as Tselé Natsok Rangdröl and Tselé Gotsangpa. According to Khenpo Tsultrim Lodrö, the dream sequence quoted here is found in his collected works.

sive appearance. There were also laymen in animal skin robes who looked like nomad types, carrying black lassos in their hands. Many of these underlings circled around me.

I then heard the chief monk utter these words:

"What a disgrace you are, sitting here so unperturbed! The monk who puts monks to their death has arrived! The one who distinguishes the law of good and evil is me! Nowadays, those of you who call yourselves lamas, masters, preceptors, and members of the monastic community, who give the appearance of Dharma practitioners and who act as refuge objects for both the living and the dead dare to take the slaughtered meat of sentient beings who have been your parents as the essence of your meals! Such great courage, ah la la!

"Delicacies of lung filled with blood, wondrous treats made of frozen liver, fried dishes cooked with live blood . . . Your ways of eating—devouring flesh and blood more voraciously than beasts of prey, guzzling wine and spirits more thirstily than beetles, and pursuing material offerings more ravenously than hungry ghosts—do you still consider yourselves ordained monks? The way you hold aloft the begging bowl while consuming flesh and blood, the way your robes and underskirts are soaked in wine, and the way you pursue business profit, wealth, and women—have you no shame even toward the Three Jewels? The pleasure you enjoyed while feasting on your donor's offerings and consuming meat and alcohol . . . having arrived at this court of karmic justice, just see whether you are happy or miserable, offering-eaters! Down yonder in that prison of dark carnivores, your own distinct ways and methods of eating and preparing meat are performed on you yourselves. Some are minced, some are beaten, some are boiled, and some are frozen. Others are scored, salted, and roasted. Now it's time you went, go!"

I did not recognize it was a dream. I was completely terrified and utterly saddened.

In this way, both the old and new tantras and their commentaries concur that meat that is killed for consumption is prohibited, both for those who want to eat meat and for use in ritual feasts and upholding samaya commitments. Thus using tantra as a pretext to heedlessly indulge in meat and alcohol only causes falling to the lower realms. Those who, craving the taste of blood and flesh, carelessly consume meat inflict extremely grave harm on both themselves and others. Moreover, if one is reincarnated in a future life as an animal or the like, due to the past habitual tendency of eating meat, one will most certainly be reborn as a carnivorous animal. What the Buddha taught is eternally infallible, and the fruition of actions in resemblance with their cause is extremely powerful. If a person is reborn as a savage animal of this kind, they will have no awareness of what should be accepted and rejected. As deeply ingrained karmic latencies spring to life, they will kill an innumerable number of beings, plunging themselves deeper and deeper into the lower realms until there is no certain escape. Direct experience tells us that savage animals prey on other animals as soon as they are born. There are some that kill tens of thousands of animals in one day. Given the abundance of nutritious food in the form of the three whites and the three sweets in the present human world, if we do not exercise ethical discernment at this time, what is there to do?

The result of failing to do so will be extremely terrifying. Apart from practitioners who have reached the acceptance stage on the path of joining[617] who need not fall to the lower states, I believe it is extremely dangerous for ordinary beings to eat meat.

In particular, in our region there are some monasteries that kill many beings for the sake of their monastic community's sustenance. This practice contravenes the pratimokṣa, bodhisattva, and tantric precepts that serve as the root of all spiritual practice and is a terrifying form of negative conduct that seriously harms the Dharma. Due to this kind of unethical behavior, slander and wrong views about the Secret Mantrayāna occurred often in the past and are extremely frequent today. As a result, many people have accumulated the negative karma of abandoning the Dharma, which is a secondary cause of falling to the lower realms. Since these are actions that bring ruin to self and other, those who consider themselves dharmic persons should abandon them. There is no fault worse than claiming to be a follower of the Buddha and intentionally harming the lives of sentient beings, despite possessing the freedom not to do so. As a sign of a lack of even a sesame-seed-sized amount of the loving-kindness and compassion at the root of the Mahāyāna teachings—or perhaps a sign of the practice of those who consider harming others an act of faith—it is extremely disheartening.

In our modern world, slaughterhouses of all kinds are like hell on earth in the way they inflict unbearable suffering on an innumerable number of beings daily. This loss of life occurs for no other reason than we eat meat. In paying a great amount of money to butchers for meat, we are in fact paying for

617. This refers to the third stage on the path of joining (Tib: *sbyor lam*), which is the second of five paths that encompass the entire spiritual journey, as relayed in the Mahāyāna, and culminate in complete enlightenment.

the intense suffering to which they subject animals. The reason that butchers subject beings to this kind suffering is precisely to obtain our money and not because there is any hatred between butchers and animals or because the animals have committed any criminal act.

For this reason, it is said that the killer and the eater of meat are both guilty of the act of killing. In the *Mañjuśrī Pradarshana*,[618] it says:

> He who kills for money
> and he who pays to eat,
> are both killers,
> so both will boil in the Crying and other hells.
>
> Killing beings for money—
> if no money were given, no killing would happen.
> Both parties have a genuine link between doer and deed,
> and are always killers of animals.
>
> If a fish were bought with money
> and the householder had no wrongdoing,
> then how could Buddha images and so on
> generate any merit?
>
> A stūpa is repaired by a worker,
> a fish is killed by a fisherman—
> the stūpa worshipper is not its repairer,
> the fish eater is not its killer.
>
> When a fish is eaten,
> if the eater has no wrongdoing,
> then when a stūpa is worshipped,
> the worshipper will have made no merit.
>
> The killer and the eater
> are separate and distinct.
> The killer craves wealth,
> the eater craves food.

618. *Teachings on Mañjuśrī's Own View* (Tib: *'Phags pa 'jam phal gyi rang gi lta ba'i 'dod pa mdor bstan pa yongs su brtag pa*).

Killers who crave wealth
will boil for one hundred thousand kalpa.
Those who crave meat
will boil for ten million kalpa.

If, for the sake of a śrāvaka,
a fisherman kills fish,
and for the sake of a brahmin,
a barmaid makes wine,
there is no one without grave wrongdoing.

Any meat eater whosoever
will first become a hungry ghost
and later descend to the Crying Hells.

In the *Laṅkāvatāra Sūtra* it says, "Moreover, Mahāmati, in this regard, since those who take lives want to attain profit, they kill and trade. All fools who eat meat buy the meat with money." The way in which we pay money for many animals to be killed is just as this says. Our need for eating meat is simply to furnish our tongue consciousness with a little taste. Since this need could be readily accomplished by many other foods in our human realm, it is not inevitable that we have to eat meat.

Causing ruin to both self and other for the sake of some trifling benefit has been the habitual nature of ordinary beings since beginningless time. This is particularly so in modern times, when people lack even the slightest belief in karmic law or compassion for sentient beings. With minds that are thoroughly stirred up by desire and ignorance, there are very few animals that humans can see that they refrain from killing or eating. Not only this, but they also engage in all kinds of inconceivably base behavior, such as cooking and eating the lower part of an animal while its upper part is still alive. Humans view animals as foodstuffs to be consumed, no different than their understanding of grains, vegetables, and so on. Born and killed to be eaten, meek and powerless animals have no freedom in their lives but come into being, live, and die for the sake of human consumption. The way they live and die is simply frightening and depressing. We need to recognize that the root of all this lies solely in the consumption of meat by humans. We also need to understand that we are among these humans. Even if all the beings of the three realms were killed for their flesh, because those who abandon eating meat refrain from partaking of a share of it themselves, they are free from any share of karmic wrongdoing.

With improved transport conditions in modern times, the world's foods are traded back and forth and carted and spread everywhere. There are now a great number of different kinds of meat products and eggs and so on that come from distant places in different shapes, colors, and attractively designed packaging. Yet since all these products are made after subjecting cows, pigs, chickens, and other animals to extremely inappropriate and unmatched torture that creates only an ocean of blood and tears, they should never be objects of free and unreflective enjoyment.

To conclude:

In this joyful human world of flourishing diverse riches,
the result of abandoning the pure foods of the three whites and three sweets,
which the Buddha praised,
and thirsting after warm flesh and blood, drooling with the saliva of barbaric sin,
is rebirth as a carnivorous beast.
If the Buddha said thus, would it not be terrifying?

Therefore, for your entire garland of lifetimes,
abstain from livelihoods that harm others,
moisten your mind with a stream of bodhicitta-amrita,
and exert yourself always for the benefit of sentient beings.

But if the force of karma and afflictions should take you among savage beings,
may you awaken to the mudrā painting of the Buddha's words sowed in your mind,
and by fully renouncing the savage attitude that harms beings for the sake of flesh and blood,
through the strength of compassion, may you unstintingly cast away life's conditioning forces.

In the terrifying ocean of saṃsāra where waves of karmic phenomenon proliferate in space,
for as long as the wind of black and white karma blows,
may the lives and bodies of sentient beings be free from harm, their minds endowed with peace, and the helpless protected.

Let this aspiration be accomplished!

Composed at the Serjong Lama Rung Hermitage of the Great Secret Liberation in a Body of Light[619] *on the tenth day of the miracle month in the iron-snake year of the seventeenth Rabjung [2001], by the servant called Tsultrim Lodrö, who brings to the crown of his head the foot dust of the embodiment of great compassion, His Holiness Dharma-Lord Wish-fulfilling Jewel [Khenpo Jigmé Phunstok], whose name I mention here only for a specific purpose. May it be auspicious!*

619. Tib: Gser ljongs bla ma rung gsang chen od skur grol ba'i dben khrod. According to Khenpo Tsultrim Lodrö, this was an early name for Larung Gar (Serta Larung Five Sciences Buddhist Academy). It refers to the attainment of the rainbow body, a sign of the highest spiritual accomplishment in the Dzokchen tradition whereby the physical body of a practitioner self-liberates into a body of light after their death.

Request in the Presence of the Noble Dharma Holders

By Khenpo Tsultrim Lodrö

Translated by Catherine Hardie

In these lowliest of times, due to the extinguishment of beings' merit, all kinds of immoral conduct is spreading and intense exertion in karmically sinful action is bringing ruin to both present and future lives. Especially here, in our snowy land of Dokham, the past few years have seen everything up to and including cattle, sheep, horses, and dogs sent to slaughterhouses without the slightest compassion. Year after year, this terrifying practice is becoming increasingly pervasive, and innocent living beings are being subjected to the most unbearable of sufferings. Committing such karmic wrongdoing and thereby strengthening the fearsome cause of descent to the lower realms for oneself and others is something that everyone clearly knows is like a blind person jumping off a cliff.

Since there are alternative means of livelihood that exist if we do not engage in karmically sinful actions of this kind, doing one's utmost to cut this stream of wrongdoing is extremely important. From the depths of my heart, I implore everyone, from impartial great beings who are holders of the teachings to pure-minded ordinary monks, not to be indifferent but to apply yourselves to this cause to the greatest degree possible. Generally speaking, since protecting the environment and animals is an undertaking that is in accordance with the law and a particularly important duty for followers of the Buddha such as ourselves, I earnestly beseech you not to forsake your compassion.

Dispatched from the Serjong Lamarung Hermitage of the Great Secret Liberation in a Body of Light [undated].

Appeal Not to Cruelly Slaughter Farm Animals

By Khenpo Tsultrim Lodrö

Translated by Catherine Hardie

Given that our snowland of Tibet has been pervaded by the Buddha's precious teachings for more than a thousand years, all people, high and low, have generally had faith in the Three Jewels, compassion for sentient beings, belief in karmic cause and effect, and a proper acquaintance with the norms of ethical conduct. This insight into the cause of eternal happiness merits great joy. However, negative customs have also manifested, and the time has come when we deeply and sincerely hope to carry out reform. In the Dokham region, most pastoral communities kill farm animals by binding their mouths and suffocating them, while in other cases the animals' throat arteries are cut. Regardless of which method is used, the animals are slaughtered in an unbearably cruel way. For instance, with suffocation approximately ten to fifteen minutes elapse from the moment the animal's mouth is bound shut to the time it dies. During this period, it experiences intense and unceasing suffering. With its front and hind legs bound with rope, it is unable to move at all. Suffocation not only causes the animal physical pain but also unbearable terror in its mind—just see how it feels to hold one's own breath for a few minutes. With each minute that passes—from the first to the second to the third to the fourth—the suffering grows increasingly intense.

A few years ago, we ransomed a yak from a butcher. Since a considerable length of time had passed since its mouth had been bound, its eyes had turned blue and it was unable to move at all—it looked as if it were dead. When we told the butchers to untie it and that we would buy it, they said it had already died. A short while after the bindings were gradually released, however, the yak revived and rose to its feet. Even after that amount of time it had still not died! Please think deeply about how it would feel if you had your own arms and legs bound for that length of time and were forced to die by suffocation.

Similarly, killing animals by cutting their throats is a cruel method of slaughter that causes tremendous suffering. A period of ten to twenty minutes elapses between the time the animal's throat is cut and its death. Death is not final until every last drop of blood from its heart has drained on the ground. After this happens, outwardly the animal looks as though it is dead, but a few still squirm around and struggle to stand up. Beings that are slaughtered by either of these methods experience extremely intense and prolonged suffering, and the karmic sin on the part of those who cruelly kill them is extremely grave.

Given this to be the case, you might ask what should be done. When we humans sustain an injury, even if the treatment needed is only very minor, we are still given a dose of anaesthesia to prevent pain. Aside from the fact they can't speak, cattle, sheep, and other animals are no different from us in this regard: they too desire even the smallest forms of comfort and dislike even the tiniest forms of pain. And yet we are indifferent to the happiness and pain of these beings. How can it be right that we subject them to all kinds of meaningless suffering? Should we do so, the infallibility of karmic cause and effect is such that we ourselves will definitely not enjoy happiness. Since these days cattle, sheep, and other animals are in such a pathetic state they could not be weaker, there is no need for us to fear them. While this may be so, it is not possible that even one brave person exists who is free from the need to fear karmic justice. Even if right now some people claim to be unafraid of karma, when the time comes for them to personally reap their dues, none of them will be able to bear it.

Therefore, regardless of what kind of animal, if a way of avoiding killing simply cannot be found, then it is extremely important to adopt a method of slaughter that minimizes suffering. If the animal's suffering is reduced, the gravity of the karmic sin committed by the killer is also slightly decreased. If you are wondering what such methods are, optimal would be to administer a drug that enables an animal to be killed painlessly, as is done in other places. However, this method is probably a bit difficult for our farmers and herders to implement in the short term. As for methods that we can practically adopt, there is one used in some places in Kham to make the suffering slightly shorter in duration and less extreme than with throat-cutting and mouth-binding.[620] The importance of this can be seen by taking ourselves as examples. Compared to dying once with immense suffering by suffocation, it would surely be better to die several times over with slightly less pain. This is much like, for example, hospital patients who suffer under extreme pain wishing over and over for a lethal medicine to help them die quickly.

They may be animals, yet they still greatly fear the pain of death. In the autumn of the metal-snake year, I visited a small slaughter yard where there

620. Khenpo Tsultrim Lodrö does not elaborate here on what this method is, but it is likely one of several methods of stunning an animal prior to bleeding it out so that it instantly becomes unconscious.

were eight yaks. Apart from these eight, three others had been killed by having their throats cut by several Chinese butchers who were in the process of quartering the meat on the skins. Among the living yaks was a young one with tears streaming from its eyes. I went right up to look at it more closely and could see that this was definitely not due to an eye illness or some other kind of injury. The other yaks' bodies were also shaking and trembling. It is therefore extremely important to find ways of reducing the suffering inflicted in the process of slaughter, and I deeply implore everyone to make this their concern and not simply shrug it off.

While generally it is impossible for killing to be free from suffering and karmic sin, finding ways to reduce the severity of both is extremely important for both oneself and other beings. However, do not misunderstand me to be saying that such methods do not entail any suffering or karmic sin whatsoever.

Written, once again, with great and sincere hope of doing some benefit for sentient beings by Khenpo Tsultrim Lodrö on the fourteenth day of the last month of autumn in the water-horse year of the seventeenth Tibetan Rabjung [2002]. By the grace of the eternally timely compassion of the Lama and the Three Jewels and the infallible cause and effect of dependent origination, may this intention be accomplished!

Source Texts

Tenzin Wangchuk (Bstan 'dzin dbang 'phyug) [Geoffrey Barstow], ed. 2016. *Bod kyi dkar zas ring lugs*. Gser thang: Gser thang bla rung lnga rig nang bstan slob gling.

Khenpo Tsultrim Lodrö (Mkhan po tshul khrims blo gros). 2016. *Bstan 'dzin gyi skyes bu dam pa dag gi zhabs drung du zhus* (*Request in the Presence of the Noble Dharma Holders*). In *Bod kyi dkar zas ring lugs*, 338–39.

———. 2016. *Sha'i kha zas gnang bkag gi bslab bya blang dor gsal ba'i me long* (*Clear Mirror of Advice on the Rules on Eating Meat*). In *Bod kyi dkar zas ring lugs*, 296–337.

———. 2016. *Sgo phyugs rnams ngan gsod mi byed pa'i re* (*Appeal Not to Cruelly Slaughter Farm Animals*). In *Bod kyi dkar zas ring lugs*, 340–43.

All three of the texts translated here are also widely available in other collections, including:

Khenpo Tsultrim Lodrö (Mkhan po tshul khrims blo gros), ed. n.d. *Sha chang tha ma kha sogs kyi nyes dmigs phyogs bsdus* (*The Faults of Meat, Alcohol, and Tobacco*). Gser thang: Gser thang bla rung lnga rig nang bstan slob gling. BDRC: W1KG18536.

———. ed. 2006. *Sha'i nyes dmigs dang srog blu'i phan yon* (*Faults of Eating Meat and Benefits of Life Liberation*). Beijing: Publishing House of Minority Nationalities.

Secondary Sources

Buffetrille, Katia. 2014. "A Controversy on Vegetarianism." In *Trails of the Tibetan Tradition: Papers for Elliot Sperling*, edited by Roberto Vitali, 113–27. Dharamsala: Amye Machen Institute.

Eckel, Malcolm David. 2008. *Bhāviveka and His Buddhist Opponents: Chapters 4 and 5 of Bhāviveka's Madhyamakahṛdayakārikaḥ with Tarkajvāla Commentary*. Harvard Oriental Series 70. Cambridge: Harvard University Press.

Gaerrang. 2016. "Tibetan Identity and Tibetan Buddhism in Trans-Regional Connection: The Contemporary Vegetarian Movement in Pastoral Areas of Tibet (China)." *Études Mongoles et Sibériennes, Centrasiatiques et Tibétaines* 47: n.p.

Gayley, Holly. 2017. "The Compassionate Treatment of Animals." *Journal of Religious Ethics* 45.1: 29–57.

Goodman, Charles, trans. 2016. The Training Anthology of Śāntideva: A Translation of the Śikṣā-Samuccaya. Oxford: Oxford University Press.

Hoornaert, Paul. 2002. "An Annotated Translation of Madhyamakahṛdayakārikā/Tarkajvālā V.69–84." Kanazawa Daigaku Bungakubu Ronshū Kōdō Kagaku.Tetsugaku hen [Bulletin of the Faculty of Letters of Kanazawa University, Behavioral Sciences and Philosophy] 22: 113–37.

Hyoung Seok Ham. 2016. "Buddhist Critiques of the Veda and Vedic Sacrifice: A Study of Bhāviveka's Mīmāṃsā Chapter of the Madhyamakahṛdayakārikā and Tarkajvālā." PhD dissertation, University of Michigan.

Newman, John R. 1985. "A Brief History of the Kalachakra." In *The Wheel of Time: The Kalachakra in Context*, edited by Geshe Lhundub Sopa, Roger R. Jackson, and John R. Newman, 51–90. Madison, WI: Deer Park Books.

Shanshan Jia. 2015. "Laṅkāvatārasūtra." In *Encyclopedia of Buddhism*, 139. Leiden: Brill.

Suzuki, D. T. 1930. *Studies in the Lankavatara Sutra*. Tokyo: Sanshusa.

Suggested Reading

Animal Ethics in Buddhism

Barstow, Geoffrey. 2019. "On the Moral Standing of Animals in Tibetan Buddhism." *Études Mongoles et Sibériennes, Centrasiatiques et Tibétaines* 50: n.p.

Finnigan, Bronwyn. 2017. "Buddhism and Animal Ethics." *Philosophy Compass* 12.7: n.p.

Ohnuma, Reiko. 2017. *Unfortunate Destiny: Animals in the Indian Buddhist Imagination.* New York: Oxford University Press.

Schmithausen, Lambert. 2005. "Meat-Eating and Nature: Buddhist Perspectives." In *Buddhism and Nature: Supplement to the Bulletin of the Research Institute of Bukkyo University*, 183–201. Kyoto.

Waldau, Paul. 2001. *The Specter of Speciesism: Buddhist and Christian Views of Animals.* New York: Oxford.

Buddhist Authors in Support of Vegetarianism

Bodhipaksa. 2016. *Vegetarianism: A Buddhist View.* Cambridge, UK: Windhorse Publications.

Geshé Thubten Soepa. 2016. *Protecting the Lives of Helpless Beings: The Udamwara Lotus Flower.* Lama Yeshe Wisdom Archive. Lama Yeshe.com. https://www.lamayeshe.com/shop/protecting-lives-helpless-beings-ebook.

Kapleau, Roshi Philip. 1981. *To Cherish All Life: A Buddhist View of Animal Slaughter and Meat Eating.* Rochester, NY: The Zen Center.

Lama Phurbu Tashi Rinpoche. 2017. *A Buddhist Perspective on the Faults of Eating Meat.* Dharamsala: Library of Tibetan Works & Archives.

Patrul Rinpoche. 1998. *The Words of My Perfect Teacher.* Translated by Padmakara Translation Group. Boston: Shambhala Publications.

Phelps, Norm. 2004. *The Great Compassion: Buddhism and Animal Rights.* New York: Lantern Books.

Ricard, Matthieu. 2016. *A Plea for the Animals: The Moral, Philosophical, and Evolutionary Imperative to Treat All Beings with Compassion.* Boston: Shambhala Publications.

Shabkar [Tsogdruk Rangdrol]. 2004. *Food of Bodhisattvas: Buddhist Teachings on Abstaining from Meat.* Translated by Padmakara Translation Group. Boston: Shambhala Publications.

Further Reading on the Authors Translated in this Volume

Achard, Jean-Luc. 2008. *Enlightened Rainbows: The Life and Works of Shardza Tashi Gyeltsen*. Leiden: Brill.

Gorvine, William M. 2019. *Envisioning a Tibetan Luminary: The Life of a Modern Bönpo Saint*. New York: Oxford University Press.

Heimbel, Jörg. 2017. *Vajradhara in Human Form: The Life and Times of Ngor chen Kun dga' bzang po*. Lumbini: Lumbini International Research Institute.

Rheingans, Jim. 2017. *The Eighth Karmapa's Life and His Interpretation of the Great Seal*. Hamburg: Numata Center for Buddhist Studies.

Shabkar Tsokdruk Rangdrol. 2001. *The Life of Shabkar: The Autobiography of a Tibetan Yogin*. Translated by Matthieu Ricard. Ithaca, NY: Snow Lion Publications.

Stearns, Cyrus. 2010. *The Buddha from Dolpo: A Study of the Life and Thought of the Tibetan Master Dolpopa Sherab Gyaltsen*. Revised and expanded edition. Ithaca, NY: Snow Lion Publications.

Yeshe Dorjé. 2013. *The Cloud of Nectar: The Life and Liberation of Nyagla Pema Düdul*. Translated by Oriol Aguilar. Arcidosso: Shang Shung Publications.

The History and Practice of Buddhist Vegetarianism

Barstow, Geoffrey. 2018. *Food of Sinful Demons: Meat, Vegetarianism, and the Limits of Buddhism in Tibet*. New York: Columbia University Press.

Buffetrille, Katia. 2014. "A Controversy on Vegetarianism." In *Trails of the Tibetan Tradition: Papers for Elliot Sperling*, edited by Roberto Vitali, 113–27. Dharamsala: Amye Machen Institute.

Gaerrang. 2016. "Tibetan Identity and Tibetan Buddhism in Trans-Regional Connection: The Contemporary Vegetarian Movement in Pastoral Areas of Tibet (China)." *Études Mongoles et Sibériennes, Centrasiatiques et Tibétaines* 47: n.p.

Gayley, Holly. 2017. "The Compassionate Treatment of Animals." *Journal of Religious Ethics* 45.1: 29–57.

Jaffe, Richard. 2005. "The Debate over Meat Eating in Japanese Buddhism." In *Going Forth: Visions of Buddhist Vinaya: Essays Presented in Honor of Professor Stanley Weinstein*, edited by William M. Bodiford, 255–75. Honolulu: University of Hawai'i Press.

Kieschnick, John. 2005. "Buddhist Vegetarianism in China." In *Of Tripod and Palate: Food, Politics, and Religion in Traditional China*, edited by Roel Sterckx, 186–212. New York: Palgrave Macmillan.

Prasad, Chandra Shekhar. 1979. "Meat-Eating and the Rule of Tikoṭiparisuddha." In *Studies in Pali and Buddhism: A Memorial Volume in Honor of Bhikkhu Jagdish Kashyap*, edited by A. K. Narain, 289–95. Delhi: B. R. Publishing Corp.

Pu Chengzhong. 2014. *Ethical Treatment of Animals in Early Chinese Buddhism: Beliefs and Practices*. Newcastle, UK: Cambridge Scholars.

Ruegg, David Seyfort. 1980. "Ahiṃsā and Vegetarianism in the History of Buddhism." In *Buddhist Studies in Honour of Walpola Rahula*, edited by Sōmaratna Bālasūriya. London: Gordon Frazer.

Stewart, James. 2015. *Vegetarianism and Animal Ethics in Contemporary Buddhism*. London: Routledge.

Tantric Samyas and the Five Meats

Barstow, Geoffrey. 2018. *Food of Sinful Demons: Meat, Vegetarianism, and the Limits of Buddhism in Tibet*. New York: Columbia University Press.

van Schaik, Sam. 2010. "The Limits of Transgression: The Samaya Vows of Mahayoga." In *Esoteric Buddhism at Dunhuang: Rites and Teachings for This Life and Beyond*, edited by Matthew T. Kapstein and Sam van Schaik, 61–83. Leiden: Brill.

Wedemeyer, Christian K. 2012. *Making Sense of Tantric Buddhism: History, Semiology, and Transgression in the Indian Traditions*. New York: Columbia University Press.

Three-Vow Theory

Dudjom Rinpoche. 1999. *Perfect Conduct: Ascertaining the Three Vows*. Translated by Gyurme Samdrup and Sangye Khandro. Boston: Wisdom Publications.

Sakya Paṇḍita Kunga Gyaltshen. 2002. *A Clear Differentiation of the Three Codes: Essential Differentiations among the Individual Liberation, Great Vehicle, and Tantric Systems*. Translated by Jared Douglas Rhoton. New York: State University of New York Press.

Sobisch, Jan-Ulrich. 2002. *Three-Vow Theories in Tibetan Buddhism*. Weisbaden: Dr. Ludwig Reichert Verlag.

Translator Biographies

Geoffrey Barstow is an assistant professor of religious studies at Oregon State University. His research focuses on the history and theory of vegetarianism in Tibet. He is the author of *Food of Sinful Demons: Meat, Vegetarianism, and the Limits of Buddhism in Tibet* (Columbia University Press, 2018).

Catherine Hardie received her doctorate in social anthropology from the University of Oxford. Her research focuses on contemporary interactions in the Sino-Tibetan Buddhist milieu in mainland China, particularly on the rise of Sino-Tibetan lay Buddhist movements in the vibrant but contested space of religion.

Jörg Heimbel received his PhD in Tibetology in 2014 from the University of Hamburg, Germany, and since then has been working as a lecturer for classical and colloquial Tibetan at the same university. His research interest lies in the religious and cultural history of Tibet and its related biographical and historiographical literature (with a special emphasis on the Sakya school of Tibetan Buddhism) and Tibetan Buddhist art. Among his recent publications is *Vajradhara in Human Form: The Life and Times of Ngor chen Kun dga' bzang po* (Lumbini International Research Institute, 2017).

Anna Wolcott Johnson is a PhD candidate at the University of Michigan. Her research interests include the nature, or ontological status, of a vow in Tibetan three-vow treatises, abhidharma karma theory as it informs the ritual generation of vows, and Tibetan representations of Indian genealogies in vow lineage histories. She has a particular interest in ethical contradiction within proscriptive content in Buddhist literature.

Rachel H. Pang is Lester D. Coltrane III Assistant Professor of Religious Studies at Davidson College. She received her PhD in Tibetan and Chinese religions from the University of Virginia. Dr. Pang's research focuses on

Buddhist auto/biography, Tibetan poetry, the nineteenth-century ecumenical movement, and the collected works of Shabkar Tsokdruk Rangdröl (1781–1851). Her research articles on these topics have been published in *Himalaya*, *Numen*, *Journal of Buddhist Ethics*, *Revue d'Etudes Tibetaines*, and *a/b: Auto/biography Studies*.

Adam Pearcey is a senior teaching fellow at the School of Oriental and African Studies, University of London, and the founder-director of Lotsawa House, an online library of Tibetan Buddhist translations. His publications (as translator) include *Mind in Comfort and Ease* by His Holiness the Dalai Lama (Wisdom Publications, 2007), *To Dispel the Misery of the World* by Ga Rabjampa (Wisdom Publications, 2012), and *Beyond the Ordinary Mind: Dzogchen Advice from Rimé Masters* (Snow Lion Publications, 2018).

Michael Sheehy is the director of scholarship at the Contemplative Sciences Center and a research assistant professor in Tibetan Buddhist studies in the Department of Religious Studies at the University of Virginia. His translations and writings largely give attention to the literary histories of marginalized traditions of Tibetan Buddhism, with an emphasis on philosophy and meditative practice. He has conducted extensive fieldwork with scholastic and contemplative communities in Buddhist Asia, including three years' training in a monastery in eastern Tibet. Most recently, his research explores contributions of Buddhism to discourses in the humanities about contemplative experience and, more specifically, the use of imagination and visualization in contemplative technique, the cultural psychology of meditation, and the Buddhism-science dialogue. He is coeditor with Klaus-Dieter Mathes of *The Other Emptiness: Rethinking the Zhentong Buddhist Discourse in Tibet* (SUNY Press, 2019).

Sangseraima Ujeed received her doctorate from the University of Oxford. She currently holds a Robert H. N. Ho postdoctoral fellowship in Buddhist Studies at the University of California Santa Barbara. Her research focuses on Tibeto-Mongolian assimilation of Buddhism and religious identity during the early Qing period.

Index

U

V

W

Y

Z

What to Read Next from Wisdom Publications

A Gathering of Brilliant Moons
Practice Advice from the Rimé Masters of Tibet
Edited by Holly Gayley and Joshua Schapiro
Foreword by Ringu Tulku

For generations, Buddhist masters in Tibet have composed *sheldam*, poignant instructions tailored to the needs of their disciples in the form of short works of advice. Often difficult to find in publication, these works cover topics ranging from practicing while ill to sitting in solitary retreat to recognizing the nature of mind. This collection focuses on an influential and inspiring generation of Buddhist teachers: the nineteenth-century ecumenical, or rimé, tradition of eastern Tibet. *A Gathering of Brilliant Moons* provides lively translations of nineteen pithy and profound works by these great masters, along with essays by their translators that explore the aesthetic qualities of their chosen works, highlight their ecumenical features, and comment on the journey of translation.

Ecology, Ethics, and Interdependence
The Dalai Lama in Conversation with Leading Thinkers on Climate Change
Edited by John Dunne and Daniel Goleman

"We need this one. Here is a book that looks at the global ecological crisis from many, many angles, each one bringing the challenge—and what to do about it—more and more into focus. This is an important book."
—Jeff Bridges, actor and environmental activist

About Wisdom Publications

Wisdom Publications is the leading publisher of classic and contemporary Buddhist books and practical works on mindfulness. To learn more about us or to explore our other books, please visit our website at wisdompubs.org or contact us at the address below.

Wisdom Publications
199 Elm Street
Somerville, MA 02144 USA

We are a 501(c)(3) organization, and donations in support of our mission are tax deductible.

Wisdom Publications is affiliated with the Foundation for the Preservation of the Mahayana Tradition (FPMT).